Saudi Arabia and the United Arab Emirates

Manchester University Press

IDENTITIES AND GEOPOLITICS IN THE MIDDLE EAST

Series editors: Simon Mabon, Edward Wastnidge and May Darwich

After the Arab Uprisings and the ensuing fragmentation of regime-society relations across the Middle East, identities and geopolitics have become increasingly contested, with serious implications for the ordering of political life at domestic, regional and international levels, best seen in conflicts in Syria and Yemen. The Middle East is the most militarised region in the world where geopolitical factors remain predominant factors in shaping political dynamics. Another common feature of the regional landscape is the continued degeneration of communal relations as societal actors retreat into sub-state identities, whilst difference becomes increasingly violent, spilling out beyond state borders. The power of religion – and trans-state nature of religious views and linkages – thus provides the means for regional actors (such as Saudi Arabia and Iran) to exert influence over a number of groups across the region and beyond. This series provides space for the engagement with these ideas and the broader political, legal and theological factors to create space for an intellectual re-imagining of socio-political life in the Middle East.

Originating from the SEPAD project (www.sepad.org.uk), this series facilitates the re-imagining of political ideas, identities and organisation across the Middle East, moving beyond the exclusionary and binary forms of identity to reveal the contingent factors that shape and order life across the region.

Previously published titles

Houses built on sand: Violence, sectarianism and revolution in the Middle East
Simon Mabon

The Gulf States and the Horn of Africa: Interests, influences and instability
Robert Mason and Simon Mabon (eds)

Transitional justice in process: Plans and politics in Tunisia   *Mariam Salehi*

The labour movement in Lebanon: Power on hold   *Lea Bou Khater*

Surviving repression: The Egyptian Muslim Brotherhood after the 2013 *coup*
Lucia Ardovini

Saudi Arabia and Iran: The struggle to shape the Middle East
Edward Wastnidge and Simon Mabon (eds)

Saudi Arabia and the United Arab Emirates

Foreign policy and strategic alliances in an uncertain world

Robert Mason

MANCHESTER UNIVERSITY PRESS

Published by Manchester University Press
Altrincham Street, Manchester M1 7JA

www.manchesteruniversitypress.co.uk

British Library Cataloguing-in-Publication Data
A catalogue record for this book is available from the British Library

ISBN   978 1 5261 4849 0   hardback

First published 2023

Typeset
by New Best-set Typesetters Ltd

Contents

Acknowledgements

Since I wrote my PhD thesis on Saudi and Iranian foreign policy a decade ago at the Institute of Arab and Islamic Studies, University of Exeter, much has changed in the Gulf, the Middle East and wider world. I have spent most of the time since 2013 living and teaching in Cairo, where I have been keenly aware how Saudi Arabia and the United Arab Emirates (UAE) have extended their economic influence and secured their long-standing alliance with Egypt.

This book is the product of a wide range of influences and experiences. As Associate Professor and Director of the Middle East Studies Center at the American University in Cairo, I had the opportunity to engage with diplomats from various countries to learn about their strategic imperatives domestically, in the Middle East (including the Gulf) and internationally. I have been fortunate to have had the opportunity to present my research on Qatar and the UAE at the Center for International and Regional Studies (CIRS), Georgetown University Qatar and the Belfer Center for Science and International Affairs at Harvard University, where I gained valuable feedback. My field research to the UAE has been funded by the London School of Economics Middle East Centre as part of their project 'Mapping Foreign Policy in the GCC'. Again, feedback from peers and scholars was extremely useful in locating the UAE's foreign policy in a wider regional context.

Another prelude to this volume came from a workshop on oil adjustment policies in the Arab Gulf since 2014, hosted in Lebanon by Martin Beck and Thomas Richter from the German Institute of Global and Area Studies (GIGA) and was published by Manchester University Press in 2021 under the title: *Oil and the Political Economy in the Middle East: Post-2014 Adjustment Policies of the Arab Gulf and Beyond*. This experience afforded me the opportunity to consider Saudi domestic reform and political consolidation in detail. I then had the opportunity to present a similar paper at the Institute for the Transregional Study of the Contemporary Middle East, Princeton University as a visiting scholar, which was an incredibly rewarding experience. Bernard Haykel was generous in hosting me and critiquing my work.

I would like to thank all those who agreed to be interviewed on or off the record for this research. Those I can mention here include a number of current or former ambassadors: Gerald M. Feierstein, Joseph W. Westphal, Seyed Hossein Mousavian, Sir William Patey, Navdeep Suri, Akihiko Nakajima, and Katsuhiko Takahashi. I am also grateful to Michael Knights, who gave up his time to discuss Gulf security issues. These contributions greatly enriched the material presented in this volume and allowed me to question, crystallise or re-evaluate key issues and concepts. Similarly, colleagues and friends have challenged my work and offered some great insights during the process of reviewing individual chapters: Ibrahim Fraihat (Iran), Jonathan Fulton (China), Christian Koch (Europe), Mark N. Katz (Russia), Talmiz Ahmed (India and Pakistan), Makio Yamada (Japan), Ikran Eum (Republic of Korea), Sumanto Al Qurtuby (Indonesia) and Asmady Idris (Malaysia). Any omissions or errors remain solely my responsibility.

There are various organisations I am indebted to for their contribution to my learning experience concerning Gulf politics. The Arab Gulf States Institute in Washington, where I am a non-resident fellow and have written a number of op-eds referenced in the research of this book, has played a vital role, first in serving as a platform for cutting-edge analysis, and second through its events from which I have been able to engage and draw a series of unique insights. The Gulf2000 project at Columbia University has been an indispensable resource for those of us in the field of Gulf studies. Thanks to Robert Byron and Lucy Burns at Manchester University Press, who have done a superb job in shepherding this project through to completion. Thanks also to my copyeditor, Judith Oppenheimer, who did a stellar job on clarifying my prose and getting the manuscript print ready.

Robert Mason
Cairo, July 2022.

Abbreviations

AED	Arab Emirates dirham
AI	artificial intelligence
ADNOC	Abu Dhabi National Oil Company
AQAP	Al Qaeda in the Arabian Peninsula
BRI	Belt and Road Initiative
CAATSA	Countering America's Adversaries Through Sanctions Act
CENTCOM	United States Central Command
CIA	Central Intelligence Agency
CPEC	China–Pakistan Economic Corridor
FATF	Financial Action Task Force
FDI	foreign direct investment
FNC	Federal National Council of the United Arab Emirates
FPA	foreign policy analysis
FTA	free trade agreement
GCC	Gulf Cooperation Council
GCTF	Global Counterterrorism Forum
GDP	gross domestic product
GERD	Grand Ethiopian Renaissance Dam
IAEA	International Atomic Energy Agency
IMF	International Monetary Fund
IONS	Indian Ocean Naval Symposium
IPO	initial public offering
IR	international relations
IRGC	Islamic Revolutionary Guard Corps
ISIS	Islamic State of Iraq and the Levant
IT	information technology
JASTA	Justice Against Sponsors of Terrorism Act
JCPOA	Joint Comprehensive Plan of Action
MB	Muslim Brotherhood
MBS	Mohammed bin Salman Al Saud
MENA	Middle East and North Africa

MESA	Middle East Strategic Alliance
MoU	memorandum of understanding
NATO	North Atlantic Treaty Organisation
NGO	non-governmental organisation
NPT	non-proliferation treaty
OIC	Organisation of Islamic Cooperation
OPEC	Organization of Petroleum Exporting Countries
PIF	Public Investment Fund
PLO	Palestine Liberation Organization
PSF	Peninsula Shield Force
ROK	Republic of Korea
RSAF	Royal Saudi Air Force
RST	rentier state theory
SANG	Saudi Arabian National Guard
SCO	Shanghai Cooperation Organization
SIPRI	Stockholm International Peace Research Institute
SME	small and medium-sized enterprises
SWF	sovereign wealth fund
THAAD	Terminal High Altitude Area Defense
UAE	United Arab Emirates
UAV	unmanned aerial vehicle
VAT	value added tax
WTO	World Trade Organization

Map

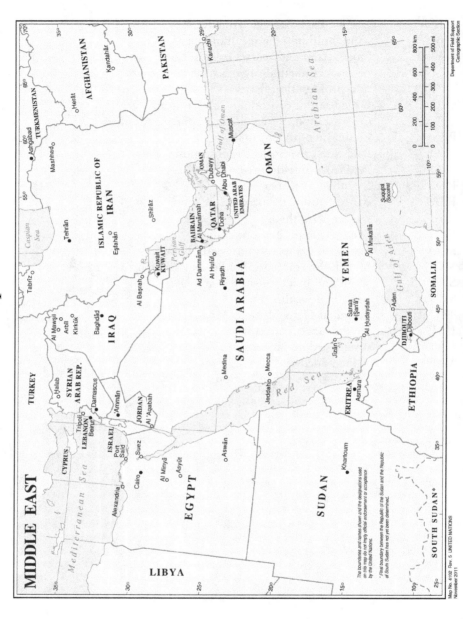

Map of the Middle East (United Nations, 2011)

Introduction

This book explores the foreign and security policies of Saudi Arabia and the United Arab Emirates (UAE), the two largest economies in the Middle East, in the context of leadership, political succession, transition and consolidation, as well as socio-economic change and other challenges taking place. The book deals with foreign policy analysis (FPA) and international relations (IR) as holistically as possible through a panoramic analysis of a series of key bilateral relations. It is not an exhaustive account, but provides an opportunity for an assessment as well as for triangulation and cross-referencing of relevant conceptual frameworks on a global basis. The research has been aided by the breakneck speed with which a series of reforms and political consolidation have been implemented following royal successions in Saudi Arabia and the UAE, giving a brief glimpse (if not a complete picture) of possible motivations, drivers and objectives of state policy making. Conducting research on the Gulf States can be challenging at the best of times, given their opaque political systems, centralised decision making and the consolidation taking place, often in securitised arenas. The task became even more challenging during COVID-19.

The Gulf region has experienced tremendous change since the oil boom of 1973 (and again in the early 2000s), including the accumulation of vast wealth, some of which has been deployed in pursuit of state foreign policy objectives. The Middle East regional order, in flux since Egypt's peace with Israel in 1979, the Iranian Revolution the same year, Iraq's invasion of Kuwait in 1990, Turkey's balancing between the EU and Arab world, domestic governance challenges and a lack of economic or security organisations, has become even more susceptible to change. The onset of the Arab uprisings in 2011 led to successive authoritarian crises, security vacuums and conflicts. Thus, Saudi Arabia, an absolute monarchy and theocratic state, and the UAE, a tribal and autocratic monarchy comprising a federation of seven emirates (Abu Dhabi, the capital, and Ajman, Dubai, Fujairah, Ras Al-Khaimah, Sharjah and Umm Al-Quwain), have gained opportunities to extend their influence and forge a strategic alliance.

The step change in push-back, counter-revolutionary or what may be called 'pro-stability' initiatives in Saudi Arabia and the UAE has been especially targeted against Islamist movements supported by Iran, Qatar and Turkey. This was accompanied by a change of leadership in the UAE in 2014 as Mohammed bin Zayed Al Nahyan took over as de facto ruler of the UAE following the incapacitation of his father, Khalifa bin Zayed al Nahyan, from a stroke. Mohammed bin Zayed became head of state in May 2022 after the death of Sheikh Khalifa, securing Al-Nahyan as the royal family of the UAE. At the time of writing, there was still debate over whether Mohammed bin Zayed's son or brother, Sheikh Tahnoun, would become the next crown prince. The kingdom also moved from a cautious gerontocracy to the more assertive policies adopted by Crown Prince Mohammed bin Salman Al Saud (also known as MBS[1]) from 2016. Both Saudi Arabia and the UAE led economic intervention in support of President Sisi of Egypt and other regional autocrats, resisted the Joint Comprehensive Plan of Action (JCPOA) agreement with Iran in 2015, prosecuted a military campaign in Yemen from 2015 and boycotted Qatar from 2017 to 2021. Saudi–UAE close coordination in regional affairs lasted until the UAE suffered battlefield defeats in Libya and unilaterally withdrew from Yemen in 2019. The lack of US military response to the attacks on Saudi oil installations at Abqaiq and Khurais the same year and withdrawal from Afghanistan in 2021 have reinforced Riyadh and Abu Dhabi's sense of US disengagement from the region and necessitated a recommitment to their traditional international balancing strategies.

This falls at a time when Asia has become the Gulf's most important energy and trading region. The Gulf[2] contains an estimated 50 per cent of the world's oil reserves, with at least 25 per cent in Saudi Arabia which is relatively cheap to extract. The kingdom is a swing producer within the Organization of Petroleum Exporting Countries (OPEC), and therefore vital for a stable supply at a stable price. The UAE is a smaller but still important oil exporter, with some natural gas reserves. Qatar ranks third in the world for natural gas reserves, after Russia and Iran. There are clear and growing connections between these Gulf Cooperation Council (GCC) states and the world, especially since all the GCC states have acceded to the World Trade Organization (WTO): the UAE in 1996 and Saudi Arabia in 2005. With growing trade and investment, plans such as Vision 2030 and UAE Vision 2021, the National Innovation Strategy and 'Designing the Next 50', which will establish the pillars and components for the UAE Centennial Plan 2071,[3] will become the touchstones for globalisation and economic opportunity in this part of the world. The Gulf and Asia regions will become vital players in international energy markets well into the twenty-first century, even when taking into consideration suppressed oil demand in major developing markets such as China and India due to COVID-19 and the rapid transition towards renewable energy. Similar to the global economic crisis in 2007–8, these economies are well placed to help lead the global recovery and may emerge stronger than before.

The volume notes the personal rapport, leadership qualities and politics of this volume's chief protagonists: Crown Prince Mohammed bin Salman of Saudi Arabia and Mohammed bin Zayed, Crown Prince of Abu Dhabi, the leading emirate in the UAE. Mohammed bin Zayed became Deputy Crown Prince in 2003, Crown Prince in 2004 and President of the UAE in 2022. Whilst Mohammed bin Salman became Deputy Crown Prince, Minister of Defence and Second Deputy Prime Minister in 2015. He went on to become Crown Prince, First Deputy Prime Minister, Chairman of the Council of Economic and Development Affairs and Chairman of the Council of Political and Security Affairs in 2017. The book highlights how nimble the UAE is as a small state, evident in its ability to secure a non-permanent UN Security Council seat 2022–23, and the election of Major General Ahmed Naser Al-Raisi as president of Interpol in 2021. This is compared to the kingdom, an economic and regional heavyweight, which plays a leading role in the Islamic world by hosting the Organisation of Islamic Cooperation (OIC) and the GCC headquarters, and participating in the G20. Russia's invasion of Ukraine in 2022, whilst calling attention to the range of diplomatic, military, economic and energy relations that have conditioned the Saudi and UAE responses, has also helped to showcase the complexity and dynamism of these states' foreign policy calculations.

Structure of the book

Following the Introduction, each chapter provides a summary of the empirical research, followed by an analytical conclusion synthesising the major themes, conceptual bases and key findings. Chapter 1 provides an overview of the existing theoretical IR and FPA literature as well as relevant conceptual innovations relevant to the study. Chapter 2 studies domestic politics in the kingdom, reflecting on Saudi statehood, survival, regional relations and contemporary transitions affecting sectarianism, secularism and liberalism. Dissent and repression are also covered, along with reference to the 'anti-corruption drive' in 2017. The chapter goes on to analyse the Saudi economy, defence and national security issues.

Chapter 3 outlines the major themes concerning UAE state consolidation, security and regional policy. It delves into the UAE's response to the Islamist threat, national security, human rights issues, its economy and defence. Chapter 4 assesses Saudi and UAE relations with Iran and how Iran has been a shaping factor that helps to drive Saudi and UAE policy at the regional and international levels. Chapter 5 is an omnibus chapter which first outlines the orientation of Saudi and UAE policy, relations and regionalism within the GCC. It then progresses to study major thematic issues such as diplomatic and economic intervention through traditional riyal politik – the use of oil revenue for political ends – and broader economic statecraft, proxy warfare and military intervention.

Chapter 6 turns to the US, assessing the impact of US policy from the Obama to the Biden administrations, and the evolution of the oil-for-security bargain. It notes the circumstances surrounding several near-death experiences in Saudi–US relations during the latest administrations and how partisan politics, carte blanche policy during the Trump administration and policy variation have played out in Saudi and UAE foreign policy decision making. Chapter 7 takes a holistic view of Chinese Middle East policy, predominantly conducted through projects associated with the Belt and Road Initiative. After some background, it covers Chinese policy under President Xi Jinping, China's approach to the Gulf, Saudi–China relations and UAE–China relations.

Chapter 8 focuses on contemporary UK and French interactions with Saudi Arabia and the UAE by situating them in their imperial pasts. Chapter 9 sketches out Russia's historically limited channels of influence in the Gulf, covering its evolving domestic and foreign policy priorities from the imperial and Soviet periods to the twenty-first century. The chapter weaves together diverse strands, incorporating energy and economic interactions, Russian relations with Iran, the conflicts in Syria and Ukraine and the changing global balance of power.

Chapter 10 directs attention to the Horn of Africa and common connections that span millennia. It adopts a case-study approach to the analysis of Saudi and UAE policy in the Horn, motivated by regional actor engagement and the Yemen conflict, and showing a common denominator of economic intervention that has maximised influence in the political marketplaces of the Horn states. The chapter shows the extent of bilateral, multilateral and military–military ties within the changing international context in the Red Sea region.

Chapter 11 surveys Saudi and UAE relations with India and Pakistan at a time when Saudi relations with these South Asian states have crossed an inversion point. The chapter notes well the rise of India, the economic opportunities which stem from that at the national as well as sub-national levels and the growing security cooperation between Saudi Arabia and India since 2006, using the 2008 Mumbai attacks to extend political and security cooperation further. It discusses a number of potential hurdles that remain at the regional level, especially India and Pakistan's policies towards each other and their respective threat perceptions over Kashmir. Chapter 12 details the broadening out of bilateral relations between Saudi Arabia, the UAE, Japan and the Republic of Korea. It assesses the interplay of energy, East Asian contributions to, and benefits from, Saudi and UAE Vision strategies, and attempts to conceptualise their contemporary relations and effects on the wider Middle East.

Chapter 13 provides an overview of Saudi and UAE engagement with Indonesia and Malaysia, referencing changes in the domestic politics of these Southeast Asian nations and the evolving bases of their long-standing interregional interaction. The Conclusion draws on these insights to deliver a coherent summary of the diverse strands of Saudi and UAE foreign policy and IR, and the most appropriate lens(es) through which to view the multifarious trends, actions and personalities.

Notes

1 Mohammed bin Salman and Mohammed bin Zayed are known by their initials MBS and MBZ respectively, but in the interests of consistency and equivalency with other leaders I have used their given names throughout the book.
2 The wider Gulf region includes Iraq and Iran. 'Gulf' will be used throughout as a politically neutral term, rather than 'Persian Gulf' or 'Arabian Gulf', given the controversy each term can engender.
3 Staff report, 'Sheikh Mohammed invites citizens, expats to help shape UAE's next 50 years', *Khaleej Times*, 29 September 2020, www.khaleejtimes.com/news/government/sheikh-mohammed-invites-citizens-expats-to-help-shape-uaes-next-50-years-. (Unless otherwise stated, all URLs were last accessed on 27 July 2022.)

1

A theoretical and conceptual framework

This study is rooted in FPA, but by necessity must relate to area studies, taking into account history, political science and IR. At the systemic level, Dickinson found that anarchy (defined as 'no common law' or 'no common force')[1] pushes states to seek supremacy, due to 'mutual fear' and 'mutual suspicion'.[2] Offensive realism has a long lineage[3] which could be fruitful to explore in the IR of the Gulf States, especially as conflict has arguably gone from being sporadic to endemic, and fear of other states, namely Iran, remains a key concern. Walt explains in *Origins of Alliances* that states form alliances to balance threats as well as counter power as traditional balance of power theory would posit, supporting the argument of defensive realists, and that fluid notions of power can be more of a threat than quantifiable elements.[4] Gause found that the most compelling reason for the use of force in the Middle East is generally related to threats that (are perceived to) challenge domestic stability and regime security.[5] Darwich and Kaarbo build on IR of the Middle East with an FPA perspective, particularly focusing on the psychology and agent-based dimensions of FPA that complement and extend IR-based frameworks.[6] A psychological approach is particularly important when dealing with threat perception and responses to ideational threats or 'ontological insecurity'. In the Saudi case, identity is found to have shifted from Islamic leadership to a greater focus on Sunni identity.[7] Identity-based analyses can also help us assess states such as Iran which adopt apparently 'irrational' positions that produce suboptimal outcomes based on revolutionary identity[8] or Shia-based identity.[9]

Stein suggests that ideological externalisation or foreign policy and international alignment augments or compensates for domestic insufficiencies in shoring up domestic support, and competitive economic and security support seeking are the state hegemonic strategies of the region's pivotal powers.[10] This has been a feature of their political relations since Pax Britannica. But, as Hinnebusch points out, the anarchy, instability and conflict prevalent in the region are rooted in the arbitrary borders and other policies of imperialism which have encouraged trans-state identities and mobilisation.[11] Only once these threats are addressed does state decision making progress onto other topics such as regional leadership, international acceptance and economic development.[12] Two of the categories of literature most applicable to this work are those on so-called 'small states' and 'middle powers', into which the UAE and Saudi Arabia, respectively, fall. Clapham notes that the category of 'small states' is problematic.[13] The size of the military, territory and economy are often used as metrics to assess state power, and yet in the Middle East sources of state power have been rather diffuse. Lustick notes that no state has been able to dominate the Middle East since the fall of the Ottoman Empire.[14] Saouli writes that states aiming for middle power require the intention, strategy, capacity to project power into the region, ideological and cultural means to influence and an ability to enable or disrupt international powers in the region.[15] The Arab uprisings created a new impetus for those with the power to intervene to cushion against ontological threats, boost their prospects towards middle powerhood and gain ground over regional adversaries.[16] Morganthau's Hobbesian view is relevant especially, in authoritarian contexts and absolute monarchies which pursue absolute power as part of their identities and values, especially within youthful leaderships whose attitude to foreign policy assertiveness and risk may not have been conditioned by conflict within living memory.

Given the relative and constantly shifting weight of threats and opportunities at the domestic, regional and international levels, David's omnibalancing concept best encapsulates these concerns and opportunities.[17] Foreign policy is necessarily multilevel, multi-causal and contextual.[18] What is generally accepted is that Middle Eastern states were far better able to manipulate the core–periphery system during the Cold War than during the post-Cold War unipolar era.[19] The opportunities on offer from growing international powers in the post-unipolar era suggest that Middle Eastern states could once again be afforded new balancing opportunities to maximise their relative autonomy.

Domestically, there has been a trend towards the centralisation of political power in the personalities of Crown Prince Mohammed bin Salman and Crown Prince Mohammed bin Zayed, which has led Davidson to regard Saudi Arabia and the UAE as having transitioned from traditional sheikdoms to contemporary sultan modes of governance and authority.[20] They preside over national economic plans, implement crackdowns, reshape civil society (notably curtailing religious forces) and engage in autocratic and repressive behaviour.[21] Yet this form of behaviour is hardly confined to the Gulf, but occurs in rentier states more broadly, including Algeria.[22] Sultanism has also been attributed to the actions of leaders in republics such as Recep Tayyip Erdoğan. There has also been a marked sense of hyper-nationalism and identity building based on shifts from traditional modes of governance. The risks of engineering such rapid changes are self-evident.[23]

A range of economic concepts are also relevant to this study. Riyal politik has already been found to have played a central role in Saudi foreign policy.[24] Baldwin argued that economic instruments in foreign policy can work to exert influence, forming economic statecraft,[25] a concept which Young points to in the analysis of UAE policies towards Egypt post-2011.[26] As Malik notes, the existing rentier state theory (RST) literature overstates the role of oil on the economy.[27] Notwithstanding the limited prospects for a rentier state to evolve into a production state, RST cannot explain domestic challenges to regime legitimacy based on other socio-economic factors. Neither, as Moritz notes, does RST explain rapidly evolving state–society relations in its entirety; co-optation can fail.[28]

A hybrid conceptual approach is therefore adopted, combining complex realism to include reference to realism, constructivism and role theory (especially shifting orders, how states perceive threats and calculate balancing strategies, and new generation identity and priorities), with economic statecraft, which has the advantage of considering the role of oil, as well as other rents, aid, remittances and state-led economic programmes and actions on foreign policy. It will also be invaluable in considering the impact of new diversification measures such as tax, renewable energy and aerospace ventures. The research is undertaken with the proviso that FPA in authoritarian contexts is more susceptible than in most contexts to 'black box' decision making and secrecy amongst relevant actors such as royals, officials and other state actors.

The following questions are expected to elicit findings which contribute to the existing literature and develop new areas to explore in the politics, FPA and IR of Saudi Arabia and the UAE:

1 What are the major impacts of regime type and leadership style (especially political consolidation) on the construct and conduct of Saudi and UAE domestic, regional and international politics?
2 What are the main sources of Saudi and UAE autonomy and external influence, especially considering new opportunities for economic, security and military relations, and how is this changing over time in line with new policy challenges and opportunities?
3 What effect(s) has/is uncertainty surrounding US policy in the region had/having on Saudi and UAE policy, as well as on international alliance patterns?
4 What other conceptual insights can be gleaned concerning key debates on the topic, including anarchy, polarity, hegemony, (relative) autonomy, dependency, defensive/offensive realism, small states, middle powers, core–periphery relations, threat perception and alliance patterns?

Notes

1 Goldsworthy Lowes Dickinson, *The European Anarchy*. London: Allen and Unwin, 1916.
2 Ibid: 'Introduction': 10.
3 See the Paul Poast thread, 21 August 2021, https://mobile.twitter.com/ProfPaulPoast/status/1429052774159945736
4 Stephen M. Walt, *The Origins of Alliance*. Ithaca, NY: Cornell University Press, 1990.
5 F. Gregory Gause III, 'Balancing What? Threat Perception and Alliance Choice in the Gulf', *Security Studies*, 13 (2), 2010: 273–305.
6 May Darwich and Juliet Kaarbo, 'IR in the Middle East: Foreign Policy Analysis in Theoretical Approaches', *International Relations*, 34 (2), 2020: 1–21.
7 May Darwich, *Threats and Alliances in the Middle East: Saudi and Syrian Policies in a Turbulent Region*. Cambridge: Cambridge University Press, 2019.
8 Thomas Juneau, *Squandered Opportunity: Neoclassical Realism and Iranian Foreign Policy*. Stanford: Stanford University Press, 2015.
9 Shahram Akbarzadeh, 'Iran and Daesh: The Case of a Reluctant Shia Power', *Middle East Policy*, XXII (3), 2015: 44–54.
10 Ewan Stein, *International Relations in the Middle East: Hegemonic Strategies and Regional Order*, Cambridge: Cambridge University Press, 2021.
11 Raymond Hinnebusch, 'Introduction to the International Politics of the Middle East', *The International Politics of the Middle East*. Manchester: Manchester University Press, 2015: 2.
12 Paul Noble, 'The Arab System: Pressures, Constraints, and Opportunities', in Bahgat Korany and Ali E. Hillal Dessouki (eds) *The Foreign Policies of Arab States: The Challenges of Change*. Boulder, CO: Westview Press, 1991: 41–78.
13 Christopher Clapham, 'Foreign Policy in International Relations', *Foreign Policy in the Twenty-First Century*. New York: Palgrave Macmillan, 2016: 15.
14 Ian S. Lustick, 'The Absence of Middle Eastern Great Powers: Political "Backwardness" in Historical Perspective', *International Organization*, 51 (4), Autumn 1997: 657.
15 Adham Saouli, 'Middling or Meddling? Origins and Constraints of External Influence in the Middle East', in Adham Saouli (ed.) *Unfulfilled Aspirations: Middle Power Politics in the Middle East*. New York: Oxford University Press, 2020: 11–30.
16 Robert Mason, 'Small State Aspirations to Middle Powerhood: The Cases of Qatar and the UAE', in Adham Saouli (ed.), *Unfulfilled Aspirations: Middle Power Politics in the Middle East*. London: Hurst/Oxford University Press: 2020: 157–183.
17 Stephen R. David, 'Explaining Third World Alignment', *World Politics*, 43 (2), January 1991: 233–256.
18 Gerd Nonneman, 'Analyzing the Foreign Policies of the Middle East and North Africa: A Conceptual Approach', *The Review of International Affairs*, 3 (2), Winter 2003: 369–373.

19 Fawaz Gerges, *The Superpowers and the Middle East: Regional and International Politics, 1955–1967*. Boulder, CO: Westview Press, 1994.

20 Christopher M. Davidson, *From Sheikhs to Sultanism: Statecraft and Authority in Saudi Arabia and the UAE*. London: Hurst/Oxford University Press, 2021.

21 Ibid.

22 See Khaled Nezzar, *Algerie, le Sultanat de Bouteflika*. Échillais: Transbordeurs, 2003.

23 Eman Alhussein, 'Saudi First: How Hyper-Natioanlism is Transforming Saudi Arabia', European Council on Foreign Relations, 19 June 2019, https://ecfr.eu/publication/saudi_first_how_hyper_nationalism_is_transforming_saudi_arabia/

24 Robert Mason, *Foreign Policy in Saudi Arabia and Iran: Economics and Diplomacy in the Middle East*. London: I. B. Tauris, 2015.

25 David A. Baldwin, *Economic Statecraft*. Princeton: Princeton University Press, 2020.

26 Karen E. Young, 'A New Politics of GCC Economic Statecraft: The Case of UAE Aid and Financial Intervention in Egypt', *Journal of Arabian Studies*, 7 (1), 2017: 113–136.

27 Adeel Malik, 'Rethinking the Rentier Curse', in Giacomo Luciani (ed.) *Combining Economic and Political Development: The Experience of MENA*. Leiden: Brill, 2017: 41.

28 Jessie Moritz, 'Reformers and the Rentier State: Re-Evaluating the Co-optation Mechanism in Rentier State Theory', *Journal of Arabian Studies*, 8, 2018, 46–64.

2

Politics in the kingdom of Saudi Arabia: state formation, political consolidation and reform

Saudi domestic politics and foreign policy-making processes are similar to those of other monarchies in the Middle East in that they generally comprise tribal, religious, economic and familial components. Where they differ, and differ with each other, are the specificities of these components, particularly what was, and still to some extent remains, the religious component, as well as aspects of political consolidation in Saudi Arabia. The Qur'an is the constitution, and the Prophet's Traditions (Sunnah) remain vital, as does Sharia, or Islamic law, as the basis for law enforcement. But across the Arab Gulf states there is an increasing focus on economic diversification in the contemporary period of (possibly extended) transition from rentier to semi-, late[1] or post-rentier statehood.

This chapter sets the tone for further discussion on Saudi foreign policy by reflecting on Saudi statehood, survival and regional relations in historical context. It then moves on to assess contemporary transitions affecting sectarianism, secularism and liberalism. This is followed by coverage on dissent and repression and the 'anti-corruption drive' in the kingdom, encompassing the Ritz Carlton episode in 2017. The chapter then turns to the Saudi economy, the role of sovereign wealth funds within that, and defence and national security issues, including with reference to counterterrorism issues. The conclusion analyses which factors are likely to have a major bearing on Saudi Arabia's foreign policy and IR well into the twenty-first century.

Saudi statehood, survival and regional relations

Muhammed Ibn Saud, also known as Ibn Saud, emir of Diriyah, was considered to be the founder of the First Saudi State and dynasty from 1727 to 1765. The puritanical views associated with Wahhabism were forged in Ibn Saud's alliance with Mohammed bin Abdul-Wahhab, a religious leader, scholar and theologian, in 1744 when the Emirate of Diriyah was established. Whilst Wahhabism is often cited as intolerant, some scholars such as DeLong-Bas take a contrary view. She notes that Wahhabism is a voice of reform, reflecting mainstream eighteenth-century Islamic thought and a vision of Islamic society based upon monotheism in which Muslims, Christians and Jews were to enjoy peaceful coexistence and cooperative commercial treaty relations.[2] The *muwahhidun* (followers of *tawhid* doctrine) relied on the House of Saud to sustain their religious influence and the House of Saud relied on Wahhabis for political leadership. As Muhammad ibn 'Abd al-Wahhab said at the time: 'You [Muhammed Ibn Saud] are the settlement's chief and wise man. I want you to grant me an oath that you will perform jihad against the unbelievers. In return you will be imam, leader of the Muslim community and I will be leader in religious matters.'[3]

By 1765, when Muhammed Ibn Saud died, most of Najd was under Saudi control. By the time of the death of Muhammad ibn Abd al-Wahhab in 1792, Saudi control extended to Rub al-Khali (Empty Quarter).[4] Abdulaziz bin Muhammad Al Saud was the eldest son of Muhammed Ibn Saud and ruled from 1765 to 1803. His rule was followed by that of Saud bin Abdulaziz Al Saud from 1803 to 1814. Saud bin Abdulaziz Al Saud sent forces to bring the Hejaz region in the west of Saudi Arabia under his control. Taif was the first city captured, followed by the holy cities of Mecca and Medina, which had been ruled over the by the Ottomans since 1517. This made him the first Al Saud ruler to receive the title of the servant of the Two Holy Cities. The first Saudi state managed the Hajj for seven seasons from 1807 to 1812,[5] and in 1807 Ibn Saud opened the prophet's tomb and seized its treasures, which he justified by citing a cessation of Ottoman aid to the people of Medina.[6] Mohammad Ali, the viceroy of Egypt, led the response to the Saudi conquest on behalf of the Ottomans. His son, Ibrahim Pasha, led Ottoman forces into the Hejaz during the Ottoman–Wahhabi War of 1811–18 and laid siege to Diriyah (on the outskirts of modern-day Riyadh) for several months over the winter of 1818. Abdullah bin Saud, who ruled from 1814 was executed in the Ottoman capital, Constantinople, in 1819, marking the end of the first state.[7]

There have been two other Saudi states. Turki bin Abdullah bin Muhammad's reconquest in 1824 against Egyptian forces marked the beginning of the second Saudi state in 1824 and covered the region of Nejd (modern-day regions of Riyadh and Ha'il). It lasted until 1891, when internal conflict between forces loyal to the last Saudi imam, Abdul Rahman ibn Faisal ibn Turki, and the Rashidi dynasty of Ha'il led to its downfall at the battle of Mulayda in 1891.[8] Prior to 1917, the British favoured Sherif Abdullah ibn Hussein of the Hashemite family of Jordan, keeper of the two Holy Places in the Hejaz, as leader of the Arab movement and head of the anti-Ottoman Arab Revolt.[9] In early 1917 ibn Saud received a modest monthly subsidy and a role in anti-Ottoman efforts, including harassing Rashidi forces. Throughout 1916 and 1917 ibn Saud began a campaign of state building in Nejd in contrast to the small local protégés supported by the British, such as Sharif Hussein, emir of Mecca and others by the Ottomans.[10] Following the 1920 plot against him by Hussein and the sheikh of Kuwait, he began a systematic campaign of conquest to first defeat the Kuwait contingent, and then, with some Shammar tribe support, laid siege to Ha'il, which collapsed in 1921. Ibn Saud is said to have inflicted a massacre on Taif in July 1924, and concluded a treaty with the Idrisi ruler that gave him control over Aseer in 1925.[11] After the occupation of the Hejaz and Wahhabi control of the Two Holy Mosques, enabled by the British, who had ended subsidies to local rulers and ceased supporting Hussein, Saudi sovereign control was endorsed by a Muslim conference convened in Mecca after Saudi occupation. Yet, there are some groups such as Hejaz Al Hur (Free Hejaz) which continue to dispute Al Saud sovereign control over the Hejaz. They point to its brief independence under the former ruler Ali bin Hussein, who ruled as king of Hejaz and Grand Sharif of Mecca from October 1924 to the time of his deposition by Ibn Saud in December 1925.

From the earliest period, Saudi state consolidation involved a symbiosis of state and religion, but marriage has also played a major role in consolidating control over the provinces. Subsidies were paid to tribal leaders and attempts were made to turn nomads into farmers, religious scholars and, ultimately, soldiers garrisoned in special settlements. These Ikhwan formed the first Saudi army, but they were difficult to control. They disliked central authority and resented Ibn Saud's association with 'infidel' foreigners. They also strayed into neighbouring provinces and across new territorial boundaries established by the British with Iraq and Transjordan. New ports in Jubail and Qatif enhanced Saudi trade, while the Jeddah Treaty of 1927 gave the nascent Saudi state (incorporating the Hejaz and Nejd) independence. After the Ikhwan Revolt in 1930, which government troops and the British in Kuwait played major roles in defeating, further Saudi institutionalisation and centralisation occurred. Still, rebellions were not uncommon in Hejaz and Aseer, given the economic depression at that time, accompanied by increased taxes. A more targeted plot involved Hejazi exiles, the Hashemites of Jordan and Iraq, and the Imam Yahya of Yemen.[12]

These developed into a full war with Yemen in early 1934 which the Saudis won quickly, pushing home the advantage by advancing on Hodieda before being repelled by a British and Italian intervention. A treaty of friendship was signed between Saudi Arabia and Yemen the same year, reflecting a propensity to do the same with Iraq (1931 and 1936) and Transjordan (1933) up to and beyond the founding of the Kingdom of Saudi Arabia by Ibn Saud in 1932. As oil companies were seeking to explore concessions in the interior, there were tensions between Saudi Arabia, Oman and the then Trucial States (now UAE), notably the Buraimi dispute in the 1940s and 1950s which culminated in the Saudi invasion of the Buraimi oasis. The British responded by occupying the oasis, which led to the clearer demarcation of British and US companies operating in the region and, after advancing onto Nizwa, extended the Sultanate of Muscat and Oman at the cost of the Ibadi theocracy, with the last rebels defeated in 1959.[13] The British move was motivated by the need to counter Saudi, Egyptian and US interests in the region.

The result of the symbiosis between monarch and outsourced Islamic jurisprudence has been a leadership which has generally been cautious, with a notable exception in 1958 when King Saud tried to have Egyptian President Gamal Abdel Nasser assassinated. This set a precedent for a brief but difficult stand-off between the Al Saud royal family with Wahhabi clergy support, and King Saud, before power was ultimately transferred to Crown Prince Faisal.[14] During King Faisal's reign, Saudi Arabia invested heavily in promoting Islam through charitable funds and religious institutions in the kingdom, such as the Muslim World League established by King Faisal as an outreach organisation to clarify the true message of Islam in 1962. The OIC was also established by King Faisal in 1969. The Higher Council of Ulama (HCU) or Council of Senior Scholars is the kingdom's highest religious body and was established in 1971. The Grand Mufti, who heads up the HCU, is always a member of the Al ash-Sheikh family. Along with the Ministry of Awqaf, Da'wa, Guidance and Islamic Affairs and the Supreme Committee of the Judiciary which is comprised of Islamic scholars from the Hanbali School of conservative Sunni interpretation favoured in the kingdom and led by a member of the HCU.[15] As a conservative and yet moderating force in Saudi Arabia, King Abdullah moved to work with the HCU on an informal basis to ensure that any fatwas would not prove embarrassing on domestic social affairs or on foreign policy issues.[16] The Kingdom of Saudi Arabia remains an absolute monarchy and theocracy.

The Saudi management of Hajj is one of religious duty, but also of consequence to Saudi nationality security and its ability to regulate relations towards states with Muslim populations regionally and globally. This has been the case from the earliest days, when there was a temporary ban the Syrian caravan bringing the *mahmal*, the wooden structure designed to carry the *keswa*, the covering of the Kaaba that was traditionally made in Egypt. Apart from being seen as an 'innovation' in Islam, it was also accompanied by hundreds of armed Ottoman/Egyptian soldiers, which represented a security threat to Ibn Saud and a challenge to his authority in the Hijaz.[17] Cairo abandoned the mahmal ceremony in 1953 and discontinued sending the keswa in 1963. Management of the Hajj, and Hajj-related incidents, have created a number of tensions over the years (some of the more severe impacts are discussed in the chapters on Iran and regional relations).

Religion continues to resonate in Saudi Arabia in a number of ways, but mainly through the king's custodianship of the Two Holy Mosques and sacred territory,[18] including responsibility for the Hajj (pilgrimage to Mecca, one of the five pillars of Islam which every Muslim should follow) and Umra. As part of Saudi political legitimacy, any notions of corruption or failings in this regard are particularly sensitive. Relatively new Islamic institutions based in the kingdom, such as the OIC, also have a role to play in advancing Saudi influence, albeit indirectly, as well as economic dimensions which have scaled up following the advent of the oil era.

Sectarianism, secularism and liberalism

The Shia minority in Saudi Arabia make up about 10 per cent of the total population, with most residing in the oil-rich Eastern Province. Whilst they are generally sympathetic to Iran and pursue reform in the kingdom, they have been securitised by the Saudi response to the Iranian Revolution and the existence of Hezbollah al-Hijaz in the 1980s and 1990s.[19] Counterterrorism and sectarianism are a complex and fluid mix of doctrinal (religious), sub-national (local), national (identity) and transnational (IR and leverage) influences. Nevertheless, there have been a number of initiatives to address the sectarian divide in the kingdom. King Abdullah's National Dialogue was founded in August 2003 to debate and remedy the social challenges associated with 9/11, terrorist attacks in the kingdom in 2003, and petitions submitted to the king. The King Abdulaziz Center for National Dialogue continues this work and had held ten meetings as of 2015. King Abdullah also initiated an interreligious dialogue, now under the auspices of the King Abdullah Bin Abdulaziz International Centre for Inter-religious and Inter-cultural Dialogue, but omits overt reference to Shia Muslims and has arranged meetings outside of the kingdom, mostly in Europe so far.

King Abdullah also tried to improve the standard of living in the Eastern Province, and Shia participation in the workforce and in lower levels of government administration such as the municipal council in the Shia-dominated Saudi city of Qatif. But since the Arab uprisings, it has not been sustained. Saudi concerns about Iranian subversion in Bahrain (about 70 per cent Shia) remain a stumbling block to better relations with the Shia domestically and with Iran. The execution of Nimr al Nimr, a Shia cleric and activist, on 2 January 2016 set the context for a rapid deterioration in Saudi–Shia relations as well as in Saudi–Iranian relations. King Salman and Mohammed bin Salman have made a number of symbolic appearances with religious leaders or officials to promote a new discourse on religious tolerance, necessary to stabilising and liberalising the kingdom. In 2017, Mohammed bin Salman promised to turn the kingdom towards moderate Islam, in replication of the UAE, instead of the 'rigid doctrines' that he attributed as a response to the Iranian Revolution.[20] Religious outreach is occurring in the context of liberalising the Saudi economy and attracting tourists, businesses and investment from around the world. The message to the US and Europe appeared to be that minorities should abide by the laws of each country, no matter which country or what the law is.[21]

Mohammed bin Salman's comment that 'Saudi national identity is the umbrella of all Saudis, and that their differences in doctrine fall within the diversity that enriches the country's culture and life' may indicate more positive relations with the Shia of the Eastern Province post-Nimr.[22] Through Vision 2030 and an economy-centric approach, the Eastern Province city of Al Khobar was the first city in the Middle East to receive a 5G wireless network, and the healthcare industry has received a boost from external funders such as the UAE.[23]

Following the Gulf War in 1991, the country became more secularised through a top-down approach that advanced state formation, historical commemoration and capital accumulation whilst focusing on Islamist movements as the great threat to the state.[24] This has affected spheres as diverse as city planning, foreign policy and regional relations. The state accumulated high oil revenues during the first decade of the 2000s, and there are suggestions that this enabled the Al Saud to restrict the clerics' budget to support Wahhabi projects and influence abroad, thereby altering their balance of power.[25] Secularisation and liberalisation have continued apace in certain spheres in the kingdom, widely favoured by hopeful and nationalistic youth and women who favour mobility, but questioned by the older generation who have found the rapid change and uncertainty less compelling. A liberalising move was already underway in 2012 after the head of the religious police (*mutawa*) was replaced with someone with a more open attitude.[26] Then the Saudi cabinet approved a new law in April 2016 that curbed the authority of the *mutawa*, ordering them to be 'gentle' and 'humane',[27] and they are no longer able to chase and arrest individuals, undermining a key coercive instrument and Wahhabi normative influence in society that has existed for centuries, not only in the kingdom but across the Islamic world.[28]

But it wasn't until Mohammed bin Salman became the de facto ruler in 2017 and his pronouncement that he would revert the kingdom to the 'moderate Islam open to the world and all religions' that the bond with Wahhabi clerics, on which the politics of the kingdom has rested for centuries, was effectively broken.[29] One scholar has noted that Saudi Arabia under Mohammed bin Salman is now 'out of the business of Islam' and that Saudi policy makers have recognised that leveraging Salafi non-state actors has only damaged the kingdom, as proven by the 2003 insurgency by Al Qaeda in the Arabian Peninsula (AQAP).[30] The kingdom doesn't fund Islamic groups in India and has given up leases on mosques in Belgium and other parts of Europe. There is 'no money in Wahhabism' except in supporting government legitimacy and in promoting religious tourism.[31] A visual metaphor of how far the kingdom has travelled down the route of secularism is the 2021 decision that Saudi shops no longer need to close at prayer times. The kingdom's focus is now on competing with other GCC states such as the UAE.

Dissent and repression

Some of the issues which have affected Saudi threat perception have been linked to actions the Al Saud have taken to combat internal criticism. For example, King Faisal allowed the World Association of Muslim Youth to be staffed by many Muslim Brotherhood (MB) figures throughout the 1960s and 1970s at the zenith of their influence in the Kingdom.[32] Those decades also saw Saudi activists establish an anti-nationalist movement in Beirut. From 1968, the Sahwa (Islamic awakening) movement, a faction of Saudi Qutbism (an ideology developed by Sayyid Qutb[33]) developed. In 1979, the takeover of the Grand Mosque in 1979 by violent Islamists intent on the overthrow of the House of Saud underscored the existential threat of dissenters in the kingdom and its reliance on foreign powers.

Sahwa gained prominence in the 1990s as religious conservatives gained influence over social institutions and the education sector to stem criticism of the Al Saud for allowing US bases in the kingdom following the Iraqi invasion of Kuwait. A small group of Saudi experts and Muslim clerics established the Committee for the Defence of Legitimate Rights, which was moved to London in 1994 following pressure from the Saudi state. The attacks on Saudi soil from AQAP in the early 2000s (endorsed through the theoretical output of various Saudi sheikhs in the 1990s[34]) again highlighted a weakness vis-à-vis extremists. Cross-border attacks by ISIS (Islamic State of Iraq and the Levant) from Iraq, as well as a campaign of terror by ISIS cells endorsed by Al-Baghdadi, the group's leader at that time, in April 2005, continued to highlight the persistent security challenges to the Al Saud.

In an attempt by some activists to try to replicate the strategies which had brought down the ruling leader in Tunisia and Egypt, 11 March 2011 was declared as a 'Day of Rage' in Saudi Arabia.[35] King Salman cut short his holiday in Morocco and returned to Saudi Arabia to spend $120 billion to secure the monarchy against any social pressure for constitutional change.

This is a red line for the monarchy and breaches the concepts of *al-bayah* – a pledge of allegiance. The Al Saud will never allow itself to become a constitutional monarchy. Prince Nayef bin Abdul-Aziz (Mohammed bin Nayef's father) famously said 'I don't want to be Queen Elizabeth'.[36] Yet, it is precisely the structural properties of absolute monarchy which create inefficiencies in the state's armed forces[37] and resentment.

A political party, Islamic Umma, was established in 2011 to challenge King Abdullah but was more an act of protest rather than a party, since there was no political infrastructure to engage with.[38] Members were conditionally released in 2011, except for the religious scholar and lawyer Abd al-Aziz al-Wuhaibi, who refused to renounce political activity and was sentenced to seven years' imprisonment.[39]

After calling for a petition in support of Mohammed Morsi in Egypt, Mohsen Al-Awaji from the Sahwa movement was briefly arrested in July 2013; he has been detained many times before and since. Mohamed Al-Arifi, a leading religious figure, has around 20 million followers on Twitter.[40] He has generally had good relations with the government, except when he was arrested in 2014 for criticising the rail network that links the holy sites of Mecca. He is known to stir sectarian tension and has been forced to backtrack on comments about Al Qaeda.[41] He is close to Salman Al-Awdah, who has supported change in other Arab countries and pushed for change domestically, including supporting a constitutional monarchy. Al-Awdah has 13 million followers on Twitter,[42] but he was arrested along with others in the September 2017 and now faces a death sentence.[43] He and others in the Sahwa group have been accused of having ties to the MB – considered a terror organisation since March 2014 – or to a 'foreign entity', i.e. Qatar, which Saudi Arabia, Bahrain, the UAE and Egypt had blockaded from 2017 to 2021. Lacroix refers to the 'scapegoating' of Sahwa to exonerate Wahhabi clerics.[44]

Following the assassination of Jamal Khashoggi at the Saudi consulate in Istanbul on 2 October 2018, the US Central Intelligence Agency (CIA) found this incident to be linked to the crown prince, Mohammed bin Salman.[45] Khashoggi wrote regular *Washington Post* articles, critical on many aspects of Saudi politics and policy. He covered topics such as repression and inequality in the kingdom, actions concerning Lebanon and 'betraying the Arab Spring' in Yemen.[46] Within a year, Khashoggi had moved from being an ontological threat to one that was neutralised by a physical response. It appears that his writings, and possibly his offer to help 9/11 victims sue the kingdom,[47] rather than his associations with the MB or Qatar, were the main reasons why he was killed. Princess Basmah, niece of King Salman, was jailed for three years for her outspoken views on women's rights and after calling for the kingdom to become a constitutional monarchy. Several women involved in the Women2Drive campaign were arrested in May 2018.[48]

Some have been released, whilst as of May 2020 there were still forty-eight women activists in five prisons.[49] Another high-profile case was that of Loujain al-Hathloul, first arrested in May 2018, but who was released following direct criticism from, and the election of, President Biden.[50] Many other activists languish in prison or are closely monitored and regularly arrested by police.

Beyond those calling for political rights or constitutional reform, one of the most common forms of popular dissent appears to be linked to land. Strong-arm tactics have often been used related to land, such as during Mohammed bin Salman's youth, when he earned the nickname 'Abu Rasasa' after allegedly sending a bullet in an envelope to a land registry official who refused to help him forcefully acquire a tract of land. Some resistance exists from locals who refuse to be evicted, one having been shot dead by security forces in Al-Khuraybah in April 2020 and subsequently labelled a terrorist.[51] Other displacements are said to be occurring in the city of Tabuk.[52] There is also evidence of contention over encroaching Al Saud consolidation in the Hejaz, such as changes of the area name to Western Area and of hospital names to reflect the patronage of specific princes. These are perceived by some to challenge the identity and history of the local region.

Saudi dissatisfaction with the ruling elite is said to be mainly among Salafis, some princes and the older generation who prefer more cautious Saudi policies.[53] Since many campaigns of political activism by dissidents and secessionists are conducted online and primarily through social media, they also tend to be dominated by youth. Given state monitoring and control, as well as societal norms, it is difficult to know how far these extend. Furthermore, technology serves as an integral part of the authoritarian toolkit, with many instances of censorship coupled with repression,[54] phone tracking[55] and grooming of informants, lobbyists or journalists at major (social) media companies.[56] This puts a different complexion on the kingdom's opening of a media city in February 2020 to attract foreign media companies. In October 2020, Saudi membership of the UN Human Rights Council was rejected on human rights grounds, while China and Russia managed to win seats. There has also been an attempt to institutionalise a political opposition and spark a transition to democracy from Saudi activists based in the UK, the US and Canada in September 2020.[57]

The 'anti-corruption drive' under Crown Prince Mohammed bin Salman

Traditional Saudi succession stopped among the brothers of Ibn Saud in April 2015, when, after just four months as Crown Prince, Muqrin bin

Abdulaziz, former director of the Saudi Intelligence Agency from 2005 to 2012, was ousted by King Salman's royal decree, overriding the former decree of King Abdullah and bypassing the Allegiance Council.[58] It was done in favour of Prince Nayef bin Abdulaziz Al Saud who became crown prince, and Prince Mohammed bin Salman, who became deputy crown prince. At this time, King Salman gave a month's bonus to all military and security personnel.[59] Whilst the change in succession reinstated the Sudairi line,[60] it also led the way for political consolidation under Mohammed bin Salman, who on 21 June 2017 ousted Prince Nayef to become crown prince.

The transition of power to Mohammed bin Salman from 2017 represented the first time one of Ibn Saud's grandsons had taken on state responsibilities. Mohammed bin Salman's rise was by no means guaranteed. It followed the premature deaths of his brothers Prince Sultan and Prince Nayef, who were next in line, but it is no secret that Mohammed bin Salman was King Salman's favourite son who preferred to be in a leadership position and ate meat with his hands, in the traditional way that his father did. Mohammed bin Salman also understands Islamic law, since he graduated with a bachelor's degree in law from King Saud University in Riyadh in 2007. Since he was not educated in the US, he may lack an affinity with the West and be unable to gauge response to some of the kingdom's policies and actions across a diverse portfolio of defence, economy, religion and oil. However, his inspirations are foreign, from Alexander the Great to UK Prime Minister Margaret Thatcher, for her restructuring of the UK economy.[61] (It's important to remember that Margaret Thatcher was removed from office by a Conservative Party rebellion against her policies, which were deemed too divisive to win the next election).

Political consolidation has been a feature of Saudi politics under Mohammed bin Salman. This has involved some subtle and not so subtle innovations. National Day, a public holiday since 2005, has become bigger each year but has faced some backlash from religious figures who deem it alien to Islamic traditions.[62] The media landscape has reflected content on social media, including accusations of treachery over activist campaigns and nationalist responses to issues of the day.[63] Further concrete steps have enhanced Muhammed bin Salman's power and control over mega projects. In 2015, after a Saudi Binladin Group crane fell and killed 100 people prior to the Hajj, the company was eventually taken over by the government and focused work on finishing Neom.[64] Even in 2001, Prince Bandar bin Sultan said that 'if you tell me that building this whole country, and spending $350 billion out of $400 billion, that we misused or got corrupted with $50 billion, I'll tell you, "Yes" ... but I'll take that anytime'.[65]

The Council of Economic and Development Affairs and the Council of Political and Security Affairs, both founded in 2015 under the direction of

Mohammed bin Salman, have consolidated the work of twelve different advisory bodies. This was a popular move because the new councils have cut through bureaucracy, which is seen by many Saudis as a barrier to progress. He has also allowed women to drive from 2018, and they were given driving licences in June 2019. The decision to allow women to drive looks to have taken place after consultation with US think-tanks in February 2016 on how to improve the kingdom's image abroad. Women have also been allowed to attend sports matches since January 2018.[66] The Saudi ambassador to the US, appointed on 23 February 2019, is the first female envoy in Saudi history. Princess Reema bint Bandar bin Sultan bin Abdulaziz Al Saud is the daughter of Bandar bin Sultan Al Saud, who was Saudi ambassador to the US from 1983 to 2005 and director general of the Saudi Intelligence Agency from 2012 to 2014.

The move to enhance the role of women in Saudi society was started by King Abdullah, who funnelled oil revenues into new centres of advanced learning, part of his agenda to give all women a higher education. King Abdullah even promoted a woman, Nora bint Abdullah al-Fayez, to the rank of deputy minister for education in 2009, an unprecedented move in the kingdom. She was fired, when King Salman came to power in 2015, over her belief that girls were entitled to physical education, to play football or swim, which is at odds with the views held by the Al ash-Sheikh-dominated clerical establishment. King Abdullah also appointed thirty women to the consultative Shura Council in 2013 and allowed Saudi women to vote and even run for office for the first time in municipal elections in 2015. Although carrying little power, with two dozen women winning office there are probably at least some Saudi men who voted for women, which indicates a changing attitude in the domestic political landscape. There are also grass-roots elements of civil society, albeit operating under a patrimonial framework, such as the King Salman Center for Local Governance, affiliated with Prince Sultan University.[67]

On 4 November 2017, the Ritz Carlton hotel in Riyadh was used as a detention centre in an anti-corruption drive or shake-down of the Saudi royal and business elite, until it reopened in February 2018. More than $100 billion was recouped by the Saudi government through various deals, including $1 billion from Prince Miteb, once seen as a contender to the throne, and Prince Alwaleed bin Talal, who was freed after paying an undisclosed amount.[68] One of the ripple effects of the Ritz Carlton episode is that some Saudis are now searching or using second nationalities in places such as Cyprus.[69] A former senior UK government official calls the Ritz Carlton episode a power play, since the anti-corruption drive was selective and corruption has always been part of the Saudi system.[70] There is also probably an element of score settling, especially with reference to the Ritz

Carlton episode, since Mohammed bin Salman did not have a fortune like other princes.[71] The anti-corruption drive may be popular, but e-government based on a unified digital identity is more popular, because it affects everyone's daily life and makes sense when trying to open up the economy.[72]

Other actions aimed at recouping lost funds involve Mohammed bin Nayef, who has been under house arrest for much of the time since he was arrested on 6 March 2020 for treason. His younger brother, Nawaf bin Nayef, was also detained, as well as one of the king's brothers, Prince Ahmed bin Abdulaziz Al Saud, who was also charged with treason,[73] probably to pave the way for Mohammed bin Salman's succession to the throne. Yet, Mohammed bin Nayef is also implicated in corruption in a secret 2007 decree signed by King Abdullah.[74] It is said to have formalised and raised from 30 to 45 per cent the amount of income he was legally allowed to receive for special activities from fines, passport and residency fees.[75] Mohammed bin Nayef's support amongst those who formerly supported King Abdullah raises the question of this being more of a power struggle than a straightforward financial issue.[76]

In November 2020, the son and daughter of Saad Al Jabri, former minister of state and long-time advisor of Mohammad bin Nayef, were sentenced to nine years in prison and six and half years, respectively, for money laundering and attempting to escape from Saudi Arabia, which the family denies.[77] The sentences are believed to have been efforts to bring Saad Al Jabri back to the kingdom.[78] The death sentence handed down to Fahd bin Turki bin Abdulaziz, a former top commander of Saudi forces in Yemen and nephew of King Salman, due to an alleged coup attempt and corruption, could similarly be used to put pressure on his family as a way to claw back billions from them.[79] Mohammed bin Salman has continued to implement reforms in this area, with ministers now banned from serving on company boards.[80]

Conspicuous consumption could yet leave Mohammed bin Salman politically exposed, especially during any extended economic downturn. He owns a $500 million super-yacht, *The Serene* which is home to a $450 million Leonardo da Vinci painting *Salvator Mundi* (bid for by the UAE ruling family, and it may yet end up there as a gift, with both Saudi Arabia and the UAE attempting to outbid Qatar). This was reported to have been given to the UAE, possibly as part of its effort to project religious tolerance (since the picture is of Jesus), in exchange for another yacht, *The Topaz*.[81] Mohammed bin Salman also owns a $300 million château in France.[82] These big-ticket items, among other assets, could leave the crown prince politically exposed, especially during a sustained economic downturn. Without a change of tack, the political consolidation that Mohammed bin Salman has undertaken has removed political options to express dissatisfaction and could be creating enemies within the kingdom. Yet, that same political consolidation is justified as having built a centre of governance that is capable of running the country but no longer in the hands of ministries.[83]

Systemic threats, including the succession process after King Salman, the youth bulge, economic and political expectations following greater liberalisation in the kingdom and external threats remain intact.[84] Therefore, it was imperative that if Mohammed bin Salman is to become king the opposition should be neutralised. That has taken place. The assassination of Khashoggi in 2018 has helped to silence domestic dissent and opposition, the Yemen conflict has spurred on hyper-nationalism, and the Qatar Crisis helped to cut, albeit temporarily, a source of contentious media influence during a period of domestic political consolidation.[85]

The Saudi economy

Saudi Arabia is the archetypal rentier economy. It is the world's largest oil exporter and the state with the world's second-largest reserves. In February 2015, when King Salman ascended to the throne, he spent $32 billion on a two-month bonus for workers and pensioners to relieve socio-economic pressure and ease into his role.[86] Previously, King Abdullah spent $130 in 2011 before public sector pay cuts were implemented as part of temporary austerity measures.[87] The kingdom is attempting to replace boom-bust cycles with a pattern of improvements in the kingdom's non-oil gross domestic product (GDP), economic recovery from COVID-19 and continued diversification of the economy, which will lead to a GDP growth forecast of 7.4 per cent in 2022.[88] This is after a budget deficit of 6.4 per cent of GDP in 2020.[89]

Economic policies have been implemented since the early 1970s with a view to moving towards a post-rentier economy. The Saudi Development Bank was created at this time, but as oil prices peaked and Saudi Arabia oil revenue rose to $22.5 billion, the appetite for heavy industrialisation diminished.[90] There have been efforts by Saudi banks to loan to large Saudi enterprises such as Ma'aden, affiliates of Aramco and to Sabic.[91] The 2002–8 oil price boom facilitated the Saudi pivot to a position of relative power in the international system amid shifts in the global energy markets towards Asia. Hydrocarbon revenues have been reinvested in new infrastructure projects in the kingdom, which have made it an attractive destination for expatriate labour, especially construction and domestic labour from the Islamic world.[92] Not all mega projects have met with positive media coverage. For instance, the systematic destruction of cultural heritage sites in Mecca and Medina over decades, but particularly since 2011, in favour of maximising

Hajj receipts, has attracted negative commentary.[93] Over 1,000 economic policy shifts are said to have occurred since 2015, most within the National Transformation Programme that was launched in 2016 as part of Vision 2030. These include reforms to the labour market, including an easing to the 'kafala' (sponsorship) system restrictions on migrant workers so they can change jobs or leave the country without their employer's permission, as well as a Premium Residency Program launched in 2019.

There are a number of structural issues which have put pressure on the Saudi economy. Hyper-centralisation, overlapping jurisdictions and other bureaucratic challenges threaten Vision 2030.[94] COVID-19 has put further pressure on Saudi Vision 2030 – Saudi Aramco profits almost halved in 2020 compared with 2019.[95] Even if prices recover following lower investments in oil infrastructure and greater demand after COVID-19, this may be the last super cycle that delivers more than $100 per barrel. Further COVID-19-related pressure has been on trade and financial markets (although the Public Investment Fund [PIF] has found opportunities[96]), limited air travel and tourism (including the Hajj) and through lost productivity. Even before COVID-19 struck, uncertainty surrounding mega projects, corporate scandal in 2009[97] and management issues have sparked questions about business practice, inward investment and economic diversification. Insecurity (particularly with regard to Iran), reputation damage after the Ritz Carlton episode in 2017 and the assassination of Jamal Khashoggi in 2018, as well as the Yemen conflict, have done the same.[98] There are also questions over how the energy transition from fossil fuels to renewable and clean sources of energy (solar, wind, water) will affect the kingdom, particularly how it attempts to extend the life cycle of oil through establishing or enhancing downstream markets and new energy projects. Amid the European rush for alternative sources of natural gas during the war in Ukraine, the Saudi and Kuwait agreement for the development of the Dorra gas field in the Neutral Zone (which lies in the onshore and offshore territory shared by Saudi Arabia and Kuwait at their border) announced in March 2022 could be significant, with the added potential for both parties to cooperate with Iran, since part of the field falls within Iran's border.

Demographics in the kingdom are also challenging the Saudi political economy. Saudi Arabia has a population of 28 million, which is larger than the other GCC states. About 70 per cent of the population is below the age of thirty.[99] The socio-economic pressure is large and growing.[100] Labour participation is just 41 per cent and productivity between 2003 and 2013 lagged behind most developing economies.[101] The kingdom will need to create another 4.5 million jobs to absorb the growing labour force by 2030.[102] Private sector jobs have grown by 11 per cent year on year from

2005 to 2017,[103] but youth unemployment among Saudis in their early twenties was still nearly 40 per cent in 2018.[104] There are various reasons for this, including skills, expectations, weaker job security in the private sector and unemployment whilst waiting for higher wages in the public sector or a higher-status job in the private sector. Whilst the prospects for young Saudi males could be improved, the common complaint against them is that they want a welfare state and are therefore not willing to engage fully in the opportunities on offer. Women's employment in the kingdom is low, at 23 per cent in 2019, but it rose to 33 per cent in 2022.[105] Given the rising education levels of Saudi women, there is the possibility that they will have higher expectations in future, although the 28,000 applicants for thirty female train-driver positions and roles in branches of the armed forces suggests that Saudi women may be willing to seek employment in non-traditional roles.[106]

There are no polls on expectations among Saudi youth, except some anecdotal evidence to suggest widespread support for Vision 2030 and a general opening up of the kingdom to the prosperity and opportunities that globalisation can provide.[107] A *nitaqat* (Saudisation) policy was introduced in 2011 and has been extended across multiple sectors, including retail from 2013, and was found to be targeting expendable expatriate labour during the pandemic, including Yemeni doctors and professors in southern Saudi Arabia in 2021, since their contracts were not renewed.[108] The kingdom has continued to seek revenues from non-oil sources, and has increased value added tax (VAT) from 5 per cent in 2018 to 15 per cent, effective from 1 July 2020.

At the October 2021 Future Investment Initiative summit in Riyadh, twenty new economic zones, with six in Riyadh, were to be announced, as well as other investor-friendly policies.[109] They are popular because they dispense with the need to implement more difficult national economic reforms.[110] Oyo and Bechtel (which is developing infrastructure in Neom) have already set up regional headquarters in Riyadh. Saudi Arabia has taken further steps to ensure this happens by not awarding government contracts to firms with regional headquarters outside of the kingdom, starting in 2024. Furthermore, under a new programme in 2021 called 'Shareek' ('Partner'), Saudi firms including Aramco and Sabic have agreed to cut dividends so as to fund a $1.3 trillion plan to contribute to domestic capital spending, boosting GDP growth and jobs.[111] Sixty per cent of the total budget allocation is expected to come from these two companies.[112] Aramco's contribution will be aided by high oil prices due to the conflict in the Ukraine, which caused its profits to soar in 2022. Although foreign direct investment (FDI) increased to reach nearly $20 billion in 2021 on the back of an oil pipeline deal, it still falls far short of the $100 billion expected by 2030. Changes to the Saudi personal data law, which prohibits data transfer outside the kingdom, may inhibit FDI further.

The role of sovereign wealth funds

Saudi Arabian Monetary Agency (SAMA), known as the Saudi Central Bank from 2020, has reserves of around $500 billion. Established in 1952, SAMA managed the kingdom's large oil surpluses and supports the national budget. It takes a much more cautious approach compared to the PIF, investing in fixed-income investments such as US treasury bonds. The PIF was established in 1971. It has used Ministry of Finance funds to help capitalise Saudi banks, including the largest bank, National Commercial Bank, so they are now effectively controlled by the PIF, which is unusual.[113] The PIF was made into a sovereign wealth fund (SWF) in April 2016 as part of Vision 2030 and invests in large-scale projects which are actively seeking to attract investment.[114]

The PIF's focus was turned inward in 2020 as a major investor in the kingdom, and expects to deliver $542 billion in projects over the coming two decades to 2040, including the $500 billion futuristic city of Neom, to ensure Vision 2030 is a success.[115] Neom sits in the north-west corner of the kingdom, on the border with Egypt and Jordan, is key in delivering on the kingdom's strategic location to link Africa, Asia and Europe.[116] It could also deliver significant advantages by combining access to the internal markets of all three states when complete. Access to Egypt expected to be through the construction of a new causeway across the Tiran Strait to Egypt. Neom Bay already includes the construction of hotels, and Neom Bay airport was inaugurated in 2019. It is expected that a new phase – a new $200 billion 170km Line City stretching from the Red Sea to the mountains and into the desert will be launched as part of Neom's growth. It will include parkland, a subterranean service level including shops and a commercial space and a second subterranean level which incorporates high-speed transport connections and a growing list of features focused on leisure and high-technology. Said to form part of the so-called 'Dubai bug' which has influenced town planning in Saudi Arabia, it follows similar economic cities developed during the reign of King Abdullah, but with only King Abdullah Economic City fully completed.[117] Saudi Arabia, like other states in the Middle East still lacks extensive transportation, mail service and a comprehensive sewage network, so there are arguments for a more integrated approach. Instead, higher oil revenues in 2022 are being used to shore up prospects for Neom and kickstart 'the line' alongside replenishing central bank reserves and supporting other counter-cyclical moves. There are, however, some good reasons why the area should be developed: there is strong tourism, agribusiness and manufacturing potential.[118] Whether a range of projects such as Neom or Amaala, as part of Vision 2030, will be enough to sustain a transition from a rentier economy to a post-rentier one is yet to be proven.

There are questions as to how the PIF will double assets over the five years from 2021 to reach $1.07 trillion[119] during the COVID-19 era, which has created great market volatility and undermined attempts to boost the Saudi tourism industry. It is expected to reach $2 trillion under management by 2030. In 2019, Saudi Arabia expanded the remit of the authority overseeing economic cities to also oversee special economic zones. The UAE, the US, France, Singapore, Japan, Kuwait and Malaysia are the main investors in Saudi Arabia.[120] Investment was up between 2018 and the first nine months of 2019, from $3.18 billion to $3.50 billion, on the back of a 54 per cent increase in the number of foreign companies setting up in the country and key aspects such as ensuring equality between Saudi and foreign investors.[121] The first Future Investment Initiative conference was hosted by PIF and took place in October 2017. Widely boycotted due to the Khashoggi affair, it has continued to attract a mix of high-profile business investors and politicians, many former officials from the Trump administration.

The main issue linking the Saudi economy and foreign policy is whether sustainable economic diversification can occur, at what level and what impact this might have on political consolidation the distributive neo-patrimonial network associated with rentierism that has maintained monarchical stability.[122] The issue will have a further bearing on which states the kingdom seeks to engage as a matter of priority as it proceeds on the path of development and diversification.

Climate change policies

In July 2020, Saudi Arabia announced plans to build a $5 billion green hydrogen plant aiming at exports.[123] The same month, the Oil and Gas Climate Initiative, to which Saudi Aramco belongs, committed to reduce the carbon intensity of upstream operations by 2025,[124] very much in line with India and China's approach of 'phase down' rather than 'phase out'. In November 2020 King Salman announced the Circular Carbon Economy National Programme as part of the Saudi presidency of the G20.[125] Mohammed bin Salman put forward a measure to 'green' Saudi Arabia and the Middle East in March 2021.[126] Ahead of the UN Climate Change Conference in Glasgow, 31 October–12 November 2021, the UK welcomed Saudi Arabia's greening initiative.[127] Saudi Arabia has committed to eliminate or offset its greenhouse gas emissions by 2060, which, even if partially achieved, could enhance its regional status and contain rising temperatures in the Gulf. However, Seznec and Mosis argue that a lack of centralised and transparent planning beyond the Saudi Ministry of Energy's Renewable Energy Project Development Office is impeding Saudi Arabia's shift to cleaner energy.[128] The kingdom has also been working with states such as Australia to avoid placing the Great Barrier Reef on an 'in danger' list due to a lack of progress in cutting pollution from the land and the impact of mass coral bleaching.[129] In a leaked document, states such as Saudi Arabia, Japan and Australia also stood accused of asking the UN to play down the need to rapidly move away from fossil fuels.[130] Whilst Mohammed bin Salman didn't attend COP26, it was notable that the Qatari emir was in attendance and held several meetings, including with British Prime Minister Boris Johnson. However, Mohammed bin Salman discussed coordinated action on climate change in the GCC summit in Riyadh in December 2021.

Defence and national security

National security challenges are tied up with monarchical interests and therefore are indistinguishable from each other. This has been the case throughout the period of Al Saud rule. Political consolidation has been a dominant theme from Ibn Saud to Mohammed bin Salman, and has led to a low level of state institutionalisation and an inability to distance or decouple the ruling elite from domestic and foreign policy blowback. The main contemporary external/internal security considerations have been the rise of violent Islamist groups such as Al Qaeda and ISIS in Iraq and the Houthis in Yemen and their attacks internally in the early 2000s. In addition, the kingdom is focused on an existential threat from Iran as a Shia republican power chafing at a US-imposed regional order that has favoured the Arab Gulf monarchies since 1979.

In the past Saudi Arabia notably used royalist Yemenis to fight Nasser's Egypt intent on pan-Arabism in the 1960s, and underwrote much of the cost of Mujahideen operations against the Soviet Union on behalf of the US in Afghanistan in the 1980s. Indeed, King Salman, who was an experienced official, having been governor of Riyadh for forty-eight years before becoming defence minister in 2011, crown prince in 2012 and king in 2015, was also a key financier of the jihad against the Soviet invasion of Afghanistan in the 1980s.[131] As prince, he raised more money privately for this campaign than the CIA and Saudi intelligence managed to do through official channels, and has raised funds for Bosnian Muslims and the Palestinians.[132] Whilst riyal politik, involvement in proxy wars and the deployment of soft power (i.e. spending $75 billion on Wahhabi doctrine abroad through funding schools, mosques and charities across the Islamic world[133]) has been a dominant theme in Saudi foreign policy, its prevalence is coming to an end. In its place, the kingdom is building a smarter, leaner military, including drones, as well as special forces with air cover, similar to the UAE. Riyadh is no longer worried about conventional war with Iraq or Iran, but it does need advanced technology materiel from the US (e.g. weaponised drones).[134]

Saudi Arabia supported on to support Iraq against Iran in the 1980s, and mobilised its forces along with Kuwaiti and US forces in the battle of Khafji and along its eastern coastline in January and February 1991. The Saudi high command admitted after the war that the Iraqi Republican Guard could have occupied the kingdom's oil-rich al-Ahsa governorate in just six hours.[135] Riyadh therefore agreed to allow US forces to be deployed in the kingdom to protect the kingdom throughout the 1990s, from Operation Desert Shield in 1990 to the Joint Task Force Southwest Asia as part of Operation Southern Watch after the Gulf War. In 2003, the US withdrew remaining non-training troops or arms purchase support from the kingdom. However, they were temporarily back again in late 2019 amid growing tensions with Iran. Arms deliveries to Saudi Arabia in 2014–18 included fifty-six combat aircraft from the US and thirty-eight from the UK. In both cases, the aircraft were equipped with cruise missiles and other guided weapons. Planned deliveries for 2019–23 include ninety-eight combat aircraft, seven missile defence systems and eighty-three tanks from the US; 737 armoured vehicles from Canada; five frigates from Spain; and short-range ballistic missiles from Ukraine.[136]

In 2015, Saudi Arabia pledged to host a thirty-five-nation Islamic military coalition (not including Iran) to fight terrorism from a joint operations command centre in Riyadh.[137] In 2016, the kingdom hosted Operation Northern Thunder, the largest military exercise in the Middle East, including 350,000 ground troops, planes and tanks from twenty nations including Malaysia, Turkey, Pakistan, Egypt, Sudan, Chad, the Comoros and the Maldives.[138]

The military forces of Saudi Arabia dominate the southern Gulf and are the best-equipped armed forces in the region. Regular forces number 227,000 troops, including 75,000 in the army, 13,500 in the navy and 20,000 in the air force. Another 16,000 assigned to air defence, 2,500 to strategic missiles and 100,000 in the National Guard come mainly from the tribes of Najd and other tribes allied with the royal family. There are 24,000 paramilitary forces.[139] The army has 600 heavy tanks, 780 light armoured vehicles and 1,423 armoured troop carriers. The air force has 150 F-15s from the US,

67 Tornadoes and 71 Typhoons from Europe.[140] Air defences include sixteen batteries of Patriot missiles, seventeen batteries of Shahine missiles, sixteen of Hawk missiles and seventy-three Crotale/Shahine missile units.[141]

Underdeveloped policy formulation and a fast-moving security environment across the region are issues which will affect Saudi foreign policy going forward. This has been evident with regard to actions against political dissidents domestically and internationally, as well as the conflict in Yemen designed to push out any last vestiges of Iranian influence. Saudi Arabia had the third-largest defence budget in the world in 2015 after the US and China.[142] This is no longer sustainable. Unlike, the UAE, the Saudis, who have around 200,000 troops, appear unwilling to send them into ground offensives, instead relying on allied troops such the Sudanese in Yemen. The army and National Guard are more for internal security, to prevent a military coup,[143] than to address interstate threats or project hard power. This may change over time, but there will be some catching up to do with the UAE in terms of building operational experience, interoperability and expertise. Saudi Arabia also needs to modernise its navy (Red Sea and Gulf fleets) in the same way that it has modernised its air force. This will be essential to projecting power more fully in the region and beyond, to counter Iran, but also to act more independently from the US and other allies.

Vision 2030 requires the General Authority for Military Industries, the regulatory authority, to achieve 50 per cent of new defence kit produced in the country by 2030. The Saudi Arabian Military Industries was launched in May 2017 to manage the production of air and land systems, weapons and missiles, and defence electronics, in a similar vein to the UAE's more established Emirates Defence Industries Company. In 2017, King Salman issued a number of royal decrees concerning the national security realm, including the consolidation of counterterrorism and domestic intelligence in a new body called the Presidency of State Security , removing important powers from the Interior Ministry.[144] Whilst the move appears to have streamlined counterterrorism activity in the kingdom, it has also secured the office of Mohammed bin Salman and removed significant powers from the Interior Ministry, formerly led by Mohammed bin Nayef. But to maintain ties to the US, Abdulaziz bin Mohammed al-Howairini, who has worked in the Interior Ministry for thirty years, was chosen to head up the new agency.[145] He and his deputy became ministers. The National Cyber Security Authority was also established at this time to combat cyber threats.

Khalid Al-Biyari has been assistant minister of defence for executive affairs since February 2018 and leads the Transformation Team which is overseeing the integration of the Saudi armed forces (army, air force, navy, air defence and the strategic missile force), similar to the UK's Joint

Operational Command.[146] But there remain significant impediments to achieving such an objective. The Saudi Ministry of Defence continues to exclude the Saudi Arabian National Guard (SANG), due to its tribal base, the Presidency of State Security (Mohammed bin Salman's praetorian guard formed in 2017 to avoid an over-reliance on the Ministry of Interior) and the Ministry of Interior, which is the largest and most influential ministry in the kingdom. There are other issues in that General Fahad bin Turki, Saudi Ministry of Defence Joint Operational Command chief, did not report to the Saudi Chief of Staff, General Fayyad Al-Ruwaili, but instead reported directly to the minister of defence, Mohammed bin Salman.[147] The National Risk Unit is unlikely to discuss terrorism and cyber attacks in the same way that its UK equivalent, the National Security Council, does.[148]

If Iran goes nuclear, Saudi Arabia has indicated that it will strive to achieve its own nuclear deterrent. But Saudi Arabia lacks the human resources to produce nuclear weapons, including the technical background to adapt conventional missiles. One aspect to consider if the JCPOA fails is the uncertainty as to whether the kingdom will pursue a Section 123 Agreement[149] (or similar) with the US or other international partners in light of its growing civil nuclear programme. If Saudi Arabia chooses to work with Russia and/or China, there are questions as to how far the US can push for this.[150] Saudi Arabia has already imported an intermediate-range ballistic missile system and manpower from China and built the underground launch facilities before western intelligence agencies knew about it. It was one of the greatest covert arms procurement deals in history. Saudi Arabia continues to work with China on developing ballistic missiles. If there were any doubt as to Saudi interest in balancing its relations with the US with other potential security partners, the fact that it hosted the World Defence Show in Riyadh in March 2022 underscored its interest in scanning for, and optimising, developmental opportunities with potential defence partners. Whether this effort will lead to tangible outcomes remains to be seen.

Counterterrorism in Saudi Arabia

As eleven out of the nineteen hijackers on 9/11 were Saudis, there has been much attention focused on the root cause(s) of their radicalisation. The xenophobic, anti-Christian and anti-Semitic teachings in Saudi schools and mosques (as well as possible radicalisation elsewhere) were identified as part of the problem, and the kingdom moved swiftly to regulate imams. The kingdom also promised to edit out hate speech from textbooks, and responded from 2017 to 2020, after years of criticism by the US, by removing hateful references to Christians, Jews and LGBT people, as well as violent and anti-Semitic language from educational textbooks.[151] Whilst more explicit language regarding Shia Islam has now been omitted, the challenge is that monotheism (*Tawhid*) at primary, middle and secondary levels is said to continue to stigmatise some practices of Shia and Sufi Islam.[152] The Saudi state was also quick to shut down its defence ministry website in 2021 whilst it removed from the same website sermons and passages which were deemed anti-American or illustrated hatred for Jews, Christians or non-Wahhabi Muslims.[153]

The Saudi government has regulated charities more tightly since 9/11, and joined other GCC states such as the UAE and Qatar in the Global Counterterrorism Forum (GCTF). This informal and multilateral organisation was launched in 2011 to share expertise and strategies and develop good practice. The kingdom announced a revision of its Counterterrorism and Counter Terror Financing Law on 4 November 2018 and has implemented UN Security Council sanctions against ISIS and Al Qaeda. Saudi Arabia is part of the international coalition against ISIS. Still, in February 2019 the kingdom was added to a European Commission list of 'high risk third countries' that are weak in combating terrorism financing and money laundering.[154] Financial regulation remains a grey area, but anything less than a robust and public attempt to crack down on terror financing may create a misperception about Saudi political will. The move by the European Commission may go some way to explaining the full Saudi membership of the Financial Action Task Force (FATF) on 21 June 2019 to help alleviate concerns and boost capacity.

Saudi counterterrorism actions also include expanded programmes and messaging to address returning foreign terrorist fighters.[155] The fragmented Islamist field in the kingdom, coupled with the war in Syria (which encouraged thousands of Saudis to join Islamist militias), domestic repression (including thousands more incarcerated since 2003 without a public trial) and sectarianism,[156] may prove to be difficult to counter through official policies aimed at addressing extremism alone. Indeed, Prince Bandar, former of Saudi intelligence, was removed partly because of Prince Nayef's increasing concern that battle-hardened young Saudis would return to the kingdom from Syria in 2014 and prosecute a similar campaign of terror to that undertaken by AQAP from 2003 to 2006.[157] From February 2014, Saudi Arabia moved to deter foreign fighters returning by issuing three- to twenty-year jail terms.[158] But, similar to the Saudi fighters and suicide bombers in Iraq from 2003 to 2005 and the 'Caravan of Martyrs' which have fought in Afghanistan, Bosnia, Tajikistan, Chechnya, and again in Afghanistan, Saudi authorities have been restricted politically by public perceptions of resistance as legitimate.[159] This is linked to Islamic solidarity (*al-tadamun al-islami*) and the pan-Islamic nationalist (*umma*) discourse which was initially mobilised to counter Nasser's pan-Arabism.[160]

Conclusion

The history of Saudi statehood highlights the existential threat that the Al Saud have faced over centuries, the need to mobilise and disband forces to consolidate territory and influence, and the Islamic leadership credentials bestowed on the Al Saud derived from its control over the Two Holy Mosques and its alliance with Wahhabi clerics. The Hajj, being a linch-pin of Saudi external engagement, along with expatriate labour, has been a vital node of interaction and influence, and could be considered a source of dependency for states with Muslim communities.

This chapter has found that the main source of Saudi autonomy and influence still relates to hydrocarbons, even if the overall orientation is from western to eastern markets. Oil is still important in the global economy and is likely to be so even after the Saudi net-zero objective of 2060 is achieved (if achieved), through upstream and downstream activities, some of which could contribute to clean energy production. For most developed economies, the opportunities on offer through Vision 2030 will be a great source of attraction and mutual benefit. Arms sales, which have traditionally been important sources of Saudi influence towards the US and some European states, could become more limited over time as the kingdom shifts to more indigenous production. This continues to be contingent on threat perception, military organisation and security relations.

Davidson has already found Crown Prince Mohammed bin Salman and Sheikh Mohammed bin Zayed to have altered the nature of their respective political systems to the point that their modes of governance can be considered to be a form of sultanism.[161] He focuses on the influence of economic expedience, anti-corruption crackdowns, altering state--religious relations, embarking on further repression and substituting consensus-driven systems for more autocratic, personal forms of governance.[162] However, this chapter has also pointed to the importance of variables such as youth and background, especially assertiveness over perceived failings in historic threat perception and passivity, and a lack of affinity for the perceptions of western allies. Personalisation of decision making, whilst addressing ministerial deficiencies, has the potential to harm longer-term cooperation on a variety of issues which require the sustained attention of a technocratic and bureaucratic elite operating in a more transparent framework.

Rapid liberalisation, political consolidation and hyper-nationalism resulting from an assertive military intervention in Yemen are altering the national identity of the kingdom without clear consequences so far concerning its sustainability and overall effect. The scorecard on liberalisation probably won't be available until 2030, when Vision 2030 will be judged on its overall merits. The effect of hyper-nationalism is far more difficult to ascertain. Whilst it may aid the rise of Mohammed bin Salman to kingship and rally social forces around the flag instead of favouring the conservative *ulema*, if hyper-nationalism extends beyond the control of the elite, the kingdom may attempt to retrench and return full circle to its co-optation of religion as its main source of political legitimacy.

The chapter has reinforced the notion that foreign policy is driven by internal as well as external threats and opportunities. Elite calculations are therefore thick composites operating in a dynamic field, with domestic calculations shown to be less susceptible to the whims of foreign interference, except when relating to national security issues. The greatest change, that towards liberalisation and secularisation, took a long time to commence and, given when it occurred, was more likely to have been driven by a combination of economic and leadership qualities, rather than by foreign inducement.

As Riyadh has shouldered new military responsibilities in the region and built up its capabilities in response to deficiencies identified during the Gulf War, the military dimension is bound to create new forms of Saudi agency in the regional system. To what end, hinges on the evolving regional security environment and threat perception, informed by outcomes from various diplomatic initiatives such as the JCPOA, as well as evolving command and control structures.

Notes

1 Matthew Gray, 'A Theory of "Late Rentierism" in the Arab States of the Gulf', Center for International and Regional Studies, Georgetown University, 2011.
2 Natana J. Delong-Bas, *Wahhabi Islam: From Revival and Reform to Global Jihad*. Oxford: Oxford University Press, 2004.
3 Madawi Al-Rasheed, 'Introduction', *A History of Saudi Arabia*. Cambridge: Cambridge University Press, 2010: 16
4 Tim Niblock, 'Introduction', in Tim Niblock (ed.) *State, Society and Economy in Saudi Arabia*. Abingdon: Routledge, 1982: 11–22 at 12.
5 Saud Al-Sarhan, 'The Saudis as Managers of the Hajj', in Eric Tagliacozzo and Shawkat M. Toorawa (eds) *The Hajj: Pilgrimage in Islam*. Cambridge: Cambridge University Press, 2015: 196.

6 Ibid: 199–200.
7 Dilip Hiro, 'Introduction', *Cold War in the Islamic World: Saudi Arabia, Iran and the Struggle for Supremacy.* Oxford: Oxford University Press, 2019: 13.
8 Ibid.
9 Bernard Reich (ed.), 'Abd al-Aziz ibn Saud', *Political Leaders of the Contemporary Middle East and North Africa: A Biographical Dictionary.* New York: Greenwood Press, 1990: 18.
10 Ibid.
11 Ibid: 19.
12 Ibid: 21.
13 Abdullah Taryam, 'Internal and External Influences and their Impact on the Arab Emirates 1950–60', *The Establishment of the United Arab Emirates 1950–85.* Abingdon: Routledge, 1987: 24–25.
14 Bruce Riedel, 'Ricochet: When a Covert Operation Goes Bad', *Studies in Intelligence*, Brookings, December 2018, www.brookings.edu/opinions/ricochet-when-a-covert-operation-goes-bad/
15 Neil Partrick, 'Domestic Factors and Foreign Policy', *Saudi Arabian Foreign Policy: Conflict and Cooperation.* London: I. B. Tauris, 2016: 5.
16 Ibid: 6.
17 al-Sarhan, 'The Saudis as Managers of the Hajj': 197.
18 Muslims associate the Mount of Mercy on the Plain of Arafat with God Forgiving Adam and Eve, the Prophet's last sermon, and many also associate it with the Judgement Day. Al-Sarhan, 'The Saudis as Managers of the Hajj': 229
19 Toby Mathiesen, *The Other Saudis: Shiism, Dissent and Sectarianism.* New York: Cambridge University Press, 2015.
20 Martin Chulov, 'I Will Return the Kingdom to Moderate Islam, Says Crown Prince', *The Guardian*, 24 October 2017, www.theguardian.com/world/2017/oct/24/i-will-return-saudi-arabia-moderate-islam-crown-prince
21 Presentation by a senior academic of Middle Eastern Studies who asked not to be named, 16 November 2021.
22 Kristin Smith Diwan, 'Saudi Nationalism Raises Hopes of Greater Shia Inclusion', Arab Gulf States Institute in Washington, 3 May 2018, https://agsiw.org/saudi-nationalism-raises-hopes-greater-inclusion-shias/
23 Simon Mabon, 'Eastern Saudi Arabia: Is De-Sectarianization a Byproduct of Vision 2030?', Italian Institute for International Political Studies, 10 September 2020, www.ispionline.it/en/pubblicazione/eastern-saudi-arabia-de-sectarianization-byproduct-vision-2030-27324
24 Rosie Bsheer, *Archive Wars: The Politics of History in Saudi Arabia.* Stanford, CA: Stanford University Press, 2020.
25 Stéphane Lacroix, 'Saudi Arabia and the Limits of Religious Reform', Cambridge Institute on Religion and International Studies, University of Cambridge, 25 February 2019: 4.
26 BBC News, 'Head of Saudi Arabia's Religious Police Replaced', 13 January 2012, www.bbc.com/news/world-middle-east-16549295

27 BBC News, 'Saudi Arabia's Religious Police Ordered to be "Gentle"', 13 April 2016, www.bbc.com/news/world-middle-east-36034807

28 Nathan Brown, 'Politics Over Doctrine: The Evolution of Sharia-based State Institutions in Egypt and Saudi Arabia', Baker Institute for Public Policy, September 2018, www.bakerinstitute.org/media/files/files/4dfadd05/cme-pub-carnegie-brown-091718.pdf

29 Lacroix, 'Saudi Arabia and the Limits of Religious Reform': 3.

30 Presentation by a senior academic of Middle Eastern Studies who asked not to be named, 16 November 2021.

31 Ibid.

32 They would be outlawed by 2014, due to their ability to mobilise support and gain strength as a transnational group, especially in the period immediately following the Arab uprisings. Other Islamist groups such as Tablighi Jamaat have also been banned in the kingdom. This extended in 2021 to ordering imams in the kingdom to identify the group as misguided, deviant and dangerous after it celebrated the Taliban victory in Afghanistan and criticised Crown Prince Mohammad bin Salman. James M. Dorsey, 'Saudi Arabia Targets Banned Ultra-Conservative Proselytisers', 10 December 2021, https://jamesmdorsey.substack.com/p/saudi-arabia-targets-banned-ultra?token=eyJ1c2VyX2lkIjo3MDEzODgyLCJwb3N0X2lkIjo0NTI3Mjg5NSwiXyI6Im82RzkrIiwiaWF0IjoxNjM5MzE0NzYzLCJleHAiOjE2MzkzMTgzNjMsImlzcyI6InB1Yi0yNDY4MjgiLCJzdWIiOiJwb3N0LXJlYWN0aW9uIn0.dP7tmB0a9z8Izap-BNCmHXWcPIdqhDQKA_2zNXQZjWY

33 Sayyid Qutb was an Egyptian author, Islamic theorist and member of the MB in the 1960s and 1970s. Qutbism is an Islamist ideology that advocates violent jihad to establish governance according to sharia law.

34 Saud Al-Sarhan, 'The Struggle for Authority: The Shaykhs of Jihadi-Salafism in Saudi Arabia, 1997–2003', *Saudi Arabia in Transition*: 206.

35 Bernard Haykel, Thomas Hegghammer and Stéphane Lacroix, 'Introduction', *Saudi Arabia in Transition: Insights on Social, Political, Economic and Religious Change*. Cambridge: Cambridge University Press, 2015: 1.

36 Bruce Riedel, 'The Prince of Counterterrorism', Brookings, 29 September 2015, http://csweb.brookings.edu/content/research/essays/2015/the-prince-of-counterterrorism.html

37 Zoltan Barany, 'Introduction', *Armies of Arabia: Military Politics and Effectiveness in the Gulf*. Oxford: Oxford University Press, 2021: 9

38 Ulf Laessing, 'Pro-reform Saudi Activists Launch Political Party', *Reuters*, 10 February 2011, https://uk.reuters.com/article/us-saudi-opposition/pro-reform-saudi-activists-launch-political-party-idUSTRE71942L20110210

39 Guido Steinberg, 'Leading the Counter-Revolution: Saudi Arabia and the Arab Spring', Stiftung Wissenschaft und Politik Research Paper, June 2014: 8, www.swp-berlin.org/publications/products/research_papers/2014_RP07_sbg.pdf

40 https://twitter.com/mohamadalarefe?lang=en (accessed 19 February 2021).

41 BBC News, 'Meet Saudi Arabia's Stars of Social Media', 3 March 2016, www.bbc.com/news/blogs-trending-35609249

42 https://twitter.com/salman_alodah?lang=en (accessed 19 February 2021).

43 Amnesty International, 'Saudi Arabia: Prominent Reformist Cleric Faces Death Sentence for His Peaceful Activism', 26 July 2019, www.amnesty.org/en/latest/news/2019/07/saudi-arabia-prominent-reformist-cleric-faces-death-sentence-for-his-peaceful-activism/

44 Lacroix, 'Saudi Arabia and the Limits of Religious Reform': 4–5.

45 Guardian Staff and Reuters, 'CIA Finds Saudi Crown Prince Ordered Jamal Khashoggi Killing – Report', *The Guardian*, 17 November 2018, www.theguardian.com/world/2018/nov/16/cia-determines-saudi-crown-prince-ordered-journalists-killing-washington-post

46 The Washington Post, 'Opinion: Read Jamal Khashoggi's Columns for The Washington Post', 7 October 2018, www.washingtonpost.com/news/global-opinions/wp/2018/10/06/read-jamal-khashoggis-columns-for-the-washington-post/

47 Michael Isikoff, 'Prior to His Murder, Jamal Khashoggi Offered to Help 9/11 Victims Suing Saudi Arabia', *Yahoo! News*, 10 July 2021, https://news.yahoo.com/prior-to-his-murder-jamal-khashoggi-offered-to-help-911-victims-suing-saudi-arabia-090018080.html

48 Suyin Haynes, 'As Saudi Women Take the Wheel, Leading Activists Remain Behind Bars', *Time*, 27 June 2018, https://time.com/5321848/saudi-arabia-women-driving-ban-activists/

49 European Saudi Organisation for Human Rights, 'Through First Half of 2020: No Sign of an End to the Persecution of Women in Saudi Arabia', 29 May 2020, www.esohr.org/en/?p=2833 (accessed 3 April 2021).

50 Joe Walsh, 'Saudi Government Frees Activist Who Campaigned for Women's Right to Drive', *Forbes*, 10 February 2021, www.forbes.com/sites/joewalsh/2021/02/10/saudi-government-frees-activist-who-campaigned-for-womens-right-to-drive/?sh=4e13b65759fc

51 Tim Stickings, 'Saudi Arabia Kills "Armed" Protestor Who Refused to be Evicted for the Crown Prince's Megacity Project Neom', *Daily Mail*, 16 April 2020, www.dailymail.co.uk/news/article-8225067/Saudi-Arabia-kills-protester-refused-make-way-megacity.html

52 The Soufan Center, 'IntelBrief: Is Mohammed bin Salman Leading Saudi Arabia into the Abyss?', 29 April 2020, https://thesoufancenter.org/intelbrief-is-mohammed-bin-salman-leading-saudi-arabia-into-the-abyss/

53 The Economist, 'Many Saudis Are Seething at Muhammad bin Salman', 6 January 2022, www.economist.com/middle-east-and-africa/2022/01/06/many-saudis-are-seething-at-muhammad-bin-salmans-reforms

54 Jennifer Pan and Alexandra A. Siegel, 'How Saudi Crackdowns Fail to Silence Online Dissent', *American Political Science Review*, 114 (1), 2020: 109–125; Bill Bostock, 'Abducted and Detained Saudi Princess Basmah Made Contact with the Outside World for the First Time in a Year, Only to Have the Call Cut When She Mentioned a Will', *Insider*, 18 May 2021, www.insider.com/detained-saudi-princess-basmah-breaks-silence-called-family-2021-5

55 Stephanie Kirchgaessner, 'Revealed: Saudis Suspected of Phone Spying Campaign in US', *The Guardian*, 29 March 2020, www.theguardian.com/world/2020/mar/29/revealed-saudis-suspected-of-phone-spying-campaign-in-us

56 Katie Benner, Mark Mazetti, Ben Hubbard and Mike Isaac, 'Saudis' Image Makers: A Troll Army and Twitter Insider', *The New York Times*, 20 October 2018, www.nytimes.com/2018/10/20/us/politics/saudi-image-campaign-twitter.html

57 Bill Bostock, 'Exiled Saudi Arabian Dissidents Have Launched a Political Party They Hope Will Dethrone MBS and Open the Door to Democracy', *Business Insider*, 25 September 2020, www.businessinsider.com/saudis-exiled-defy-mbs-rule-new-political-party-demand-democracy-2020-9

58 The Allegiance Council was created in 2006 to facilitate communication across the royal family.

59 Reuters Staff, 'Saudi King Orders One-month Salary Bonus for Security Personnel', *Reuters*, 29 April 2015, www.reuters.com/article/us-saudi-military-bonuses/saudi-king-orders-one-month-salary-bonus-for-security-personnel-idUSKBN0NK0MW20150429

60 Prince Ahmed and King Salman are the survivors of the so-called Sudairi Seven – sons of one of Ibn Saud's favourite wives, Hassa al-Sudairi.

61 Ben Hubbard, 'MBS: The Rise of Saudi Prince', *The New York Times*, 21 March 2020, www.nytimes.com/2020/03/21/world/middleeast/mohammed-bin-salman-saudi-arabia.html

62 Eman Alhussein, 'Saudi First: How Hyper-Nationalism is Transforming Saudi Arabia', European Council on Foreign Relations, 19 June 2019, www.ecfr.eu/publications/summary/saudi_first_how_hyper_nationalism_is_transforming_saudi_arabia

63 Ibid.

64 Stephen Kalin, Tom Arnold and Reem Shamseddine, 'Saudi Arabia's Government has Taken Control of the Construction Giant Owned by Osama Bin Laden's Family, *Reuters*, 11 January 2018, available at www.businessinsider.com/saudi-state-take-control-of-binladin-construction-giant-2018-1

65 Nicholas Kulish and Mark Mazzetti, 'Saudi Royal Family is Still Spending in an Age of Austerity', *The New York Times*, 27 December 2016, www.nytimes.com/2016/12/27/world/middleeast/saudi-royal-family-money.html

66 Spencer Feingold, 'Saudi Women Attend Soccer Match for First Time', *CNN*, 12 January 2018, https://edition.cnn.com/2018/01/12/middleeast/saudi-women-attend-first-soccer-match/index.html

67 King Salman Center for Local Governance, www.ksclg.org/en/

68 Stephen Kalin, 'Saudi Ritz Reopens After Stint as a Gilded Prison of Princes', *Reuters*, 11 February 2018, www.reuters.com/article/us-saudi-arrests-ritz/saudi-ritz-reopens-after-stint-as-gilded-prison-of-princes-idUSKBN1FV0AW. The Public Investment Fund (PIF) has since bought a $1.5 billion stake in Prince Alwaleed's holding company, bringing him under closer government influence after years of relative independence. Aman Malik, 'Saudi PIF to Buy $1.5 bn Stake in Prince Alwaleed's Kingdom Holding', *The Capital Quest*, 23 May 2022, https://thecapitalquest.com/2022/05/23/saudi-pif-to-buy-1-5-bn-stake-in-prince-alwaleeds-kingdom-holding/#:~:text=Saudi%20PIF%20to%20buy%20%241.5%20bn%20stake%20in%20prince%20Alwaleed's%20Kingdom%20Holding,-Private%20Equity%20West&text=Saudi%20Arabia's%20prince%20and%20billionaire,68%20billion).

69 Sebastian Castelier, 'Rich Families Buy Second Citizenship in Post-Ritz Saudi Arabia', *Al-Monitor*, 28 September 2020, www.al-monitor.com/pulse/originals/2020/09/saudi-arabia-ritz-carlton-second-citizenship-passport.html

70 Author's interview with a senior UK government official who asked not to be named, 18 November 2021.

71 Hubbard, 'MBS: The Rise of Saudi Prince'.

72 Ibid; see the Yesser program at www.yesser.gov.sa/en/for-citizens/gov-sa

73 Alasdair Sandford, 'Saudi Arabia: Three Senior Royals "Detained", in Latest Clampdown', *Euronews*, 7 March 2020, www.euronews.com/2020/03/07/saudi-arabia-three-senior-royals-detained-in-latest-clampdown

74 David Ignatius, 'Opinion: The Dazzling Rise and Tragic Fall of Saudi Arabia's Mohammed bin Nayef', *The Washington Post*, 5 July 2020, www.washingtonpost.com/opinions/2020/07/05/dazzling-rise-tragic-fall-saudi-arabias-mohammed-bin-nayef/

75 Ibid.

76 Karen Elliot House, 'Profile of a Prince: Promise and Peril in Mohammed bin Salman's Vision 2030', Belfer Center for Science and International Affairs, April 2019, www.belfercenter.org/publication/profile-prince-promise-and-peril-mohammed-bin-salmans-vision-2030

77 David Ignatius, 'Opinion: The Biden Administration's Saudi Problem', *The Washington Post*, 25 January 2021, www.washingtonpost.com/opinions/2021/01/24/biden-saudi-arabia-mbs-saad-aljabri/

78 Raya Jalabi, 'The Legal War Between the Saudis and Their Former Spymaster', *Reuters*, 22 April 2021, https://web.archive.org/web/20210422125640/https:/www.reuters.com/world/legal-war-between-saudis-their-former-spymaster-2021-04-22/

79 Ali AlAhmed, 'Exclusive: Senior Saudi Prince Sentenced to Death in Military Trial', Gulf Institute, 27 June 2021, www.gulfinstitute.org/2021/06/27/exclusive-senior-saudi-prince-sentenced-to-death-in-military-trial/

80 Zawya, 'Saudi Arabia Bans Ministers from Serving on Company Boards', 12 September 2021, www.zawya.com/saudi-arabia/en/legal/story/Saudi_Arabia_bans_ministers_from_serving_on_company_boards-ZAWYA20210912051258/

81 Ryan Parry and Josh Boswell, 'Exclusive: The World's Most Expensive Painting Cost $450 Million because Two Arab Princes Bid against Each Other by Mistake and Wouldn't Back Down (But Settled It by Swapping a Yacht)', *Mail Online*, 28 March 2018, www.dailymail.co.uk/news/article-5554969/Two-Arab-princes-cost-450MILLION-bidding-war-Da-Vincis-Salvator-Mundi.html

82 Katie Warren, 'The Saudi Crown Prince has Reportedly Detained 3 Royal Family Members for Unknown Reasons. Meet 34-Year-Old Mohammed bin Salman, Who's at the Center of Human Rights Issues and Drops Millions on Yachts and Mansions', *Business Insider*, 9 March 2020, www.businessinsider.com/mohammed-bin-salman-saudi-prince-net-worth-yacht-private-jet-lifestyle-2019-5

83 Reuters, 'Saudi Crown Prince Says He Will Further Centralise Policy-Making', 28 April 2021, www.reuters.com/world/saudi-crown-prince-says-he-will-further-centralise-policy-making-2021-04-28/

84 Bruce Riedel, 'The Prince of Counterterrorism', Brookings, 29 September 2015: 2.

85 Presentation by a senior academic of Middle Eastern Studies who asked not to be named, 16 November 2021.

86 Ben Hubbard, 'Saudi King Unleashes a Torrent of Money as Bonuses Flow to the Masses', *The New York Times*, 19 February 2015, www.nytimes.com/2015/02/20/world/middleeast/saudi-king-unleashes-a-torrent-as-bonuses-flow-to-the-masses.html

87 BBC News, 'Saudi Arabia Unveils First Public Sector Pay Cuts', 27 September 2016, www.bbc.com/news/world-middle-east-37482690

88 Massoud A Derhally, '2022 Budget Returns Saudi Arabia to Surplus for First Time in Eight Years', *The National*, 12 December 2021, www.thenationalnews.com/business/economy/2021/12/13/2022-budget-returns-saudi-arabia-to-surplus-for-first-time-in-eight-years/

89 Ibid.

90 Jean-François Seznec, 'Money Matters: The State of Financial Markets in the Gulf', 7 March 2019, www.youtube.com/watch?v=c2hIZnd92GA; Jean-François Seznec and Samer Mosis, *The Financial Markets of the Arab Gulf: Power, Politics and Money*. Abingdon: Routledge, 2018.

91 Seznec, 'Money Matters'.

92 Although there have been tensions and a series of incidents when foreign workers come into the closest contact with Gulf nationals as domestic workers, especially due to dependence created by the Kafala system. This system requires all unskilled labourers to have an in-country sponsor, usually their employer, who is responsible for their visa and legal status. Various human rights organisations have criticised it for the potential for exploitation, especially as worker passports are confiscated and there have been relatively few legal safeguards for workers' rights.

93 Carla Power, 'Saudi Arabia Bulldozes Over its Heritage', *Time*, 14 November 2014, https://time.com/3584585/saudi-arabia-bulldozes-over-its-heritage/

94 Hadi Fathallah, 'Challenges of Public Policymaking in Saudi Arabia', Carnegie Endowment for International Peace, 22 May 2019, https://carnegieendowment.org/sada/79188

95 BBC News, 'Saudi Aramco's Profits Slide Nearly 45% after Lower Oil Demand', 21 March 2021, www.bbc.com/news/business-56474925

96 Financial Times, '"Never Waste a Good Crisis": Inside Saudi Arabia's Shopping Spree', 26 May 2020, www.ft.com/content/af2deefd-2234-4e54-a08a-8dbb205f5378

97 The Economist, 'The Algosaibi Affair: A Saudi Saga', 19 March 2015, www.economist.com/business/2015/03/19/a-saudi-saga

98 See Robert Mason, 'The Nexus Between State-Led Economic Reform Programmes, Security, and Reputation Damage in the Kingdom of Saudi Arabia', in Martin Beck and Thomas Richter (eds) *Oil and Political Economy of the Middle East: Adjustment Policies of the Arab Gulf and Beyond Since 2014*. Manchester: Manchester University Press, 2021.

99 Zahraa Alkhalisi, 'Saudi Arabia's Reforming Crown Prince has Youth on his Side', *CNN*, 20 November 2017, https://money.cnn.com/2017/11/20/news/economy/saudi-crown-prince-young-people/index.html

100 Jack Goldstone found that revolutions are usually driven by 'ecological crises' resulting from cumulative population growth and limited available resources. Jack A. Goldstone, *Revolution and Rebellion in the Early Modern World*. Berkeley: University of California Press, 1993.

101 McKinsey, 'Saudi Arabia Beyond Oil: The Investment and Productivity Transformation: Executive Summary', December 2015, www.mckinsey.com/~/media/McKinsey/Featured%20Insights/Employment%20and%20Growth/Moving%20Saudi%20Arabias%20economy%20beyond%20oil/MGI%20Saudi%20Arabia_Executive%20summary_December%202015.ashx

102 Ibid.

103 Harvard Kennedy School, 'The Labor Market in Saudi Arabia: Background, Areas of Progress and Insights for the Future': 10, https://epod.cid.harvard.edu/sites/default/files/2019-08/EPD_Report_Digital.pdf

104 Ibid: 20.

105 World Bank, 'Labour Force Participation Rate, Female – Saudi Arabia', https://data.worldbank.org/indicator/SL.TLF.CACT.FE.ZS?locations=SA

106 Christopher M. Davidson, 'Saudi Women Train Drivers: MbS's Ultimate Constituency', *Arab Digest*, 25 February 2022, https://arabdigest.org/sample-newsletters/saudi-women-train-drivers-mbss-ultimate-constituency-2/

107 Marc Thompson, *Being Young, Male and Saudi: Identity and Politics in a Globalized Kingdom*. Cambridge: Cambridge University Press, 2019.

108 Mohammed Ghobari and Reyam Mokhashef, 'Mass Job Terminations Hit Hundreds of Yemenis in Saudi Arabia', *Reuters*, 17 August 2021, www.reuters.com/world/middle-east/mass-job-terminations-hit-hundreds-yemenis-saudi-arabia-2021-08-17/

109 Arab News, 'FII: Saudi Arabia Eyes 20 Free Economic Zones, Six in Riyadh', 28 January 2021, www.arabnews.com/node/1800041/business-economy

110 Robert Mogielnicki, 'Flexibility, Multifaceted Objectives Contribute to Persistence of Gulf Free Zones', Arab Gulf States Institute in Washington, 28 June 2021, https://agsiw.org/flexibility-multifaceted-objectives-contribute-to-persistence-of-gulf-free-zones/

111 Arabian Business, 'Saudi Firms, Including Aramco, To Cut Dividends to Fund $1.3 Trillion Plan', 31 March 2021, www.arabianbusiness.com/politics-economics/461137-saudi-firms-including-aramco-to-cut-dividends-to-fund-13-trillion-plan

112 Ibid.

113 Ibid.

114 Yousef Saba and Davide Barbuscia, 'Saudi Sovereign Wealth Fund Scopes Banks for ESG Framework – Sources', *Reuters*, 12 July 2021, www.reuters.com/business/sustainable-business/saudi-sovereign-wealth-fund-scopes-banks-esg-framework-sources-2021-07-12/

115 Abeer Abu Omar and Matthew Martin, 'Saudi Wealth Fund Making Another Splash, This Time at Home', *Bloomberg*, 16 November 2020, www.bloomberg.com/amp/news/articles/2020-11-17/saudi-wealth-fund-is-making-another-splash-but-this-time-at-home#click=https://t.co/dD2f50366Y

116 Kingdom of Saudi Arabia Vision 2030, 'The Vision Themes', www.vision2030.gov.sa/en/vision/themes

117 Financial Times, 'Why Saudi Arabia is Building a 170km Line City Through the Desert', 25 February 2021, www.youtube.com/watch?v=REYtqZIRiR0&feature=youtu.be

118 Ibid.

119 Marwa Rashad and Saeed Azhar, 'Saudi Sovereign Fund to Double Assets in Next Five Years to $1.07 trln – Crown Prince', *Reuters*, 24 January 2021, www.reuters.com/article/us-saudi-pif-assets-idUSKBN29T0MC

120 Nordea, 'Foreign Direct Investment in Saudi Arabia', www.nordeatrade.com/en/explore-new-market/saudi-arabia/investment (accessed 2 February 2021).

121 Arabian Business, 'Saudi Arabia Sees Biggest Rise in FDI in 10 Years', 20 January 2020, www.arabianbusiness.com/banking-finance/438121-saudi-arabia-sees-biggest-rise-in-fdi-in-10-years

122 Courtney Freer, 'The Symbiosis of Sectarianism, Authoritarianism, and Rentierism in the Saudi State', *Studies in Ethnicity and Nationalism*, 19 (1), April 2019: 88–108.

123 Air Products, 'Air Products, ACWA Power and NEOM Sign Agreement for $5 Billion Production Facility in NEOM Powered by Renewable Energy for Production and Export of Green Hydrogen to Global Markets', 7 July 2020, www.airproducts.com/news-center/2020/07/0707-air-products-agreement-for-green-ammonia-production-facility-for-export-to-hydrogen-market

124 Oil and Gas Climate Initiative, 'Our Milestones', n.d., https://oilandgasclimateinitiative.com/about-us/ogci-at-a-glance/#milestones

125 'G20 Saudi Arabia 2020 Riyadh Summit', n.d., https://twitter.com/i/broadcasts/1BRKjBbwdBvKw

126 Arab News, 'Saudi Crown Prince Announces Green Saudi Initiative, Green Middle East Initiative', 27 March 2021, www.arabnews.com/node/1832861/saudi-arabia

127 Dominic Raab, https://twitter.com/DominicRaab/status/1377323730414800901?s=20, 31 March 2021.

128 Jean-François Seznec and Samer Mosis, 'The Energy Transition in the Arab Gulf: From Vision to Reality', Atlantic Council Global Energy Center, July 2021, www.atlanticcouncil.org/wp-content/uploads/2021/08/AC_GulfTransitions_FINAL.pdf

129 Graham Readfearn, '"Fossil Fuel Friends": Saudi Arabia and Bahrain Back Australia's Lobbying on Great Barrier Reef', *The Guardian*, 14 July 2021, www.theguardian.com/environment/2021/jul/14/fossil-fuel-friends-saudi-arabia-and-bahrain-back-australias-lobbying-on-great-barrier-reef-unesco

130 Justin Rowlatt and Tom Gerken, 'COP26: Document Leak Reveals Nations Lobbying to Change Key Climate Report', *BBC News*, 21 October 2021, www.bbc.com/news/science-environment-58982445

131 Bruce Riedel, 'Saudi Arabia and the Future of the Middle East', Centre for International Governance Innovation, 31 March 2016, www.youtube.com/watch?v=fS6xpmg-3u4

132 Ibid.

133 Mai Yamani, 'Saudi Arabia Goes to War', *The Guardian*, 23 November 2009, www.theguardian.com/commentisfree/2009/nov/23/saudi-arabia-yemen-houthi-war

134 Presentation by a senior academic of Middle Eastern Studies who asked not to be named, 16 November 2021.

135 Stephanie Cronin, 'Tribes, Coups and Princes: Building a Modern Army in Saudi Arabia', *Armies and State-Building in the Modern Middle East: Politics, Nationalism and Military Reform.* London: I. B. Tauris, 2014: 213–214.

136 Pieter D. Wezeman et al, 'Trends in International Arms Transfers, 2018', SIPRI Fact Sheet, March 2019, www.sipri.org/sites/default/files/2019-03/fs_1903_at_2018.pdf

137 Rory Miller, '(In)Capacitated', *Desert Kingdoms to Global Powers: The Rise of the Arab Gulf*, Newhaven, CT: Yale University Press, 2016: 302.

138 Ibid.

139 Agence France Presse, 'Saudi Arabia: The Gulf's Best Equipped Military', *Defense News*, 26 March 2015, www.defensenews.com/global/mideast-africa/2015/03/26/saudi-arabia-the-gulf-s-best-equipped-military/

140 Kenneth Katzman, 'Arms Sales in the Middle East: Trends and Analytical Perspectives for U.S. Policy', CRS Report for Congress, 23 November 2020: 23, https://fas.org/sgp/crs/mideast/R44984.pdf

141 Agence France Presse, 'Saudi Arabia: The Gulf's Best Equipped Military'.

142 Sam Perlo-Freeman, Aude Fleurant, Pieter Wezeman and Siemon Wezeman, 'Trends in World Military Expenditure, 2015', SIPRI Fact Sheet, April 2016: 2, www.sipri.org/sites/default/files/EMBARGO%20FS1604%20Milex%202015.pdf

143 The Saudi military planned four coups attempts in 1954, 1962, 1969 and 1977.

144 Hadeel Al Sayegh, 'Saudi King Overhauls Security Services Following Royal Shakeup', *Reuters*, 20 July 2017, www.reuters.com/article/us-saudi-decrees-idUSKBN1A52N9

145 Ibid.

146 Neil Partrick, 'Saudi Arabia's Elusive Defense Reform', Carnegie Endowment for International Peace, 14 November 2019, https://carnegieendowment.org/sada/80354

147 Ibid.

148 Ibid.

149 'Section 123 of the U.S. Atomic Energy Act generally requires the conclusion of a peaceful nuclear cooperation agreement for significant transfers of nuclear material or equipment from the United States.' U.S. National Nuclear Security Administration, '123 Agreements for Peaceful Cooperation', www.energy.gov/nnsa/123-agreements-peaceful-cooperation

150 Author's interview with various diplomats, December 2021.

151   Ben Hubbard, 'In Saudi Arabia, Quiet Changes May Ease Tensions with Biden', *The New York Times*, 19 January 2021, www.nytimes.com/2021/01/19/world/middleeast/saudi-reforms-biden.html

152   Human Rights Watch, 'Saudi Arabia: Further Textbook Reforms Needed', 15 February 2021, www.hrw.org/news/2021/02/15/saudi-arabia-further-textbook-reforms-needed

153   Ali Al-Ahmed, 'Saudi Government Shuts Down Defense Website, Removes Hate', Institute for Gulf Affairs, February 2021, www.gulfinstitute.org/wp-content/uploads/2021/02/IGA-Impact_report.pdf

154   Natasha Turak, 'Saudi Arabia's Inclusion on European Terror Finance Risk List Could Threaten Vision 2030 Investment', *CNBC*, 14 February 2019, www.cnbc.com/2019/02/14/saudi-arabia-on-europe-terror-finance-risk-list-threatens-investment.html

155   Refworld, 'Country Reports on Terrorism 2017 – Saudi Arabia', 19 September 2018, www.refworld.org/docid/5bcf1f85c.html

156   Toby Mathiesen, 'The Domestic Sources of Saudi Foreign Policy: Islamists and the State in the Wake of the Arab Uprisings', Brookings, August 2015, www.brookings.edu/wp-content/uploads/2016/07/Saudi-Arabia_Matthiesen_FINALFINALFINAL.pdf

157   Ian Black, 'End of an Era as Prince Bandar Departs Saudi Intelligence Post', *The Guardian*, 16 April 2014, www.theguardian.com/world/2014/apr/16/prince-bandar-saudi-intelligence-syria

158   Reuters Staff, 'Saudi Arabia to Jail Citizens Who Fight Abroad', *Reuters*, 3 February 2014, www.reuters.com/article/us-saudi-law-idUSBREA121302014 0203

159   Thomas Hegghammer, 'Saudis in Iraq: Patterns of Radicalization and Recruitment', *Cultures and Conflicts*, 12 June 2008, https://journals.openedition.org/conflits/10042

160   Ibid.

161   Christopher M. Davidson, *From Sheikhs to Sultanism: Statecraft and Authority in Saudi Arabia and the UAE*. London: Hurst, 2021.

162   Ibid.

3

Politics in the United Arab Emirates: state consolidation, security and ambition

Introduction

The UAE, which celebrated its fiftieth anniversary in 2021, is one of the smallest countries in the world, with a population of about 1.5 million citizens. It is also one of the wealthiest countries per capita, due to possessing about 6 per cent of the world's oil reserves, and has achieved rapid economic expansion.[1] Personal politics, oil and urbanisation have dominated the UAE's political culture. British engagement with what were then the Trucial States throughout the nineteenth and twentieth centuries was conducted with only a handful of tribal chiefs, thus supporting a personal approach. They ruled by consultation and consensus building, but with limited authority, and were put in charge of implementing maritime agreements. They lacked autonomy, even to the extent of not being able to approve a succession without securing British consent.[2]

In 1968 Britain announced that it would withdraw from the Gulf in 1971. In the three-year interval the seven emirates had to overcome mutual suspicion and rivalry in order to guarantee their security and form the UAE. Security was perceived mainly to come from Britain, and riyal politik was employed in an attempt to finance the expenses of British troops and thereby persuade Britain not to withdraw.[3] Ras Al-Khaimah also reportedly offered military facilities to the US in return for recognition as an independent state in 1971.[4] Since its founding, the UAE has relied on informal institutions and balanced interests between the different ruling families, different tribes and unitary diversity. Over time, seven emirates have become more cohesive as a state under a common and strengthening national identity. Bahrain and Qatar became independent states. This has not been without periods of instability and contention.

The UAE gained independence in December 1971, but it took another six months for the formal nationalisation of seven emirates – Abu Dhabi, Dubai, Ajman, Fujairah, Ras Al-Khaimah, Sharjah, and Umm Al-Quwain – to occur. Ras Al-Khaimah was the emirate to delay state consolidation.

It lacked the hydrocarbon revenues that would make it an equal partner in the federation, and although its ruler, Sheikh Saqr bin Muhammad al-Qasimi, attempted to play off Abu Dhabi against Dubai to secure a more favourable deal, his attempts failed because he simply did not have the economic resources to support such equality.[5] Still, there is variation across the emirates in terms of governance. The ruler of Fujairah has for a long time held an open *majlis* during which anyone from the local community may come to present their case to the ruler.[6]

Khalifa bin Zayed bin Sultan al-Nahyan assumed the position of president of the UAE in 2010, and is only the second incumbent since the founding of the state. However, he was incapacitated by a stroke in 2014, leading Mohammed bin Zayed al-Nahyan to become the de facto president of the UAE as well as crown prince and heir apparent of Abu Dhabi until he became de jure president in May 2022. Mohammad bin Rashid Al Maktum is the UAE vice president, prime minister and defence minister as well as the ruler of Dubai emirate. Others in the UAE leadership include: Sultan bin Mohammad Al Qassimi, ruler of Sharjah emirate; Saud bin Saqr Al Qasimi, ruler of Ras al-Khaimah; Humaid bin Rashid Al Nuami III, ruler of Ajman emirate; Saud bin Rashid Al Mu'alla, ruler of Umm Al-Quwain emirate; Hamad bin Mohammed Al Sharqi, ruler of Fujairah emirate; which are collectively known as the Federal Supreme Council. They are joined in the leadership team by Abdullah bin Zayed Al Nahyan, foreign minister; deputy prime minister Mansur bin Zayed; minister of interior Sayf bin Zayed; national security advisor Sheikh Tahnoun bin Zayed; and Yousef al-Otaiba, ambassador to the US and son of long-time UAE oil minister Mani Saeed al-Otaiba.[7] There is also a UAE Cabinet.

Unlike many states, the UAE (and indeed Saudi Arabia) have embarked on state building only from the second half of the twentieth century, which raises questions about social and political adaptation, transition and readjustment. From independence, the UAE political system has been found to exhibit traits of a bifurcated executive branch, encompassing high national security-related issues where cabinet ministers and two federal authorities dominate, and low politics, encompassing areas that are not vital to the survival of the state.[8] As this chapter shows, this bifurcation of politics has also been accompanied by an increasing personalisation of the domestic political environment (sultanism) under Sheikh Mohammed bin Zayed, as well as a shifting balance of power within the emirates due to the exposure of Dubai to external economic shocks, versus the more manageable impact of lower (and higher) oil prices on Abu Dhabi.

The UAE has become an active player in the Middle East and internationally. As a member of the GCC[9] it is a vital part of the sub-regional security system, but its policy towards Qatar has called into question the strength of the GCC after the so-called Qatar Crisis in 2014 and from 2017 to 2021. In the decade from the Arab uprisings to 2021, the UAE has become so assertive that it has challenged our very notion of what a 'small state' is and where the dividing line between a small state and 'middle power' lies.[10] This chapter outlines the major themes affecting UAE foreign policy, including its struggle with Islamism, national security and human rights issues, the economy and defence. The conclusion sums up the conceptual issues most applicable in this case.

The struggle with Islamism

The MB in the UAE dates to the 1950s and 1960s, when President Nasser cracked down on the group in Egypt. Like Saudi Arabia, the UAE required educated labour, and members of the group quickly became active in education, religious and social affairs, filling key positions in the education sector and judiciary. In 1974, foreign-educated Emiratis with an Islamist agenda officially launched the MB in the UAE, calling it Al-Islah Reform and Social Guidance Association.[11] It was financially supported by the Kuwaiti Reform Society.[12] The ruler of Ras Al-Khaimah, Sheikh Saqr bin Mohammed Al Qasimi, was an important patron of Al-Islah in the UAE and was said to be a member.[13] Al-Islah's founding member, Sheikh Said Abdullah Salman of Ras Al-Khaimah, served as minister of housing from 1971, and then as minister of education from 1979, when he also became chancellor of the new UAE University. The impact on education was particularly marked, seeking to stop English teaching in primary schools, music courses, and urging females not to attend music or dance classes.[14] Westernisation was also perceived as a real threat within the group.[15]

Al-Islah was initially tolerated. But by the late 1980s its regular magazine became increasing sharp in its criticism of Emirati education policy, which led to the suspension of its publication for six months in 1988. By the mid-1990s, a number of issues converged which sparked a government crackdown because Al-Islah maintained the education ministry and judiciary as a state within a state; they had a significant influence on youth through education, summer camps and other activities such as Scout troops; and the politicised Friday prayers became problematic in terms of growing sectarian tensions with Iran. Al-Islah was overt in its lack of tolerance for non-Muslims in the UAE – which was problematic for a state focused on becoming a global hub with inward tourism, and businesspeople visiting and staying as part of the UAE's efforts at diversification and integration in global markets. Al-Islah's headquarters in Dubai was shut down in 1994 and transferred to Ras Al-Khaimah. Despite this, Al-Islah remained active in

Dubai, Fujairah and Ras Al-Khaimah, and Irshad continued activities such as Qur'an recitation competitions in Ajman.[16] UAE relations with Egypt could also have informed decision making about the group, as President Mubarak was fighting an insurgency by the MB at the time.

Further crackdowns and reform-oriented measures occurred throughout the 2000s, especially after 9/11, when Emirati youth became more serious about Islam, but whereby some became radicalised.[17] The threat posed by Al Qaeda was a socio-economic, religious and security issue, since the terror group recruited two UAE nationals in the 9/11 attacks. Fayez Banihammad was possibly born in Khor Fakkan in Sharjah[18] and Marwan al-Shehhi was from Ras Al-Khaimah.[19] In response, the UAE authorities focused on counterterrorism and began working more intensively with western military partners such as the US, while they also reformed and internationalised the education system[20] and forced imams to adhere to pre-approved sermons. In 2002, the State Security Directorate arrested 250 Emiratis on terrorism charges.[21]

Since Al-Islah refused to disband or divulge its membership following 9/11, talks began in 2003 between Abu Dhabi's Crown Prince Sheikh Mohammed bin Zayed Al Nahyan and Al-Islah to cease operating in the UAE and cut relations with other branches in exchange for state support.[22] Of particular contention was the pledge of allegiance (*bayah*) that Al-Islah reserves for the MB's General Guide, who at the time of writing is Mohammed Badie, the eighth Supreme Guide, and not the state. The UAE has since sought to undermine the group's cohesion through transferring known members to different departments in government.

The rise in terrorist activity was met with a specific and general crackdown on all perceived threats to the state. Hundreds of teachers, academics and ministry employees associated with Al-Islah were fired in 2006, which led to protest rallies, online articles and media appearances.[23] The mid-2000s became a turning point in the political economy of the UAE. The death of the UAE's founding president, Sheikh Zayed bin Sultan Al Nahyan, in 2004, followed by the death of Dubai's ruler, Sheikh Maktoum bin Rashid Al Maktoum, in January 2006, coincided with an upswing in international oil prices from 2002.[24] Utilising the increase in oil wealth, the UAE has become more adept at responding to internal and external threats and opportunities, particularly towards states affected by the Arab uprisings in the Middle East, and internationally, to secure its national interest. Part of these measures included helping to establish the Hedayah Center, an extension of the UAE's involvement in the GCTF.

The UAE government cracked down on Al-Islah in 2012 in light of the MB's election win in Egypt, even though Al-Islah had been non-violent since its establishment in 1974. The UAE government went on to outlaw the MB in 2014, categorising it as a terrorist organisation along with eighty-five other entities that included Al Qaeda and Islamic State.[25] Such a move has contributed greatly to tensions with Qatar, and informed UAE policy in Yemen, which will be explored in the following chapter. The UAE has also challenged the conservative Islamic and anti-western tenets of Al-Islah. In response to ISIS, the UAE launched the Sawab Center with the US in 2015, used and staffed by several nations to produce and counter ISIS narratives aimed at youth. As an international business centre, the country has paid close attention to implementing anti-money-laundering initiatives and has generally avoided global watch lists which could be detrimental to its economic as well as political interests. The UAE is being especially focused on using new technology to address a security challenge rooted in political Islam, but also potentially a function of its involvement in conflicts such as Libya, and as the country becomes an increasingly popular tourism destination.[26] A new border security body will merge the functions of emirate-level border authorities, each with slightly different tolerances on extremists or even individuals aligned with Islamist parties, whilst providing more commercial opportunities to the UAE defence conglomerate EDGE as part of emiratisation (*Taawteen*).[27]

National security and human rights

Since at least 2009, the UAE authorities have launched a major online cyber-surveillance campaign, including installing spyware on BlackBerrys,[28] purchasing spyware from Israel[29] and a new Development Research Exploitation Analysis Department staffed by former US National Security Agency operatives.[30] Deployed in the name of counterterrorism, the spyware has appeared on devices used by human rights activists such as Ahmed Mansour,[31] and relentlessly targeted Qatar during the Qatar Crisis, threatening to imprison any UAE national expressing sympathy with Qatar.[32] In December 2021 a UAE agency was found to have placed spyware from the NSO Group onto the phone of Hanan Elatr, the fiancée of Jamal Khashoggi, when she was arrested by UAE officials in Dubai in 2018.[33] However, by 2019 the Emirates signals intelligence agency and Pax AI, a data-mining firm, were linked to ToTok. Promoted as a secure way to chat by video or text message, the app was found to be a spying tool, highlighting a new development in indigenous spyware capabilities, able to reach users in the Middle East, Europe, Asia, Africa and North America.[34]

The UAE government's response to the Arab uprisings was, and remains, informed by its intensely anti-Islamist agenda. It continues to view Islamism as a direct threat to the political legitimacy of the ruling monarchy. This includes groups such as Al-Ishlah and the MB, as well as Al Qaeda and Islamic State. Whilst secularism is championed as a way to separate Islamist influence in politics and modern state decision making on policy issues such as energy and infrastructure,[35] democracy is not. Throughout this period there was also some social pressure for an elected parliament. For example, in March 2011, 133 Emirati intellectuals petitioned against the lack of democratic progress in the Federal National Council (FNC) and called for an elected chamber.[36] Critics pointed to headway being made in other Arab nations such as Palestine, Iraq and Saudi Arabia. In response, the UAE government pledged to support the poorer emirates with $1.6 billion in infrastructure investments.[37] There are also signs that the public and expatriates will be permitted to submit ideas on 'health, education, social development, economy, environment, housing, tourism, entrepreneurship, investment, skill development, societal values, culture, family relations, sports, youth, food security, science and advanced technologies' for the UAE Centennial Plan 2071.[38] Whilst this doesn't address elections, it shows some movement on consultation and consensus building, which have been the hallmarks of UAE/Trucial State policy throughout its history. It also marks growing connections between UAE ministries that are emblematic of its joined-up economic statecraft approach. Adopting such ideas could create new synergies and open up areas to explore with external partners, leading to new forms of cooperation and collaboration.

The UAE government has encouraged female participation in the FNC. Sheikha Lubna bint Khalid bin Sultan Al Qasimi became the first woman to hold a ministerial post in the UAE when she became minister of economics and planning in 2004. Since then she has been minister of state for international cooperation from 2004 to 2016 and minister of state for tolerance from 2016 to 2017. Other female ministers include Her Excellency (HE) Reem Al Hasimi, minister of state for international cooperation; HE Noura Al Kaabi, minister of culture and knowledge development; HE Hessa Buhumaid, minister of community development; HE Jameela Al Muhairi, minister of state for public education affairs; HE Dr Maitha Al Shamsi, minister of state and former chair of the Marriage Fund; HE Ohood Al Roumi, minister of state for happiness and wellbeing; HE Shamma Al Mazrui, minister for youth; HE Maryam Al Mehairi, minister of state for food security; and HE Sarah Al Amiri, minister of state for advanced sciences.[39] Women make up some of the ambassadorships to countries such as Denmark, Latvia, Finland and Brazil. The UAE permanent representative to the UN is Lana Nusseibeh, who has served there since 2013. The motivation for inclusivity is partly in recognition of the UAE's small population.

Anwar Gargash, UAE minister of state for foreign affairs in 2020, said at the time that the UAE's single most important achievement is growing equality for women.[40] This also feeds into the UAE's Human Rights Plan which was in the consultative process as of 2020 and is engaging in the Universal Periodic Review of the UN Human Rights Council.[41] It's no coincidence that human rights forms a pillar of a state whose foreign policy interests need to align with NATO (North Atlantic Treaty Organisation) allies who often promote human rights as part of their foreign policy agendas, and that needs to differentiate itself from adversaries such as Iran. Yet, these positive norm-setting practices have been undermined through the UK High Court's finding that Sheikh Mohammed bin Rashid Al Maktoum, ruler of Dubai, was responsible for a campaign of intimidation against his former wife, Princess Haya (the half-sister of Jordan's King Abdullah II). He was also found responsible for the abduction and forced return of two of his daughters by a different marriage, including Princess Latifa. Evidence to support allegations of the princess's ongoing detention in 2021 led the UN High Commissioner for Human Rights to raise the case with the UAE's permanent mission in Geneva.[42] Princess Latifa has since been viewed free and abroad. However, a UAE human rights activist, Ahmed Mansour, who has been detained since December 2017, remains in isolation.[43] The US State Department's Arab Emirates 2019 Human Rights Report mentions arrest without charge linked to alleged violations of state security regulations, lack of due process on occasion, poor conditions and overcrowding in prisons and two cases of arbitrary detention in 2020, both related to members of Al-Islah who had completed their sentences back in 2017.[44]

Post the Arab uprisings, the Gulf monarchies have been able to position themselves as the only viable alternative to an Islamist takeover. But the catch-all term of political Islam as a monolithic threat belies the diversity of ways in which Islamists have engaged in the region.[45] Furthermore, the liberal application of the term 'terrorist', particularly against Islamists and minority Shia communities, has extended the internal parameters of sectarianism and inflamed regional tensions in a zero-sum game.

The economy: state-led capitalism and diversification

The UAE has the second-largest economy in the Arab world after Saudi Arabia. Its strategic location in the Gulf and large SWF give it increased clout in the global economy. Inward investment into the UAE increased by 32 per cent between 2018 and 2019, to reach $13.8 billion, helped by the UAE acting as an entrepôt for broader regional trade.[46] Political and economic stability has been key to attracting investment from other parts of the region racked by conflict. With a GDP of over $421 billion and a GDP per capita of $69,958 in 2020, the UAE ranks high in global league tables.[47] However, masked by the richer emirates of Abu Dhabi and Dubai, the GDP figures across all the emirates present a more diverse picture. Abu Dhabi's GDP was around $253.85 billion in 2018 (AED 932.4 billion),[48] Dubai's was around $108.38 billion in 2018 (AED 398.1 billion),[49] Sharjah's was $25.23 billion in 2017 (AED 92.7 billion),[50] Ras Al-Khaimah's was $9.55 billion in 2016 (AED 35.1 billion),[51] Fujairah's was $4.1 billion in 2017,[52] Ajman's was $5.71 billion in 2019 (AED 21.00 billion)[53] and Umm Al-Quwain's was $632 million in 2013.[54] The disparity is largely offset by small local populations – Umm Al-Quwain had a population of just 49,159 in 2005[55] – and access to the richer emirates for education and work opportunities.

The UAE has the seventh-largest oil reserves in the world and oil exports make up 20 per cent of its export revenue, contributing around $65 billion to the economy in 2019.[56] The oil industry is centred on Abu Dhabi, which holds about 96 per cent of reserves. It exported more than 881 million barrels in 2019, making it the third-largest petroleum producer in OPEC after Saudi Arabia and Iraq. It was aiming for over 1 billion barrels in 2020 and seeks to boost its low-cost production to full capacity to fund a rapid economic transition and diversification. However, the UAE has been constrained by OPEC production quotas, particularly during the COVID-19 crisis, which suppressed its baseline production and limited exports to two-thirds of its operating capacity.[57] The UAE minister of energy and infrastructure, Suhail Al Mazouei, said production cuts to 2018 levels 'wasn't a good deal'[58] and has sought assurances that post-April 2022 its baseline quota will be lifted, allowing it to export 5 million barrels per day through refinery and petrochemical plants in Ruwais.[59] Saudi Arabia and the UAE were for a short period in disagreement over the matter, which, if allowed to continue, could have spelled the end of UAE membership in OPEC after fifty-four years. In the event, a compromise was made to allow the group to boost output in 2021. Still, the UAE attempt to have its grade of crude used as a benchmark to price world supply could also fuel a split with Saudi Arabia over OPEC policy.[60] Further division could also be possible after Abu Dhabi introduced futures trading for its oil in 2021. The port of Fujairah is under expansion, with anticipated boost in capacity by 42 million barrels by 2022.[61]

The UAE has some of the largest capabilities of solar energy in the world, with more in the pipeline. It has a mixed approach to energy, feeding a low-carbon economy, including nuclear, gas (from Qatar through the Dolphin Project because consumption outstrips production) and renewables. In 2017, the UAE launched 'Energy Strategy 2050', which aims to increase the contribution of clean energy to the UAE's total energy mix from 25 per cent to 50 per cent by 2050.[62] In 2020 the UAE announced that it would reduce its greenhouse gas emissions by 23.5 per cent by 2030, making it the first Gulf state to peak its emissions by that date.[63] In October 2021, the UAE was the first country in the Middle East and North Africa to announce a net-zero strategic initiative to be carbon neutral by 2050.[64] In this effort, Abu Dhabi has committed $15 billion to Masdar, the world's largest alternative energy programme. Its projects include a solar-powered desalination project in the UAE; solar farms in the UAE, Egypt, Jordan, South Pacific Islands and the Caribbean; and wind farms in Jordan, Oman, Serbia, Montenegro, the US, UK and the South Pacific Islands.[65]

Building on renewables, Robin Mills, chief executive of Qamar Energy, notes that the manufacture of green hydrogen will play a role as renewable power generation and gas projects take off.[66] It could be used domestically and develop as part of international projects.[67] On 1 August 2020, Barakah, the UAE nuclear power plant, went on line. Here too, the UAE has taken a collaborative approach, working with Korea Electric Power Corporation, the International Atomic Energy Agency (IAEA) and a host of other stakeholders to ensure a high degree of confidence and acceptance, including with the US, which culminated in an exceptionally stringent Section 123 ('gold standard') agreement.[68] The UAE will continue to carve out a niche in renewable and clean energy, partly based on its commitment to funding renewables, including its success in attracting the International Renewable Energy Agency to have its headquarters there from 2009. This was the first time any Middle East and North Africa (MENA) state had been able to attract an international agency to its territory. The UAE has continued to build its international relevance and climate credentials by linking its leadership of the region in aiming for carbon neutrality by 2050 to being chosen to host the UN Climate Change Conference, COP28, in 2023.[69]

Regime security is advanced through advancing the twin agendas of Arab secularism and state-led capitalism. The latter is a direct consequence of the UAE's rentier roots, the accumulation of capital which it invests through SWFs such as the Abu Dhabi Investment Authority (valued at $696 billion in 2020 and the largest externally focused SWF of the emirate), which takes a more traditional investment approach; the Investment Corporation of Dubai (valued at $239 billion in 2020), which makes a contribution to the federal budget; and Mubadala Investment Company (valued at $228 billion in 2020), which is focused on domestic technology and (renewable) energy investments worldwide as a legacy from the International Petroleum Investment Corporation which merged with it to become Mubadala Development Co. in 2017.[70] Mubadala Investment has sparked a number of UAE industries: aerospace, under Abu Dhabi Aircraft Technologies; electronics, under Advanced Technology Investment Company; ship-building, under Abu Dhabi Ship-building Company; and defence, under Abu Dhabi Systems Integration and al-Yah Satellites. Many have developed from investments in British, French and Italian firms.

The Emirates Investment Authority is smaller (valued at $45 billion in 2020) but is the only federal SWF and invests domestically and internationally.[71] The Emirates Investment Authority's concentration in Abu Dhabi contributes to political consolidation and the emirate's power. Many UAE SWFs were formed in 2007 but invest in many different asset classes, commercial companies (including domestic ones such as Du and Etisalat) and ventures (including building new export-orientated industries such as aerospace components with support from Boeing and Airbus). They span a large number of countries and serve to attract further international capital investment and expatriate labour, economic development and status. In doing so, they contribute to the Emirates' sovereignty, autonomy and ultimately, security.

As the UAE reaches for greater economic diversification there are individuals within the royal family who are well placed to combine politics, defence and economic statecraft. Their inclusion is also important for Sheikh Zayed to consolidate control. For example, Sheikh Tahnoun is the son of Sheikh Zayed bin Sultan Al-Nahyan, the UAE founding father and full brother of Sheikh Mohammed bin Zayed, giving him almost unequalled influence in state affairs. He is on the board of the Supreme Council for Financial and Economic Affairs; is chair of First Abu Dhabi Bank; and is chair of International Holdings Company (a conglomerate with interests in a range of industries including fisheries and healthcare), which acquired Trust International Group (a defence company) in 2019 when he was chair of the Royal Group (another conglomerate).[72] He is also chair of Group 42 (a cloud-computing and artificial intelligence [AI] company with links to China[73]) and ADQ (a state holding company and active investor).[74] Another example is Sheikh Mansur bin Zayed Al Nahyan. He is the deputy prime minister of the UAE, minister of presidential affairs and also a billionaire. He is chairman of the Emirates Investment Authority and the Emirates Racing Authority, sits on the Supreme Petroleum Council and the Supreme Council for Financial and Economic Affairs. He is also a member of the board of Abu Dhabi National Oil Company and Abu Dhabi Investment Authority (ADIA) and is vice-chairman of Mubadala Investment Company. The UAE is also well placed through its proximity to conflict zones and its status as an economic safe haven. For example, many foreign leaders or officials come to the Cleveland Clinic Abu Dhabi, a multi-speciality hospital, during which time UAE government officials can use the visitor's down time to negotiate and reduce tensions in other states.[75] The downside is that growing FATF concern about money laundering, particularly by Russian oligarchs relocating to hubs such as Dubai, has translated into the UAE being placed on its grey watch list in March 2022 after the Russian invasion of Ukraine.

Since 1999, a National Human Resource Development and Employment Authority was established to accelerate the movement of UAE nationals into the private sector to address the imbalance in the workforce in favour of foreign labour. Quotas were initiated from 2002, along with access to a special pension fund and changes to working hours which have proved costly to business. High state benefits and better wages in the public sector have skewed the labour market, but this was being addressed by the UAE spending $6.5 billion in September 2021 to reduce unemployment and make private sector jobs more attractive.[76] There are questions about citizenship for the future descendants of families who have emigrated to the UAE (mainly Abu Dhabi and Dubai). The ruling elite will be cognizant of the need to avoid or reduce any socio-economic schism that may exist between the more cosmopolitan emirates and the more conservative ones. COVID-19 has temporarily relieved pressure on the expatriate imbalance in some cities. Longer term, the UAE will want to avoid job losses which could spark a brain drain, loss of tax revenues and a slow-down of economic growth associated with white collar worker output.

The UAE, like Qatar, sees the GCC as being beneficial as a common market more than as a political platform.[77] The ending of the Qatar Crisis will see a return to – and perhaps more healthy – competition (e.g. for foreign investment), and also more cooperation.[78] All GCC states are intent on attracting more revenue through diversification efforts, streamlining fiscal expenditure, raising taxes, attracting foreign investment and resident investors; but amid lower oil revenues they have also taken on more debt. The UAE implemented a VAT system (5 per cent) along with Saudi Arabia in 2018. The UAE has also announced a 9 per cent corporation tax, not including free zones, effective from June 2023. Oil companies and banks already pay corporation tax, and tourist companies pay associated taxes.

A senior UAE official noted in 2021 that the UAE is pursuing economic liberalisation through a number of ways, including increasing legal transparency (on aspects such as inheritance) so that residents will move from staying in the UAE temporarily to permanently.[79] The UAE is also adjusting its economic and social laws on aspects such as longer-term visas,[80] cohabitation, alcohol and cancelling provisions for leniency concerning 'honour killings', with an eye both to retaining talent and to fuelling economic growth post COVID-19.[81] Abu Dhabi is also introducing a secular family law.[82]

Dubai has focused on expanding tourism, real estate development and economic deal-making, including establishing new industries which, along with Abu Dhabi, support a substantial expatriate population and more international interests than the other more conservative emirates. For example, Changpeng Zhao, chief executive of Binance Holdings Ltd, has called the UAE the 'Wall Street of Crypto', due to it becoming a global hub for digital currencies.[83] The size and pace of change has led many nationals to question the merits of globalisation, just as they have been questioned in the West, especially following periods of instability. These include the 2008–9 financial crisis, which affected the tourism industry, free zones and the real estate market in Dubai and forced it to accept a $10 billion financial bailout from Abu Dhabi.[84] Buoyed by being the largest emirate and holding 94 per cent of the UAE's oil reserves[85] and associated revenues, Abu Dhabi has been relatively insulated from such shocks, leading it to consolidate its power over Dubai. The same pattern has been repeated during COVID-19, when the tourism and aviation industries have been disproportionately affected in Dubai along with, temporarily, food security and migrant labour. The Emirates Food Security Council was set up in January 2020 to coordinate and implement the UAE's National Food Security Strategy. The Abu Dhabi-based company Pure Harvest is set to expand in the GCC precisely because of the need for local food production highlighted by COVID-19.[86] Dubai has moved quickly to keep the emirate in the limelight, including by attracting social media 'influencers' from around the world, whilst establishing a New Media Academy, founded by Sheikh Mohammed bin Rashid al-Maktoum, to train a new generation of social media experts and influencers locally.[87]

Abu Dhabi has not been immune from structural constraint. Indeed, the precipitous drop in oil prices from 2014 gave new impetus to a range of emirate and state-wide diversification strategies, including Vision 2021, Hope Mars Mission 2021, UN Agenda 2030 (sustainable development), Abu Dhabi Economic Vision 2030, Dubai Industrial Strategy 2030, Fujairah 2040 Plan, UAE Energy Strategy 2050 and Centennial Plan 2071.[88] In Abu Dhabi, the *majlis* has moved online, where government officials, experts and entrepreneurs meet with youth in an interactive dialogue, especially about shaping the next fifty years.[89] In 2020, the UAE launched 'Hope Probe', its first mission to Mars. Commanded from the Mohammed Bin Rashid Space Centre in Dubai, the mission fits with UAE ambition and results-orientated objectives. Supported by US experts at the Laboratory for Atmospheric and Space Physics at the University of Colorado and companies such as Mitsubishi Heavy Industries, the mission is expected to deliver fresh insights into the atmosphere on Mars.[90] Increasingly, Dubai and Abu Dhabi have worked in tandem to advance their soft-power influence, Dubai attracting the World Expo and the Asian Infrastructure Investment Bank sixth Annual Meeting and Abu Dhabi hosting IDEX in 2021.

Defence

The UAE maintains a deployable ground force of fewer than 20,000 troops.[91] Typically, just hundreds or a couple of thousand troops (sometimes including special forces) have been deployed to support NATO campaigns in Kosovo, Afghanistan and, more recently, in Libya. The UAE has also been active in Syria and in Yemen. The UAE's Presidential Guard is said to be the best fighting force in the Gulf and is comprised of the Emiri Guard, the Special Operations Command, the Marine Battalion of the UAE navy and reconnaissance forces of the Directorate of Military Intelligence, mostly trained by the US Marine Corps.[92]

Due to its shortage of manpower, the UAE military relies on foreign nationals within its ranks, as trainers and military planners, as well as on private security firms and mercenaries. These have been deployed in Somalia, Yemen and Libya and represent a rather unique feature of UAE defence policy in the region, and an area of weakness in terms of command and control, with implications for foreign partners. Long-term national defence planning has enabled the UAE to build assets such as its air force, special forces and high-tech weaponry. The decisions to make Abu Dhabi the UAE's capital city and to make the constitution permanent were confirmed only in 1996, along with the amalgamation of the defence forces.[93] This helped to spur on the UAE armed forces' rapid development, modernisation and professionalisation under a General Headquarters in Abu Dhabi, and with troops receiving better pay as part of a national force.[94] The Stockholm International Peace Research Institute (SIPRI) estimates that the UAE spent $22.8 billion on military spending in 2014 (latest available figure), mainly from the US and Western Europe.[95] But figures from 2018 are likely to be equal or higher than this, due to the UAE's engagement in the Yemen conflict up to February 2020, continued involvement in Libya and its ongoing interest in modernising and expanding its armed forces.

In June 2014, the UAE introduced mandatory military conscription for males aged eighteen to thirty. For those who have completed high school, their service is nine months (the same for women who choose to volunteer) and for those who have not, it is two years. For military personnel from Dubai and Abu Dhabi the primary social bonds may no longer be tribal, but more cosmopolitan networks such as education or business activities. The interventions that the UAE has been associated with have also had the domestic effect of enhancing nationalism and introducing a new national military ethos based on duty, service, sacrifice and patriotism.[96] These attributes could be useful in influencing and mobilising public discourse (i.e. social engineering projects) in greater support of socio-economic objectives towards establishing a post-rentier state, or simply wresting more financial assets from generous fiscal policies to spend on increased defence spending and outward investment partnerships in a lower oil era. But, as Herb and Lynch note, there are likely to be differences between the framing of the regime and the framing of the citizens which could seriously impact on the political economies of the UAE, the Gulf and MENA states reliant on foreign labour remittances.[97]

IDEX, inaugurated in 1993, is the only international defence exhibition and conference in the MENA region. It has grown to become the platform for joint military cooperation. For example, in 2017, Russia and the UAE announced the purchase an undisclosed number of advanced Sukhoi Su-35 Flanker-E fighters from Russia,[98] and a new programme to jointly develop the next generation of fighter jet for the UAE air force.[99] This may have played a role in the Biden administration's choosing not to cancel the $23 billion stealth F-35 order secured during the Trump administration in the context of the Abraham Accords. The development of the UAE's indigenous defence industry will eventually reduce reliance on arms imports, boost local employment and increase the opacity of its military procurement programme, which will be useful in contributing to deterrence. In 2014–18 the UAE was the seventh-largest arms importer in the world. The US accounted for 64 per cent of arms imports by the UAE. Deliveries in 2014–18 included five missile defence systems, 124 short-range ballistic missiles and 1,671 armoured personnel carriers from the US, and three corvettes from France. Some of the armoured vehicles were subsequently supplied by the UAE to militias in Yemen.[100] The UAE has also been making great strides in missile defence domestically through the development of the SkyKnight rocket system manufactured by Halcon, part of the EDGE group.

The UAE navy is the last service to experience expansion. It lacks a blue water fleet and so its combined ports host more naval ships than any other port outside the US. The UAE has 2,500 sailors, eleven–fourteen corvettes, ten submersibles, thirty-four coastal defence craft and twenty-eight amphibious vehicles.[101] Project Liwa is expected to cost $2 billion and will involve a three-phase acquisition of frigates, offshore patrol vessels and naval shipyard facilities. Combined, UAE military programmes and companies such as Emirates Defence Industries Company can be viewed as part of a wider stimulus programme in the UAE economy. There are issues in that both Saudi Arabia and the UAE still lack skilled workforces in this area, and so they need to create and implement training policies.[102] But moving from the Maquiladora System to an indigenous capability with the right levels of spending, cooperation and focus could yield significant results.

As well as these hard-power capabilities, the UAE also have a range of soft-power tools through which they can project influence and build partnerships in fields such as education, science and technology, culture, religion and sports. Dubai International Academic City is the Middle East's largest education hub, bringing together universities from Australia, the UK, India and elsewhere. But one of the UAE's standout contribution has been through its interest in building religious tolerance. In 2019, as part of the UAE's campaign to make the country a model for religious and ethnic tolerance, the government announced the Abrahamic Family House in Abu Dhabi. This compound will contain a mosque, church and synagogue and is to be designed by David Adjaye, who designed the National Museum of African American History and Culture in Washington, DC.[103] Pope Francis visited the same year, the first-ever visit by the pontiff to the Arabian Peninsula, for an interfaith conference.[104] Both the UAE and Qatar have attempted to bolster their Islamic credentials through hosting international associations of Islamic scholars. The Muslim Council of Elders is based in Abu Dhabi, whilst the International Union of Muslim Scholars is based in Doha, showing how religious statecraft is dynamic and part of soft power and national branding.[105]

Diplomacy and statecraft, particularly hybrid political–economic statecraft, became more pronounced after 9/11, facilitating a shift from the common personal approach, still dominant within the GCC,[106] to a more institutionalised approach internationally. The key components appear to bind states to the UAE through a hub-and-spokes model, increasing the vested national interests at stake and thereby the security and protection on offer.

Conclusion

Rapid economic development and relatively early use of oil revenue to underwrite economic projects has afforded the UAE multiple opportunities to diversify its economy and to consolidate its federation and the individual's place within it, whilst harnessing new forms of state-led development. The UAE's existential crisis vis-à-vis Islamism and those states which support it, such as Qatar, Turkey and Iran, has been the main driving force behind its national security measures and unusual, for a small state, hard-power projection. This appears to be changing from 2021, with a greater weight on economic statecraft over more the muscular responses seen since the Arab uprisings. Indeed, the UAE has been consistent in exploring all sources of hard and soft power as two sides of the same coin. The UAE's vulnerable position between two sparring partners in the Gulf (Saudi Arabia and Iran), and instability in the wider region, with no recourse to a reliable regional security architecture, has contributed to its high arms imports and search for a series of defensive relationships. This trend looks set to continue.

Due to its federal nature, the UAE government has tolerated some traditional discrepancies between the emirates on various policy issues. However, over time there appears to be a convergence and consensus building on major foreign policy issues and the necessity to act in concert, especially on issues concerning national security. Liberalism has been spurred on by the necessity to attract highly qualified expatriate labour to contribute to the UAE's vision strategy, while secularism helps to support monarchical stability versus the Islamist threat. The unique federal decision making in the UAE, having traversed through periods of tension and contest between the emirates, and still with distinct differences between them, appears to be set on a course dominated by youth at many levels. There also appears to be an increasing intermingling of economic statecraft and politics, due to sheikhs who hold multiple positions across officialdom, conglomerates and defence companies. Certainly, the UAE has set in motion a series of developments in its political economy to address the needs of its citizenry, and there are signs that the UAE has become more competitive in attracting global talent post-COVID-19.

Although this chapter has shown the beginnings of a possible cleavage in OPEC+ between Saudi Arabia and the UAE, the UAE remains a core element in the GCC and has good relations with the kingdom. The social contract as far as these rentier states are concerned remains intact, with the UAE attempting to engage its citizenry in ambitious visions and new forms of consultation. The UAE is one of the more diversified GCC states. But, due to the centrality of Abu Dhabi in UAE politics, and Abu Dhabi still deriving most of its income from oil, RST cannot be ignored as a cogent form of analysis even if it is diminishing as the industrial sector grows.

Notes

1 Hussein Ibish, 'Executive Summary', *The UAE's Evolving National Security Strategy*, Arab Gulf States Institute in Washington, 6 April 2017.

2 Andrea B. Rugh, 'The Political Culture of Leadership', *The Political Culture of Leadership in the United Arab Emirates*. New York: Palgrave Macmillan, 2007: 218.

3 See John Duke Anthony, *Arab States of the Lower Gulf: People, Politics, Petroleum*. Washington, DC: Middle East Institute, 1975.

4 Ibid.

5 Joseph A. Kechichian, 'Succession Challenges in the Arab Gulf Monarchies: The United Arab Emirates and the Al-Nahyan–Al Maktoum Duopoly', Asian Institute for Policy Studies, 2015: 78.

6 Kristian Coates-Ulrichsen, 'State Formation', *The United Arab Emirates: Power, Politics and Policymaking*. Abingdon: Routledge, 2017: 17–43, at 29.

7 Kenneth Katzman, 'The United Arab Emirates (UAE): Issues for U.S. Policy', CRS Report for Congress, 28 October 2021: 1.

8 Athol Yates, 'Challenging the Accepted Understanding of the Executive Branch of the UAE's Federal Government', *Middle Eastern Studies*, 14 October 2020.

9 Abu Dhabi hosted the meeting in 1981 which established the GCC. Gulf News, 'Timeline of the GCC Summit', 5 December 2010, https://gulfnews.com/world/gulf/timeline-of-the-gcc-summit-1.723199

10 See Robert Mason, 'Small State Aspirations to Middle Powerhood: The Cases of Qatar and the UAE', in Adham Saouli (ed.) *Unfulfilled Aspirations: Middle Power Politics in the Middle East*. London: Hurst/Oxford University Press, 2020: 157–183.

11 Joseph Braude, 'The UAE's Brotherhood Problem', Al Mesbar Studies and Research Center, https://mesbar.org/the-uaes-brotherhood-problem/

12 Hedges and Cafiero, 'The GCC and the Muslim Brotherhood': What Does the Future Hold?', *Middle East Policy Council*, XXIV (1), Spring 2017, https://mepc.org/journal/gcc-and-muslim-brotherhood-what-does-future-hold

13 Kristian Coates Ulrichsen, 'Politics', *The United Arab Emirates: Power, Politics and Policymaking*. Abingdon: Routledge, 2017: 74.

14 Sultan Sooud Al Qassemi, 'The Brothers and the Gulf', *Foreign Policy*, 14 December 2012, https://foreignpolicy.com/2012/12/14/the-brothers-and-the-gulf/

15 Ibid.

16 Courtney Freer, 'Rentier Islamism After Pan-Arabism', *Rentier Islamism: The Influence of the Muslim Brotherhood in Gulf Monarchies*. Oxford: Oxford University Press, 2018: 130.

17 Fatma Al Sayegh, 'Post 9/11 Changes in the Gulf: The Case of the UAE', *Middle East Policy*, XI (2), Summer 2004: 107–135, at 114.

18 Jim Krane, 'Notes', *City of Gold: Dubai and the Dream of Capitalism*. New York: St. Martin's Press, 2010: 333.

19 Frontline, 'Inside the Terror Network: Introduction', 17 January 2002, www.pbs.org/wgbh/pages/frontline/shows/network/etc/synopsis.html

20 Ryan Bohl, 'What I Taught in the Emirates – and What It Taught Me', *New Lines Magazine*, 30 November 2021, https://newlinesmag.com/first-person/what-i-taught-in-the-emirates-and-what-it-taught-me/

21 Courtney Freer, *Rentier Islamism: The Role of the Muslim Brotherhood in the Gulf*. LSE Middle East Centre, Series 9, November 2015.

22 Matthew Hedges and Giorgio Cafiero, 'The GCC and the Muslim Brotherhood: What Does the Future Hold?', *Middle East Policy Council*, XXIV (1), Spring 2017.

23 Ibid.

24 Kristian Coates Ulrichsen, 'International Relations', *The United Arab Emirates: Power, Politics and Policymaking*. Abingdon: Routledge, 2017: 137.

25 Katzman, 'The United Arab Emirates (UAE)': 3.

26 Isabel Debre, 'UAE Announces Relaxing of Islamic Laws for Personal Freedoms', AP News, 7 November 2020, https://apnews.com/article/dubai-united-arab-emirates-honor-killings-travel-islam-bce74c423897dc77c7beb72e4f51a23a

27 Agnes Helou, 'UAE Pursues Better Border Security Collaboration, More Domestic Capabilities', *Defense News*, 8 November 2021, www.defensenews.com/global/ mideast-africa/2021/11/08/uae-pursues-better-border-security-collaboration-more-domestic-capabilities/?utm_campaign=Socialflow%20DFN&utm_ medium=social&utm_source=twitter.com&fbclid=IwAR3xEsuf4Zj1Hpa3qJ RLTS3qoHuzATYadygR68mU6SwxgCrrttGZmyrkiu4

28 Ben Thompson, 'UAE Blackberry Update Was Spyware', *BBC News*, 21 July 2009, http://news.bbc.co.uk/2/hi/8161190.stm

29 Chaim Levinson, 'With Israel's Encouragement, NSO Sold Spyware to UAE and Other Gulf States', *Haaretz*, 25 August 2020, www.haaretz.com/middle-east-news/.premium-with-israel-s-encouragement-nso-sold-spyware-to-uae-and-other-gulf-states-1.9093465

30 Christopher Bing and Joel Schectman, 'Secret Hacking Team of American Mercenaries', *Reuters*, 30 January 2019, www.reuters.com/investigates/special-report/usa-spying-raven/

31 Ibid.

32 BBC News, 'Qatar Crisis: UAE Threatens Sympathisers with Prison', 7 June 2017, www.bbc.com/news/world-middle-east-40192730

33 Dana Priest, 'A UAE Agency Put Pegasus Spyware on Phone of Jamal Khashoggi's Wife in Months before His Murder, New Forensics Show', *The Washington Post*, 21 December 2021, www.washingtonpost.com/nation/interactive/2021/ hanan-elatr-phone-pegasus/

34 Mark Mazzetti, Nicole Perlroth and Ronen Bergman, 'It Seemed Like a Popular Chat App. It's Secretly a Spy Tool', *The New York Times*, 14 August 2020, www.nytimes.com/2019/12/22/us/politics/totok-app-uae.html

35 'UAE Ambassador Youssef Otaiba on the Separation of Religion and State in the Middle East', *Twitter*, 18 April 2021, https://twitter.com/Adlamassoud/ status/1383602266767192069

36 Hedges and Cafiero, 'The GCC and the Muslim Brotherhood'.

37 Reuters, 'UAE to Invest in Poorer Northern Emirates', 2 March 2011, www. reuters.com/article/oukwd-uk-emirates-utilities-idAFTRE72121720110302

38 Staff Report, 'Sheikh Mohammed Invites Citizens, Expats to Help Shape UAE's Next 50 Years', *Khaleej Times*, 29 September 2020, www.khaleejtimes.com/news/ government/sheikh-mohammed-invites-citizens-expats-to-help-shape-uaes-next-50-years-

39 Emma Day, 'Meet the Nine Female Ministers in the UAE's Current Cabinet', *Emirates Women*, 15 February 2018, https://emirateswoman.com/meet-the-nine-female-ministers-in-the-uaes-current-cabinet/

40 Council on Foreign Relations, 'A Conversation with Anwar Gargash', 29 September 2020, www.cfr.org/event/conversation-anwar-gargash

41 Reem Krimly, 'UAE Launches Consultative Process for UAE National Human Rights Plan', *Al Arabiya News*, 10 December 2020, https://english. alarabiya.net/News/2020/12/10/UAE-launches-consultative-process-for-UAE-National-Human-Rights-Plan

42 Ibid.

43 The Independent, 'UAE Human Rights Activist Ahmed Mansour Kept in 2m
 * 2m Cell for 4 Years', 27 January 2021, www.independent.co.uk/news/world/
 middle-east/uae-ahmed-mansoor-jail-human-rights-b1793501.html

44 US Department of State, 'United Arab Emirates 2019 Human Rights Report',
 www.state.gov/wp-content/uploads/2020/03/UNITED-ARAB-EMIRATES-
 2019-HUMAN-RIGHTS-REPORT.pdf

45 Frederic Volpi, 'Political Islam in the Mediterranean: The View from Democratization Studies', *Democratization*, 16 (1), 2009, 20–38.

46 Nordea, 'Foreign Direct Investment (FDI) in the United Arab Emirates',
 www.nordeatrade.com/dk/explore-new-market/united-arab-emirates/investment
 (accessed 2 February 2021).

47 US News, 'Overview of the United Arab Emirates', www.usnews.com/news/
 best-countries/united-arab-emirates

48 Staff Report, 'Abu Dhabi GDP Continues to Achieve Significant Growth',
 Khaleej Times, 12 January 2020, www.khaleejtimes.com/business/economy/
 abu-dhabi-gdp-continues-to-achieve-significant-growth

49 Emirates NBD, 'Dubai's GDP Growth Slowed to 1.9% in 2018', 28 March
 2019, http://emiratesnbdresearch.com/research/article/?a=dubais-gdp-growt
 h-slowed-to-19-in-2018–1320#:~:text=Dubai's%20real%20GDP%20grew%20
 to,from%202.8%25%20to%203.1%25.

50 Sharjah Update, 'Sharjah GDP Rises to AED 92.7b in 2017', www.sharjahupdate.
 com/?s=sharjah+gdp#:~:text=Sharjah%20GDP%20rises%20to%20
 AED92,the%20Sharjah%20Economic%20Development%20Department.

51 Ras Al Khaimah Government Media Office, 'Facts about Ras Al Khaimah',
 www.rakmediaoffice.ae/en/about-ras-al-khaimah/facts/#:~:text=Ras%20Al%20
 Khaimah's%20GDP%20reached,%2C%20contributing%2030%25%20
 towards%20GDP.

52 Emirates News Agency, 'UAE's Fujairah Records GDP of $4.1bln in 2017',
 www.zawya.com/uae/en/economy/story/UAEs_Fujairah_records_GDP_of_
 41bln_in_2017-WAM20180410130029951/#:~:text=FUJAIRAH%20%2D%20
 The%20Annual%20Statistical%20Book,foreign%20trade%20amounted%20
 to%20AED6.

53 UAE Government, 'About Ajman', https://u.ae/en/about-the-uae/the-seven-
 emirates/ajman#:~:text=In%202019%2C%20the%20GDP%20of,economic%20
 growth%20of%20the%20emirate.

54 MEED, 'Doing Business in Umm al-Quwain', 1 February 2013, www.meed.com/
 doing-business-in-umm-al-quwain/

55 UAE Government, 'Umm Al Quwain', https://u.ae/en/about-the-uae/
 the-seven-emirates/umm-al-quwain

56 Export.gov, 'United Arab Emirates – Oil and Gas Field Machinery and Services',
 7 August 2019, www.export.gov/apex/article2?id=United-Arab-Emirates-Energy-
 Power

57 Simeon Kerr, Anji Raval and Derek Brower, 'UAE–Saudi Brinkmanship Threatens
 OPEC Unity as Oil Prices Soar', *Financial Times*, 7 July 2021, www.ft.com/
 content/d0b77371-fdd3-4650-81e7-9b5e51f27bb9?sharetype=blocked

58 Dan Murphy and Hadley Gamble, 'UAE "Unconditionally" Supports OPEC+ Supply Increase, But Says Not to a Bad Deal', *CNBC*, 4 July 2021, www.cnbc.com/2021/07/04/uae-unconditionally-supports-opec-supply-increase-minister-says.html

59 Kerr, Raval and Brower, 'UAE–Saudi Brinkmanship Threatens OPEC Unity'.

60 Rania El Gamal, 'Analysis: UAE's Oil Expansion Gives it New Weight within OPEC', *Reuters*, 3 December 2020, www.reuters.com/article/us-oil-opec-emirates-adnoc-analysis/analysis-uaes-oil-expansion-gives-it-new-weight-within-opec-idUSKBN28D1PM

61 US Energy Information Administration, 'Country Analysis Executive Summary: United Arab Emirates', 6 May 2020: 4, www.eia.gov/international/content/analysis/countries_long/United_Arab_Emirates/uae_2020.pdf

62 UAE Government, 'UAE Energy Strategy 2050', https://u.ae/en/about-the-uae/strategies-initiatives-and-awards/federal-governments-strategies-and-plans/uae-energy-strategy-2050#:~:text=The%20strategy%20aims%20to%20increase,AED%20700%20billion%20by%202050.

63 Emirates News Agency, 'UAE Announces Ambitious Climate Commitments as Part of Second Nationally Determined Contribution', 30 December 2020, https://wam.ae/en/details/1395302898670

64 Arabian Business, 'UAE Chosen as Host of COP28 in 2023', 13 November 2021, www.arabianbusiness.com/industries/industries-culture-society/uae-chosen-as-host-of-cop28-in-2023#:~:text=Sheikh%20Abdullah%20bin%20Zayed%20Al,Parties%20(COP28)%20in%202023.

65 Masdar, 'Our Projects', https://masdar.ae/en/masdar-clean-energy/projects

66 The Oxford Institute for Energy Studies, 'The Role of Hydrogen in the Energy Transition', *Forum*, 127, May 2021, www.oxfordenergy.org/wpcms/wp-content/uploads/2021/05/OEF-127.pdf

67 Ibid.

68 Robert Mason, 'As UAE Nuclear Power Plant Comes On Line, Attention Turns to Saudi Plans', Arab Gulf States Institute in Washington, 19 August 2020, https://agsiw.org/as-uae-nuclear-power-plant-comes-on-line-attention-turns-to-saudi-plans/

69 Arabian Business, 'UAE Chosen as Host of COP28 in 2023'.

70 Stanley Carvalho, 'Abu Dhabi Creates $125 Billion Fund by Merging Mubadala, IPIC', *Reuters*, 21 January 2017, www.reuters.com/article/us-emirates-abudhabi-funds-idUSKBN1550R2

71 Matthew Amlot, 'Here are the Top 10 Sovereign Wealth Funds in the Arab World', *Al Arabiya News*, 20 May 2020, https://english.alarabiya.net/business/economy/2019/08/28/Here-are-the-top-10-sovereign-wealth-funds-in-the-Arab-world

72 Andrew England and Simeon Kerr, 'The Abu Dhabi Royal at the Nexus of UAE Business and National Security', *Financial Times*, 25 January 2021

73 Intelligence Online, 'Abu Dhabi's Spymaster Fashions Local Palantir 2.0 with Chinese Help', 27 January 2021, www.intelligenceonline.com/government-intelligence/2021/01/27/abu-dhabi-s-spymaster-fashions-local-palantir-20-with-chinese-help,109638008-eve

74 England and Kerr, 'The Abu Dhabi Royal at the Nexus of UAE Business and National Security'.

75 Discussion with a senior UAE official who asked not to be named, 19 January 2021.

76 Zainab Fattah, 'UAE to Spend $6.5 Billion to Boost Private-Sector Jobs', *Bloomberg*, 12 September 2021, www.bloomberg.com/news/articles/2021-09-12/uae-to-spend-6-5-billion-luring-citizens-to-private-sector-jobs

77 Discussion with a senior UAE official who asked not to be named, 19 January 2021.

78 Ibid.

79 Ibid.

80 Modernisation of the visa regime, economic agreements with global markets, digital initiatives and other aspects to enhance UAE competitiveness such as investment summits are part of the first set of 'Projects of the 50', https://u.ae/en/about-the-uae/initiatives-of-the-next-50/projects-of-the-50/first-set-of-projects-of-the-50. The second set of 'Projects of the 50' was launched in September 2021, https://u.ae/en/about-the-uae/initiatives-of-the-next-50/projects-of-the-50/second-set-of-projects-of-the-50

81 Reuters, 'New UAE Criminal Code "Most Sweeping Reform in Gulf State's History"', *The Jerusalem Post*, 27 November 2021, www.jpost.com/middle-east/new-uae-criminal-code-most-sweeping-reform-in-gulf-states-history-687140

82 Ibid.

83 Ben Bartenstein, 'Bankers Quit Jobs for Shot at Riches in "Wall Street of Crypto"', Bloomberg, 6 May 2022, www.bloomberg.com/news/articles/2022-05-06/bankers-quit-jobs-for-shot-at-riches-in-wall-street-of-crypto

84 Richard Spencer, 'Dubai Accepts $10bn Bail-Out from Abu Dhabi in Dramatic Climb Down', *The Telegraph*, 14 December 2009, www.telegraph.co.uk/news/worldnews/middleeast/dubai/6807939/Dubai-accepts-10bn-bail-out-from-Abu-Dhabi-in-dramatic-climbdown.html

85 Export.gov, 'United Arab Emirates – Oil and Gas Field Machinery and Services', 8 July 2019, www.export.gov/apex/article2?id=United-Arab-Emirates-Energy-Power#:~:text=Abu%20Dhabi%20holds%2094%20percent,million%20barrels%20of%20oil%2C%20respectively.

86 Sarmad Khan, 'Abu Dhabi's Pure Harvest Raises $60m to Fund GCC Growth', *The National*, 16 March 2021, www.thenationalnews.com/business/technology/abu-dhabi-s-pure-harvest-raises-60m-to-fund-gcc-growth-1.1184264#click=https://t.co/1st373uZH2

87 Ruth Michaelson, '"In This World, Social Media is Everything": How Dubai Became the Planet's Influencer Capital', *The Guardian*, 17 April 2021, www.theguardian.com/world/2021/apr/17/in-this-world-social-media-is-everything-how-dubai-became-the-planets-influencer-capital

88 UAE Government, 'Future', https://u.ae/en/about-the-uae/uae-future#:~:text=UAE%20Energy%20Strategy%202050&text=The%20strategy%20aims%20to%20increase%20the%20contribution%20of%20clean%20energy,AED%20700%20billion%20by%202050.

89 Emirates News Agency, 'Mohamed Bin Zayed Majlis for Future Generations Opens with Great Turnout of UAE Youth', 14 March 2021, https://wam.ae/en/details/1395302918091

90 Jonathan Amos, 'Hope Probe: UAE Launches Historic First Mission to Mars', *BBC News*, 19 July 2020, www.bbc.com/news/science-environment-53394737

91 Michael Knights, 'Lessons from the UAE War in Yemen', *Lawfare*, 18 August 2019, www.lawfareblog.com/lessons-uae-war-yemen

92 Zoltan Barany, 'Military Politics: The Absolute Monarchy, Domestic Threats, and Civil-Military Relations', *Armies of Arabia: Military Politics and Effectiveness in the Gulf*. Oxford: Oxford University Press, 2021: 90.

93 Courtney Freer, 'National Identity and the Emirati State', LSE Middle East Centre, 11 December 2018, https://blogs.lse.ac.uk/mec/2018/12/11/national-identity-and-the-emirati-state/

94 David B. Roberts, 'Bucking the Trend: The UAE and the Development of Military Capabilities in the Arab World', *Security Studies*, 29 (2): 301–334, at 321–322.

95 Pieter D. Wezemaan and Alexandra Kuimova, 'Military Spending and Arms Imports by Iran, Saudi Arabia, Qatar and the UAE, SIPRI Factsheet, May 2019, 6, www.sipri.org/sites/default/files/2019-05/fs_1905_gulf_milex_and_arms_transfers.pdf

96 Eleonora Ardemagni, 'Militarised Nationalism in the Gulf Monarchies: Crafting the Heritage of Tomorrow', LSE Middle East Centre, 16 May 2020, https://blogs.lse.ac.uk/mec/2020/05/16/militarised-nationalism-in-the-gulf-monarchies-crafting-the-heritage-of-tomorrow/

97 Michael Herb and Marc Lynch, 'The Politics of Rentier States in the Gulf', *The Politics of Rentier States in the Gulf*, January 2019, 7, available at http://eprints.lse.ac.uk/101386/1/Hertog_what_would_the_saudi_economy_have_to_look_like_to_be_post_rentier_published.pdf

98 Middle East Monitor, 'UAE Buys Advanced Fighter Jets from Russia', 22 February 2017, available at www.scribd.com/article/340073480/Uae-Buys-Advanced-Fighter-Jets-From-Russia

99 Military Watch Magazine, 'What Happened to the Joint Russia–UAE Next Generation Stealth Fighter Program?', 7 June 2019, https://militarywatchmagazine.com/article/what-happened-to-the-joint-russia-uae-next-generation-stealth-fighter-program

100 Pieter D Wezeman et al, 'Trends in International Arms Transfers, 2018', SIPRI Fact Sheet, March 2019, www.sipri.org/sites/default/files/2019-03/fs_1903_at_2018.pdf

101 Hussein Ibish, *The UAE's Evolving National Security Strategy*: 20.

102 David B. Des Roches, 'Can Saudi Arabia and the UAE Develop National Arms Industries?', Arab Center Washington, 22 July 2020, http://arabcenterdc.org/policy_analyses/can-saudi-arabia-and-the-uae-develop-national-arms-industries/

103 Lizzie Crook, 'David Adjaye Designs Trio of Multifaith Temples in Abu Dhabi', *Dezeen*, 26 September 2019, www.dezeen.com/2019/09/26/david-adjaye-the-abrahamic-family-house-temples-abu-dhabi-architecture/

104 BBC News, 'Pope Francis Arrives on Historic Visit to the UAE', 3 February 2019, www.bbc.com/news/world-middle-east-47106204

105 Kristin Diwan, 'Clerical Associations in Qatar and the United Arab Emirates: Soft Power Competition in Islamic Politics', *International Affairs*, 97 (4), July 2021, 945–963.

106 A point reinforced in an interview with a foreign affairs analyst, Abu Dhabi, 25 March 2015.

4

Iran: a supreme ontological threat

Introduction

This chapter explores Saudi and UAE relations with Iran, outlining the key shaping factors that drive their contemporary interactions, and provides some additional context for their IR at the wider regional and global levels. The chapter, coupled with the following one on regional relations, underscores the main dynamics of Saudi–Iranian contestation and expression, contributing to what Gause labels a new Cold War,[1] and Fraihat a conflict.[2] Saudi–Iranian relations have been impacted upon by a number of factors, including but not limited to historical and religious contentions, differences in structural power and threat perception since the Iranian Revolution in 1979.

Following the Gulf War, US has become a local actor in Gulf politics, and therefore the historic, complex and multilayered contentions primarily between Saudi Arabia and Iran have been extended to include the US. Thus, Iranian support for Hezbollah and Syria within the 'resistance axis', and changes to US policy, including the Global War on Terror, the JCPOA and the Trump administration's 'maximum pressure policy' all feature in this chapter to provide context. The Arab uprisings have contributed further disorder, conflict and uncertainty about the regional balance of power, whilst internal sectarian policies set the scene for external sectarian escalation, followed by Saudi alliance construction and consolidation. The chapter ends with a discussion of diplomacy taking place in 2021.

Saudi–Iranian relations

The range of Saudi–Iranian contentions is long: Shia mistrust, partly based on the death of Hussain ibn Ali during the battle of Karbala in 680 AD, which has created a collective memory and strong sense of sacrifice and struggle. Indeed, the Shia sect ('the party of Ali') venerates the Prophet, his Nephew Ali and a host of others according to the Shia hierarchy. This aspect of Shia identity has been reinforced by episodes such as the sacking of Karbala in 1801–2 by the first Al Saud dynasty, which destroyed the shrine of saints and monuments and killed more than 5,000 Shia civilians.[3] The Saudis attribute their actions to an earlier perceived injustice over trading routes and an attack that left 300 Wahhabis dead.[4] Abdul-Aziz bin Muhammad, the second ruler of the first Saudi state, who led the attack, was assassinated by a Shia in 1803.

Leadership of the Muslim *Ummah* is another area of contention. Before 1979, the secular ambitions of the shah of Iran and the Saudi objective of leading the Muslim world rarely, if ever, clashed, except for the shah's support for Israel. Iran and Saudi Arabia enjoyed close relations with the US and were encouraged to spend billions of dollars on US arms under the US 'twin pillars' policy. After decades of cooperation (especially on Soviet influence in the Middle East and Arab radicalism; although on Iranian influence in the Gulf, Saudi positions matched those of Arab radicals) and through mutual visits the two states had learnt to live with one another.

In 1979, the major concern in Saudi Arabia was the speed with which the shah was abandoned by Washington, and whether the revolution would turn communist.[5] As Ghattas notes, the Saudis were probably unfamiliar with Khomeini's 1945 book *Kashf al-Asrar*, in which he labels them 'the camel grazers of Riyadh and barbarians of Najd, the most infamous and wildest members of the human family'.[6] The combination of the Iranian Revolution, the takeover of the Grand Mosque in 1979 and a Shia uprising in Qatif the same year, made the Al Saud feel especially vulnerable. This was later added to by Khomeini's rhetoric. In a twenty-nine-page document which formed part of his will after he died in 1989, he writes: 'Muslims should curse these tyrants, including the Saudi royal family, these traitors to God's great shrine, may God's curse and that of his prophets and angels be upon them … King Fahd spends a large part of the people's wealth every year on the anti-Qorani totally baseless superstitious faith of Wahhabism. He abuses Islam and the dear Qoran.'[7] The emphasis was then very much on containing the revolution and identifying it as Shia rather than Islamic, leaving the Saudis to maintain their position as defenders of the faith. For example, Saudis often refer to Iranians as 'Majus' (Zoroastrian), thereby questioning their Muslim faith and reflecting sectarian and ethnic factors.[8] The states then became diametrically opposed, activating conservative religious discourse to advance their state agendas.

From 1979, the regional order was thrown into flux by the new policies pursued by the Iranian government, and a new struggle for legitimacy and hegemony along religious lines took shape.[9] The framing of these pursuits has been vital to both sides in containing the perceived threat and building alliances across the Gulf, the Middle East, South Asia and beyond. Iran, which has a hierarchy of threat perception including the US, Israel, terrorism and the reformulation of the regional order, was generally isolated by regional parties. This became clearly apparent during the Iran–Iraq War. For example, although Saudi Arabia engaged Iran in diplomacy and appeasement throughout the war[10] and beyond, Saudi Arabia supported Iraq against Iran during that war 'with billions of dollars in civilian and military supplies ... $20–27 billion by the end of 1982'.[11] Tensions mounted further as Saudi Arabia shot down two Iranian fighter jets that it accused of entering Saudi airspace on 5 June 1984.[12] Iran was reliant on large numbers of troops, with little coordination between the Islamic Revolutionary Guard Corps (IRGC) and the army or support from heavy weapons, which translated into extensive losses and casualties.[13] Iran's dichotomous political system, where state entities are shadowed and often undermined by IRGC equivalents, has proven to be a persistent hurdle in stabilising relations. Iran's revolutionary policies since the 1979 Iranian Revolution through *Velayat-e faqih*, which describes a theocratic republic governed by a *marja* or grand ayatollah, make IRGC policies even more problematic through their disproportionate influence.[14] Ayatollah Khamenei has favoured hard-liners turning the Iranian political system from a theocracy to a system more akin to a military dictatorship.[15]

Iran has found it easier to work with, predominantly, non-state actors such as the Islamic Front for the Liberation of Bahrain, and Hezbollah from its creation in 1985, in pursuit of its foreign policy interests. Iran, Syria and Hezbollah also joined forces in the so-called 'resistance axis' to counter US hegemony and advance Ayatollah Khomeini's agenda concerning the liberation of Palestine.[16] According to some accounts, the MB offered to pledge allegiance to Khomeini and elevate him as the leader of the Muslim nation. 'Short of appointing him a caliph, men like Youssef Nada indicated they at least hoped Khomeini could be spiritual leader of millions across the world.'[17] This was then undermined by article 12 of the 1979 Iran constitution, which declared Iran's state religion to be Shia Islam. Even so, the Alawis of Syria were never a natural fit with Twelver Shiism, but geopolitical concerns have dominated.

Mabon asserts that there is an 'incongruence of identity' between Riyadh and Tehran which leads to an internal security dilemma.[18] This causes Saudi Arabia and Iran to attempt to delegitimise each other through religious narratives, symbols and institutions (including Saudi support for Wahhabi teaching in mosques and madrassas in a range of states) so as to undercut Shia Islam. Iran's strong sense of civilisation, population size and actions in the Gulf following the British withdrawal 'East of Suez' in 1971 have also led to tensions. External security guarantees affected through transitions in the international balance of power from British to American, as well as regional conflict and upheavals, play a part. Thus, Iran's ideology and regional behaviour came into play in terms of compromising expanding US energy interests in the Gulf as well as close security relations with Israel. US–Iran tensions have been an important factor contributing to Iran–Saudi tensions as Iran has sought to escape from Saudi and US encirclement.

Iranian threat perception is derived from American Christian missionaries sent to Iran between 1834 and 1934, the Anglo-Soviet invasion of Iran in 1941 and the CIA/British intelligence-sponsored coup against the nationalist prime minister, Mossadegh, in 1953. It has been exacerbated by the US hostage crisis in 1979, Iranian support for violent non-state actors such as Hezbollah and actions towards the Arab Gulf monarchies, US-led sanctions and the Global War on Terror when US forces were in neighbouring Afghanistan and Iraq. Saudi Arabia was able to reflect on the use of the oil weapon in 1973 and support US policy to isolate Iran after the US hostage crisis, through the Iran–Iraq War and into dual containment of Iran and Iraq throughout the 1990s.

Rapprochement

After the Gulf War in 1991, the 1990s was a period of relatively low threat perception, and convergence of interests was accompanied by a more pragmatic, moderate and reformist Iranian leadership under president Rafsanjani (1989–97), and then under president Khatami. Diplomatic relations moved up to the ambassadorial level in 1991, laying the foundation for a golden period for bilateral relations from 1996. It was almost derailed by the bombing of the Khobar Towers housing US forces in Saudi Arabia in 1996, which was initially assumed to be work of Iran and the IRGC, but which was later suggested to be the work of Al Qaeda.[19]

Ambiguity about the US–Saudi security partnership may have also contributed to the Saudi–Iranian rapprochement, but there were also other areas of converging interest, such as Bosnia. Bilateral relations made great strides; for example, Crown Prince Abdullah hosted President Khatami in 1999, which marked the first visit of an Iranian president to Saudi Arabia since the 1979 revolution. Saudi Arabia and Iran concluded a political, economic and security package in 2001, when both sides began to view their security as being dependent on the other. Prince Nayef, then Saudi interior minister, was noted at the time as saying that Iran's security was akin to Saudi Arabia's security and vice versa.[20] Rafsanjani said later that King Salman is not anti-Iranian, stating that 'When [King Salman bin Abulaziz Al Saud] was governor of Riyadh province, he hosted me. Everything was brotherly and constructive.'[21]

The rapprochement lasted until the mid-2000s, when a combination of challenges coalesced to undermine relations and the potential in a collective security mechanism which Saudi Arabia proposed in 2004, similar to the Organisation for Security and Cooperation in Europe.[22] These factors included: the US War on Terror following 9/11, when President G. W. Bush labelled Iran as part of the 'Axis of Evil' in 2002; the US intervention in Iraq in 2003, which facilitated Iranian influence in the country; and uranium enrichment under President Ahmadinejad – although even this didn't prevent Ahmadinejad from visiting Saudi Arabia in 2007. It did, however, lead King Abdullah of Saudi Arabia to exhort the Obama administration in 2010 to 'cut off the head of the snake' by launching military strikes to destroy Iran's nuclear programme.[23]

Tensions due to Hajj incidents

Tensions between Saudi Arabia and Iran have also been clearly apparent in the pilgrimage to Mecca, which all Muslims should undertake at least once in their lifetime: the Hajj. The Hajj was quickly affected by hostility between the two states. Clashes are recorded between Saudi police and Iranian pilgrims 'distributing pictures of Khomeini and chanting "*Allahu Akbar va Khomeini rahbar*" (God is great, Khomeini is leader)' in 1981.[24] Some 150,000 Iranian pilgrims were allowed to demonstrate peacefully one mile from the Grand Mosque in Mecca in 1984 when Khomeini called on pilgrims to 'strive for the liberation of Jerusalem'.[25] But in 1986 Iranian and Libyan pilgrims were arrested with explosives, signifying another potential takeover of the Holy Mosque.[26] The threat was felt so keenly in the kingdom that King Fahd decided in 1986 to change his title from His Majesty to Custodian of the Two Holy Mosques, a title that had hitherto never been officially used. Tolerance and restraint broke down again in 1987, when 400 Iranian protestors were killed when they clashed with Saudi security forces.[27] Hajj quotas for Iran were reduced from this point on. In response to the incident, Khomeini stated:

> It is not surprising to see the contaminated hands of the United States and Israel emerging from the sleeves of devious people, the ringleaders of Saudi Arabia and the traitors to the two holy shrines, and then taking aim at the hearts of the best Moslems, the dear ones, the guests of God. It is not surprising to see those who lay claim to guarding Mecca and the House of God drenching Mecca's streets and side streets with the blood of Moslems.[28]

Other incidents since then, such as the 24 September 2015 stampede, in which more than 400 of at least 2,000 pilgrims who were crushed or suffocated were Iranian, caused similar anger, expressed by Khamenei.[29] Such unfortunate events and a lack of publicly expressed Saudi sympathy have fed into hard-line Iranian rhetoric aimed at undermining the Saudi monarchy, thereby perpetuating mistrust and sectarian antipathies. They form one of a string of issues which could derail Saudi–Iranian diplomacy at any point, especially in a period of escalating insecurity or heightened political tensions.

Contemporary issues

Only after the US intervention in Iraq in 2003 did sectarianism become a more salient feature of relations between Saudi Arabia and Iran.[30] This was reinforced by Saudi Arabia as a useful basis for the counter-revolution that began in response to the Arab uprisings and the opportunities posed by weak, collapsing or failed states. The inability of Saudi Arabia to work with other Sunni states such as Turkey in theatres such as Syria is a salient reminder that sectarianism is limited in explaining the current geopolitics of the region. Furthermore, Haddad draws attention to the term sectarianism being too generic and ineffective in explaining its occurrence in doctrine as well as sub-national, national and transnational dimensions.[31]

Iranian military expenditure is far less than that of Saudi Arabia and the UAE. Iran spends under $13 billion a year on defence,[32] compared to more than $60 billion spent by Saudi Arabia.[33] Saudi Arabia doesn't have the troops to match Iran's and is therefore dependent on the US security umbrella to even out the balance of power in the Gulf. Still, Iran is decades ahead in building its regional influence through a network of state and non-state actors and it is these actors which are so contentious regarding acquisition of weapons technology from Iran. Iran also maintains a broad range of missiles such as Shahab1 (300km range), Fateh-110 (300km range), Shahab2 (500km range), Zolfaghar (700km range), Qiam-1(800km range), Shahab3 (2,000km range), Sejjil (2,000km range) and Soumar (cruise missile with a 2,500km range). Most short-range missiles are capable of targeting the GCC states. Composites are improving to increase range, and precision-guided technology is improving, which is clearly a concern to the GCC states, Israel and the US military in the region. The Houthis claimed to have used cruise missiles and drones to hit the Abqaiq and Khurais oil-processing facilities in Saudi Arabia on 14 September 2019, but the indication from the US intelligence community is that the attack came from the north, implicating Iran.[34] Furthermore, Iran targeted Aramco facilities 2012 as well as the UAE; perhaps more concerning, the 2019 attacks on Sheybah and Aramco oil and gas facilities, according to Iranian sources, were alleged to have been carried out with help from Saudi dissidents.[35]

Continued US-led sanctions against Iran have drained the economic resources of the Iranian state, and yet its regional adventurism gives the IRGC and Iran significant leverage vis-à-vis the Arab Gulf states and the

US. Iran appears more willing to use force more than most other Gulf states, which makes any arms trade with Iran more impactful. Furthermore, its ability to reverse-engineer systems within twenty years makes those exports even more sensitive. After the UN arms embargo on Iran expired on 18 October 2020, Iran may export the Mersad air defence system, which was first reverse-engineered (at great expense) from US Hawks sold to the shah in the 1970s. Iran also appears able to incorporate advancements in technology across its ballistic and cruise missile range.[36] Therefore, even a token purchase for political or military reasons will have a disproportionate effect on the Arab Gulf states' threat perception.

In contrast to the kingdom, Iran has proved adept at times in circumventing sectarian differences to maximise influence. For example, during Yasser Arafat's visit to see Khomeini in Iran, Al Quds Day was added to the Iranian calendar, designed to contrast with Israel's Jerusalem Day. Palestine continues to feature high on the Iranian foreign policy agenda, and yet 'Today Iran, tomorrow Palestine'[37] has given way to greater Iranian public concerns about domestic economic needs in a period of heightened US-led sanctions. Such concerns have been reflected in slogans such as 'Let go of Palestine' and 'Not Gaza, not Lebanon, I'd give my life (only) for Iran' in rare protests in 2017.[38] In 2021, Iran appointed a naval commander who is a Sunni Kurd, again highlighting Iran's willingness to cross sectarian boundaries, but maybe also a de-escalatory signal to the kingdom.

Whenever Saudi Arabia has attempted to influence state and non-state actors, the result has often been suboptimal: in support of Allawi in Iraq in 2005, trying to mediate unity talks between Hamas and Fatah in 2007, and in support of Hariri and the brief March 14 coalition in 2009.[39] There is no hierarchy in Sunni Islam, and, due to close Saudi security relations with the US, the Al Saud have ended up being targeted by groups such as Al Qaeda, which sees them as illegitimate rulers. Saudi Arabia and the UAE have, along with the US, attempted to leverage Iran's ethnic diversity by supporting Jundallah's cross-border attacks from Pakistan, encouraged by the US since 2005,[40] and Mujahedeen-e Khalq (MEK)[41] – two Sunni elements – as well as other militant groups in Iran, as part of their deterrence and Middle East policies, respectively. These groups are blamed for the deaths of thousands of Iranian civilians and instability along Iran's borders.[42] In 2015, the Islamic Military Counter Terrorism Coalition was set up, with its headquarters in Riyadh, to counter ISIS, but it continues to exclude Iran from its membership.

John Bolton was one of the chief architects of a more hawkish US policy on Iran and was part of a team, along with secretary of state Pompeo, that would not be in a position to initiate or advance negotiations with Iran. Bolton was undersecretary of state for arms control and international security affairs from 2001 to 2005, US ambassador to the UN from 2005 to 2006 during the G. W. Bush administration and national security advisor to President Trump from April 2018 to September 2019. In the Trump administration he supported the Saudi-led Middle East Strategic Alliance (MESA) in 2017 and oversaw a manifesto for the US to withdraw from the JCPOA and support Kurdish independence. He is known to have worked with secretary of state Pompeo and Brian Hook through the Iran Action Group, formed on 16 August 2018, which was tasked with coordinating US policy toward Iran.

Iran has accused Saudi Arabia of funding, arming and training the Arab Struggle Movement for the Liberation of Ahwaz, which claims to represent the minority Iranian Arabs in Khuzestan and to have carried out attacks in January 2006, May 2015, June 2016, January 2017 and October 2018.[43] The last attack also came after Mohammed bin Salman threatened in May 2017 that he would not wait until Saudi Arabia becomes a battleground before taking action.[44] Khuzestan continues to demonstrate the interplay between sectarianism, securitisation, social movement(s) aimed at regime change, environmental damage and degradation, water scarcity and climate change.

The execution of Sheikh Nimr al-Nimr was inevitably followed by Iranian protests and the storming of the Saudi embassy in Tehran and consulate in Mashhad in January 2016. Saudi Arabia and other Muslim majority states (Bahrain, Bangladesh, Djibouti, Somalia, Sudan) responded by closing their embassies in Tehran and cutting diplomatic relations, whilst the UAE downgraded its diplomatic relationship with Iran. Hajj quotas represent one of the few areas in which Saudi–Iranian dialogue has continued. The Saudi view at the time was that Iran was trying to interfere in regional conflicts, with Mohammed bin Salman comparing Ayatollah Ali Khamenei with Hitler in November 2017, and also stating that 'appeasement doesn't work'.[45]

Indeed, the view informed Saudi (and Israeli) opinion about the Obama administration's policy of negotiating the JCPOA in 2015, based on a clear set of observations by the then Saudi foreign minister, Adel al-Jubeir, in 2017: namely, that Iran took advantage of the resources it received from sanctions relief to fund its nefarious activities in the region; it stepped up its aggressive behaviour in Syria, Iraq, Yemen, Pakistan, Afghanistan and Africa; there was supposed to be no enrichment but it was able to keep some enrichment capability; there was no limit in the JCPOA on Iran's ability to conduct nuclear research; and the sunset provision after twelve years would lift limits on how many centrifuges Iran could operate.[46] All this, for Saudi Arabia, meant that Iran would have the research capability and resources to set up centrifuges and create enough material for a nuclear weapon within weeks (a breakout capacity).[47] The Saudi preference is therefore for a strict inspections regime of military and non-declared sites, changes on sunset provisions and accountability in its support of terrorism, including attacks on embassies, and ballistic missile programme.[48]

Saudi Arabia continues to fear a JCPOA which would give Iran higher oil and gas revenues to distribute in its asymmetric warfare machinery and which could affect the global energy market and compromise the kingdom's economic transition. Any JCPOA which does not address Iran's missile capabilities, its asymmetric warfare capabilities, particularly precision-guided missiles and capabilities for manufacturing missiles in Yemen and Lebanon is problematic for the kingdom. It is too much to assume that these will be on the table in any snapback or new agreement. As Iran's foreign ministry said in 2021: 'No negotiation has been, is being, or will be held about Iran's defence power.'[49] Thus, Iran's Hormuz Peace Endeavour (HOPE), encompassing freedom of navigation and energy security, regional endeavours to prevent war and violence, countering terrorism and expanding cooperation, presented to the UN in 2019, does not affect Saudi strategic calculations. However, then Iranian foreign minister Zarif did echo Prince Nayef's comments by stating in 2021: 'Our neighbourhood doctrine is that we are bound to live together forever. We will remain in the neighbourhood; others come and go.'[50] As Keynoush notes, Iran's lack of bridge-building across the region complicates its interactions.[51] It also creates an environment less conducive to Iran's diplomatic efforts such as HOPE.

Absent an attractive investment environment, with the high costs of rapidly ramping up piped gas or liquefied natural gas exports, negative past experiences and uncertainty about the next US presidential election, it is unlikely that Iran will be able to quickly replace a portion of the Russian gas lost from European markets due to sanctions or revised energy policies in 2022. Budding P5–Iran[52] political and economic relations could nevertheless form an interesting dynamic in the years ahead whilst also perhaps serving to strengthen Russian and Saudi/UAE energy cooperation.

Diplomacy

Saudi Arabia took steps in late 2019, including the acknowledgement of ongoing talks with the Houthis, which helped to diffuse some tensions with Iran. As the Biden administration talked about rejoining the JCPOA in Vienna, ending US support for the war in Yemen and pulling out of Afghanistan, there were also signs of fresh Saudi–Iranian bilateral engagement in Baghdad in April 2021 in the lead-up to Raisi winning the Iranian presidential election in June 2021. But this was only after the kingdom had been attacked 84 times by Iran and Iranian proxies by April 2021 and after talks to purchase Turkish drones fell through.[53] This was also in the context of Bahrain and the UAE having concluded their respective Abraham Accords with Israel in 2020, and the continued uncertainty surrounding US–Saudi relations, thereby putting the kingdom in a more isolated position.

In a television interview in April 2021 to commemorate the fifth anniversary of inaugurating Vision 2030, Mohammed bin Salman said that he hoped for better relations with Iran, once militias and nuclear and ballistic missiles issues had been addressed.[54] This has been followed up by tributes from the Saudi energy minister on the departure of his Iranian colleague from OPEC. Prince Abdulaziz bin Salman called Bijan Zanganeh a 'personal friend'.[55] Many analysts remain dubious about the sincerity of both sides. Certainly, Saudi–Iranian talks could improve the atmosphere at a time when the Saudi homeland is being attacked from three directions, but, similar to the 'resolution' of the Qatar Crisis, it is unlikely to amount to a comprehensive de-escalation. Saudi Arabia is said to be more 'clear eyed' about Iran than the US. It knows the JCPOA will be enough for Iran to continue to sell oil, develop relations with China and continue with its missile programme.[56]

President Raisi has also stated that regional factors and ties will be important.[57] The Supreme Leader and his office, plus the IRGC, will determine the way forward on this front. Saudi Arabia used President Raisi's swearing-in ceremony in July 2021 as an opportunity both to attend and to support the process of normalised relations between the countries. The Iraq Summit in August 2021 was the first time Saudi foreign minister Faisal bin Farhan was at the same table as Iran's foreign minister Hossein Amirabdollahian. Whilst Iran labelled these talks as having achieved 'remarkable progress' on the issue of Gulf security in September 2021,[58] it may have been early posturing in an attempt to get the US to revert quickly to the JCPOA. In the same month, King Salman was at the UN General Assembly, telling members that the kingdom supports efforts to prevent Iran from obtaining nuclear weapons.[59] The IRGC has similarly attempted to influence, but in this case undermine, the JCPOA through attacks on US targets such as the US consulate in Irbil.

Whilst Saudi Arabia has indicated that it may reopen the Iranian consulate in Jeddah, as of November 2021 the talks did not have enough 'substance' for the kingdom to commit to reopening its consulate in Mashhad.[60] Yemen has not been publicly disclosed as an agenda issue, but, as one former senior UK official has noted, Yemen is a freebie for Iran, it has no strategic issue there, so there could be concessions.[61] The Saudi–Iranian dialogue is likely to lead to the re-establishment of diplomatic relations that were cut in 2016. But if it can begin to tackle the more thorny issues of Yemen and other activities affecting regional security, then it could be all the more significant.

Ambassador Frank G. Wisner is one of those who believe that the Trump administration had a hand in radicalising Iranian politics (and removing reformists from the political scene), which has contributed to an escalation in regional tensions, just as the Biden administration's willingness to return to JCPOA discussions has helped to reduce tensions.[62] President Raisi will be operating from a position of strength in Iraq, Afghanistan, Syria and Yemen. The likely outcome in Iran is an entrenchment of the 'resistance economy'. If a JCPOA deal is secured, a cold peace may become the new status quo between Saudi Arabia and Iran, but only if the IRGC is reined in and if conflicts in states under contention can be managed and drawn to a close. Without the JCPOA, Saudi Arabia will stand closer to GCC allies and aim at building a new consensus against Iran. Mohammed bin Salman looked to be doing precisely that in December 2021.[63] The fundamental question remains: does Iran want state-based relations through a Helsinki type of agreement, or relations with violent non-state actors and a deteriorating regional security environment?

The UAE and Iran

Like Saudi Arabia, the UAE, since its independence in 1971, has been deeply concerned about Iranian foreign policy and distrusts Iranian intent, but its position has been tempered by long-standing people-to-people and business connections and cultural influences from Iran, especially in Dubai.[64] UAE policy on Iran has also been affected by a multitude of considerations such as US Middle East policy, the Abraham Accords and considerations within the GCC. Like other small states in the GCC, the UAE is caught between two aspiring regional hegemons and, like most of these states, had charted a path of diplomacy under Sheikh Zayed bin Sultan Al-Nahyan, ruler of Abu Dhabi and president of the UAE, until his death in 2004. Absent sectarian tensions, the only direct contention between these two Gulf states is competing claims over Greater Tunb, Lesser Tunb islands and Abu Musa, occupied by Iran since 30 November 1971, the day after the British officially withdrew. Iran then constructed military installations on the geostrategically significant islands in the Strait of Hormuz. Abu Dhabi has been more hawkish on Iran than Dubai has been, for the reasons already mentioned, and although four of the emirates (Abu Dhabi, Ajman, Fujairah and Ras Al-Khaimah) supported Iraq during the Iran–Iraq War (in line with GCC policy), three of the emirates have shown greater sympathy towards Iran (Dubai, Sharjah, Umm Al-Quwain), mainly for reasons related to trade.[65] Dubai became a transit hub for supplies to Iran whilst Jebel Ali received a boost to its dry dock operation through damaged ships being forced to seek repair.[66]

There are other threat perceptions which inform UAE policy. Iranian regional behaviour and the size of Iran's military, but particularly its missile capabilities, remain key concerns for the UAE. Thus, the UAE has pushed to achieve air superiority over Iran, which it has achieved through consistently high arms imports. In 2010, the UAE ambassador to Washington, Yousef al-Otaiba, said 'Our military, who has existed for the past 40 years, wake up, dream, breathe, eat, sleep the Iranian threat ... there's no country in the region that is a threat to the UAE, it's only Iran.'[67] Saudi Arabia, the UAE, Bahrain and Israel were the only states to support President Trump's withdrawal from the JCPOA. The UAE decision reflected its continued suspicions and concerns about Iranian activities in the Gulf. However, the UAE has been consistent in its assessment that pushing Iran to the brink through 'maximum pressure' could risk a confrontation.[68] UAE policy aligned with Saudi policy on Iran and in the Quartet against Qatar which demanded Doha to curb its diplomatic ties with Iran and close its mission there, expel members of the IRGC from Qatar and cut joint military cooperation with Iran, as well as any trade that does not comply with US sanctions.[69]

The Trump administration's 'maximum pressure' policy quickly ran aground during the Abqaiq and Khurais attack in 2019. Sabotage attacks in UAE waters and to Saudi infrastructure heightened UAE security concerns even though Abu Dhabi did not publicly blame Iran for them. As the UAE pulled forces out of Yemen, an Emirati 'peace delegation' visited Tehran on 26 July 2019 for discussions on a range of topics, and a few days later this was followed up with a delegation discussing maritime security.[70] A UAE official has stated that the UAE 'cannot afford a conflict' and 'prefers diplomacy and de-escalation but there is a need to find a process'.[71] At the Manama Dialogue in 2020 there was a 'consensus', at least in the GCC, that the JCPOA is no longer enough as a basis of engagement with Iran. This includes the UAE, which views a return to the JCPOA as needing to be accompanied by negotiations on missiles and movement on other aspects of Iran's regional activities. The UAE is therefore taking a 'wait and see approach' on US Iran policy.[72] Certainly, the UAE is hopeful that Iran will become more enmeshed in the regional and the international political economy, which would increase the costs associated with visions of hegemony and belligerent behaviour in the Strait of Hormuz. Whether this is what Iran wants remains to be seen. But it does need to alleviate some economic pressure so as to better manage socio-economic stability.

The UAE has used its economic relations with Iran and built new pathways of diplomacy with Tehran. For instance, when the COVID-19 crisis hit, the UAE sent 7.5 tonnes of aid in cooperation with the World Health Organization and 33 tonnes of medical equipment to Tehran in March 2020, plus another 16 tonnes in June 2020.[73] In August 2021, Sheikh Mohammed bin Rashid al-Maktoum is said to have met with Iran's foreign minister, Hossein Amirabdollahian, on the sidelines of a Baghdad summit aimed at easing regional tensions.[74] In November 2021, Iran and the UAE agreed to open a new chapter in bilateral relations, according to Iran's deputy foreign minister, Ali Bagheri Kani.[75]

Sheikh Tahnoun bin Zayed Al Nahyan travelled to Tehran in early December 2021, reflecting the UAE's political, security and economic interests, especially should a JCPOA deal go ahead. In 2018, Iran–UAE trade was at a not insignificant $19 billion, and far more than Saudi–Iran trade, which is negligible.[76] Under pressure from US sanctions, tensions in the Gulf, a collapse in the Iranian currency and COVID-19, the UAE remains one of Iran's largest trading partners. The UAE is already ramping up investments, including a 300MW power project in Khuzestan.[77] Should the JCPOA talks fail, the UAE will be well placed to avoid confrontation with the IRGC and possibly help de-escalate on certain other issues between Saudi Arabia, Israel and the US on the one hand, and Iran on the other. As such, it is a win-win policy for the UAE within the broader context of its close cooperation with the US, Saudi Arabia, Israel and China.

Conclusion

This chapter has shown the centrality of Saudi–Iranian relations in the regional system and the strong civilisation and political–religious roots of their mutual antipathy. Any resolution of the conflict will have tremendous implications for the global political economy, energy security (particularly affecting East Asia) and political stability. In modern times, even post-1979, it is shown that bilateral relations can function along new lines of pragmatic engagement, encouraged by external engagement such as Iranian trade and dialogue with Europe in the 1990s and a relatively low regional threat perception. Relations have become more complex and contentious since the Gulf War, the 2003 US-led intervention in Iraq and the JCPOA, making regional relations triangular: US–Saudi–Iranian. Iranian strategic depth in Iraq and Syria (perceived in the kingdom as Iranian encirclement), Quds Force pronouncements on Bahrain and the challenge of ISIS on Saudi Arabia's northern border remain formidable threats.

The instability highlighted and facilitated by the Arab uprisings, especially the Syria and Yemen conflicts, Iran's missile development programme, nuclear intentions and relations with local proxies are at the core of continued hostility. Saudi Arabia and Iran have vied for broader influence in Asia and, increasingly, Africa. The GCC as an organisation has failed to address the Iranian threat and, as will be discussed in the following chapter, alternative sub-regional groupings have become more prominent, including deepening Israel–Arab Gulf ties, although how deep and durable these will be and how they end up impacting on the Biden administration's calculations and Iranian foreign and security policy remains to be seen. Iran often points to the Qatar Crisis and the anxieties of Oman and Kuwait becoming sub-states under Saudi hegemony like Bahrain, which makes Riyadh's policies appear problematic,[78] although, from Tehran's perspective, the Qatar Crisis made Doha more dependent on Iran for trade and airspace access, which was an advantage.

Given the complexity of relations and the sensitivities to national security, the only viable option is direct talks, leading to new negotiations and agreements. Mousavian states that this should be based on UN Security Council Resolution 598, drafted in July 1987 after the Iran–Iraq War. Whilst the concept of regional security is debatable, it is also fluid, with potential for the Abraham Accords to influence decision making in Tehran to pragmatically consider broader views about its regional activities. Domestic politics and economic conditions that have historically played an important role in curtailing and advancing relations,[79] and macro-economic transitions, especially oil revenue, raise the stakes of this centuries-old rivalry. There are a growing array of contentions, especially related to nuclear proliferation, as well as a range of regional and international stakeholders involved in their futures. A lack of dialogue, divergent identities and the process of political consolidation underway in Iran and Saudi Arabia have contributed to the status quo. The legacy of the Iranian Revolution and fears of Saudi or Iranian hegemony will continue to dominate concerns about Gulf security.

What is most interesting in thinking through Saudi–Iranian relations and, indeed, GCC–Iran and US–Iran relations, is the mirroring taking place. Iran perceives US encirclement and responds with a similar strategy towards Saudi Arabia, and even to some extent the US (i.e. relations with Venezuela). Saudi Arabia is seeking to import missile defence technology to generate the strategic depth that Iran has established through its networks with militia groups. The UAE is using Socotra in a similar way to the Iranian occupation and militarisation of Abu Musa and the Tunb Islands in 1971, and so on. Foreign policy behaviour is observed and informs responses throughout the region and internationally. A new norms-based approach could do likewise. It is less clear if the Al Saud have learnt lessons from Shah Mohammad Reza Pahlavi, who implemented the White Revolution from 1963 to 1973, in which he embarked on aggressive modernisation, including redistributing wealth to Iran's working class, deconstructing Iran's feudalist system and the enfranchisement of women. The antagonism that land and democratic reforms had on the clergy and elite ultimately contributed to the shah's downfall. The issues may not be identical, but the breakneck speed is similar.

Notes

1 F. Gregory Gause, 'Beyond Sectarianism: The New Middle East Cold War', *Brookings*, 22 July 2014, www.brookings.edu/research/beyond-sectarianism-the-new-middle-east-cold-war/

2 Ibrahim Fraihat, *Iran and Saudi Arabia: Taming a Choatic Conflict.* Edinburgh: Edinburgh University Press, 2020.

3 Dilip Hiro, 'Introduction', *Cold War in the Islamic World: Saudi Arabia, Iran and the Struggle for Supremacy*. Oxford: Oxford University Press, 2019: 8.

4 Kim Ghattas, 'Mecca is Mine', *Black Wave: Saudi Arabia, Iran, and the Forty-Year Rivalry that Unraveled Culture, Religion, and Collective Memory in the Middle East*. New York: Henry Holt and Company, 2020: 172.

5 Kim Ghattas, 'Darkness', *Black Wave: Black Wave: Saudi Arabia, Iran, and the Forty-Year Rivalry that Unraveled Culture, Religion, and Collective Memory in the Middle East*. New York: Henry Holt and Company, 2020: 81.

6 Ibid: 82.

7 Ghattas, 'Mecca is Mine': 181.

8 Shireen Hunter, 'Iran's Relations with Saudi Arabia: Rivals for Regional Supremacy', *Arab–Iranian Relations: Dynamics of Conflict and Accommodation*. London: Rowman and Littlefield, 2019: 208.

9 Anoushiravan Ehteshami, 'The Foreign Policy of Iran', in Raymond Hinnebusch and Anoushiravan Ehteshami (eds) *The Middle East in the International System*. London: Lynne Reiner, 2002: 284.

10 Shahram Chubin and Charles Tripp, *Iran and Iraq at War*. Boulder, CO: Westview Press, 1988: 160.

11 Ghattas, 'Mecca is Mine': 167.

12 Richard Halloran, '2 Iranian Fighters Reported Downed by Saudi Air Force', *The New York Times*, 6 June 1984, www.nytimes.com/1984/06/06/world/2-iranian-fighters-reported-downed-by-saudi-air-force.html

13 Rob Johnson, 'Human Waves: Iran's Counter-Offensives into Iraq', *The Iran–Iraq War*. New York: Palgrave Macmillan, 2011: 71–80.

14 Confirmed in a leaked audiotape of Mohammad Javad Zarif, Iran's foreign minister, speaking about the IRGC. Farnaz Fassihi, 'Iran's Foreign Minister, in Leaked Tape, Says Revolutionary Guards Set Policies', *The New York Times*, 26 April 2021, www.nytimes.com/2021/04/25/world/middleeast/iran-suleimani-zarif.html

15 Ali Alfoneh, *Iran Unveiled: How the Revolutionary Guards Is Transforming Iran from Theocracy into Military Dictatorship*. Washington, DC: AEI Press, 2013.

16 John K. Cooley, 'Iran, the Palestinians, and the Gulf', *Foreign Affairs*, 57 (5), Summer 1979: 1017–1034.

17 Kim Ghattas, 'Today Tehran, Tomorrow Jerusalem', *Black Wave: Saudi Arabia, Iran, and the Forty-Year Rivalry that Unraveled Culture, Religion, and Collective Memory in the Middle East*. New York: Henry Holt and Company, 2020: 44.

18 Simon Mabon, *Saudi Arabia and Iran: Soft Power Rivalry in the Middle East*. London: I. B. Tauris, 2013.

19 The New York Times, 'Al Qaeda is Now Suspected in 1996 Bombing of Barracks', 14 May 2003, www.nytimes.com/2003/05/14/world/al-qaeda-is-now-suspected-in-1996-bombing-of-barracks.html

20 Khaled Al-Maeena, 'Kingdom, Iran Sign Historic Agreement', *Arab News*, 18 April 2001, www.arabnews.com/node/211187

21 Akbar Hashemi Rafsanjani, 2015, http://hashemirafsanjani.ir/en

22 Awadh AlBadi, 'Saudi-Iranian Relations: A Troubled Trajectory', in Anoushiravan Ehteshami, Neil Quilliam and Gawdat Bahgat (eds), *Security and Bilateral Issues between Iran and its Arab Neighbors*. New York: Palgrave Macmillan, 2017: 189–209.

23 Ross Colvin, '"Cut Off Head of Snake" Saudis Told U.S. on Iran', *Reuters*, 29 November 2010, www.reuters.com/article/us-wikileaks-iran-saudis-idUSTRE6AS02B20101129

24 Ghattas, 'Mecca is Mine': 168–169.

25 Dilip Hiro, 'Postscript', *Iran Under the Ayatollahs*. Abingdon: Routledge, 1985: 371.

26 Ghattas, 'Mecca is Mine': 169.

27 John Kifner, '400 Die as Iranian Marchers Battle Saudi Police in Mecca; Embassies Smashed in Tehran', 2 August 1987, www.nytimes.com/1987/08/02/world/400-die-iranian-marchers-battle-saudi-police-mecca-embassies-smashed-teheran.html

28 The New York Times, 'Excerpts from Khomeini Speeches', 4 August 1987, www.nytimes.com/1987/08/04/world/excerpts-from-khomeini-speeches.html

29 The Independent, 'Hajj: Iran Says Saudi Arabia "Murdered" Pilgrims during 2015 Stampede', 7 September 2016, www.independent.co.uk/news/world/middle-east/iran-saudi-arabia-murdering-pilgrims-hajj-stampede-a7228466.html

30 Gause, 'Beyond Sectarianism'.

31 Fanar Haddad, 'Sectarian Identity and National Identity in the Middle East', *Nations and Nationalism*, 26 (1), January 2020: 123–137.

32 The World Bank, 'Military Expenditure (current USD) – Iran', https://data.worldbank.org/indicator/MS.MIL.XPND.CD?locations=IR

33 The World Bank, 'Military Expenditure (current USD) – Saudi Arabia', https://data.worldbank.org/indicator/MS.MIL.XPND.CD?locations=SA

34 Humeyra Pamuk, 'Exclusive: U.S. Probe of Saudi Oil Attack Shows it Came from North – Report', *Reuters*, 19 December 2019, www.reuters.com/article/us-saudi-aramco-attacks-iran-exclusive-idUSKBN1YN299

35 Fars News Agency, 'Nasrollah: Declaring War on Iran IS Declaring War against Entire Axis of Resistance', 27 July 2019.

36 Dave Des Roches, 'After the Embargo: Iran's Weapons Agenda and its Regional Impact', Arab Gulf States Institute in Washington, 15 October 2020, www.youtube.com/watch?v=2Hu5wZIa_1c

37 Ghattas, 'Today Tehran, Tomorrow Jerusalem': 39.
38 Reuters Staff, 'Price Protests Turn Political in Iran as Rallies Spread', *Reuters*, 29 December 2017, www.reuters.com/article/us-iran-economy-protests-idUSKBN1EN0P0
39 Greg Gause, 'Saudi Arabia in the New Middle East', Council on Foreign Relations, www.cfr.org/event/saudi-arabia-new-middle-east
40 Reuters Staff, 'Pakistani Militants Staging Raids Inside Iran: ABC', *Reuters*, 4 April 2007, www.reuters.com/article/us-iran-pakistan-militants/pakistani-militants-staging-raids-inside-iran-abc-idUSN0329667420070404?pageNumber=2
41 Removed from US terrorist list in 2012.
42 Hossein Musavian, 'The Typology of Disputes in the Persian Gulf', *A New Structure for Security, Peace, and Cooperation in the Persian Gulf*. London: Rowman and Littlefield, 2020: 117.
43 Saeed Kamali Dehghan, 'Terrorists Kill Iranian Children and Soldiers in Military Parade Attack', *The Guardian*, 22 September 2018, www.theguardian.com/world/2018/sep/22/elite-iranian-soldiers-killed-in-attack-on-military-parade-revolutionary-guard-ahvaz
44 Associated Press, 'Iran Is Seeking "to Control Islamic World" Says Saudi Arabian Prince', *The Guardian*, 2 May 2017, www.nytimes.com/2018/09/24/world/middleeast/iran-attack-military-parade.html
45 BBC News, 'Iran Hits Back Over Saudi Prince's "Hitler" Comment', 24 November 2017, www.bbc.com/news/world-middle-east-42117134
46 Chatham House, 'In Conversation with HE Adel al-Jubeir, Minister of Foreign Affairs, Saudi Arabia', 25 October 2017, www.youtube.com/watch?v=Xw4AWD_7Dl4
47 Ibid.
48 Ibid.
49 Al Manar News, 'Talks on Iran's Defense Power Out of Question: Spokesman', 4 January 2021, https://english.almanar.com.lb/1239196
50 Tehran Times, 'Saudis May See Opportunity in Raisi Win to Mend Ties with Iran', 20 June 2021, www.tehrantimes.com/news/462223/Saudis-may-see-opportunity-in-Raisi-win-to-mend-ties-with-Iran
51 Banafsheh Keynoush, 'Iran's Regional Dynamics: A Piecemeal Approach', *Middle East Policy*, 27 (2), Summer 2020: 94–107.
52 P5: the five permanent members of the UN Scurity Council.
53 Kenneth M. Pollack, 'The Middle East Abhors A Vacuum', Foreign Affairs, May/June 2022, www.foreignaffairs.com/guest-pass/redeem/rRa5HDZb6gs
54 Tom O'Connor, 'Saudi Arabia's MBS Wants 'Good' Relations with Iran as Rivals Reportedly Talk in Iraq', *Newsweek*, 27 April 2021, www.newsweek.com/saudi-arabias-mbs-wants-good-ties-iran-rivals-reportedly-talk-iraq-1586943
55 Fareed Rahman, 'Saudi Arabia's Energy Minister Praises Iranian Oil Minister's Contribution to OPEC', *The National*, 2 July 2021, www.thenationalnews.com/business/2021/07/02/saudi-arabias-energy-minister-praises-iranian-oil-ministers-contribution-to-opec/
56 Interview with Michael Knights, Jill and Jay Bernstein Fellow of the Washington Institute, 25 May 2021.

57 Sabena Siddiqui, 'Raisi to Enter Maze of Regional Factors in Guiding Diplomacy with Riyadh', *Al-Monitor*, 4 July 2021, www.al-monitor.com/originals/2021/07/raisi-enter-maze-regional-factors-guiding-diplomacy-riyadh

58 Al-Monitor, 'Iran Says "Remarkable Progress" Made in Saudi Arabia Talks', 23 September 2021, www.al-monitor.com/originals/2021/09/iran-says-remarkable-progress-made-saudi-arabia-talks

59 Reuters, 'Saudi King Tells U.N. Kingdom Supports Effort to Prevent Nuclear Iran', 22 September 2021, www.reuters.com/world/middle-east/saudi-king-says-kingdom-worked-with-opec-allies-stabilise-oil-market-2021-09-22/

60 Andrew England, 'Saudi Arabia "Serious" About Talks with Iran', *Financial Times*, 15 October 2021.

61 Author's interview with a former senior UK official who asked not to be named, 18 November 2021.

62 Remarks in a discussion titled 'Viennese Waltz: How Can the U.S. Balance Its Priorities With Gulf Arab Concerns as it Engages Iran?', Arab Gulf States Institute in Washington, 16 June 2021, https://agsiw.org/programs/viennese-waltz-how-can-the-u-s-balance-its-priorities-with-gulf-arab-concerns-as-it-engages-iran/

63 Summer Said and Stephen Kalin, 'Saudi Crown Prince Tours Gulf as Iran Nuclear Talks Stall', *The Wall Street Journal*, 6 December 2021, www.wsj.com/articles/saudi-crown-prince-tours-gulf-as-iran-nuclear-talks-stall-11638801218

64 See Jim Krane, *Dubai: The Story of the World's Fastest City*. London: Atlantic Books, 2009.

65 Kristian Coates Ulrichsen, 'Politics', *The United Arab Emirates: Power, Politics, and Policymaking*. Abingdon: Routledge, 2017: 67; Christopher M. Davidson, 'Sheikh Zayed the Second: Prosperity and Unity', *Abu Dhabi: Oil and Beyond*. London: Hurst, 2011: 66.

66 Karim Sadjadpour, 'The Battle of Dubai: The United Arab Emirates and the U.S.–Iran Cold War', The Carnegie Papers, July 2011: 6, https://carnegieendowment.org/files/dubai_iran.pdf; John Rice, 'Dubai Looking for Economic Boom After Persian Gulf War with AM-Dubai Dhows', *AP News*, 26 July 1988, https://apnews.com/article/5227827b923723731d764bda3dd26b32

67 Karim Sadjadpour, *The Battle of Dubai: The United Arab Emirates and the U.S.–Iran Cold War*, July 2011, 11, https://carnegieendowment.org/files/dubai_iran.pdf

68 In 1995, a UAE official warned then Secretary of State Warren Christopher that this could happen. National Security Archive, 'Excessive U.S. Sanction could push Iran "Over the Brink": UAE Official to U.S. in 1995', https://nsarchive.gwu.edu/briefing-book/iran/2018-08-08/excessive-us-sanctions-could-push-iran-over-brink-uae-official-us-1995

69 AP, 'What are the 13 Demands Given to Qatar?', *Gulf News*, 23 June 2017, https://gulfnews.com/world/gulf/qatar/what-are-the-13-demands-given-to-qatar-1.2048118

70 Hussein Ibish, 'UAE Outreach to Iran Cracks Open the Door to Dialogue', Arab Gulf States Institute in Washington, 1 August 2019, https://agsiw.org/uae-outreach-to-iran-cracks-open-the-door-to-dialogue/

71 Discussion with a senior UAE official who asked not to be named, 19 January 2021.

72 Ibid.

73 Anam Rizvi, 'Coronavirus: UAE Sends 16 Tonnes of Aid to Medics in Iran', *The National*, 29 June 2020, www.thenationalnews.com/uae/government/coronavirus-uae-sends-16-tonnes-of-aid-to-medics-in-iran-1.1039951

74 Reuters, 'UAE Vice President Meets Iran Foreign Minister at Baghdad Summit', 28 August 2021, www.reuters.com/article/iraq-summit-emirates-iran-idUSL4N2PZ069

75 Reuters, 'Iran and the UAE Agree to Open New Chapter in Relations', 24 November 2021, www.reuters.com/world/middle-east/iran-uae-agree-open-new-chapter-relations-2021-11-24/

76 Andrew England and Simeon Kerr, 'US Sanctions Put Chill on Iranian Trade with UAE', 26 July 2019, www.ft.com/content/bbe3c99a-aee9-11e9-8030-530adfa879c2

77 Press TV, 'UAE to Build 300MW Power Projects in Iran's Khuzestan', 8 December 2021, www.presstv.ir/Detail/2021/12/08/672236/Iran-renewables-power-plant-UAE-Khuzestan

78 Author's interview with Seyed Hossein Mousavian, 10 April 2019, Princeton.

79 Fahad Alsultan and Pedram Saeid, *The Development of Saudi–Iranian Relations Since the 1990s: Between Conflict and Accommodation*. Abingdon: Routledge, 2016.

5

The Middle East:
counter-revolutionaries united?

Introduction

With the main domestic influences and state responses to a key regional adversary, Iran, already established, this omnibus chapter turns to the wider regional level. It begins with an outline of the orientation of Saudi and UAE policy and regionalism within the GCC and sources of contrast and rivalry between these protagonists. Due to space considerations, the chapter utilises a limited number of case studies to illustrate the dominant paradigms of diplomatic and economic intervention through traditional riyal politik and broader economic statecraft, proxy warfare and military intervention. Special attention is given to Jordan, Egypt, Iraq, Turkey, Lebanon, Israel, Palestine, Syria, Libya and Yemen.

The Arab uprisings are a major point of reference, whereby states such as Saudi Arabia and the UAE perceived their interests in binary terms: stability versus radicalism. These events also provided a point of acceleration and metamorphosis from overriding domestic security concerns to a more active, robust and expansive series of foreign policies targeting states or areas of instability. For example, when coupled with the more laissez-faire approach of the Trump administration from 2017, the UAE was able to hire foreign mercenaries led by Erik Prince, founder of Blackwater, to deploy in theatres of conflict such as Somalia, Yemen and Libya. The Saudi and UAE foreign policy *modus operandi* is noted whereby these states are able to dial up or down their policy responses according to the issue, level of national or security resources and interest, nature of the relationship with the target state(s) and available sources of leverage.

The GCC

The greatest achievement of the GCC has been in the economic realm, with a unified economic agreement in 1981, economic agreement in 2001, the signing of the customs union agreement in 2003 and the adoption of the common market in 2008. The completion of a region-wide electricity grid took place from 2009, and the GCC implemented a customs union (free trade area) from 1 January 2015. This has added a standard 5 per cent levy on goods imported from outside the GCC, paid at the first point of entry.[1] It took twelve years to reach an agreement, which was delayed by disagreements over the division of customs revenue and protection for local agents.[2] The customs union is modelled on the EU, with no internal tariffs, and should boost internal and external trade. Yet, under pressure from Saudi policy changes, the agreement could be revised further. New transport and infrastructure projects are planned, such as the GCC Railway, which is expected to connect the GCC states by 2024. Saudi Arabia and the UAE play important roles in ports such as Duqm and Salalah in Oman.[3] In addition, the Saudi Fund for Development began funding three projects in Oman with a total value of $244 million from February 2022. There is still potential in a common GCC currency, but geopolitical risk, political expediency and fluctuating oil prices could create liquidity crises or currency events that continue to impinge on economic integration.

In the security realm, the GCC had little success in developing a common approach, which was recognised following the Iraqi invasion of Kuwait in 1990. There are some good reasons why this approach initially failed, including 'coup proofing' regimes with praetorian guards which have been able to counterbalance the role of the army. As John Duke Anthony has noted, territorial disputes, dynastic competition and radical–conservative contest have dominated relations among the Gulf States.[4] Saudi hegemony in the GCC and GCC state preferences for bilateral relations with the US, led especially by those states seeking to balance Saudi and Iranian relations, such as Qatar, and to a lesser extent the UAE, Kuwait and Oman, have impeded collective security arrangements. Gulf dynamics are therefore at the core of Saudi and UAE IR and dependence on western security partners, both bilaterally and through initiatives such as NATO's Istanbul Cooperation Initiative, which Kuwait, Bahrain, Qatar and the UAE joined.

Nevertheless, a number of broad and overarching agreements have been concluded: an early warning system, the Cooperation Belt, came into effect in 2001 and provides better communication between air defence systems. In 2000, the GCC Joint Defence Agreement meant that an attack on one GCC was construed as an attack on all, and was operationalised as part of a common GCC Peninsula Shield Force (PSF) deployment in Kuwait ahead of the Iraq War in 2003, and again in Bahrain in 2011. After the Kuwaiti police infiltrated a terrorist cell in January 2005, and amid an increased threat from jihadi groups such as AQAP, a GCC Counterterrorism Agreement was signed in May 2005 that provided for intelligence sharing and cross-border cooperation. A proposal for centralised command and decentralised forces has never been taken forward, but a joint naval force was created in 2009 to combat piracy. The GCC proposed extending membership to Jordan and Morocco in 2011 to secure the interests of the Sunni monarchies. There has remained a lack of clarity about whether the move had political or military integration at its heart. In the end, broadening GCC membership was not achieved, due to a number of reasons related to geography, political and economic interests, and questions it would raise about the League of Arab States. In November 2012, the GCC members signed an Internal Security Pact giving powers to share personal information, integrate security apparatuses and operational commands, allowing security forces to be deployed on one another's territory searching for wanted criminals, and permitting the extradition of alleged criminals. In 2013 a GCC Unified Military Command was set up under a Saudi military commander to support the interoperability of GCC militaries, post-conflict reconstruction and counterterrorism efforts. It could go further in coordinating GCC defence rather than following the piecemeal approach that has been prevalent. In 2014 the GCC continued to build a military alliance with Jordan and Morocco which also involved Egypt.

'Arab Gulf Security 1', the first series of GCC-wide security exercises, was conducted in 2016. Higher threat perception during the Arab uprisings has generally spurred new initiatives or consolidated existing GCC cooperation, and Qatar has participated in training exercises in the PSF, despite the rift at the time with Saudi Arabia and the UAE. By 2018, the direction of cooperation with Morocco, Jordan and Egypt looked to have been established in Arab Shield I, which took place in western Egypt and also involved Saudi Arabia, the UAE, Bahrain, Kuwait and Jordan, with Morocco and Lebanon as observers. They were the largest joint Arab military drills up to that point.

Centrifugal pressures in the GCC continue to undermine the grouping; for example, Kuwait ultimately chose not to ratify the 2014 security pact, due to its more plural political environment and to protect its sovereignty. Qatar was left out of the joint military exercise Tuwaiq-2 in 2021 which included Saudi Arabia, the UAE, Jordan and Oman, with Kuwait and Bahrain as observers. Any future 'Middle East NATO' looks set to be dominated by an informal alliance of Israel, Saudi Arabia, UAE, Jordan, Egypt and possibly Iraq at the margins.[5] Operation Freedom's Sentinelle in Afghanistan from 1 January 2015 to 11 September 2021 had GCC state forces working in parallel with European forces, and this could be replicated in other theatres of conflict.[6] In the short term, the recovery of Gaza and regional missile defence are likely to remain priorities, with the potential to expand GCC naval cooperation.

Saudi–UAE rivalry

The political dynamics between Saudi Arabia and the UAE underscore an essential feature of the GCC, which is the power differential between hegemonic Saudi Arabia and the small(er) states of the UAE, Bahrain, Qatar, Kuwait and Oman. It is one of the reasons why Sheikh Shakhbut bin Sultan Al Nahyan, then ruler of Abu Dhabi, chose to build up his defence forces instead of relying on the Trucial Oman Scouts or the British military.[7] Territorial issues have also dominated. For example, there have been tensions in the past over the 1974 border agreement which allocated most of the Shaybah oil field to Saudi Arabia in exchange for recognition of the UAE.[8] Following a discrepancy between the oral agreement and the final text of the treaty, due to the absence of lawyers, technicians and geographers on its negotiation team, the UAE has attempted, so far unsuccessfully, to bring Saudi Arabia back to the negotiating table.

In the 2000s, Saudi Arabia objected to a plan to link the UAE and Qatar through a causeway, as the most likely route would run through waters offshore of the Saudi coastal strip. The 1974 Agreement on the Delimitation of Boundaries grants 'joint sovereignty' over coastal waters and a right of passage for Saudi Arabia to international waters, but the Saudis see the causeway as compromising its full access to international sea lanes.[9] The Saudis also tried to block the Dolphin pipeline between Qatar, the UAE and Oman. Construction started in 2002, and the first gas was carried by the pipeline to the UAE in 2007. The Saudi–UAE dynamic was also affected by UAE's President Khalifa bin Zayed Al Nahyan, who sought greater equality with its larger neighbour and reignited a territorial dispute with the kingdom over its claim to parts of the Eastern Province. The UAE decision to withdraw from the GCC single currency after the decision to locate the GCC Central Bank's headquarters in Riyadh also created consternation. Saudi, Emirati and Omani tribal tensions over Al Buraimi exist to the present day (2022), and there were brief clashes between Saudi Arabia and the UAE over the maritime border in 2010.[10]

During a period of rapid economic diversification and under youthful leadership intent on making their mark through policy making, there is evidence of growing competition between Saudi Arabia and the UAE. Saudi Arabia amended its import rules to exclude goods made in free zones or using Israeli input from preferential tariffs in a challenge to the UAE, which is widely regarded as the leading trade hub in the region.[11] New levies could range from 3 to 15 per cent and apply to companies which do not include 10–25 per cent Saudi nationals in their workforce, in an attempt to undermine cheap foreign labour in neighbouring countries.[12] Free zones play an important and growing role in UAE diversification efforts, encouraged by 100 per cent foreign ownership. The UAE business response to the new Saudi tariff regime has been largely negative, especially in Dubai, which has some thirty free zones, and where the lure of investment has been exports to neighbouring markets such as Saudi Arabia.[13] Whilst the eventual effect may be to 'lift all boats',[14] given the existing power differential, the rush to diversify and the stakes involved, it may take time before economic competition becomes constructive.

Saudi–UAE tensions played out in 2020 and in rare public disagreement at the OPEC summit in 2021. The substantial and long-term differences in Saudi and UAE energy approaches as a function of their economic objectives could yet see the UAE leave the OPEC+ grouping, which could exacerbate other economic and political tensions. Saudi Arabia and the UAE, by investing in carbon capture and in clean hydrogen, may increasingly compete for market share in states which will pursue these options as they transition to carbon-neutral status. This could include a possible pipeline(s) from the Gulf to the Eastern Mediterranean and into Europe. Importantly, Saudi–UAE rivalry does not exhibit the same ideological chasm as the UAE–Qatari rivalry, and could therefore be expected to be managed more effectively.

Bahrain

The sectarian divide unites Saudi Arabia and Bahrain, since instability in the archipelago could easily track into the kingdom. This was evident from the 1980s, when Shia unrest moved easily between Bahrain, Saudi Arabia and Kuwait, and groups such as International Front for the Liberation of Bahrain, Organization of the Islamic Revolution and Shiraziyyun, respectively.[15] There were also Saudi concerns from 1994 to 1999, when there was an ongoing push by leftists, liberals and Islamists for greater political and civil rights in Bahrain after decades of calls for a transition to a constitutional monarchy. Saudi Arabia, fearful of protests spreading to the Shia community in the Eastern Province took action to help suppress the unrest.

Saudi Arabia intervened in the Bahrain uprising from 14 February to 2 March 2011, this time using the deployment of the PSF to bolster the security of key ministries, freeing up the Bahrain security services to focus on protestors who were drawn to the Pearl Roundabout in Manama. The intervention was led by 1,200 Saudi armoured forces and 600 UAE police, and naval forces from Kuwait were used to secure Bahrain's maritime borders.[16] After a three-year political deadlock up to 2014, Bahrain's crown prince met with the main Shia opposition party, al-Wefaq, and other parties.

The kingdom has cause to remain concerned over Bahrain: Iran has maintained a long-standing territorial claim to Bahrain up to 1970, followed by statements about Bahrain being Iran's 'fourteenth province', and alleged Iranian involvement in an attempted coup in Bahrain in 1981.[17] In response to Bahrain revoking the citizenship of a leading Shiite opposition cleric in 2016, General Qasem Soleimani vowed 'a bloody intifada' in Bahrain.[18] Bahrain's participation in the Abraham Accords in 2020 has given Iran another tool for mobilisation of the Shia against their ruler, and terror plots are routinely linked back to the IRGC.

Qatar

Doha has differentiated itself from other GCC members through its pragmatic and assertive foreign policy after Sheikh Hamad bin Khalifa Al Thani took power in June 1995. He and his then experienced prime minister, Hamad bin Jassim bin Jaber Al Thani, engaged in 'subtle power' through the combination of strategic international investments, financial influence and diplomacy.[19] Qatar has a close but discrete security relationship with the US, whilst being able to showcase its pan-Arab credentials through Al Jazeera to most of the Arab world. In 2009 the country won the bid to host the 2022 FIFA World Cup, and it has established itself as a mediator. Key diplomacy in which Qatar has been involved includes negotiating with Hamas to provide aid, reconstruction and reconciliation in Gaza, defusing sectarian tensions in Lebanon and addressing genocide and peace building in Darfur. Senior Taliban leaders have been based in Qatar since the early 2010s.

As a small state, Qatar engages in the same sort of soft power and national branding strategies that the UAE engages in. They create international ties, primarily through arms imports and hosting foreign troops (Qatar hosts foreign forces at Al Udeid, the largest US forward base in the Middle East). They also raise the economic and political stakes of allies through a web of strategic investments, joint ventures, hosting of important transport hubs, global events and summits. They also seek to imbed themselves in nodes of global governance. For example, Qatar was responsible for turning the Gas Exporting Countries Forum into an intergovernmental agency in 2001, and its headquarters are based in Doha.[20] Qatar went on to join the Global Redesign Initiative of the World Economic Forum, hosted a Global Redesign Summit in 2010 and hosted the Climate Change Conference in 2012. Although all GCC states except Saudi Arabia signed the COP21 Paris Agreement with other UN members in 2016, Qatar was one of the first to craft a climate change policy in 2012, as part of its state branding programme.[21]

Whilst Qatar is a well-known host of Islamist groups leaders such as Hamas leader Khaled Meshaal and Sheikh Yusuf al-Qaradawi, the ideologue of the MB who left Cairo for Qatar in 1961, there are a multitude of other personalities based in Qatar. The wife of former Iraqi president Saddam Hussein, Sajida Khairallah Talfah; Hussein's last foreign minister, Naji Sabri al-Hadithi; and Hussein's long-term aide, Arsah Yassin, all live in Qatar.[22] Doha continues to benefit from a small, homogeneous population where 'high-modernism' or social engineering through generous financial ties has contributed to elite autonomy domestically.[23]

Even before the diplomatic rupture in 2014 and the Qatar Crisis from 2017, Qatar–Saudi relations looked to be in peril. They were impacted upon early on by a border clash in 1992 which led to the deaths of two guards in 1995 Saudi Arabia and the UAE were accused of trying to reinstall Emir Hamad's father, Khalifa bin Hamad Al Thani, and in 1996 Saudi Arabia was implicated in an attempted coup in Qatar. In 2001, Qatar proposed a gas pipeline to Kuwait that required Saudi approval, which was first denied and then granted in 2003, only to be denied again in 2006.[24] In 2000, the then crown prince Abdullah boycotted a summit of the OIC in Doha, due to Qatar allowing Israel to set up a trade office there. Riyadh withdrew its ambassador to Doha from 2002 to 2008 over anti-Saudi programming broadcast on Al Jazeera. In 2003, one US cable mentioned that Mohammed bin Zayed had asked the commander of US Central Command to 'bomb Al Jazeera'.[25] In 2007 Qatar–Saudi relations began to improve after the then Qatari prime minister, Sheikh Hamad bin Jassim bin Jaber Al Thani, accompanied the emir to Riyadh. The border issue was resolved, and in 2010 Qatar pardoned the Saudis implicated in the 1996 coup attempt – despite another allegation of a Saudi-linked coup attempt in 2009. In 2008, Qatar's attempt at summit diplomacy to help mediate the Lebanon crisis led to the Doha Agreement, but tensions with Saudi Arabia arose once again, as Doha's summit-style diplomacy with Syria and Hezbollah was vetoed by Saudi Arabia and Egypt, who organised their own summit in Riyadh. Another alleged Saudi-linked coup attempt took place in Qatar in 2011.

Doha continues to engage with Iran, partly linked to their share in the North Dome/South Pars gasfield and by having to navigate its tankers through the Persian Gulf, and has had a free-trade agreement with Iraq since 2002. Qatar and the UAE both participated in the NATO intervention in Libya from 19 March to 31 October 2011. But their interests over support for Islamist groups have diverged, and it was Qatar which was well placed to secure an influential position when the MB came to power in Egypt from 30 June 2012 to 3 July 2013. Doha spent $8 billion in grants and soft loans in support of the Morsi government,[26] overreaching in Egypt after the MB was deposed and in Syria, where its support for opposition groups has not resulted in the overthrow of President Assad.

Tamim bin Hamad Al Thani, born 3 June 1980, and son of the former emir, Hamad bin Khalifa Al Thani, became emir of Qatar in 2013, signifying a step change to a youth-orientated leadership. By January 2014, Saudi Arabia, Bahrain and the UAE were attempting to push Qatar onto a new policy track through the Riyadh Agreement, which has never been disclosed but which was expected to contain provisions about Qatar's non-interference in regional affairs, cooperation on regional issues, and a guarantee on not supporting extremist groups.[27] By March 2014, Qatar was already deemed to have been non-compliant and so Saudi Arabia, the UAE and Bahrain cut diplomatic relations. The move was the first coordinated severing of diplomatic relations in GCC history.

Qatar appears to have done little to present a united front within the GCC from this point up to the more serious 'Qatar Crisis' in 2017. Doha maintained relations with Iran; Azmi Bishara, the Palestinian Arab nationalist, received funding in the interim period; and Yusuf al-Qaradawi, the MB preacher, remained on air in Qatari media. Hamas was still based in Doha. The alleged $1 billion paid to secure the release of twenty-eight members of a royal hunting party kidnapped in Iraq in 2015 ,which may have ended up in the bank accounts of Kataib Hezbollah in Iraq, Qasem Soleimani, the then leader of the IRGC, and Hayat Tahrir al-Sham in Syria, once known as al-Nusra Front, must have made matters worse.[28]

Mohammed bin Zayed repeatedly called on the G. W. Bush and Obama administrations to take a tougher stance with Qatar, and Ben Rhodes has been clear that the Obama administration had to 'spend a lot of time to prevent that [break with Qatar] from happening'.[29] In 2017 Yousef Al Otaiba's personal e-mail account was hacked, possibly by agents working for Doha, and Qatar alleged that hackers were responsible for posting fake remarks by its emir against US policy, just days before President Trump arrived in Riyadh for a GCC summit. Egypt, Yemen and others then joined Saudi Arabia, Bahrain and the UAE in cutting diplomatic relations.

Saudi Arabia almost invaded Qatar to seize control of Doha, restrained only by then US secretary of state Rex Tillerson, who lost his job in the diplomatic fallout and due to possible lobbying activities by the UAE.[30] Tillerson seems to have taken the view at the time, along with then defense secretary James Matthis, that this crisis simply detracted from the focus on Iran.[31] The self-named Anti-Terror Quartet of Saudi Arabia, the UAE, Bahrain and Egypt issued Qatar with thirteen demands, including: curbing diplomatic ties and joint military cooperation with Iran, severing ties to 'terrorist organisations' such as the MB, ISIS and Al Qaeda, shutting down Al Jazeera and its affiliates (since blocked in the Quartet states), terminating the Turkish military presence in Qatar and stopping contact with political opposition groups of the Quartet.[32] The demands were extensive, with little room for negotiation.

Few of the original thirteen demands have been met over the years since, probably because Qatar could withstand the economic boycott. Following the election of President Biden, Mohammed bin Salman moved quickly to resolve the crisis by hosting a meeting at Al Ula in January 2021. The resulting agreement was said to be a 'gift' to the Biden administration.[33] Like the Riyadh Agreement, the details of the Al Ula Agreement are unknown and the situation could quickly deteriorate again. The prognosis for more positive steps being achieved improved with Saudi Arabia sending a new ambassador to Doha in June 2021. In September 2021, a picture was circulated in the media featuring a much-publicised informal meeting between Mohammed bin Salman, Sheikh Tahnoun, UAE national security advisor, and Sheikh Tamim Bin Hamad Al Thani.

The UAE and Qatar have resumed trade and cooperation, but they continue to support rival groups in Libya, as well as competing political forces in Libya, Sudan and Somalia. In January 2021, UAE ambassador Omar Ghobash said that the UAE will give Qatar 'the benefit of the doubt' on changing its foreign policy behaviour and await Saudi-led diplomacy with Qatar.[34] Following years of bilateralism and mistrust, the enduring legacy of the Qatar Crisis might well be an end to regionalism in the Gulf and the demise of the GCC organisation as a potential security institution. Qatar may be a beneficiary of reorientating gas markets following the Russian invasion of Ukraine in 2022. But, as gas industry expert Wayne Ackerman suggests, producers such as Qatar are unlikely to be involved in European attempts to find alternative sources of gas, as Doha tends to take a more conservative and long-term approach to commercial contracts and has little spare capacity prior to 2025.[35] Qatar was, however, quick to step in to mediate between the US and Iran during the final stages of the JCPOA renegotiation in 2022, showing its continued relevance in diplomatic circles.

Diplomatic and economic intervention

This section analyses the highly personalised and economic-dominated relations with Jordan, Egypt, Iraq and Turkey, which each stand out for different reasons. Egypt, Morocco and Jordan all remain important for the GCC states in terms of their manpower, and in the latter two cases for their similar monarchical interests. Since 2013, the kingdom and the UAE have buttressed the Egyptian political economy with billions in aid to maintain its weight as part of *their* Arab core. Iraq has become a case study of what happens when ties are cut due to the overtly sectarian agenda of Prime

Minister Maliki, and then re-established with a view to balancing out Iranian influence in a more normalised political economy. Turkey and Lebanon are intriguing cases, as predominantly economic relations have given way to deadlock and more robust methods in 2016 and 2017, possibly salvaged by fresh diplomacy in 2021.

Jordan

Jordan's stability is important for Saudi Arabia, with which it shares a border and monarchical interests, allowing limited Saudi power projection into the Levant. Amman was able to re-establish diplomatic ties with Qatar in 2019, due to Jordan's neutrality on the Qatar Crisis, which stems from a more balanced threat perception (favouring economic opportunity with Qatar) and its overriding regime security imperative. Jordan is generally viewed with suspicion and animosity by the Saudis since the Hashemites[36] were expelled from the Hijaz region by Abdulaziz Al Saud. When King Hussein allied with Iraq during the Iran–Iraq War, it was viewed as an attempt to retake the Hijaz for the Hashemites. Another difficult period occurred when Jordan refused to support US-led military intervention against Iraq after it occupied Kuwait in 1990, which led Saudi Arabia to suspend aid. Like Lebanon, Jordan is viewed by Riyadh as a dependent state without any particular payoff. This factor, combined with the decline of oil prices from 2014, meant that the Jordan protests in 2018 were met with only $2.5 billion in loan guarantees and central bank deposits rather than direct budget support from Kuwait, Saudi Arabia and the UAE.[37]

Biateral relations became critical during the Trump administration, when the Haram Al Sharif in Jerusalem, of which Jordan has been custodian since 1924, was at risk of being negotiated away to Saudi custodianship.[38] Any change to the custodianship of the site, which includes the Al-Aqsa mosque, the third most important site for Muslims after Mecca and Medina, could form part of a deal to facilitate a normalisation in Israel–Saudi relations. For Jordan, beyond regime survival and influence in Palestine, which is part of its national identity, the emphasis will remain on protecting access for its large educated expatriate labour force of more than 400,000 in the kingdom post-COVID-19 – more so since Jordan is said to lack the same evidence-based active labour market policies which might mitigate against future labour market issues.[39] The emerging tripartite economic and political partnership with Egypt and Iraq is thus ideal to boost trade and their relative autonomy in their somewhat one-sided relations with the GCC states. Meanwhile, meetings such as those of the Jordanian, Egyptian, Iraqi and UAE leaders in Aqaba in March 2022 presented a united front and brotherly exchange.

Egypt

Given its large population, ancient civilisation, borders with Israel, Saudi Arabia and Libya, status as a member of the US-backed alliance since 1979 and control over the Suez Canal, Egypt remains a vital node of Middle East influence. During 1956 the Suez Crisis it is reported that Sheikh bin Sultan Al Nahyan communicated to the British agent that 'Britain should do to Cairo what the Russians did to Budapest',[40] i.e. lay siege to it. Egypt, by intervening in the North Yemen civil war for five years during the war of 1962–70, marked a decisive clash between republic and monarchy over regional power and legitimacy. Nasser's presidency, which espoused pan-Arabism, encouraged the kingdom to engage in pan-Islamism and set the tone for the Islamisation of Saudi foreign policy. Ferris argues that the Egyptian intervention in Yemen at this time led to the brinkmanship which ignited the 1967 war with Israel and a reordering of the Arab regional political system.[41]

More recently, Egypt has been shaped by domestic and international factors during the Arab uprisings. After President Morsi's vocal criticism of Abu Dhabi's persecution of al-Islah in 2013, the power struggle between the Egyptian military and the Morsi government became an existential issue for Saudi Arabia and the UAE. It was imperative to bring Egypt back into the Arab fold and to stem the tide of Islamist militants in Sinai, the Western Desert and on the border with Libya. Saudi support was directed by Prince Bandar as one of his last tasks in office. Saudi, UAE and Kuwait moved decisively to support the then defence minister Sisi with a $12 billion package of direct cash injections to support the central bank, as well as grants, mainly in the form of energy transfers.[42] This is partly attributable to the time Sisi spent in the kingdom as Egyptian military attaché and the relationship he has with Saudi intelligence. There was little by way of US government action to the military's regaining of power, since it would continue to benefit from deeply entrenched interests amongst their military and intelligence communities. Egypt's limited participation in the Saudi-led intervention in Yemen repays an economic debt to the kingdom, papers over divergent positions on Syria, Qatar, Turkey and Russia and sends a clear message to the MB and other designated terrorist groups about challenging an incumbent regime.

Egypt repaid the last batch of debt owed to Qatar, $3 billion, in 2016.[43] Deposit draw-downs such as this were met with new deposits from Saudi Arabia and the UAE. They each deposited $2 billion in April 2015 and a further $5 billion in 2016 and 2017.[44] But these alone were not enough to float the whole Egyptian economy. Cairo was forced to seek International Monetary Fund (IMF) financing: a $12 billion loan agreement was reached in 2016 and a $5.4 billion standby arrangement in 2020. Saudi Arabia has continued to support President Sisi with $3 billion deposited with Egypt's central bank in October 2021, and extended the term of another $2.3 billion from previous deposits.[45] The same month, Egypt and Saudi Arabia agreed a $1.8 billion deal to build electric transmission plants and link their power grids.[46] Whilst Egypt–Qatar trade has been affected by the new political environment, Egyptian–UAE trade accelerated rapidly after 2010 to reach $4.1 billion in 2020.[47]

Although Egypt joined Saudi Arabia, the UAE and Bahrain to form the so-called 'Quartet' in the Qatar Crisis, it has tried to maintain pragmatic relations with Doha for reasons related to continued Qatari investment and Egyptian expatriate labour in Qatar, as well as cooperation on Gaza. Labour remittances from the Gulf remain important to Egyptian families and the economy, averaging $20 billion per year over the five years to 2019, equivalent to a quarter of the country's current account receipts.[48] Remittances were at their highest level in 2019 – $30 billion in total, of which 39 per cent came from Saudi Arabia alone.[49]

Saudi Arabia and the UAE are also likely to continue to fund strategic arms sales to Egypt, which helped to make Egypt the third-largest arms importer globally between 2014 and 2018[50] and thirteenth in terms of military strength in 2021.[51] They financed Russian arms sales to Egypt in 2014.[52] The UAE and other GCC states, including Saudi Arabia, Kuwait and the UAE, helped to finance a $5.9 billion deal for twenty-four Rafale fighter jets from France in 2015. This enabled Egypt to diversify its supply away from the US after the Obama administration froze military aid during the period following Morsi's ousting in 2013 until shortly just after the conclusion of the Rafale deal in 2015.[53] They also co-financed the €950 million deal for Mistral amphibious assault ships from France in 2015.[54] Saudi Arabia agreed to fund a $2 billion deal between Egypt's Ministry of Defence and Germany's ThyssenKrupp Marine Systems, initially for two corvettes,[55] but later switching to four MEKO A-200 frigates,[56] with one to be manufactured in Egypt. But due to a deterioration of relations between Riyadh and Berlin in 2018 after the Khashoggi incident, the deal was blocked.[57] By 2020, the rift appears to have passed, as the German parliament approved the sale of four frigates in April 2019, and in 2020 the Alexandria Shipyard Company announced that local manufacturing of the first MEKO-class frigate would commence in 2021.[58] Saudi Arabia and the UAE are also likely to transfer their military hardware which is surplus to requirements. For example, the UAE donated a dozen counter-insurgency aircraft to Egypt in 2015 for use in the Sinai – but they were seen in only 2018.[59]

UAE (joint) ventures have also benefited Egypt. For example, in 2017 the Dubai-based Minerva Special Purpose Vehicles (MSPV) was building between 2,000 and 3,000 Panthera T6 light armoured vehicles for Egypt's police and army.[60] Egyptian air force Mirage-2000 fighter jets appeared with Al-Tariq precision-guided munitions in 2021. Al-Tariq is bomb kit produced by a joint venture between Denel Dynamics of South Africa and EDGE Group of the UAE.[61]

Saudi Arabia remains active in its maritime influence throughout Egypt. El Dekheila port is run by Hutchison Port Holdings, a joint venture between Hutchison (Hong Kong), the Alexandria Port Authority and Al Blagha Group (Saudi Arabia). Saudi Arabia will use the islands of Tiran and Sanafir, the transfer of which the Egyptian parliament approved the in 2017, to help it replicate the success of Egypt's tourism industry in nearby Sharm El Sheikh and in neighbouring Jordan. The move will allow the Saudis to build a causeway from Neom across the Tiran Strait, linking North Africa to the Arabian Peninsula, bypassing Israel. Egypt requires Saudi and UAE support not only economically, but also politically, with regard to the Grand Ethiopian Renaissance Dam (GERD). GERD was being filled in July 2020 and could be operational before the end of 2022. Indeed, in 2021 there was evidence to suggest that the UAE was seeking to mediate between Egypt, Sudan and Ethiopia to break the deadlock in negotiations.

Iraq

After meeting Nuri al-Maliki in 2006, then King Abdullah chose not to engage further in Iraq, viewing him as an Iranian proxy. The Saudi withdrawal left Iraq fully open to Iranian influence. As Sir William Patey, former UK ambassador to Iraq and Saudi Arabia, stated, 'I told them [the Saudis] it [not engaging the Iraqi leadership] was a mistake.'[62] Riedel and Harvey agree that engaging with Maliki, an Iraqi nationalist first and foremost, could have done more to divert Iraqi attention back to the Arab world at an earlier point, which could have paid more dividends than waiting until 2020 to engage more fully.[63] Relations between Saudi Arabia and Iraq turned a corner in 2014 when Haider al-Abadi showed a firm commitment to rolling back ISIS and proving to Saudi Arabia that Iraq was not beholden to Tehran. The Saudi and Emirati view was also aided by Abadi's quietist approach of keeping religion out of politics but still making Shiite–Sunni relations a cornerstone of Saudi engagement. This was done primarily through the establishment of a Saudi consulate in Najaf to facilitate Shiite pilgrimage there, as well as Iraqi Shiite pilgrimage to Mecca and Medina for Hajj and Umra. The Saudis sent an ambassador to Iraq in 2015 after a twenty-five-year hiatus, opened a consulate in Basra in 2019 and opened the main border crossing at Arar in November 2020.[64] Iraq will no longer be under default Iranian influence, but, unless there are further Saudi shifts in cross-sectarian engagement, the status quo is likely to persist.

UAE concern over Iraq is also part of its concern related to Iran. To bolster its relations with the US, the UAE offered training to hundreds of Iraqi troops between 2004 and 2005, and may have allowed the US to use Al-Dhafra air base outside Abu Dhabi to operate surveillance aircraft over Iraq.[65] The UAE hosted the first Preparatory Group Meeting for the International Compact with Iraq in September 2006 and funded reconstruction efforts through the UN and World Bank. It wrote off $7 billion of Iraqi debt in 2008 and hosted a German mission to train Iraqi police.[66] The UAE hosted Abadi in 2014 and delivered COVID-19 supplies to Iraq in 2020. However, when Iraqi Prime Minister Mustafa al-Kadhimi visited Saudi Arabia and the UAE in March and April 2021 in search of aid, he instead received a commitment of $3 billion investment from each state, including in renewable energy.[67] Along with concurrent changes taking place in Saudi policy on Lebanon, this appears to spell the end of riyal politik for states still susceptible to Iranian influence. Energy cooperation may help Saudi Arabia and the UAE compete more effectively in Iraq vis-à-vis other actors such as Russia and Iran. But the calculation looks tentative and reflects the reality that if other actors in the international community do not take action to stabilise the Iraqi economy, an existential economic crisis in Iraq could undermine relations.

Turkey

The Saudi–Turkey dynamic is informed by Ottoman acquisitions in the Arabian Peninsula in the sixteenth and seventeenth centuries. In the modern era, Turkey's secular republicanism is perceived to be a threat to the absolute monarchies of the Gulf. Saudi Arabia maintains a sensitivity to cooperation with Turkish forces even when it might be expedient, and especially on Saudi territory, as was proposed during the Iraq invasion of Kuwait in 1990. Turkey and Saudi Arabia went on to help contain Iraq throughout the 1990s, maintaining generally positive relations apart from during the one-year premiership of Necmettin Erbakan from 1996 to 1997. Erbakan founded the Milli Görüş, the Turkish MB, in 1969, and quickly tried to facilitate the rise of new Islamic power including in Libya, Iran, Egypt, Pakistan, Indonesia, Nigeria, Bangladesh and Malaysia.

Turkey came back into the GCC fold orbit with a wide-ranging strategic dialogue with GCC states in 2008. However, trade potential has remain unrealised. Having initially put economics first through a rapid expansion of international trade and investment, securing middle-income status and acting as a model between western democracies and the Islamic world, Erdoğan won the directly elected presidency in 2014, after which his control over foreign affairs expanded.[68] King Abdullah's death in 2015 gave President

Erdoğan an opportunity to reset relations with Saudi Arabia, with comments from the then Saudi foreign minister, Saud al-Faisal, that the kingdom's issue was with the MB rather than with Turkey per se.[69] Turkey has also indicated that it supports Saudi policy in Yemen and wants Iranian influence out.[70] The reset was short lived, however. After the toppling of President Morsi in Egypt, Turkey became a preferred place of refuge for MB figures, along with Qatar. Turkey is said to actively incite against Egypt by allowing the MB to broadcast content into Egypt on multiple channels.[71] Turkey's overt support for Pakistan over Kashmir and their cooperation on Ankara potentially securing and operating Kabul's international airport, coupled with growing Turkish–Azerbaijani relations, shows that Turkish geopolitical influence is stretching from North Africa to Central Asia.

For the kingdom, Turkey's use of intelligence surrounding the assassination of Jamal Khashoggi in the Saudi consulate in Istanbul in 2018 was another major barrier to the thawing of relations. Relations only improved in May 2021 after both sides committed to working on a common agenda and holding regular consultations. For the UAE, it is more complicated. As one UAE official put it, there are clear issues: Turkey's activities in the Gulf (i.e. support of Qatar in 2017) were a concern and came with a cost attached – economic contraction, currency issues and polarisation of the population.[72] Turkey's involvement in Libya, Iraq, Qatar and Syria is also seen to have been a problem. The UAE says it must respect the sovereignty of these states.[73] The level of UAE contention with President Erdoğan's regional policies may be evident in the attempted coup of 2016. Turkish foreign minister Mevlut Cavusoglu accused the UAE of channelling $3 billion to the coup plotters.[74] This has been followed up with an assertion that Saudi and UAE 'dark money' is being used to fund the Turkish Democracy Project.[75]

The UAE continues to view 5,000 Turkish soldiers stationed on Iraqi territory for a decade as a concern, with the only other states that tolerate this being Qatar and Somalia. The UAE also fears a Turkish permanency in north-west Syria.[76] Yet the UAE is still one of Turkey's largest trade partners in the Middle East, with bilateral trade valued at around $8 billion in 2019.[77]

Turkey has expressed a greater willingness to engage with Egypt, Saudi Arabia and the UAE to resolve some of the tensions, even if the rhetoric changes from time to time depending on what is happening in places such as Libya and Gaza. The visit by Sheikh Mohammed bin Zayed Al Nahyan to Turkey in November 2021 may signal a reduction in tensions with Turkey, and a number of commercial agreements have been signed aimed at con-solidating gains, including a $10 billion fund to support investments in Turkey.[78] Whether this shift is sustainable depends to a large degree on political will and ambition. Given the downturn in Turkey's economy and relative isolation in the MENA region, the motivation in Ankara should be there, but whether an agreement can transcend ideological and specific issues with Emirati allies such as Egypt (i.e. handing over wanted Egyptians and withdrawing from Libya) remains to be seen. From Abu Dhabi's perspective, the move is consistent with the UAE's attempts to bolster relations with key economies regionally and internationally and welcoming leaders to Abu Dhabi, as it did with President Erdoğan in February 2022. In January 2022, Turkey and Saudi Arabia implemented a currency-swap deal to help ease Turkey's financial crisis, and in March 2022, Turkey suspended the trial in absentia of those it accused of the murder of Jamal Khashoggi and transferred it to Saudi Arabia, leaving the door open for a more complete rapprochement.

Lebanon

Lebanon has occupied a central position in the struggle between Saudi Arabia and Iran in the Middle East since the Lebanese civil war of 1975–1990. In September 1989 Saudi Arabia played a prominent role through the Arab League to end the civil war, with the conclusion of the Taif Agreement. But it led to Syria being the powerbroker in the country and an overrepresentation of the Christian minority in parliament to reassure them and persuade them to sign on to the deal. Until 2005 this exacerbated political deadlock. The kingdom managed by maintaining a long-standing relationship with the Sunni Hariri family, first with Rafic Hariri, who had made a fortune as a contractor in the kingdom in the 1980s, and who served as prime minister from 1992 to 1998 and from 2000 until 2005, when he was assassinated by Hezbollah. Saudi Arabia picked up influence through Saad Hariri, who set up the Future Movement Party in 2005. Saudi Arabia and Kuwait were instrumental in post-conflict reconstruction, depositing $2.5 billion in Lebanon's central bank between 2006 and 2008.[79] Hezbollah, which emerged as a node of Iranian influence in Lebanon in 1982 after Israel's massive invasion to attack the Palestine Liberation Organization (PLO) and lay siege to Beirut, has entrenched itself in Lebanese politics, causing a new political deadlock. The GCC states remain vital to the Lebanese economy. They have been the primary investors in Lebanon, accounting for billions of dollars of transfers and 76 per cent of all FDI from 2003 to 2015.[80] Foreign labour remittances from the Gulf accounted for 60 per cent of all remittances, in turn accounting for 20 per cent of Lebanon's annual GDP.[81]

With a change of Saudi leadership from 2015, Riyadh has taken a tougher position. Unlike his predecessors, Mohammed bin Salman is keenly aware that the cost of supporting Lebanese institutions such as the army has yet to bear any fruit. In terms of geopolitics, the fate of Lebanon will have little impact on the kingdom, whereas other regional states such as Bahrain, Yemen and Egypt will. The Lebanese government refused to condemn the Iranian authorities for the Iranian attack on the Saudi embassy in January 2016. In response, the kingdom stopped $3 billion in French arms sales to Lebanon and suspended a further $1 billion financing package for Lebanese security forces in February 2016.[82] In March 2016 it cut off $4 billion worth of military aid to Lebanon.[83] In the same month the kingdom designated Hezbollah a terror organisation and got the Arab League to do the same. In April, Lebanese citizens with alleged links to Hezbollah were expelled from the kingdom.[84] On 9 November 2017, Saudi Arabia, Bahrain, the UAE and Kuwait asked their citizens to leave Lebanon. Since none of this appeared to achieve the Saudi aim of pressuring a rethink in the Lebanese government, Saad Hariri was detained in December 2017 during a visit to Riyadh, where he was forced to announce his immediate resignation. The situation was ameliorated only by the intervention of President Macron.

Following the Lebanese liquidity crisis in 2019, Saudi Arabia pledged its economic support to Lebanon less than a day after Qatar said that it planned to purchase $500 million of sovereign bonds.[85] The UAE was active in carrying aid, including food, medical supplies and personal protective equipment to Lebanon following the Beirut port explosion in 2020. Beyond basic support, Anwar Gargash, speaking as UAE foreign minister in 2020, said that there was 'a deterioration of Lebanon's Arab relations and Gulf relations over the past 10 years' and that 'Lebanon is partly paying the price for that right now'.[86]

In November 2021, Saudi Arabia applied new pressure on Lebanon in response to George Kordahi's remarks about the Saudi-led war in Yemen.[87] The Saudi and Lebanese ambassadors were recalled, along with the ambassadors of the UAE, Bahrain and Kuwait. Saudi Arabia has indefinitely banned Lebanese agricultural imports and sanctions were adopted by Bahrain, Kuwait and the UAE. As part of a French–Saudi deal to draw a line under the incident, Kordahi resigned from his position as information minister in December 2021, and fresh contact with Lebanese Prime Minister Najib Mitaki was made. But, as the Lebanese foreign minister, Abdallah Bou Habib, stated in November 2021, 'If they [Saudi Arabia] just want Hezbollah's head on a plate, we can't give them that.'[88]

Israel, Palestine and the Abraham Accords

The UAE interest in building good relations with US evangelicals and projecting itself as a bastion of religious tolerance as part of its soft-power strategy towards the US appears to be the primary motive for its signing up to the Abraham Accords, alongside containment of Iran and recognition of de facto relations with Israel.[89] The UAE also looked to Egypt and Jordan as having relevance in the Middle East peace process and saw an opportunity to extend its own influence and become an interlocutor. However, limited GCC elite-level relations with Israel have not cascaded down to Arab public opinion.

Most UAE–Israel cooperation has been economic based, apart from overt political cooperation since 2015 through Israel stationing a permanent diplomat, Rami Hatan, in Abu Dhabi, accredited to the International Renewable Energy Agency, but not to the UAE government.[90] Economic cooperation has included critical infrastructure for Emirati oil and gas installations, such as the $816 million contract signed between Abu Dhabi's Critical National Infrastructure Authority (CNIA) and AGT International in 2008.[91] In 2010, a Hamas operative was assassinated in Dubai by a group of Israeli agents. The crisis in relations ended only upon assurances that assassinations by Israeli agents would not take place in the UAE ever again. A partial reimbursement and offset programme for Israeli military hardware was established and an enhanced security and intelligence dialogue took place. In 2011, CNIA agreed to purchase unmanned aerial vehicles (UAVs) from Israel's Aeronautics Defence Systems, but the Israeli Ministry of Defence refused the sale.[92] This was due to a combination of caution over selling sensitive technology to the UAE and US reservations. AGT International was again linked to UAE companies in Abu Dhabi for an emirate-wide surveillance system called Falcon Eye.[93] There have also been Israeli arms sales to Saudi Arabia and the UAE which have generally remained secret. Only when a US employee of Israel's Elbit Systems Ltd was found dead in the kingdom during an inspection of Elbit-made missile launchers in 2015 was attention generated about the deal and the circumstances surrounding his death.

Economic ties continue to be discreet, often with imports via Cyprus, Jordan or Palestine. Israel's trade with its Arab neighbours, estimated to be around $1 billion in 2018, is estimated to have the potential to reach $25 billion.[94] The main trade is in agriculture, including irrigation supplies, homeland security-related products, medical technology, the diamond industry and computer systems, including cyber security.[95] However, cyber cooperation is coming under increasing investigation, as GCC states such as Saudi Arabia, Bahrain and the UAE were found to be making use of Israeli companies such as NSO Group in 2021 to hack cellphones used by journalists, activists and US officials such as the Biden administration's lead negotiator with Iran.[96] A glitch in the cellphone of Saudi women's rights activist Loujain al-Hathloul helped to expose the work of NSO Group. The Israeli Ministry of Defence has since curtailed its cyber export list, including the removal of Saudi Arabia and the UAE.[97] In November 2021 NSO Group was added to the US Commerce Department's 'entity list', effectively blacklisting it for malicious cyber activity. While attention was drawn to such covert activity and awareness was raised among potential targets, many similar companies are expected to continue to operate through the use of existing or new technologies.

Prime Minister Netanyahu's 2020 West Bank annexation plan was considered to be in contravention of 'a principle in international law', according to a UN human rights panel,[98] and yet no action was taken by President Trump to put pressure on Netanyahu as President Obama had done. Instead, the result was to bring forward the date by which some Arab Gulf states chose to conclude normalisation agreements with Israel. If President Trump had won a second term, the Abraham Accords could have boosted UAE standing in Washington, DC. Even in one term, the Abraham Accords have had a tangible effect on UAE defence policy through the fast-tracking of the UAE's purchase of fifty F-35 aircraft from the US. Indeed, Martin Indyk, US Special Envoy for Israeli–Palestinian negotiations from 2013 to 2014, tweeted: 'Bibi just can't admit what everybody knows: that his deal with the UAE was not "peace for peace" but "peace for F35s and no annexation". It's a good deal for Israel. Why continue to lie about something of which he should be proud?'[99]

The Abraham Accords, by building closer political and security relations between their participants, are likely to further entrench securitisation in Israel, especially in light of ISIS attacks, and against Iran. This feature appears to be becoming evident in meetings between the signatories of the Abraham Accords, along with the logic of growing trade and people-to-people connections. The UAE is said to be attempting to use Mohammed Dahlan, a former Palestinian official turned critic of President Mahmoud Abbas, as its Palestine and broader Middle East fix-it person, with reference to his role in Gaza, the alleged Turkish coup attempt, Nile Dam diplomacy between Sudan, Ethiopia and Egypt, in Libya and against Islamists in Yemen.[100] It is uncertain how effective this policy will be if the Palestinian view reflects that of senior PLO officials, who accused the UAE of 'selling out' the Palestinians.[101]

The Abraham Accords do give the Arab states who signed on more trade and investment possibilities in a period of increasing economic pressure to diversify, secure water and food supplies and jointly address climate and health challenges during COVID-19. The UAE proposed setting up 'Silicon Wadi' in East Jerusalem in August 2020.[102] The first UAE company to open an office in Israel was G42, a company which has links to the UAE government through Sheikh Tahnoun and which seeks to replicate the Israel Defence Force's (IDF) incubation of tech companies which work closely with the defence industry.[103] In March 2021, the UAE set up a $10 billion fund to invest in Israel.[104] The first UAE ambassador to Israel arrived that same month, looking for an embassy in the Tel Aviv area.

In November 2021, the UAE, Israel and Jordan, assisted by US climate envoy John Kerry, signed an important energy deal which included the UAE building a massive solar farm in Jordan to supply electricity to Israel, and Israel building a desalination plant to provide water to Jordan.[105] The project, the biggest renewable energy project in the Middle East so far, is said to have attracted Saudi pressure first to stop it and then to change the language of the deal, since it upset Mohammed bin Salman over his 'Green Middle East' vision.[106]

Crown Prince Mohammed bin Salman might yet be tempted to use normalisation with Israel as a way to alter the narrative and thaw tense relations with Washington. He will have to take into account the views of different generations, and even young people may not be ready for normalisation. But, managed well, it could help to realise Palestinian statehood. For example, Sir William Patey said that 'It wouldn't surprise me' if Saudi Arabia committed to the Abraham Accords after King Salman, but that the kingdom would have to extract a price.[107] Restarting the moribund peace process might be enough to warrant a venture down this route, effectively putting the Arab Peace Plan into reverse: recognition for a commitment to peace. It would be an act of faith, since there would be no guarantee or legal requirement for Israel to follow through on the deal. The risk of failing to secure an agreement is that it would be a further blow to establishing a viable political horizon for Palestinian autonomy. It could also risk conflation between Saudi recognition of Israel and Israeli operations against the IRGC and Iranian nuclear programme, whilst potentially serving to coalesce and mobilise Saudi forces of dissent on the domestic front.

Proxy warfare

The cases of Syria and Libya highlight the extent to which Saudi Arabia and the UAE have engaged in proxy warfare, the regional and international context of such decision making and why it was necessary, as opposed to the more traditional and benign aspects of economic and diplomatic intervention.

Syria

Syria was an early test for Saudi Arabia and Iran in their pursuit of regional influence and hegemony, amounting to what Gause defines as a 'new Middle East Cold War', bearing striking similarities to the battles of influence fought in the sphere of domestic politics during the 1950s and 1960s.[108] Syria is a key battleground because it forms part of the 'axis of resistance' with Iran which provides Tehran with strategic depth across Syrian territory, to Hezbollah in southern Lebanon. This has taken on an increasingly embedded and transnational dimension along the Syrian border with Iraq, and in conjunction with allied militia groups in Iraq, from which the IRGC can conduct strikes against Israel and US forces. Saudi Arabia has had a difficult relationship with Syria's President Bashar al-Assad since the assassination of its long-time Lebanese ally, Rafic Hariri, in 2005, although the Saudi–Syrian agreement on the make-up of the Lebanese government in 2009 led to a short-lived harmony.

Certainly the Al Saud wanted to see Assad go, and stand accused of arming the Syrian opposition, even extreme elements within it. As the Syrian conflict became more sectarian, for example, through atrocities perpetrated by both sides, King Abdullah needed to be seen to be protecting the Sunni community.[109] This in the context of Saudi Arabia's having lost influence in Iraq and the capabilities to protect the Iraqi Sunni community.[110] Saudi Arabia was always going to engage under US leadership, so to be hawkish on Syria without implementing a new Saudi-led alliance left the kingdom frustrated but ultimately constrained. Instead, Riyadh has taken a number of steps aimed mainly at preventing domestic blowback from Syria, similar to that related to returning jihadis from Afghanistan in the 1980s. It moved to prevent certain clerics from preaching in 2012 and banned young Saudis from travelling to fight in Syria in 2014.

The pivotal moment for the Saudis came in the summer of 2013, when the US reversed its intention to attack Assad for its use of chemical weapons. This caused Prince Bandar, then in charge of the Syria dossier, to re-evaluate the Saudi position on Syria. He moved from supporting the Free Syrian Army to support for Jaysh al-Islam, which was considered to be more effective, given the rise of other violent rebel groups such as Al-Nusra Front, possibly supported by Qatar,[111] and ISIS. Indeed, they battled with ISIS and still have a tense relationship with Al Qaeda affiliate Jabhat Fateh al-Sham. Private Gulf families, including those in Kuwait have been cited as supporting violent groups such as Ahrar with financial donations through organisations such as the Popular Commission to Support the Syrian People.[112]

The reliance on pro-Saudi interlocutors in an attempt to gain representation during the US and Russian talks of 2015 and 2016 ignored the broader Syrian representation which would be required to advance peace talks. In February 2016, Saudi Arabia threatened to switch from covertly funding, supplying or training the armed opposition groups supported by western states, to supporting some groups regarded as extreme by Washington, and to introduce Saudi ground forces in Syria.[113] Saudi troop deployment would probably have been in coordination with Turkey and Qatar to fight ISIS, which was gaining ground to reach its peak of territorial control in early 2017. In the event, Saudi Arabia didn't send troops, probably because the risks were so great for a military with little battlefield experience, already committed in Yemen and with little on-the-ground intelligence in Syria. The kingdom again reverted to leveraging domestic options, including implementing more restrictive policies on Umrah, Hajj and work visas for Syrian nationals from 2016.[114] Riyal politik was also reportedly used in 2018 by offering reconstruction investments to Assad if he should break ties with Iran and Hezbollah.[115] Saudi Arabia has since left military intervention to Israel's IDF, who have conducted a number of strikes against Iranian targets in Syria.

During 2014–15, the UAE, as part of the US coalition against ISIS, conducted – and even commanded on occasion – air strikes against ISIS positions in Syria, and hosted French jets at Al Dhafra air base.[116] Like Qatar and Saudi Arabia, the UAE sought to remove Assad from power in 2011. But, unlike Saudi Arabia, the UAE did not provide weapons to the Syrian opposition, but contributed to a multilateral mechanism to fund approved rebel groups in Syria.[117] Post Russian intervention in 2015, the UAE believes that it must embrace Assad as the best way to stem Iranian influence in Syria and Lebanon. The UAE reopened its embassy in Damascus in December 2018, offered assistance to Syria after the outbreak of COVID-19 and indicated, along with Russia, that US sanctions against the Syrian government challenge a potential rapprochement.[118] That rapprochement appears to be based on the calculation that Syria is still a 'functioning pillar of Arab security'[119] and that embracing Assad will help to level out any Iranian gains from a new nuclear deal. Abu Dhabi's position may be reinforced by a growing assertion that US sanctions against Assad under the Caesar Act are hurting Syrian civilians more than the government. The UAE could use its non-permanent seat on the UN Security Council 2022–23 to pursue this line. There are questions about whether other Arab states will continue to condemn Assad's use of chemical weapons, including formally in the Organisation for the Prohibition of Chemical Weapons. There is also speculation that Syria will be readmitted into the Arab League.

Libya

Libya and Saudi Arabia had highly contentious relations during the Gaddafi era, specifically in 1984, when Saudi police interrupted an attempt to assassinate Libyan dissidents in Mecca.[120] This was followed in 2003, when Libya was accused of plotting to assassinate the then Crown Prince Abdullah,[121] and in 2009, when Gaddafi confronted then King Abdullah to proclaim he was 'king of kings of Africa and the imam of the Muslims' during a diatribe at the 2009 Arab League Summit.[122] A leaked recording from an unknown date found that Gaddafi and Hakem al-Mutairi, preacher and leader of the Kuwaiti Ummah Party, an unrecognised political party, discussed going after Saudi oil wealth and oil reserves during the instability in Iraq.[123] A recording between Gaddafi and Sheikh Hamad bin Jassim, the former prime minister of Qatar, exists from 2017, with the Sheikh defending the discussion about attacking the kingdom as a way to appease Gaddafi.[124]

The Emirati and Egyptian strategic objective is to establish stability in post-Gaddafi Libya, the number one security threat for Egypt.[125] It might also be to avoid a repeat of the MB winning control of Libyan state apparatus as it did in Egypt in 2012. The stakes are high, as the Brotherhood has not been as engaged with the public as it was in the lead-up to its 2012 electoral win in Egypt, but nevertheless is pushing for control and power in Libya at all costs. Saudi Arabia threw its diplomatic weight behind the Arab League during the NATO intervention, but has since supported Khalifa Haftar, commander of the Tobruk-based Libyan National Army (LNA) with tens of millions of dollars as he advanced on the capital, Tripoli, in 2019.[126] Its motives for doing so revolve around keeping Libya in the Arab fold and establishing stability in the country and in the Eastern Mediterranean, including rolling back Turkish influence. Following Haftar's defeat by Government of National Accord (GNA) forces in June 2020, Riyadh will be looking to enhance its communication with the GNA in an attempt to achieve its objectives in Libya and the Eastern Mediterranean.

The UAE believes there is a legacy issue after its participation in NATO intervention, so it is now involved in the political situation. Libya represents a continuity of UAE influence from the Horn of Africa to North Africa through Sudan, Cairo and the Mezzan, and on into the Mediterranean through further port projects and deepening strategic relations with France. The UAE has become a catalyst for the movement of Sudanese rebels to Libya by making direct contact with Darfurian Libya-based commanders of rebel groups, bypassing the LNA leadership, and inviting them to Abu Dhabi.[127] These groups have been involved in military operations in Tripoli and Sirte, have a significant number of troops at their disposal, numbering 3,000 in 2019, and are recruiting, allegedly through Black Shield Security Services, an Emirati company.[128] The UAE and Egypt are focused more on diplomatic, military and economic cooperation with the LNA only, leaving intelligence and social media disinformation to Russia.[129] This stands in contrast to Turkey which looks to be playing a more comprehensive diplomatic, military, economic, intelligence, counterterrorism and social media role with the GNA.

Foreign actor engagement in Libya has been destabilising to the achievement of a rapid political transition and contributed to poor relations between the UAE, Egypt, Saudi Arabia and Russia, on the one hand, which support Haftar, and Turkey and Qatar, on the other, which support the UN-recognised interim GNA in Tripoli. The approach of the UAE, Saudi Arabia and Egypt in Libya is summarised by Wehrey: 'What was needed was a tighter ruling grip and a healthy dose of Islamic orthodoxy for the wayward youth who'd been led astray by terrorists – and by the Brotherhood, which they considered one and the same.'[130]

The clash of UAE and Turkey's agenda became more pronounced after Haftar launched a war against the UN-endorsed government in Tripoli in 2019. He was defeated, partly due to weeks of persistent Turkish drone strikes,[131] and had few options other than to support a ceasefire deal. Ankara reportedly sent 3,800 fighters to Libya from Syria in 2020.[132] Ankara may also be sending weapons[133] and deploying air defence systems in preparation for the deployment of fighter jets.[134] There is also an allegation from the US Defense Intelligence Agency that the UAE may provide some financing for Wagner Group operations in Libya.[135] Wagner Group has been active in Libya since 2018, deploying hundreds of mercenaries to training sites, airfields, forward bases, energy and infrastructure sites.[136] Any accusation of the UAE supporting Russian attempts to gain another Mediterranean foothold and being better placed to challenge NATO is sensitive. So much so, that Yousef Al Otaiba, Emirati ambassador to the US, issued a statement denying any financing arrangements with Wagner Group.[137]

Direct military intervention

Yemen is the most clear and visible sign that Saudi hegemony and homeland security on the Arabian Peninsula had been fundamentally challenged, and that it would use whatever levers were at its disposal in order to re-establish its position and order. Relevant to the kingdom's evolving relations with the UAE, this section also covers points which resonate in subsequent chapters, in particular, how international actors have engaged with the kingdom on this issue and how the kingdom has sought to influence decision making in various forums and capitals.

Yemen

In dealing with Yemen, the Saudis had utilised an eclectic approach of tribal funding (which reached thousands of schools in villages and towns across

Yemen), aerial drones and links to the Yemeni Salafi party to maintain control.[138] Riyadh had also relied on the political loyalty of Yemen's President Saleh, who was Zaidi Shia but managed to contain Yemen's problems for two decades. He governed from Yemen's unification on 22 May 1990, using distributive patronage in the almost equally divided Sunni–Shia nation. The diffusion of control inside Yemen, coupled with a lower ranking of the Yemen portfolio after the border agreement in 2000, which moved from the Saudi ministry of defence to the ministry of interior and the Saudi intelligence services, may have created a sense of security which proved unfounded in 2009.

Houthi clashes with the Yemeni government were reported six times between 2004 and 2010 and there have been tensions spanning decades. After the Houthis conducted incursions into Saudi territory from 4 November 2009, Saudi Arabia deployed military units and aerial attacks to ensure hostile elements were 'cleansed'.[139] This stood in contrast to Qatari diplomatic efforts with the Houthis. It was the first time Saudi forces had crossed a border without an international power such as the US taking a leading role. The kingdom also helped to finance the Yemeni military Operation Scorched Earth in Saada governorate from August 2009 to February 2010, and provided some international political cover for the Yemeni government.[140]

President Saleh's policies were a key element in sparking the 2011 uprising in Yemen. The GCC transition agreement, signed in December 2011 with US and other external support, was spearheaded by King Abdullah and managed to avert further hostilities in Yemen, until it was disrupted by the Houthis in 2014.[141] Abdrabuh Mansour Hadi Mansour was selected as the transitional president, and President Saleh resigned on 25 February 2012. Saleh's assassination on 4 December 2017 then made it more difficult for an accommodation to be reached with the Houthis amid a collapsing economy, attacks from Al Qaeda and secessionism in the south.

Iranian involvement in support of the Houthis has consisted of financial support, weapons and training to the Houthi group from 2011, but also proselytism of the Shia religion.[142] The commonality of Shia religion does not make the Houthis and Iran allied by extension. The Houthis practise Zaydism, the oldest branch of the Shia and not traditionally associated with Twelver Shiism. But by 2014, as the Houthis took over the capital, Sana'a, Iran, as one of the few states to support the Houthi mission, started supplying heavy weapons and delivering more significant economic support.[143] The Saudi-led intervention in Yemen, Operation Decisive Storm, was announced on 26 March 2015 to restore the rule of President Abd Rabbo Mansour Hadi along the lines of the GCC agreement and to secure its southern border against attacks. It has been suggested that the UAE and other Saudi allies were given just twenty-four hours' notice to join the Saudi-led coalition in Yemen.[144] Riyadh's intention to destroy the Houthis marked a significant escalation in an overtly militaristic era in Saudi foreign policy.

The Saudi-led intervention included a joint military operation of 100 warplanes and 150,000 troops,[145] including border forces, naval contingents and air support, mobile and rotated troops from some GCC states, Sudan and Yemen.[146] States involved included Egypt, which sent warships to support the Saudi naval blockade but no troops; Morocco, Jordan, Sudan, Kuwait, Qatar and Bahrain.[147] UAE support, which consisted of 3,500 troops with another 3,000 providing in-theatre support[148] and the utilisation of transport planes,[149] was a vital component. The UAE was always reliant on Saudi Arabia for war planning and propaganda, which meant a certain loss of control, although it suited the UAE that Saudi leadership of the campaign meant that it also became a lightning rod for international criticism.

Houthi attacks on Saudi troops and territory between 2016 and 2021 have included reports of: Houthi shells in southern Saudi Arabia which killed seven civilians in August 2016;[150] a Houthi missile which killed more than fifty Saudi soldiers in Najran the same month;[151] and the Houthis killing and wounding several Saudi soldiers after capturing a Saudi military base in Raboah, Asir province in May 2017.[152] Further attacks were reported on Saudi oil refineries in Yanbu province, Saudi Arabia causing a major fire in July 2017[153] and a Volcano H-2 missile is claimed to have hit King Khalid International Airport in Saudi Arabia.[154] Some analysts believe that the Saudi-led campaign following such cross-border attacks amounts to 'collective punishment of civilians' through the use of large munitions or indiscriminate weapons in built-up areas.[155] After the Houthis fired a missile at Riyadh on 4 November 2017, Saudi Arabia has maintained a large naval presence in the Red Sea and Gulf of Aden as part of its operations in Yemen, including as part of a land, sea and air blockade to cut the flow of weapons to the Houthis, but which has had grave humanitarian consequences.[156] The UN Security Council has continued to give the kingdom the exclusive right to inspect shipping and imports into Yemen, although by 2017 UN leaders were calling for a full lifting of the blockade,[157] and by 2018 a UN Security Council panel of experts was calling for improvements to this process.[158] In 2021 the blockade was seen to be the key to unlocking a peace deal with the Houthis.[159] As the conflict continued into 2022, President Hadi was removed and replaced with a twelve-person Presidential Leadership Council. The move reflected the factionalisation of Yemen politics (including President Hadi's association with the Islah Party, which the UAE disapproved of) and was also packaged as a diplomatic gesture designed to support UN-led efforts to end the war.

The UAE completed the withdrawal of its troops from the Yemen conflict on 9 February 2020, on the basis that it had trained enough Yemeni forces, along with other forces such as those from Sudan, to secure its counterterrorism interests (including against Islamist groups such as Islah) and had supported the Saudi mission.[160] As a legacy, the UAE has an indirect presence of 90,000 fighters across the Shabwani and Hadrami Elite Forces in the east, the Joint Forces, including Guards of the Republic (National Resistance) in the west, Security Belt Forces in the south and Abu al-Abbas Fighters in the south-west.[161] By formalising the Southern Transition Council as a political party to the Riyadh Agreement, the UAE cemented its future role in Yemeni politics before its withdrawal.

The UAE achieved 'maximum strategic expansion' in Yemen with influence in Assab, Djibouti, Somalia, Socotra and a foothold in Ethiopia and Eritrea.[162] That expansion has not been cost free, and, like Saudi Arabia, the UAE remains exposed to drone attacks. It makes air defence a top prority for the UAE. Yemen has been a leading recipient of UAE aid ever since the UAE was established, including Socotra, where there have been UAE developmental projects since the late 1990s.[163] The UAE has expanded its footprint on Socotra and Mayun, which is ideally located to monitor shipping in the Red Sea and still allows force projection into the Horn of Africa. This could become a fixed UAE outpost if the Biden administration allows such de facto control to occur. The same is true of Saudi control over al-Mahrah, which it has controlled since 2017.[164]

Conclusion

Monarchical interest, Saudi hegemony, continued preference for close security relations with the US, and GCC-wide security exercises keep the GCC grouping together on hard security issues. Terrorism, air defence and manpower issues have all spurred the GCC states to integrate in the security realm. But there is diversity in the GCC system which could turn into centrifugal forces, especially dynastic and personalised competition (with economic competition possibly becoming a new source of existential threat), and Saudi Arabia and the UAE maintain a heavy Iran focus versus states such as Kuwait, Oman and Qatar which balance Iran in their relations with the kingdom.

UAE policy sits almost as a mirror image to that of Qatar, which has been effective in mobilising state resources and has driven similar responses in turn, echoing Newton's Third Law of Motion. COVID-19 has been used opportunistically to disparage competitors[165] or used as a convenient segue into more meaningful diplomacy. Such manoeuvres, as well as bringing 'insiders' to advise on specific foreign policy issues, could be considered a hedge from a small state.

Other forms of diversity in the GCC include the Abraham Accords, which only Bahrain and the UAE from the GCC have signed on to so far. Saudi hegemony was shown to be a source of apparent unification during the GCC Al Ula summit, but can also be a source of division or uncertainty, as was evident especially in the 2016 diplomatic fracture with Iran, but also in the detention of Saad Hariri in 2017, the OPEC disagreement in 2020 and the Saudi response to Lebanese criticism in 2021.

Riyal politik and economic statecraft have been vital to these states in pursuing counter-revolutionary objectives during and after the Arab uprisings. In the context of lower oil prices from 2014, there is a question as to whether an exclusively economic approach can be replicated. Saudi support of Lebanon has already changed following renewed cost-benefit calculations, leading to withdrawal in the same vein as from Iraq. Whilst riyal politik and economic statecraft saved Egypt from the clutches of Qatari influence, and provided a bridge to further economic support from the IMF, Egypt provides far more return on investment in economic, political and spillover terms. So-called dark money and covert activities have also been apparent in Libya, Turkey, Sudan and in other parts of the region, with the aim of undermining adversaries (some being challenger states) and promoting the joint interests of Saudi Arabia and the UAE. Support for arms sales, working in tandem on foreign policy issues such as Libya and Sudan, and the long-term prospects of enhancing collective influence with Egypt and Israel in other parts of the Middle East and Africa make the Saudi–UAE relationship increasingly interdependent as well as highly personalised.

Notes

1   The Economist, 'Saudi Arabia: GCC Customs Union Up and Running', 13 January 2015, http://country.eiu.com/article.aspx?articleid=1522653936
2   Ibid.
3   Karen Young, 'China Is Not the Middle East's High Roller', *Bloomberg Opinion*, 2 July 2020, available at www.aei.org/op-eds/china-is-not-the-middle-easts-high-roller/
4   John Duke Anthony, 'Aspects of Saudi Arabia's Relations with Other Gulf States', in Tim Niblock (ed.), *State, Society and Economy in Saudi Arabia*. Abingdon: Routledge, 1982: 148–170.
5   Interview with Michael Knights, 25 May 2021.
6   Ibid.

7   Ash Rossiter, 'Local Forces and Britain's Silver Age in the Gulf', *Security in the Gulf: Local Militaries Before British Withdrawal*. Cambridge: Cambridge University Press, 2020: 192

8   'Joint Embassy Riyadh–Embassy Abu Dhabi Cable', 10 September 2005, available at https://wikileaks.org/plusd/cables/05ABUDHABI3851_a.html

9   Ibid.

10 See Noura Saber Mohammed Saeed Al-Mazrouei, 'UAE–Saudi Arabia Border Dispute: The Case of the 1974 Treaty of Jeddah', PhD thesis, October 2013, https://core.ac.uk/download/pdf/19743733.pdf

11 Aziz El Yaakoubi, Marwa Rashad and Davide Barbuscia, 'Saudi Arabia Amends Import Rules from Gulf in Challenge to UAE', *Reuters*, 5 July 2021, https://mobile.reuters.com/article/amp/idUSKCN2EB0PL?__twitter_impression=true

12 Simeon Kerr, 'Trade Emerges as Latest Flashpoint in Deepening Saudi–UAE Rivalry', *The Financial Times*, 14 July 2021, www.ft.com/content/0cb64e0b-fcad-4992-beed-191261caa406

13 Ibid.

14 Omar Al-Ubaydli, 'Saudi Arabia's Economic Transformation Benefits the UAE Too', 25 October 2021, www.atlanticcouncil.org/blogs/menasource/saudi-arabias-economic-transformation-benefits-the-uae-too/

15 Lourence Louer, 'Exporting the Revolution', *Transnational Shia Politics: Religious and Political Networks in the Gulf*. London: Hurst, 2012: 179.

16 Congressional Research Service, 'Bahrain: Unrest, Security, and U.S. Policy', 26 June 2020: 4, https://fas.org/sgp/crs/mideast/95-1013.pdf

17 International Crisis Group, 'Popular Protests in North Africa and the Middle East (III): The Bahrain Revolt', Middle East/North Africa Report No. 105, 6 April 2011, available at www.files.ethz.ch/isn/128331/105-%20Popular%20Protests%20in%20North%20Africa%20and%20the%20Middle%20East%20-III-The%20Bahrain%20Revolt.pdf

18 Thomas Erdbrink, 'Iranian General, Denouncing Move by Bahrain, Threatens "Bloody Intifada"', *The New York Times*, 21 June 2016, www.nytimes.com/2016/06/22/world/middleeast/iran-bahrain.html

19 Mehran Kamrava, 'Qatar's Moment in History', *Qatar: Small State, Big Politics*. Ithaca, NY: Cornell University Press, 2013: 165–174.

20 Kristian Coates Ulrichsen, 'The Gulf Goes Global: The Evolving Role of Gulf Countries in the Middle East and North Africa and Beyond', FRIDE Working Paper No. 121, December 2013: 9

21 Crystal A. Ennis, 'Reading Entrepreneurial Power in Small Gulf States: Qatar and the UAE', *International Journal*, 73 (4), 2018: 588.

22 Courtney Freer, 'Who's Actually in Qatar? – Analysis', *Gulf State Analytics*, 10 August 2017, available at www.eurasiareview.com/10082017-whos-actually-in-qatar-analysis/

23 Mehran Kamrava, 'State Capacity and High Modernism', *Qatar: Small State, Big Politics*. Ithaca, NY: Cornell University Press, 2013: 140–164.

24 Sultan Sooud Al Qassemi, 'How Saudi Arabia and Qatar Became Friends Again', *Foreign Policy*, 21 July 2011, https://foreignpolicy.com/2011/07/21/how-saudi-arabia-and-qatar-became-friends-again/

25 Caroline Mortimer, 'UAE Crown Prince Asked US to Bomb Al Jazeera During War on Terror', *The Independent*, 29 June 2017, www.independent.co.uk/news/world/middle-east/uae-crown-prince-us-bomb-al-jazeera-mohammed-bin-zayed-al-nahyan-wikileaks-qatar-a7814691.html

26 Michelle Dunne, 'Foreign Policy Shaped by Donors', Carnegie Endowment for International Peace, 3 April 2014, https://carnegieendowment.org/sada/55230

27 Hussein Ibish, 'Unfulfilled 2014 Riyadh Agreement Defines Current GCC Rift', Arab Gulf States Institute in Washington, 6 June 2017, https://agsiw.org/unfulfilled-2014-riyadh-agreement-defines-current-gcc-rift/

28 Paul Wood, '"Billion Dollar Ransom": Did Qatar Pay Record Sum?', *BBC News*, 16 July 2018, www.bbc.com/news/world-middle-east-44660369

29 Susan B. Glasser, 'The Full Transcript: Ben Rhodes and Samantha Power', *Politico*, 15 January 2018, www.politico.com/magazine/story/2018/01/15/the-full-transcript-ben-rhodes-and-samantha-power-216322/

30 Simon Henderson, 'Qatar Diplomacy: Unraveling a Complicated Crisis', Washington Institute for Near East Policy, PolicyWatch 2941, www.washingtoninstitute.org/policy-analysis/qatar-diplomacy-unraveling-complicated-crisis

31 Ibid.

32 AP, 'What are the 13 Demands Given to Qatar?', 23 June 2017, available at https://gulfnews.com/world/gulf/qatar/what-are-the-13-demands-given-to-qatar-1.2048118

33 Simeon Kerr and Katrina Manson, 'Saudi Arabia Seeks to Resolve Qatar Crisis as "Gift" to Joe Biden', *Financial Times*, 27 November 2020, www.ft.com/content/ae7e041f-ff4b-4df7-8b2b-06488e17a91c

34 Hadley Gamble, 'As Saudi Arabia, the UAE and now Qatar all push for a seat at Biden's negotiating table with Iran their three year rift hasn't healed "It's not going to be rosy straight away," says @omarsaifghobash @cnbcinternational #exclusive', 19 January 2021, https://twitter.com/_HadleyGamble/status/1351438907754344448

35 Wayne Ackerman, Middle East Institute Expert Voices, 7 February 2022, www.youtube.com/watch?v=r7bqg0SK-gw

36 Hashemites claim lineage to the Prophet Mohammed. Their leaders in the Hijaz region held the titles of Custodians of the Muslim holy cities of Mecca and Medina.

37 Marwan Muasher, 'Jordan: Fallout from the End of an Oil Era', Carnegie Endowment for International Peace, 9 June 2020, https://carnegieendowment.org/2020/06/09/jordan-fallout-from-end-of-oil-era-pub-82008

38 Martin Chulov and Michael Safi, 'Phone Intercepts Shine More Light on Jordanian Prince's Alleged Coup Attempt', *The Guardian*, 30 May 2021, https://amp.theguardian.com/world/2021/may/30/phone-intercepts-jordanian-prince-alleged-coup-attempt#click=https://t.co/s3LokTRZFp

39 Laith Al-Ajlouni, 'Overcoming Unemployment in Jordan: The Need for Evidence-Based Policies', Middle East Institute, 13 October 2021, www.mei.edu/publications/overcoming-unemployment-jordan-need-evidence-based-policies

40 Christopher M. Davidson, 'Sheikh Shakhbut and the Great Decline', *Abu Dhabi: Oil and Beyond*. London: C. Hurst & Co., 2011: 38.

41 Jesse Ferris, *Nasser's Gamble: How Intervention in Yemen Caused the Six-Day War and Decline of Egyptian Power*. Princeton: Princeton University Press, 2013.

42 David Butter, 'Egypt and the Gulf: Allies and Rivals', Chatham House, 20 April 2020, www.chathamhouse.org/2020/04/egypt-and-gulf/sisis-debt-his-gulf-arab-backers

43 Ahram Online, 'Egypt Repays Qatar Final $1 Bln in Outstanding Debt: CBE Governor', 1 July 2016, https://english.ahram.org.eg/News/232304.aspx

44 Butter, 'Egypt and the Gulf'.

45 Reuters, 'Saudi Deposits $3bln in Egypt's Central Bank', 31 October 2021, www.reuters.com/world/middle-east/saudi-deposits-3-bln-egypts-central-bank-extends-previous-facilities-2021-10-31/

46 Kamal Tabikha, 'Egypt and Saudi Arabia Sign $1.8 Billion Deal to Link Their Power Grids', *The National*, 5 October 2021, www.thenationalnews.com/business/2021/10/05/egypt-and-saudi-arabia-sign-18-billion-deal-to-link-their-power-grids/

47 Business Today Egypt, 'Egypt–UAE Trade Partnership Saw $4.1B in 2020, Total Exports Recorded at $2.8B', 28 June 2021, www.businesstodayegypt.com/Article/1/782/Egypt-UAE-trade-partnership-saw-4-1B-in-2020-total

48 Butter, 'Egypt and the Gulf': 11.

49 Dina Abdel-Fattah, 'The Covid-19 Pandemic and Egyptian Migrant Workers', ERF The Forum, 3 May 2020, https://theforum.erf.org.eg/2020/05/03/covid-19-pandemic-egyptian-migrant-workers/

50 Butter, 'Egypt and the Gulf'.

51 Global Firepower, '2021 Egypt Military Strength', www.globalfirepower.com/country-military-strength-detail.php?country_id=egypt

52 Al-Masry Al-Youm, 'KSA, UAE to Finance Russia Arms Deal with Egypt', 7 February 2014, https://egyptindependent.com/ksa-uae-finance-russian-arms-deal-egypt/

53 Noah Rayman, 'The Real Reason Egypt is Buying Fighter Jets from France', *Time*, 15 February 2015, https://time.com/3710118/egypt-rafale-fighter-jet-france/

54 Jean-Baptiste Vey and John Irish, 'France, Egypt Agree 950 Million Euro Mistral Warship Deal', *Reuters*, 23 September 2015, www.reuters.com/article/us-france-egypt-mistral-idUSKCN0RN18Z20150923

55 Small warships normally used for naval patrols.

56 These are larger vessels, usually with a mix of offensive and defensive capabilities, used for naval patrols or to escort larger ships.

57 Michel Cabirol, 'L'Arabie Saoudite Bloque le Contrat des Corvettes Meko A200 en Egypte', *La Tribune*, 11 May 2018, www.latribune.fr/entreprises-finance/industrie/aeronautique-defense/l-arabie-saoudite-bloque-le-contrat-des-corvettes-meko-a200-en-egypte-796222.html

58 Rasha Mahmoud, 'Egypt Boosts Naval Power in Deal with German Shipbuilder', *Al-Monitor*, September 2020, www.al-monitor.com/originals/2020/09/egypt-germany-contract-produce-frigate-navy-regional-tension.html

59 Defence Web, 'Egyptian AT-802 Acquisition Confirmed', 24 January 2018, www.defenceweb.co.za/aerospace/aerospace-aerospace/egyptian-at-802-acquisition-confirmed/

60 Defence Web, 'Egypt Getting MSPV Panthera T6 Armoured Vehicles', 24 February 2017, www.defenceweb.co.za/land/land-land/egypt-getting-mspv-panthera-t6-armoured-vehicles/

61 Mahmoud Gamal, 5 July 2021, https://twitter.com/mahmouedgamal44/status/1411903321766514690

62 Author's interview with Sir William Patey, former UK Ambassador to Saudi Arabia (2007–10), 18 November 2021.

63 Bruce Riedel and Katherine Harvey, 'Why is Saudi Arabia Finally Engaging with Iraq?', Brookings, 4 December 2020, www.brookings.edu/blog/order-from-chaos/2020/12/04/why-is-saudi-arabia-finally-engaging-with-iraq/

64 Ibid.

65 Jon B. Alterman, 'The United Arab Emirates', United States Institute of Peace Special Report 189: 10.

66 Kenneth Katzman, 'The United Arab Emirates (UAE): Issues for U.S. Policy', CRS Report for Congress, 4 September 2020: 10, https://fas.org/sgp/crs/mideast/RS21852.pdf

67 Karen E. Young, 'Iraq Wants Aid, but Saudi Arabia and the UAE See Investment Opportunity', *Foreign Policy*, 30 April 2021, https://foreignpolicy.com/2021/04/30/saudi-arabia-uae-iraq-investment-energy/

68 Soner Cagaptay, *The New Sultan: Erdogan and the Crisis of Modern Turkey*. London: I. B. Tauris, 2017.

69 Mohamed Moktar Qandil, 'The Muslim Brotherhood and Saudi Arabia: From Then to Now', Fikra Forum, Washington Institute for Near East Policy, 18 May 2018, www.washingtoninstitute.org/policy-analysis/muslim-brotherhood-and-saudi-arabia-then-now

70 France 24, 'Turkey Supports Saudi Mission in Yemen, Says Iran Must Withdraw', 26 March 2015, www.france24.com/en/20150326-turkey-support-saudi-yemen-erdogan-interview-france-24

71 Discussion with a senior UAE official who asked not to be named, 19 January 2021.

72 Council on Foreign Relations, 'A Conversation with Anwar Gargash', 29 September 2020, www.cfr.org/event/conversation-anwar-gargash.

73 Discussion with a UAE official who asked not to be named, 19 January 2021.

74 Gönül Tol, 'Turkish–Emirati Tensions Continue to Simmer', Middle East Institute, 4 May 2020, www.mei.edu/blog/turkish-emirati-tensions-continue-simmer

75 Eli Clifton and Murtaza Hussain, 'Dark Money Network Pushes Pro-UAE/Saudi Policies from New York', *Responsible Statecraft*, 26 November 2021, https://responsiblestatecraft.org/2021/11/26/dark-money-network-pushes-pro-uae-saudi-policies-from-new-york/

76 Council on Foreign Relations, 'A Conversation with Anwar Gargash'.

77 Firat Kozok, Zainab Fattah and Sylvia Westall, 'UAE, Saudi Arabia Reach Out to Turkey's Erdogan in Wary Move to Ease Tensions', *Bloomberg*, 4 February 2021, www.bloomberg.com/news/articles/2021-02-04/gulf-states-reach-out-to-erdogan-in-wary-move-to-ease-tensions

78 Orhan Coskun, 'Turkey, UAE Sign Investment Accords Worth Billions of Dollars', *Reuters*, 24 November 2021, www.reuters.com/world/middle-east/turkey-hopes-uae-investment-deals-during-ankara-talks-2021-11-24/

79 Ibid.

80 Maha Yahya, 'Lebanon: Not Expecting Gulf Aid to Come Back', Malcolm H. Kerr Carnegie Middle East Center, 9 June 2020, https://carnegie-mec.org/2020/06/09/lebanon-not-expecting-gulf-aid-to-come-back-pub-82009

81 Ibid.

82 Staff Writer, 'Saudi Halts $3 Billion in Aid to Lebanon Army', *Al Arabiya News*, 19 February 2016, https://english.alarabiya.net/News/middle-east/2016/02/19/Saudi-halts-3-bn-in-aid-to-Lebanon-army-official#:~:text=the%20Lebanese%20republic'-,Saudi%20Arabia%20said%20Friday%20it%20has%20stopped%20a%20%243%20billion,in%20support%20of%20Syria's%20regime.

83 Ben Hubbard, 'Saudis Cut off Funding for Military Aid to Lebanon', *The New York Times*, 19 February 2016, www.nytimes.com/2016/02/20/world/middleeast/saudis-cut-off-funding-for-military-aid-to-lebanon.html

84 Sami Aboudi, 'Lebanese Expats Fearful as Gulf Expels Dozens Accused of Hezbollah Links', *Reuters*, 8 April 2016, www.reuters.com/article/us-gulf-hezbollah-lebanon-idUSKCN0X51R2

85 Natasha Turak and Sam Meredith, 'Saudi Arabia Promises Full Support for Lebanon after Qatar Offers Aid Package', 22 January 2019, www.cnbc.com/2019/01/22/saudi-arabia-prepared-to-go-all-the-way-to-help-lebanon-finance-minister-says.html

86 Reuters Staff, 'Lebanon Paying Price for Deteriorating Gulf Ties, Says UAE Official', *Reuters*, 25 June 2020, www.reuters.com/article/uk-lebanon-crisis-emirates/lebanon-paying-price-for-deteriorating-gulf-ties-says-uae-official-idUKKBN23W1FL

87 Reuters, 'Yemen Comments Put Fresh Strain on Lebanon's Gulf Ties', 27 October 2021, www.reuters.com/world/middle-east/lebanon-pm-says-ministers-criticism-saudi-is-not-govt-position-2021-10-27/

88 Reuters, 'Lebanon Says It Wants Dialogue with Saudi Arabia, Not Demands about Hezbollah' 3 November 2021, available at https://english.alarabiya.net/News/middle-east/2021/11/03/Lebanon-says-it-wants-dialogue-with-Saudi-Arabia-not-demands-about-Hezbollah

89 Joel C. Rosenberg, *Enemies and Allies: An Unforgettable Journey inside the Fast Moving and Immensely Turbulent Modern Middle East*. Carol Stream, IL: Tyndale House Publishers, 2021.

90 Ali Younes, 'Israel to Open Office for Renewable Energy in Abu Dhabi', *Al Jazeera*, 27 November 2015, www.aljazeera.com/news/2015/11/27/israel-to-open-office-for-renewable-energy-in-abu-dhabi.

91 Nissar Hoath, 'Security Expo Closes with Mega Contracts', Emirates 24/7, 5 March 2008, www.emirates247.com/eb247/news/security-expo-closes-with-mega-contracts-2008-03-05-1.214771.

92 UPI, 'Emirates "has Security Links with Israel"', 27 January 2012, www.upi.com/Defense-News/2012/01/27/Emirates-has-security-links-with-Israel/73471327687767/.

93 Rori Donaghy, 'Falcon Eye: The Israeli-Installed Mass Civil Surveillance System of Abu Dhabi', *Middle East Eye*, 28 February 2015.

94 Tony Blair Institute for Global Change, 'Assessing Israel's Trade with its Arab Neighbours', August 2018, https://institute.global/advisory/assessing-israels-trade-its-arab-neighbours

95 Ian Black, 'Just Below the Surface: Israel, the Arab Gulf States and the Limits of Cooperation', LSE Middle East Centre, 13, http://eprints.lse.ac.uk/100313/7/JustBelowtheSurface.pdf

96 Dana Priest, Craig Timberg and Souad Mekhennet, 'Private Israeli Spyware Used to Hack Cellphones of Journalists, Activists Worldwide', *The Washington Post*, 18 July 2021, www.washingtonpost.com/investigations/interactive/2021/nso-spyware-pegasus-cellphones/

97 CTech, 'Israel Defence Ministry Slashes Cyber Export List, Drops Saudi Arabia, UAE', 25 November 2021, www.calcalistech.com/ctech/articles/0,7340,L-3923361,00.html

98 Die Welt, 'UN Panel: Israel Annexation of West Bank 'Violates International Law', 16 June 2020, www.dw.com/en/un-panel-israel-annexation-of-west-bank-violates-international-law/a-53830668

99 Martin Indyk, Twitter, 24 October 2020, https://twitter.com/Martin_Indyk/status/1320072707833270274

100 Neri Zilber, 'The Talented Mr Dahlan', *New Lines Magazine*, 11 November 2020, https://newlinesmag.com/reportage/the-talented-mr-dahlan/

101 Jack Khoury and Noa Landau, 'Palestinians Slam "Betrayal" by UAE in Deal with Israel: "Reward of the Occupation's Crimes"', *Haaretz*, 13 August 2020, www.haaretz.com/israel-news/.premium-plo-official-lashes-out-at-uae-for-selling-out-palestinians-in-israel-agreement-1.9071095

102 Hadeel Al Sayegh and Steven Scheer, 'Israeli Tech's "Thirst" for UAE Cash Must Overcome Old Enmity', *Reuters*, 27 August 2020, www.reuters.com/article/us-israel-emirates-investment-idUSKBN25N0PN

103 Andrew England and Simeon Kerr, 'The Abu Dhabi Royal at the Heart of UAE Business and National Security', *Financial Times*, 25 January 2021, www.ft.com/content/ce09911b-041d-4651-9bbb-d2a16d39ede7

104 Arab News, 'UAE Sets up $10 Billion Fund to Invest in Israel', 11 March 2021, www.arabnews.com/node/1823961/middle-east

105 Barak Ravid, 'Scoop: Saudis Tried to Stop UAE-Israel-Jordan Solar Energy Deal', *Axios*, 24 November 2021, www.axios.com/saudis-uae-solar-farm-israel-d836a165-b901-4cc7-a929-377555784ec6.html

106 Ibid.

107 Author's interview with Sir William Patey, 18 November 2021.

108 F. Gregory Gause III, 'Beyond Sectarianism: The New Middle East Cold War', Brookings Doha Center Analysis Paper 11, July 2014, www.brookings.edu/wp-content/uploads/2016/06/english-pdf-1.pdf

109 Christopher Phillips, 'Gulf Actors and the Syria Crisis', in *The New Politics of Intervention of Gulf Arab States,* Middle East Centre, London School of Economics, 2015: 45, http://eprints.lse.ac.uk/61772/

110 Ibid.

111 Amena Bakr, 'Defying Allies, Qatar Unlikely to Abandon Favored Syrian Rebels', *Reuters*, 20 March 2014, www.reuters.com/article/instant-article/idusbrea2j0wm20140320

112 William McCants, 'Gulf Charities and Syrian Sectarianism', *Foreign Policy*, 30 September 2013, https://foreignpolicy.com/2013/09/30/gulf-charities-and-syrian-sectarianism/

113 Abdulrahman al-Rashid, 'Saudi Boots on the Ground in Syria?', *Al Arabiya News*, 6 February 2016, https://english.alarabiya.net/views/news/middle-east/2016/02/06/Saudi-Arabian-boots-on-the-ground-in-Syria-

114 Dahlia Nehme, 'Syrians on Haj Pray for Peace; Damascus Says Riyadh Plays Politics', *Reuters*, 8 September 2016, www.reuters.com/article/us-saudi-haj-syrians-idUSKCN11E2B6

115 Tehran Times, 'MBS Urged Assad to Cut Ties with Iran, Hezbollah: Lebanese MP', 26 August 2018, www.tehrantimes.com/news/426818/MBS-urged-Assad-to-cut-ties-with-Iran-Hezbollah-Lebanese-MP

116 Kenneth Katzman, 'The United Arab Emirates (UAE): Issues for U.S. Policy', CRS Report for Congress, 4 September 2020: 9, https://fas.org/sgp/crs/mideast/RS21852.pdf

117 Ibid.

118 Isabel Debre, 'UAE Minister: US Sanctions on Syria Challenge Rapprochement', *The Washington Post*, 9 March 2021, www.washingtonpost.com/world/middle_east/uae-minister-us-sanctions-on-syria-challenge-rapprochement/2021/03/09/1ca404b2-80ca-11eb-be22-32d331d87530_story.html

119 Reuters, 'Syria's Assad Visits UAE, First Trip to Arab States Since War Began', 19 March 2022, www.reuters.com/world/middle-east/syrian-president-assad-met-dubai-ruler-syrian-presidency-2022-03-18/

120 Brian Lee Davis, 'Appendix: The Qaddafi Regime on Terrorism: A Sampling', *Qaddafi, Terrorism, and the Origins of the U.S. Attacks on Libya*. New York: Praeger, 1990: 183.

121 The Irish Times, 'Libya "Plotted to Kill" Saudi Crown Prince', 31 July 2004, www.irishtimes.com/news/libya-plotted-to-kill-saudi-crown-prince-1.986510

122 The Sunday Morning Herald, 'Libya's Gaddafi Hurls Insults at Saudi King', 31 March 2009, www.smh.com.au/world/libyas-gaddafi-hurls-insults-at-saudi-king-20141031-9h9r.html

123 Alarabiya News, 'Gaddafi, Extremist Preacher Discuss Going After Saudi Wealth, Oil in Leaked Recording', 25 June 2020, https://english.alarabiya.net/features/2020/06/25/Gaddafi-extremist-preacher-discuss-going-after-Saudi-wealth-oil-in-leaked-recording

124 Ibid.

125 A Conversation with H.E. Motaz Zahran, Ambassador of Egypt to the United States, Arab Gulf States Institute in Washington, 11 March 2021, https://agsiw.org/programs/a-conversation-with-h-e-motaz-zahran-ambassador-of-egypt-to-the-united-states/

126 Jared Malsin and Summer Said, 'Saudi Arabia Promised Support to Libyan Warlord in Push to Seize Tripoli', *The Wall Street Journal*, 12 April 2019, www.wsj.com/articles/saudi-arabia-promised-support-to-libyan-warlord-in-push-to-seize-tripoli-11555077600

127 United Nations Security Council, 'Letter Dated 113 January 2021 from the Panel of Experts on the Sudan Addressed to the President of the Security Council', 13 January 2021: 23, https://undocs.org/S/2021/40

128 Andrew England and Simeon Kerr, 'The Abu Dhabi Royal at the Nexus of UAE Business and National Security', *Financial Times*, 25 January 2021, www.ft.com/content/ce09911b-041d-4651-9bbb-d2a16d39ede7

129 U.S. Department of Defense, 'East Africa Counterterrorism Operation: North and West Africa Counterterrorism Operation', Lead Inspector General Report to the United States Congress, 1 July 2020–30, September 2020: 36, https://media.defense.gov/2020/Nov/25/2002541626/-1/-1/1/LEAD%20 IG%20EAST%20AFRICA%20AND%20NORTH%20AND%20WEST%20 AFRICA%20COUNTERTERRORISM%20OPERATIONS.PDF.

130 Frederic Wehrey, 'This Is Disunity', *The Burning Shores: Inside the Battle for the New Libya*. New York: Farrar, Straus and Giroux, 2018: 194

131 Declan Walsh, 'In Stunning Reversal, Turkey Emerges as Libyan Kingmaker', *The New York Times*, 18 June 2020, www.nytimes.com/2020/05/21/world/middleeast/libya-turkey-russia-hifter.html

132 Isabel Debre, 'Pentagon Report: Turkey Sent up to 3,800 Fighters to Libya', *AP News*, 18 July 2020, https://apnews.com/article/c339f71bf029f36b1091ee31c9f0171a

133 An attempted EU Operation Irini inspection of a Turkish vessel suspected of carrying military equipment had to aborted on 24 November 2020 due to tacit consent being required to board a ship, as required under international law.

134 International Crisis Group, 'Foreign Actors Drive Military Build-Up amid Deadlocked Political Talks', 24 December 2020, www.crisisgroup.org/middle-east-north-africa/north-africa/libya/crisis-group-libya-update-2

135 U.S. Department of Defense, 'East Africa Counterterrorism Operation': 37.

136 Brian Katz, 'Moscow's Next Front: Russia's Expanding Military Footprint in Libya', Center for Strategic and International Studies, 17 June 2020, www.csis.org/analysis/moscows-next-front-russias-expanding-military-footprint-libya

137 Amy Mackinnon and Jack Detsch, 'Pentagon Says UAE Possibly Funding Russia's Shadowy Mercenaries in Libya', *Foreign Policy*, 30 November 2020, https://foreignpolicy.com/2020/11/30/pentagon-trump-russia-libya-uae/

138 Neil Partrick, 'Saudi Arabia and Yemen', in Neil Patrick (ed.), *Saudi Arabian Foreign Policy: Conflict and Cooperation*. London: I. B. Tauris: 250.

139 Mohammed Aly Sergie, Summer Said and Margaret Coker, 'Saudi Raids Persist, Aiding Yemeni Fight', *Wall Street Journal*, 6 November 2009, www.wsj.com/articles/SB125755652567935179

140 Christopher Boucek, 'Operation Scorched Earth', *Yemen: On the Brink: War in Saada: From Local Insurrection to National Challenge*, Carnegie Endowment for International Peace Middle East Program Number 110, April 2010, 9, https://carnegieendowment.org/files/war_in_saada.pdf

141 UN, 'Agreement on the Implementation Mechanism for the Transition Process in Yemen in Accordance with the Initiative of the Gulf Cooperation Council (GCC)', 5 December 2011, https://peacemaker.un.org/sites/peacemaker.un.org/files/ YE_111205_Agreement%20on%20the%20implementation%20mechanism%20 for%20the%20transition.pdf

142 Gerald M. Feierstein, 'The United States–Saudi Arabian Relationship', 97th Middle East Policy Council Conference on Capitol Hill, 19 July 2019, https:// mepc.org/hill-forums/united-states-saudi-arabian-relationship

143 International Institute of Strategic Studies, 'Yemen', *Iran's Network of Influence in the Middle East*, November 2019, 159–178, www.iiss.org/publications/ strategic-dossiers/iran-dossier/iran-19-07-ch-5-yemen

144 Peter Salisbury, 'Risk Perception and Appetite in UAE Foreign and National Security Policy', Chatham House, 1 July 2020, www.chathamhouse.org/2020/07/ risk-perception-and-appetite-uae-foreign-and-national-security-policy-0/8-case-study-uae

145 NBC News, 'Yemen Crisis: Saudi Arabia Masses 150,000 Troops to Support Airstrikes', 26 March 2015, www.nbcnews.com/news/world/saudi-arabia-masses-150-000-troops-support-airstrikes-yemen-n330416

146 Interview with Michael Knights, 25 May 2021.

147 Reuters Staff, 'Factbox: Saudi-Led Coalition Against Yemen's Houthis', *Reuters*, 10 April 2015, www.reuters.com/article/us-yemen-security-coalition-factbox-idUSKBN0N11F220150410

148 Michael Knights, 'Lessons from the UAE War in Yemen', *Lawfare*, 18 August 2019, www.lawfareblog.com/lessons-uae-war-yemen

149 Michael Knights and Alex Almeida, 'The Saudi–UAE War Effort in Yemen (Part 1): Operation Golden Arrow in Aden', Washington Institute for Near East Policy, PolicyWatch 2464, 10 August 2015, www.washingtoninstitute.org/ policy-analysis/saudi-uae-war-effort-yemen-part-1-operation-golden-arrow-aden

150 Reuters Staff, 'Houthi Shelling Kills Seven in Saudi Arabia, Nine Yemenis Die in Air Strike', *Reuters*, 16 August 2016, www.reuters.com/article/us-yemen-security-idUSKCN10R17K

151 Leith Aboufadel, 'Houthi Missile Attack Kills 50+ Saudi Soldiers in Najran', *Al Masdar News*, 21 August 2016, www.almasdarnews.com/article/houthi-missile-attack-kills-50-saudi-soldiers-najran/

152 Middle East Monitor, 'Houthis Capture Military Base in Saudi Arabia', 11 May 2017, www.middleeastmonitor.com/20170511-houthis-capture-military-base-in-saudi-arabia/

153 Iran Daily, 'Yemen Targets Saudi Oil Refinery with Ballistic Missile', 23 July 2017, www.iran-daily.com/News/197125.html?catid=9&title=197125

154 Tim Lister, Ammar Albadran, Hakim Al-Masmari, Sarah El Sirgany and Eric Levenson, 'Saudi Arabia Intercepts Ballistic Missile Over Capital', *CNN*, 5 November 2017, https://edition.cnn.com/2017/11/04/middleeast/saudi-arabia-ballistic-missile/index.html

155 Michael Knights and Alex Almeida, 'The Saudi–UAE War Effort in Yemen (Part 2): The Air Campaign', Washington Institute for Near East Policy,

PolicyWatch 2465, 11 August 2015, www.washingtoninstitute.org/policy-analysis/saudi-uae-war-effort-yemen-part-2-air-campaign

156 Selam Gebrekidan and Jonathan Saul, 'In Blocking Arms to Yemen, Saudi Arabia Squeezes a Starving Population', *Reuters*, 11 October 2017, www.reuters.com/investigates/special-report/yemen-saudi-blockade/

157 UNICEF, 'United Nations Leaders Call on the Saudi-Led Coalition to Fully Lift Blockade of Yemeni Red Sea Ports', 2 December 2017, www.unicef.org/press-releases/united-nations-leaders-call-saudi-led-coalition-fully-lift-blockade-yemeni-red-sea

158 UN Security Council, 'Letter Dated 26 January 2018 from the Panel of Experts on Yemen Mandated by the Security Council Resolution 2342 (2017) Addressed to the President of the Security Council', 26 January 2018: 3, https://reliefweb.int/sites/reliefweb.int/files/resources/N1800513.pdf

159 Aziz Yaakoubi, 'End of Yemen Quagmire? Saudi-Led Coalition, Houthis Near Peace Deal', *Reuters*, 21 June 2021, www.reuters.com/world/middle-east/end-yemen-quagmire-saudi-led-coalition-houthis-near-peace-deal-2021-06-21/

160 Feierstein, 'The United States–Saudi Arabian Relationship'.

161 Ibrahim Jalal, 'The UAE May Have Withdrawn from Yemen, but Its Influence Remains Strong', Middle East Institute, 25 February 2020, www.mei.edu/publications/uae-may-have-withdrawn-yemen-its-influence-remains-strong

162 Interview with Gerald M. Feierstein, 23 April 2021.

163 Council on Foreign Relations, 'A Conversation with Anwar Gargash'.

164 Ibid.

165 Marc Owen Jones, 'Disinformation Superspreaders: the Weaponisation of Covid-19 Fake News in the Persian Gulf and Beyond', *Global Discourse*, 10 (4), November 2020: 431–437.

6

United States: partisan politics, carte blanche and policy variation

Introduction

In the following sections, which concentrate on the history of US–Arab Gulf relations and Saudi, UAE and US relations during the Obama, Trump and Biden administrations, a detailed picture is built up about the extent to which US policy, including uncertainty, has conditioned Saudi and UAE foreign policy. At the political level, differences in US policy have become discernible between pro-business Republicans, who tend to favour large arms-sales contracts, Saudi Arabia's central position as a swing producer in OPEC and its financial clout, and Democrats, who have tended to be more circumspect on human rights, Middle East conflicts and US arms sales.[1] There is also a structural issue in US policy about the extent to which Saudi Arabia still represents vital US interests or petro-alignment in terms of it being a swing producer in OPEC. As Robert Vitalis notes, the oil-for-security bargain is based on a myth of scarcity and how moving beyond fossil fuels will have major implications for the US–Saudi relationship going forward.[2]

Special relations have developed between the US and Saudi Arabia since formal diplomatic relations were established in 1933 and a Mutual Defense Assistance Agreement in 1951 provided a bulwark in the Arab Gulf against Soviet influence.[3] They have been based on the formation of the Arabia American Oil Company (Aramco), which became strategic in searching for oil from the 1940s onwards, but also the way the profits were split 50/50, enhancing Saudi economic power. Relations became more functional at the political level after an important meeting took place between President Franklin D. Roosevelt and King Abdulaziz on the Great Bitter Lake in Egypt on 11 February 1945. This meeting focused on Palestine, post-war independence for Lebanon and Syria, and agricultural development in Saudi Arabia.[4] Relations would build on shared global interests against Soviet influence during the Cold War in the warm waters of the Gulf and Indian Ocean and in Afghanistan.

The withdrawal of the British in 1971 was addressed by the Nixon Doctrine – arms and political support to selected allies to protect core US interests. Saudi Arabia and Iran became part of the 'Twin Pillars' policy, which also accounted for a greater US presence in the Gulf in diplomatic terms, but not in military terms. Although there were tensions in the 1980s over sales of the airborne warning and control system (AWACS) and lack of progress on Arab–Israeli peace,[5] relations have continued to develop in a relatively consistent manner. Bilateral relations continued to be close during the 1960s, when Saudi Arabia and the US cooperated to support the North Yemen Arab Republic with a trilateral military assistance programme (e.g. F-5s), paid for by the Saudi government, although early on in the North Yemen Civil War the Kennedy administration preferred to remain on good terms with Egypt's Nasser and his policy of Arab nationalism to preserve its interests in the Middle East.[6] The 1973 oil crisis underscored at once Saudi Arabia's global interest in the oil market versus its regional interest, and US interest in negotiating disengagement of the key protagonists in the Yom Kippur/Ramadan War through Henry Kissinger's 'shuttle diplomacy'.[7]

US–Saudi relations post-1979

Saudi and US threat perception increased markedly by the end of 1979: the Marxist coup in Afghanistan in 1978, followed by the Soviet invasion in December 1979; the Iranian Revolution, which removed the pro-American Shah; and the Second Yemenite War laid the foundations for the reassertion of US influence in the Middle East. The Carter Doctrine in 1980 stated that the US would use force if necessary to defend its national interests in the Gulf. The US quickly sent AWACS to Saudi Arabia. The intensity and severity of the threats being faced by the Carter administration, especially with US hostages on the line, kept the Gulf in the spotlight at the White House. The Three Mile Island nuclear meltdown, also in 1979, affected US energy calculations as the US became more dependent on the Arab Gulf states for oil imports. US Central Command (CENTCOM) was established in Florida in 1983.

Thus, US and Saudi policy continued to dovetail throughout the 1980s and 1990s. The model of US assistance, underwritten by Saudi Arabia, was replicated in other Cold War theatres, notably in Afghanistan in support of the Afghan resistance to the Soviet occupation. The Saudis are said to have given nearly $4 billion in aid to the *mujahideen* between 1980 and 1990, not including aid from Islamic charities, foundations or private donors.[8]

Cooperation has extended beyond these actions. The US and Saudi Arabia mainly supported Iraq against Iran during the Iran–Iraq War from 1980 to 1988, with US military aid leaving Iraq as the fourth-largest military in the world by the end of the war. Covert CIA operations have been funded with Saudi petrodollars, such as the Iran–Contra affair in which Prince Bandar played a key role. He also consulted with President Mikhail Gorbachev to secure Soviet withdrawal from Afghanistan, helped to negotiate an end to the Iran–Iraq War and, along with Nelson Mandela, is said to have resolved the diplomatic crisis resulting from the bombing of Pan Am Flight 103 over Lockerbie in 1988.[9]

The GCC's inability to address chronic and persistent insecurity in the Gulf has sustained a GCC-state reliance on US security guarantees. These have not been without cost, since dual containment policies pursued by the, US coupled with US bases and deployments in the Gulf and Central Asia, have contributed to the notion that Iran is encircled, have Iranian responses in turn and have contributed to offensive realist assumptions as well as a security dilemma. More than 500,000 US troops were deployed to Saudi Arabia as part of Operation Desert Shield from 1990 in case Iraqi troops attacked the kingdom. Their mission was to protect the Saudi oil fields and to use Saudi territory to drive Saddam's forces out of Kuwait. But, after the conflict, about 5,000 US combat troops and air crews remained in the kingdom to enforce the containment of Iraq through a 'no-fly zone', utilising at least seven bases.[10]

The presence of US forces was one of Osama Bin Laden's key issues, and contributed to a rallying cry against the Al Saud and recruitment into Al Qaeda.[11] US presence on Saudi territory was one of the stated motivations for Al Qaeda's attacks, including a 1995 car-bomb attack which killed seven, including five US servicemen, and the June 1996 bomb attack on the Khobar Towers in Dharan, where nineteen US servicemen were killed and 400 injured. US–Saudi relations were clearly strained after 9/11, when fifteen of the nineteen hijackers were found to be Saudi citizens. The 9/11 attacks enhanced the security focus on the kingdom, re-emphasised regime legitimacy and national security and increased the Al Saud's willingness to engage with the US (by offering its territory and bases for their use) and by cooperating with other partners on counterterrorism. Yet there has been a post-9/11 legacy of a gap between official policy and limited social support for attacks on US forces in Afghanistan and Iraq[12] and/or funding transfers to proscribed groups.[13]

The US has exerted pressure on the kingdom to shut down charities and organisations that could be responsible for channelling funds to terror groups. Saudi imams became state regulated, and attention was paid to textbooks.

After 9/11 then Crown Prince Abdullah refused President G. W. Bush's requests for a summit, threatened a break in relations and even hinted at the use of the oil weapon.[14] The G. W. Bush and Obama administrations were both in intense dialogues with the Saudis on private funds which make their way to terror groups. This continues to be a grey area and an irritant in the bilateral relationship.[15] The relationship at this time was salvaged only by President G. W. Bush's promise to support a two-state solution, including King Abdullah's Arab Peace Plan in 2002, in the middle of the second Palestinian Intifada. After 9/11, the US sought to broaden out Task Force 150, which served as part of CENTCOM, to encourage multilateralism and burden sharing under Combined Task Force (CTF) 150, aimed at interdicting suspect shipping in the Gulf, North Arabian Sea and in the Horn of Africa pursuant to the Global War on Terror. This task force was joined by CTF 151 (counter-piracy) in 2009 and CTF 152 (Gulf maritime security), established in 2004, with the aim of upholding the international rules-based order.

The UAE response to 9/11 was robust and with clear intentions towards upholding and strengthening its relations with the US. The UAE deployed peacekeeping and special operations troops in the Kosovo Force, where it has played both a humanitarian and development role.[16] For more than a decade from 2001, UAE special forces fought alongside US and coalition soliders in Afghanistan, supported by some of the six Boeing C-17 Globemaster IIIs, a large military transport aircraft, and four Lockheed C-130 Hercules sold to it by the US. In 2011 the UAE participated in air force sorties over Libya, and has participated in the Global Coalition against ISIS in Syria. UAE forces have also deployed to Yemen from 2015 to 2020. The UAE hosts the Gulf Warfare Center, Al Dhafra air base, which it operates with CENTCOM and which is home to 3,800 US military personnel, and an Integrated Air and Missile Defence Center at Al Bateen air base. Called 'Little Sparta' by former secretary of defense James Mattis for its military skills, commitment and preparedness,[17] the UAE long-term mission appears to be to build up military experience (including urban warfare, amphibious landings and precision-,strike operations as seen in Yemen for example) and the level of military competence and capability. In some ways the UAE military now approaches the capabilities of a first-rank military.

As the US signalled its withdrawal of US troops from the kingdom in April 2003, from 5,000 to 400,[18] Al Qaeda's insurgency began and struck at the heart of the Saudi government's efforts to counter such groups. In the lead-up to the US-led intervention in Iraq in 2003, the Saudis warned the US that it would be seen as an act of aggression. There was also friction over the US effectively handing Iran the advantage in Iraq, and to some extent subsequently in Syria.

The Obama administration

The Obama administration created a new crisis for Saudi Arabia and the UAE by supporting regime change in Egypt in 2011. The situation became even more serious during the crisis in Bahrain, whereby it risked US–Saudi relations, Saudi oil cooperation and access to its Bahrain base. The situation was salvaged by President Obama backtracking on the US reform agenda in that case. Further irritants included President Obama's pursuit of the JCPOA within the P5+1 (the permanent five members of the UN Security Council plus Germany)–Iran framework first set up during the G. W. Bush administration in 2006. This was done without adequate coordination with the GCC states, due to fears that it would face resistance. To secure their assent once the deal was ready, President Obama considered designating Saudi Arabia, the UAE, Oman and Qatar as Major Non-NATO allies in 2015, but this was not actioned.

As one former senior UK official noted, the Saudi view was incompatible with the JCPOA deal, the US was already signalling its retreat from the Middle East and it was impossible to broaden out the JCPOA to include aspects such as Iran's regional behaviour or its missile programme.[19] That view, surprisingly, is not universally held, including by a former US ambassador to Saudi Arabia. Dr Joseph W. Westphal said 'I do think they [the Saudis] should have been better informed [on the JCPOA]', that the US should have negotiated a broader agreement and that it could have involved a peace agreement on Yemen.[20] Although Dr Westphal was not party to the JCPOA negotiations and recognises that it would have been 'absolutely a tough sell', this does raise interesting possibilities, not least for a deal on Yemen and the JCPOA negotiations under way in 2021.[21]

The extent of the covert talks and the concession of not forcing Iran to suspend the enrichment of uranium, in line with IAEA demands, was what Suzanne Maloney, vice president and director of foreign policy at the Brookings Institution, called a 'poison pill' for Israel and others across the region, due to their fears of a possible rapprochement.[22] In response the Obama administration's diplomacy with Iran, King Salman and other Gulf leaders snubbed President Obama's Camp David summit in May 2015.[23] As Ben Rhodes, former deputy national security advisor in the Obama administration, has noted, 'MbZ [Mohammed bin Zayed] and MbS [Mohammed bin Salman] were ascendant voices in the Gulf, and they didn't care for Obama or his policies. He was someone to be tolerated and waited out.'[24]

Obama administration support for the Saudi-led intervention in Yemen has given way to rising frustration on both sides. Saudi Arabia has recognised social, economic and political differences as well as unfavourable public polling figures and has invested in broad-based lobbying activities in the

US. In 2016, the US Congress passed the Justice Against Sponsors of Terrorism Act (JASTA) and overrode President Obama's veto, allowing the families of 9/11 victims to sue the kingdom. Seven major court cases are under way and the UAE is also being sued. These legal actions place limits on Saudi Arabia floating companies on the US stock exchanges, such as Aramco on the New York Stock Exchange, because it could potentially lose control of those companies if a US judge were to award a plaintiff a massive fine which the kingdom failed to pay.[25] This is a particularly sensitive area because, as part of Vision 2030, Saudi Arabia needs to realise investment opportunities and raise funds from US stock markets to sustain economic growth. In response, the kingdom has gone to extraordinary lengths by paying US veterans to lobby Congress against adapting a law allowing 9/11 families to sue the kingdom.[26]

The Trump administration

The US–UAE relationship has been rooted in close military–military contact, but also expanding political–military ties, and the UAE has shown adeptness at navigating the halls of power in Washington, DC. A high-water mark was achieved by lobbying President Trump to accept Mohammed bin Salman as a reformer in Saudi Arabia and in isolating Qatar. President Trump could have continued his predecessor's policies, including in building on the JCPOA and a dialogue on regional security with Iran. He could also have adopted the hawkish stance of Hillary Clinton towards Saudi Arabia and Qatar. As a presidential candidate in 2016 she noted that 'we need to use our diplomatic and more traditional intelligence assets to bring pressure on the governments of Qatar and Saudi Arabia, which are providing clandestine financial and logistical support to ISIL and other radical Sunni groups in the region'.[27] Instead, he drew a line under the Obama era, primarily by withdrawing the US from the JCPOA in 2018, and adopted a hawkish 'maximum pressure' policy against Iran in 2019 which would end up costing the Iranian economy $1 trillion.[28] His administration undermined the two-state solution and adopted a nonchalant attitude towards international concerns such as human rights, arms sales and the transfer of nuclear power technology. Unusually, there was no US ambassador installed in Saudi Arabia from 8 January 2017 to 17 April 2019, when Christopher Henzel was chargé d'affaires ad interim.[29] Instead, US–Saudi relations during this time were conducted primarily through the personal relations of Jared Kushner, President Trump's son-in-law, and Mohammed bin Salman.[30]

President Trump gave a clear indication of pursuing a preferential or 'blank cheque' policy towards Saudi Arabia, tweeting in November 2017:

'I have great confidence in King Salman and the Crown Prince of Saudi Arabia, they know exactly what they are doing' and 'Some of those they are harshly treating have been "milking" their country for years!'[31] President Trump's first overseas trip was to Saudi Arabia, where he had one bilateral meeting with the Saudis in which he signed a $110 billion arms deal, was honoured with the Collar of Abdulaziz Al Saud and visited the National Museum of Saudi Arabia. But according to Bruce Riedel, senior advisor on South Asia and the Middle East to four US presidents, the headline-grabbing arms deal was simply a wish list of potential arms sales, some of which the Saudis were interested in, but for which no contract existed and which was not mentioned in joint statements.[32] Furthermore, there was no notification to the Department of State or the Senate.

In May 2019, President Trump invoked emergency authority codified in the Arms Export Control Act, citing 'the need to deter further Iranian adventurism in the Gulf and throughout the Middle East', to offer the UAE immediate sales of precision-guided missiles worth $1 billion. The same month, the State Department approved the sale to the UAE of the Blackjack UAV, valued at around $80 million, also under the emergency notification. The Trump administration sold up to eighteen MQ-9 Reapers to the UAE in 2020, the first American transfer of lethal unmanned aerial systems to an Arab ally.[33] This sale was suspended in January 2021, subject to review under the Biden administration. One of the most consequential pieces of technology which the UAE did import from the US was the EA-18 Growler, which is the US navy's newest attack aircraft and integrates the latest electronic attack technology, including jamming pods, communication countermeasures and satellite communications.[34] It would be a useful tool in the UAE's arsenal against Iran, in particular.

The then national security advisor, Michael Flynn, initially encouraged US nuclear technology transfer to Saudi Arabia without safeguards.[35] The US could have been in contravention of Article 3 of the Non-Proliferation Treaty (NPT), had such a transfer(s) taken place. Unlike the UAE, the kingdom lacks a Section 123 Agreement with the US over its nuclear power plans. Whether or not the kingdom will sign up to a Section 123 Agreement is uncertain. Some Asian states have said it would be 'helpful' when considering civil nuclear cooperation with the kingdom,[36] but no states are in a position to push the US on this.

During his trip, President Trump also attended one multilateral meeting of the GCC and one multilateral meeting of the OIC, after which he opened a Global Center for Combating Extremist Ideology.[37] Given that his visit was quickly followed by the onset of a more serious Qatar Crisis in 2017, it is clear that Saudi Arabia and the UAE joined Israel in being given carte blanche over regional matters, including and beyond Iran, and supported them by undermining secretary of state Tillerson and his attempts to draw the Qatar Crisis to an early end.[38] The Trump presidency therefore represented a high-water mark of disruptive foreign policies, often favouring the foreign policy objectives of Saudi Arabia and the UAE. The narrow interests at play, working at cross purposes within the US administration, were successful only in contributing to regional instability. MESA, established in 2017, could have been a step towards addressing Obama-era 'free rider' concerns and building a broader-based alliance with regional security utility, but the perception of it as being premised on an anti-Iranian agenda has caused it to falter.

The inability of the Saudis to dominate in the Yemen conflict and the assassination of Jamal Khashoggi in the Saudi embassy, Istanbul on 2 October 2018 did not sway the Trump administration. Indeed, when Mohammed bin Salman renewed calls for US support after a Houthi missile was intercepted over Riyadh in December 2017, a small team of US Green Berets were sent to help locate and destroy training sites and caches of Houthi missiles.[39] Saudi Arabia has employed its US-trained military, US arms, US logistical assistance and intelligence in Yemen.[40] Unlike President Biden, who as a presidential candidate labelled the ruling Saudi monarchy a 'pariah',[41] President Trump took a different perspective and protected Mohammed bin Salman from congressional scrutiny and bypassed Congress to sell more arms to Saudi Arabia and the UAE.[42] Despite US intelligence concluding that Mohammed bin Salman probably approved the operation against Khashoggi, the US chose not to sanction the crown prince directly in case it put the US in a 'hostile' position vis-à-vis the kingdom.[43]

Saudi Arabia's image in the US took another knock in December 2019 when Royal Saudi Air Force (RSAF) Lieutenant Al-Shamrani killed three people and wounded eight in a shooting spree at the Pensacola Naval Air Station. He was later found to have been a long-term Al Qaeda operative, who joined the RSAF in 2015 with the aim of conducting such an attack,[44] although this case, as one which was self-directed and enabled by Al Qaeda, appears to differ from many which involve direction by groups such as Al Qaeda or inspiration by online jihadist ideology.[45] According to a JASTA lawsuit, Saudi Arabia knew of Al-Shamrani's radicalisation and anti-American sentiments and did not act.[46] In response, then US attorney general William Barr, deported twenty-one Saudi military cadets said to have been found with jihadist material and indecent images of children in their possession.[47]

This raises the issue of people-to-people connections. After 9/11, King Abdullah and President Bush established a major scholarship programme, the Saudi Arabian Cultural Mission Scholarship Fund, to boost people-to-people connections, including cultural connections, and the numbers of Saudi students studying in the US. In 2006–7 there were 3,035 Saudi students studying in the US, a 129 per cent increase from the year before.[48] This number rose to 61,287 in 2016–17 or twenty times higher than 2006–7.[49] But by 2017, Trump's immigration policies, the rising value of the US dollar and the Saudi Arabian government's decision in early 2016 to cut back on scholarships abroad meant that numbers fell by almost half in 2018–19, to 37,080.[50] Saudi scholarships are still offered, but the range of countries where Saudis are now studying has increased considerably, whilst the kingdom also aims to attract outstanding scholars from around the world to its universities.

There was no US military response to the attacks on Abqaiq and Khurais oil installations in 2019, although the US did later deploy Patriot missiles and troops temporarily in the kingdom. The US also launched Operation Sentinel, comprising small naval vessels with air support to protect shipping in the Gulf in November 2019 amid rising tensions. The US military package for the kingdom was withdrawn in September 2021, leaving Riyadh to seek support from other countries such as Russia, albeit perhaps only temporarily and with signalling to Washington a key motivation. The Terminal High-Altitude Area Defense System (THAAD), part of a $15 billion agreement signed in October 2017 which will be delivered to the kingdom around 2023, will enable the kingdom to target intercontinental ballistic missiles.[51] But the greatest threat is bound to remain regional, where hardware such as Patriot missiles will continue to be vital, and where an integrated air and missile defence system in the GCC states is still lacking.

US–Saudi shared interests encompass economic, energy,[52] political and defence and security elements. Bilateral trade in 2019 was $38.7 billion, with approximately two-thirds being US exports to the kingdom.[53] Leading export categories include aircraft, vehicles, machinery and arms.[54] Arms sales are facilitated by the Pentagon's US Training Mission to Saudi Arabia, intelligence sharing and emerging concerns in the cyber domain. The Technical Cooperation Agreement between the US and Saudi Arabia, signed on 15 May 2008, signalled a shift towards greater US support for Saudi critical infrastructure. US arms sales to Saudi Arabia reached $64.1 billion between 2015 and 2020, or around $10 billion per year, with $3 billion worth of arms transferred in the five years before 2015.[55] Saudi and UAE investments are also important to the US jobs and the economy, for example in companies such as Uber, Magic Leap or in film production firms such as William Morris Endeavour Entertainment LLC.[56]

In recent years US oil and gas fracking has made it relatively independent from Saudi Arabia and the UAE for energy supplies, but the US still imports about 5 million barrels per day, so is still somewhat involved the global energy market. The US can also be impacted upon by disruption of international oil, and indeed other, supplies. Evidence has come to light that suggests President Trump did take pre-emptive steps on 2 April 2020, which could have seriously undermined the bilateral relationship, by threatening Mohammed bin Salman with the withdrawal of US troops from the kingdom if he did not take action on OPEC pricing which was affecting the US fracking industry.[57] Such crises highlight some of the red lines in the bilateral relationship, but also its resilience. Saudi Arabia still retains ownership of the largest refinery in the US, in Port Arthur, Texas. Aramco has exclusive rights to sell Shell-branded gasoline and diesel in Georgia, North Carolina, South Carolina, Virginia, Maryland, most of Florida and in eastern Texas.[58]

On 14 October 2020 both parties implemented a Strategic Dialogue, seventy-five years after President Roosevelt met King Abulaziz Al Saud aboard the *USS Quincy*, laying the groundwork for the bilateral relationship to develop.[59] The kingdom continues to be a valuable US partner across a host of US priorities, including those outlined by CENTCOM: deterring Iran, countering violent extremist organisations in Afghanistan, Iraq, Syria and Yemen, taking into account strategic competition with China and the 'destabilizing influence of Russia', developing regional partnerships and COVID-19-related interventions.[60]

The Biden administration

Even before President Biden's inauguration day, and partly in response to reputation damage, Saudi Arabia was modifying its foreign policy by reaching out to Turkey, Qatar and Iran. The kingdom will drop a ban on Turkish goods, overtly resolved the Qatar Crisis by inviting Qatar to the GCC summit in Al Ula in January 2021 and, in the face of the Biden administration's return to talks on the JCPOA, has since engaged in a series of talks with Iran. The speed of these foreign policy U-turns has been incredible. One of the first measures which the Biden administration took towards Saudi Arabia and the UAE, as part of the transfer of power but also in line with congressional support to slow or limit arms sales to the kingdom, was to suspend US arms sales. Sales to the UAE were quickly resumed in April 2021, although US participation at IDEX 2021, the UAE's international defence exhibition, was notably low key.

The UAE trades with all fifty US states, with bilateral trade standing at $17.83 billion in 2020.[61] Electronics imports was a leading category and counted for $2.58 billion or 17 per cent of trade, followed by passenger vehicles, aircraft and spacecraft.[62] UAE infrastructure projects also have an impact, specifically the UAE's new railway, civil nuclear energy programme, new airport construction in Abu Dhabi and Dubai and seaport construction.[63] The UAE will continue to ingratiate itself with the Democrats by focusing on secularism, peace efforts and religious tolerance and avoid negative public relations such as that generated by ambassador Yousef Al Otaiba, who was allegedly so angry about Representative Ro Khanna's push to end US support for the Yemen War that he is said to have shouted at him during a meeting.[64] Concentrating on a broader range of common interests might go some way to undoing damage resulting from UAE involvement in the Yemen War and help to address some human rights concerns. Economic cooperation will be paramount to both parties as they implement a rapid recovery from COVID-19. To this end, the UAE added another $17 billion worth of T-bonds (government debt securities issued by the US government) to its stockpile of more than $50 billion in May 2021.[65] This stands in contrast to Saudi Arabia, which has been selling positions through the PIF amounting to a similar figure in order to increase investments domestically.

JASTA, combined with the Yemen War, is making it increasingly difficult to get US arms sales to Saudi Arabia through Congress. Cluster bomb sales were stopped during the Trump administration, and it's possible that precision-guided munitions may be held back in future as well.[66] Indeed, they were almost stopped through bipartisan opposition in 2016, but the move in Congress was just a few votes short.[67] It is unlikely that the suspension of arms sales to Saudi Arabia will remain in place for long, since the US would lose out to the UK, France and China. If the US were to walk away from Saudi Arabia on defence, it 'would send shockwaves around the world'.[68] The Saudi defence architecture is based on US systems, so major changes could compromise Saudi security, whilst the US aim in 2021 was to go 'back to basics' by not pursuing maximal unachievable objectives, and to focus on maintenance and management of alliances and enable allies to defend themselves.[69] The Saudi aim is to take its lobbying efforts to middle America[70] and develop a new digital news platform in the US, with a studio in Washington, DC.[71]

In February 2021, under in the Biden administration, seventy-six Saudi citizens were added to a US list of sanctioned Saudis for their activities against journalists and dissidents abroad.[72] Former deputy Saudi intelligence chief Ahmed al-Asiri is on the list, as is the Saudi Royal Guard's rapid intervention force, also known as the Tiger Squad or Firqat el-Nemr.[73] This group, it is argued in a civil suit filed by Saad Al Jabri in the United States District Court for the District of Columbia, are noted as the personal mercenaries of the crown prince. They are alleged to have been sent to execute Saad Al Jabri where he resides in Canada for what he may know about the royal family, which could undermine Mohammed bin Salman's relations with the White House.[74] One might imagine that these cases reflect a problem for the Biden administration to secure individuals who have contributed to US security whilst maintaining cordial ties with the Al Saud. Bruce Riedel has stated that Prince Nayef 'has exceptional expertise and institutional memory as a leading counterterrorist in the region. He is also America's best friend in the family.'[75] He successfully defeated Al Qaeda in Saudi Arabia, and was responsible for foiling its planned attack over Chicago, President Obama's home town, on the eve of the 2012 presidential election. He was also engaged in countering ISIS, which ultimately seeks to take over Mecca.[76] But ambassador Joseph W. Westphal notes that Nayef's detention is 'ancient history' and that the US can't run the kingdom, but needs to be engaged with it.[77] In a rare move in the Jabri case, the US director of national intelligence made an extraordinary intervention in September 2021, citing US national security interests, in an attempt to prevent the disclosure of classified information[78] which could attract a Saudi response which would be harmful to US interests.

By far the most important arms transfers will be the US facilitating missile defence technology, which is expected to include short- to medium-range Iron Dome and Barak-8 missile defence systems.[79] The US army has been testing this system and its batteries should be available from late 2021.[80] The UAE already has an advanced air defence system incorporating Patriot missiles (which the US used to protect Al Dhafra air base in February 2022), THAAD (which was used to intercept at least one Houthi missile in January 2022), as well as Russian built Pantsir-S1s, which are capable of engaging aircraft, helicopters and UAVs.[81] The integrated UAE air defence systems are said to already cover Bahrain, Qatar and parts of Oman and Saudi Arabia.[82] But large parts of the kingdom remain unprotected and in 2021 experienced high levels of Houthi attacks. In 2021, Saudi Arabia expanded US access to the kingdom's airports and seaports in the west of the country to give CENTCOM more room to operate in a potential war with Iran, reducing exposure in the east of the country as Iran's ballistic missiles improve. The US Naval Forces Central Command launched Task Force 59 in September 2021, aimed at integrating unmanned systems and AI into the Fifth Fleet area of operations. This could also give the US and its allies a competitive advantage in the Gulf, especially vis-à-vis Iran. After the Abraham Accords, there is also more opportunity to involve Israel, at least in joint exercises in the Red Sea if not in Gulf waters specifically.

On 23 September 2021, the House of Representatives passed the FY22 National Defense Authorization Act which included the Protection of Saudi Dissidents Act provision. This imposes temporary limits on US arms to Saudi Arabia and requires various reports and actions related to the death of Jamal Khashoggi.[83] In the summer of 2021 Prince Khalid bin Salman, deputy minister of defence of Saudi Arabia, cut short a trip to Washington, DC after failing to make headway on Saudi air defence. Subsequently, a visit by US secretary of defense, Lloyd Austin, was cancelled in the autumn of 2021, and the kingdom welcomed a Russian politician instead. At the time of writing Biden's policy is to sell defensive weapons: Patriot missiles, THAAD etc., but not offensive weapons or precision-guided missiles. The State Department was set to approve $650 million of advanced medium range air-to-air missiles in November 2021.[84] But there is a grey area, such as spare parts for Saudi aircraft, which the administration has been less clear about. After ending the Trump-era designation of the Houthis as a terrorist organisation, possibly to support a cease-fire and peace talks, the Biden administration was said to be mulling its reclassification in January 2022. This could also be done in the context of improving bilateral US–Saudi relations.

The Biden administration decided to move ahead with the F-35 sale to the UAE, but US security requirements, including restrictions on the use of the warplane and relations with Chinese technology companies such as Huawei, were seen to be too arduous and the UAE suspended talks in December 2021. If the F-35 deal does eventually go through, it will significantly boost UAE defence. It will mean that the UAE air force will likely shed some of its F-16s to Greece[85] and/or possibly to Egypt, as it continues to upgrade its own air capabilities.

The actions taken by the Biden administration have in fact been more nuanced than the rhetoric, but still represent an element of continuation from the Obama administration, especially on the JCPOA, which was not universally welcomed by the kingdom even though the Biden administration has promised to consult more closely with GCC allies this time. Nevertheless, with all the congressional activity, fraught relations have occurred and are already taking a toll on petrol prices at the pump in the US, exacerbated by the main cause which has been the war in Ukraine in 2022. President Biden was rebuffed by Mohammed bin Salman and Mohammed bin Zayed when trying to discuss increases in their respective oil production. Saudi Arabia pointed to the need to maintain the OPEC+ agreement, but the UAE could have moved closer to its OPEC quota sooner. When asked in an interview with *The Atlantic* if President Biden misunderstood things about him, Mohammed bin Salman said 'Simply, I do not care'.[86] That attitude appears to have extended to Saudi TV, with some programmes mocking President Biden during Ramadan 2022. Saudi Arabia and Israel have both offered to mediate between the US and Russia on Ukraine, but, given the kingdom's limited experience in this field and current difficulties with the Biden administration, this may be more a gesture of goodwill. In the mean time, economic linkages such as US electric vehicle maker Lucid Group establishing its first overseas factory in Saudi Arabia may be well placed to drive an improvement to the political context. The next US presidential election, in 2024, will confirm whether there can be continuity under President Biden, which may include a degree of reciprocation and rapprochement, or if a Republican candidate may succeed in upending US Middle East policy once more.

Conclusion

From the earliest contact between the US and Arab Gulf states, there was a clear connection between engagement and the local need for arms and defence in the pursuit of domestic and/or regional interests. This has been a remarkably persistent theme in the evolution of the Gulf States. The chapter has unearthed the role that domestic legislation, political turbulence and domestic policy can play in undermining or advancing trade and security relations. The US–Saudi relationship in particular has experienced numerous periods of cordial and tense relations over many different issues: over Israel–Palestine; oil in the 1970s; military hardware and arms in the 1980s; after 9/11, the 2003 US-led intervention in Iraq; and due to the Obama administration pursuing the JCPOA with Iran over its nuclear programme.

Core contentions still remain and could be joined by new ones. The bilateral relationship has nevertheless been important to the global economy, the Global War on Terror and regional security. The US remains a key security and defence broker for the Arab Gulf states even during a period of shifting energy interests, antagonisms over Yemen and human rights, and a possible trend towards US de-prioritisation of the Middle East. One could expect the continuation of the Nixon Doctrine: high levels of arms sales to specified or implicit states or group of states and political support (also known as offshore balancing) to address dynamic threats to US core interests. After the US failed to respond to the attacks on Saudi Arabia in 2019, the geostrategic calculations of the Carter Doctrine appear to have expired.

Given the existential questions being faced by Saudi Arabia, whether pursuing dissidents abroad or continuing to prosecute a war in Yemen, it is unclear whether US policy direction will have a major impact. It was notable that Prince Khalid, Mohammed bin Salman's brother, held top-level meetings with the Biden administration in July 2021, possibly as a precursor to a visit by Mohammed bin Salman to Washington.[87] It is worth noting that for US allies such as Canada, which has taken a more robust approach on human rights, Mohammed bin Salman has refused to engage in dialogue. Saudi Arabia remains well placed to exert influence on the oil market, but there are limits to what it can do, especially in a period when congressional pressure has been building.

Gulf State foreign policy is flexible when it needs to be, with decision makers willing to sacrifice peripheral interests where necessary in order to sustain key alliance patterns and opportunities. The UAE has responded to changes in US politics and the region by right-sizing its military footprint and re-engaging with the Democrats, as well as building up important strands of co-dependence. Increasingly, there is evidence of hedging by the UAE, with the partial construction of a Chinese military facility. This may become a more common strategy if the US remains intent on not selling it lethal UAVs or imposes too much conditionality on arms such as the F-35 sale, or if the US remains unconvinced that it should be engaging in the Middle East to secure energy supplies.

Both Saudi Arabia and the UAE have fundamental economic interests at stake in the US, but the concentration of economic interests in the PIF, relative lack of diversification and JASTA give Saudi Arabia little room to manoeuvre vis-à-vis the US, as compared to the UAE. Saudi economic interests could be further constrained by any arms control legislation that is passed by the US Congress. This would have a disproportionate effect on the bilateral relationship. The stakes are high and will require ongoing lobbying in Washington, DC.

The Yemen conflict and the JCPOA led Mohammed bin Salman to undertake alliance enhancement activities by taking a five-day tour of Oman, Bahrain, Qatar, the UAE and Kuwait in December 2021, in the lead-up to the forty-second GCC summit in Riyadh on 14 December 2021.[88] Whilst prospects for the US returning to the JCPOA are unknown at the time of writing, the combination of a laissez-faire political approach in the kingdom, pushback against conditionality, ire at US policy on Yemen and the Iran nuclear deal, and diminishing cohesion on economic issues could stretch ties to a breaking point. Resisting US policy imperatives is unlikely to contribute to Saudi and GCC defences, and without immediate alternative states to balance with, which could prove a dangerous gambit. Saudi Arabia is not Afghanistan, and so, should there be more reciprocity in bilateral relations coupled with new nodes of interaction, the US–Saudi relationship could be salvaged.

Notes

1 Marwa Rashad, Ghaida Ghantous and Jonathan Landay, 'Honeymoon Over? Saudi Arabia–U.S. Ties Face Reset with Biden Win', *Reuters*, 22 October 2020,

www.reuters.com/article/usa-election-gulf-idUSKBN2770MP; Ryan Nobles, 'Congressional Democrats Call on Biden Administration to Demand Saudi Arabia Lift Blockade on Yemen', *CNN*, 7 April 2021, https://edition.cnn.com/2021/04/07/politics/democrats-reaction-yemen-blockade/index.html

2 Robert Vitalis, *Oilcraft: The Myths of Scarcity and Security that Haunt U.S. Energy Policy*. Stanford: Stanford University Press, 2020.

3 The US extended security guarantees to other Middle East states in the event of armed aggression through the Eisenhower Doctrine in 1957.

4 For more on this meeting see Thomas W. Lippman, *Arabian Knight: Colonel Bill Eddy USMC and the Rise of American Power in the Middle East*. Vista, CA: Selwa Press, 2008.

5 William B. Quandt, 'Riyadh Between the Superpowers', *Foreign Policy*, No. 44, Autumn 1981: 37–56.

6 Fawaz A. Gerges, 'The Kennedy Administration and the Egyptian–Saudi Conflict in Yemen: Co-Opting Arab Nationalism', *Middle East Journal*, 49 (2), Spring 1995: 292–311.

7 Rachel Bronson, 'Double, Double, Oil and Trouble', *Thicker than Oil: America's Uneasy Partnership with Saudi Arabia*. Oxford: Oxford University Press, 2006: 120.

8 Greg Bruno, 'Saudi Arabia and the Future of Afghanistan', Council on Foreign Relations, 10 December 2008, www.cfr.org/backgrounder/saudi-arabia-and-future-afghanistan

9 William Simpson, *The Prince: The Secret Story of the World's Most Intriguing Royal, Prince Bandar bin Sultan*. New York: HarperCollins, 2006.

10 Sharon Otterman, 'Saudi Arabia: Withdrawal of U.S. Forces', Council on Foreign Relations, 7 February 2005, www.cfr.org/backgrounder/saudi-arabia-withdrawl-us-forces

11 F. Gregory Gause III, 'Be Careful What You Wish For: The Future of U.S.–Saudi Relations', *World Policy Journal*, 19 (1), 2002, 37–50.

12 David Ottoway, 'The King and US: U.S.–Saudi Relations in the Wake of 9/11', *Foreign Affairs*, 88 (3), May/June 2009: 121–131.

13 Christopher M. Blanchard and Alfred B. Padros, 'Saudi Arabia: Terrorist Financing Issues', CRS Report for Congress, 14 September 2007, https://fas.org/sgp/crs/terror/RL32499.pdf

14 Bruce Riedel, 'Whither Saudi Arabia', *Kings and Presidents: Saudi Arabia and the United States since FDR*. Washington, DC: Brookings Institution Press, 2017: 188.

15 The US and Saudi Arabia do cooperate in the Saudi-based US–GCC Terrorist Financing Targeting Center (TFTC) but this mainly focuses on targeting Iranian financial transactions. The Embassy of the Kingdom of Saudi Arabia in Washington, DC, 'Riyadh Based Terrorist Financing Targeting Center Concludes Exercise on Disrupting Illicit Finance', 1 April 2019, www.saudiembassy.net/news/riyadh-based-terrorist-financing-targeting-center-concludes-exercise-disrupting-illicit-finance

16 Gulf News, 'UAE Forces' Role in KFOR Explained', 11 October 2001, https://gulfnews.com/uae/uae-forces-role-in-kfor-explained-1.426896

17 Rajiv Chandrasekaran, 'In the UAE, the United States has a Quiet, Potent Ally Nicknamed "Little Sparta"', *The Washington Post*, 9 November 2014, www.washingtonpost.com/world/national-security/in-the-uae-the-united-states-has-a-quiet-potent-ally-nicknamed-little-sparta/2014/11/08/3fc6a50c-643a-11e4-836c-83bc4f26eb67_story.html

18 Oliver Burkeman, 'America Signals Withdrawal of Troops From Saudi Arabia', 30 April 2003, *The Guardian*, 30 April 2003, www.theguardian.com/world/2003/apr/30/usa.iraq

19 Author's interview with a former senior UK official, 18 November 2021.

20 Author's interview with Joseph W. Westphal, 19 November 2021.

21 Ibid.

22 Remarks in a discussion titled 'Viennese Waltz: How Can the U.S. Balance Its Priorities With Gulf Arab Concerns as it Engages Iran?', Arab Gulf States Institute in Washington, 16 June 2021, https://agsiw.org/programs/viennese-waltz-how-can-the-u-s-balance-its-priorities-with-gulf-arab-concerns-as-it-engages-iran/

23 BBC News, 'Gulf Leaders Back Out of Camp David Summit in "Snub" to Obama', 12 May 2015, www.bbc.com/news/world-us-canada-32694184

24 Ben Rhodes, 'A Fatal Abandonment of American Leadership', *The Atlantic*, 12 October 2018, www.theatlantic.com/ideas/archive/2018/10/jamal-khashoggi-and-us-saudi-relationship/572905/

25 Spencer S. Hsu, 'Saudi Crown Prince Girds for Legal Battle in a Changing Washington Over Human Rights Allegations', *The Washington Post*, 2 November 2020, www.washingtonpost.com/local/legal-issues/saudi-crown-prince-lawsuits/2020/11/02/ca23820a-1a06-11eb-aeec-b93bcc29a01b_story.html

26 CBS News, 'Saudis Paid U.S. Veterans to Lobby Against Law Allowing 9/11 Families to Sue Kingdom', 11 May 2017, www.cbsnews.com/news/saudis-paid-u-s-veterans-to-lobby-against-law-allowing-911-families-to-sue-kingdom/

27 Liz Goodwin, 'In Leaked Email, Clinton Claims Saudi and Qatari Governments Fund ISIS', Yahoo! News, 12 October 2016, news.yahoo.com/in-leaked-email-clinton-claims-saudi-and-qatari-governments-fund-isis-221758254.html

28 Seyed Hossein Mousavian, 'Two Steps to Revive-and Sustain-the Iran Nuclear Deal', *Bulletin of the Atomic Scientists*, 7 December 2021, https://thebulletin.org/2021/12/two-steps-to-revive-and-sustain-the-iran-nuclear-deal/

29 US Department of State Office of the Historian, 'Chiefs of Mission for Saudi Arabia', https://history.state.gov/departmenthistory/people/chiefsofmission/saudi-arabia

30 Kushner would go on to secure $2 billion for his private equity firm from the Saudi PIF in return for a 28 percent stake in the investment vehicle just months after he left the White House. David E. Kirkpatrick and Kate Kelly, 'Before Giving Billions to Jared Kushner, Saudi Investment Fund Had Big Doubts', *The New York Times,* 10 April 2022, www.nytimes.com/2022/04/10/us/jared-kushner-saudi-investment-fund.html

31 Peter Jacobs, 'Trump Tweets His Support for the Massive Upheaval in Saudi Arabia, Says Those Arrested Have Been "Milking" the Country for Years', *Business Insider*, 7 November 2017, www.businessinsider.com/trump-saudi-arabia-tweets-2017-11

32 Bruce Riedel, 'Obama and Trump, Abdallah and Salman, 2009 to 2017', *Kings and Presidents: Saudi Arabia and the United States Since FDR*. Washington, DC: Brookings Institution Press, 2017: 178.

33 Natasha Turak, 'UAE to Get its First Reaper Drones, Clinches F-35 deal as Trump Administration Pushes Through Final Arms Sales', *CNBC*, 12 November 2020, www.cnbc.com/2020/11/12/uae-set-to-get-its-first-reaper-drones-clinch-f-35-deal-as-trump-administration-pushes-through-final-arms-sales-.html

34 Hussein Ibish, 'Arab States Should Avoid an Arms Race with Iran', *Bloomberg*, 22 October 2020, www.bloomberg.com/opinion/articles/2020-10-22/saudi-arabia-uae-should-avoid-an-arms-race-with-iran?srnd=opinion&sref=tp95wk9l

35 Die Welt, 'White House Pushed Saudi Nuclear Power Plan: Report', 20 February 2019, www.dw.com/en/white-house-pushed-saudi-nuclear-power-plan-report/a-47593923

36 Interview with an Asian diplomat who asked not to be named.

37 'Saudi Arabia and the Visit of President Trump – 2017 Report', www.saudiembassy.net/sites/default/files/WhitePaper_TrumpVisit_June2017.pdf

38 Robbie Gramer, Dan De Luce and Colum Lynch, 'How the Trump Administration Broke the State Department', *Foreign Policy*, 31 July 2017, https://foreignpolicy.com/2017/07/31/how-the-trump-administration-broke-the-state-department/

39 Mythili Sampathkumar, 'US Special Forces Secretly Deployed to Assist Saudi Arabia in Yemen Conflict', *The Independent*, 3 may 2018, www.independent.co.uk/news/world/americas/us-politics/us-special-forces-saudi-arabia-yemen-war-green-berets-houthi-rebels-mohammed-bin-salman-a8335481.html

40 Congressional Research Service, 'Saudi Arabia: Background and U.S. Relations', 18 February 2020, https://fas.org/sgp/crs/mideast/RL33533.pdf

41 David E. Sanger, 'Candidate Biden Called Saudi Arabia a "Pariah". He Now Has to Deal with It', *The New York Times*, 24 February 2021, www.nytimes.com/2021/02/24/us/politics/biden-jamal-khashoggi-saudi-arabia.html

42 Sonam Sheth and John Haltiwanger, '"I Saved his A–": Trump Boasted that He Protected Saudi Crown Prince Mohammed bin Salman after Jamal Khashoggi's Brutal Murder, Woodward's New Book Says', *Business Insider*, 10 September 2020, www.businessinsider.com/trump-woodward-i-saved-his-ass-mbs-khashoggi-rage-2020-9

43 See Twitter thread from Hassan Hassan, 26 February 2021, https://mobile.twitter.com/hxhassan/status/1365369356675350530

44 US Department of Justice, 'Attorney General William P. Barr and FBI Director Christopher Wray Announce Significant Developments in the Investigation of the Naval Air Station Pensacola Shooting', 18 May 2020, www.justice.gov/opa/pr/attorney-general-william-p-barr-and-fbi-director-christopher-wray-announce-significant

45 Michael LaForgia and Eric Schmitt, 'The Lapses that Let a Saudi Extremist Shoot up a U.S. Navy Base', *The New York Times*, 21 June 2020, www.nytimes.com/2020/06/21/us/politics/saudi-gunman-vetting.html

46 Aaron Katersky, '3 Service Member's Families, 13 Wounded Sue Saudi Arabia Over NAS Pensacola Shooting', *ABC News*, 22 February 2021, https://abcnews. go.com/Politics/service-members-families-sue-saudi-arabia-nas-pensacola/ story?id=76049252

47 BBC News, 'US Expels 21 Saudi Military Cadets After Gun Attack', 13 January 2020, www.bbc.com/news/world-us-canada-51095771

48 A. Celeste Gaia and Marcelo de Silva Leite, 'International Education in the Twenty-First Century: Lessons Learned from 9/11 and Cautious Hope for the Future', in Mark Finney and Matthew Shannon (eds) *9/11 and the Academy: Responses in the Liberal Arts and the 21st Century World*. New York: Palgrave Macmillan, 2019: 285.

49 Ibid.

50 Study International Staff, 'Is Trump to Blame for the Decline of International Students in the US?', 20 November 2019, www.studyinternational.com/news/ trump-blame-decline-international-students-us/

51 Patrick Schmidt, 'The Saudi Air Defense Problem is a U.S. Opportunity', The Washington Institute for Near East Policy, PolicyWatch 3450, 17 March 2021, www.washingtoninstitute.org/policy-analysis/saudi-air-defense-problem-us-opportunity

52 Especially after the 1973 Arab boycott against states in support of Israel during the Arab–Israeli War, and after the Three Mile Island nuclear accident and partial meltdown on 28 March 1979.

53 Office of the United States Trade Representative, 'Saudi Arabia', https://ustr.gov/ countries-regions/europe-middle-east/middle-eastnorth-africa/saudi-arabia

54 Ibid.

55 Bruce Riedel, 'It's Time to Stop US Arms Sales to Saudi Arabia', Brookings Institution, 4 February 2021, www.brookings.edu/blog/order-from-chaos/2021/02/04/ its-time-to-stop-us-arms-sales-to-saudi-arabia/

56 Karen E. Young, 'U.S.–Saudi Economic Ties: Why Saudi Arabia Matters', Arab Gulf States Institute in Washington, 19 March 2018, https://agsiw.org/u-s-saudi-economic-ties-why-saudi-arabia-matters/

57 Timothy Gardner, Steve Holland, Dmitry Zhdannikov and Rania El Gamal, 'Special Report: Trump Told Saudi: Cut Oil Supply or Lose U.S. Military Support – Sources', *Reuters*, 30 April 2020, www.reuters.com/article/us-global-oil-trump-saudi-specialreport-idUSKBN22C1V4

58 Young, 'U.S.–Saudi Economic Ties'.

59 US Embassy and Consulates in Saudi Arabia, 'Joint Statement of the U.S.– Saudi Arabia Strategic Dialogue', 21 October 2020, https://sa.usembassy.gov/ joint-statement-of-the-u-s-saudi-arabia-strategic-dialogue/

60 US Central Command, 'Statement of General Kenneth F. McKenzie, Jr, on the Posture of U.S. Central Command–HASC Hearing, 10 March 2020, www.centcom.mil/ABOUT-US/POSTURE-STATEMENT/

61 Embassy of the United Arab Emirates, Washington D.C., 'UAE–US Trade', www.uae-embassy.org/uae-us-relations/uae-us-trade

62 Ibid.

63 Ibid.

64 Ryan Grim, 'Gulf Ambassador Yelled at Member of Congress Pushing to End Yemen War', *The Intercept*, 12 February 2021, https://theintercept.com/2021/02/12/ro-khanna-yemen-uae-ambassador/

65 Christopher M. Davidson, 'The UAE's US T-Bond Drive: A Judicious Approach?', Diligencia, 17 May 2021, www.diligenciagroup.com/insights-resources/the-uae-s-us-t-bond-drive-a-judicious-approach/

66 Warren P. Strobel, 'Biden Re-Examining U.S. Arms Sales to Saudi Arabia, U.A.E.', *The Wall Street Journal*, 27 January 2021, www.wsj.com/articles/biden-freezes-u-s-arms-sales-to-saudi-arabia-uae-11611773191

67 Aria Bendix, 'U.S.–Saudi Arms Deal Narrowly Escapes Bipartisan Opposition', *The Atlantic*, 14 June 2017, www.theatlantic.com/news/archive/2017/06/us-saudi-arms-deal-narrowly-escapes-bipartisan-opposition/530232/

68 Interview with Gerald M. Feierstein, 23 April 2021.

69 Remarks by a senior US official under the Chatham House rule, 9 December 2021.

70 Deirdre Shesgreen, 'After Kashoggi Murder, Saudi Arabia Shifts Lobbying Firepower to "Middle America" with Women's Rights Message', *USA Today*, 6 March 2021, www.usatoday.com/story/news/politics/2021/03/06/after-khashoggi-murder-saudi-arabia-shifts-lobbying-middle-america/4497449001/

71 Brian Schwartz, 'Saudi Arabia Funds New Digital News Platform in the U.S., Launches White House Lobbying Effort', *CNBC*, 8 July 2021, www.cnbc.com/2021/07/08/saudi-arabia-funds-digital-news-platform-in-us-lobbies-white-house.html

72 Phil Stewart, 'U.S. Imposes Sanctions, Visa Bans on Saudis for Journalist Khashoggi's Killing', *Reuters*, 26 February 2021, www.reuters.com/article/us-usa-saudi-khashoggi-sanctions-idUSKBN2AQ2QI

73 Ibid.

74 The Canadian Press, 'Saudi Crown Prince Sent Hit Squad to Kill Former Spy, Lawsuit Claims', 6 August 2020, www.cbc.ca/news/canada/toronto/saudi-hit-squad-aljabri-1.5676650

75 Bruce Riedel, 'Saudi Arabia's King Promotes His Son – and Ousts the Best Counter-terrorist in the Mideast', *The Daily Beast*, 21 June 2017, available at www.brookings.edu/opinions/saudi-arabias-king-promotes-his-son-and-ousts-the-best-counter-terrorist-in-the-mideast/

76 William Young, 'ISIS Aims to Occupy Mecca', RAND, 19 January 2015, www.rand.org/blog/2015/01/isis-aims-to-occupy-mecca.html

77 Author's interview with Joseph W. Westphal, 19 November 2021.

78 Alex Marquardt, 'US Intelligence Chief Intervenes to Block State Secrets in Saudi Crown Prince's Feud with Former Saudi Official', *CNN*, 2 September 2021, https://edition.cnn.com/2021/09/02/politics/haines-state-secrets-privilege-court-case/index.html

79 Paul Iddon, 'What Weapons Systems Won't the U.S. Sell the UAE?', *Forbes*, 17 January 2021, www.forbes.com/sites/pauliddon/2021/01/17/what-weapons-systems-wont-the-us-sell-the-uae/?sh=54e309827db3

80 John W. Miller, 'Biden's Mideast Drawdown Poses Perils', *Defense News*, 15 April 2021, www.defensenews.com/opinion/commentary/2021/04/15/bidens-mideast-drawdown-poses-perils/

81 Iddon, 'What Weapons Systems Won't the U.S. Sell the UAE?'

82 Awad Mustafa, 'All You Need to Know About the UAE's Missile Defense and Houthi Attack Propaganda', *Al Arabiya News*, 3 December 2017, https://english.alarabiya.net/News/gulf/2017/12/03/All-you-need-to-know-about-the-UAE-s-missile-defense-and-Houthi-attack-propaganda

83 Congressman Gerry Connolly, 'Press Releases', 23 September 2021, https://connolly.house.gov/news/documentsingle.aspx?DocumentID=4380

84 Defense Security Cooperation Agency, 'Saudi Arabia – AIM-120C Advanced Medium Range Air-to-Air Missiles (AMRAAM)', 4 November 2021, www.dsca.mil/press-media/major-arms-sales/saudi-arabia-aim-120c-advanced-medium-range-air-air-missiles-amraam

85 EurAsian Times, 'Why Is the UAE Planning to Sell Its Latest F-16 Fighter Jets to Greece', 24 September 2020, https://eurasiantimes.com/why-is-the-uae-planning-to-sell-its-latest-f-16-fighter-jets-to-greece/

86 Maher Chmaytelli, 'Saudi Crown Prince Says He Does Not Care if Biden Misunderstands Him – The Atlantic', *Reuters*, 3 March 2022, www.reuters.com/world/saudi-crown-prince-says-do-not-care-if-biden-misunderstands-him-atlantic-2022-03-03/

87 Frank Gardner, 'Khashoggi Murder: US Softens towards Saudi Leader', *BBC News*, 14 July 2021, www.bbc.com/news/world-middle-east-57760786

88 Asmahan Qarjouli, 'Saudi Crown Prince MBS to Visit Qatar in Coming Days: Reports', *Doha News*, 5 December 2021, www.dohanews.co/saudi-crown-prince-mbs-to-visit-qatar-in-coming-days-reports/

7

China's Belt and Road Initiative: bilateralism versus alliances

Introduction

China's soft-power influence in the Middle East is centuries old. Indeed, even by the ninth century trade was quite developed, with dhows travelling from across the Gulf to and from China.[1] China–Iran political contacts might date as far back as the pre-imperial Chinese era, and are evident in the blue glazing for Chinese pottery sourced from Iran. Contact extended into the first and the Han dynasty, the second imperial dynasty (206 BC to 220 AD), which developed land and sea routes connecting East Asia, Southeast Asia, South Asia, Persia, the Arabian Peninsula, East Africa and Southern Europe. The enterprise would continue up to the eighteenth century. From 1405 to 1433, China's fleet made seven voyages which included the Gulf, but after the emperor forbade ship building, such contact would not resume for another century.[2]

The form of China's modern engagement with the world has been a function of communist rule from 1949. This was quickly elaborated on during the Cold War, when the Bandung conference of 1955 led to China's participation, helping to spur Asian–African cooperation spanning political, economic and cultural spheres. Within this framework, China, India and Myanmar laid out the Five Principles of Peaceful Coexistence, including mutual respect for sovereignty and territorial integrity, mutual non-aggression, non-interference in each other's internal affairs, equality and mutual benefit and peaceful coexistence.[3] China was opposed to European colonialism, which included trade discrimination and infrastructure in Africa, whereby 'roads and railways led down to the sea' instead of being focused on developing internal markets.[4] Chinese labourers were responsible for building some of the first roads in Yemen and helped to build the modern port of Hodeida, along with Soviet engineers.[5] Arabic and Persian language training has been a policy of the Chinese government since 1964, interrupted by the cultural revolution from 1966 to 1976, and then pursed in Chinese higher education institutions such as Beijing International Studies University, Northwest

University (Xi'an), Peking University and Shanghai International Studies University.[6] This has helped to build a high level of mutual understanding and trust over time, based on personal communication.

Deng Xiaoping was a major influence on de-ideologising Chinese foreign policy, seeking trading partners, defusing potential for global confrontations with the US and competing with the USSR as it built relations with Iraq and India in the early 1970s.[7] This was in line with China becoming a member of the UN Security Council in 1971, solidifying its status as an international actor. After the 1973 Arab–Israel War, as the US and European states sought to diversify energy supplies, the Gulf state's interest in new oil markets increased, closely matching China's search for energy resources to support annual economic growth rates of 10 per cent from 1978, sparked by its 'open door policy'. Further integration into global markets from the 1980s (including accession to the WTO in 2001) sustained this approach, along with China's mercantilist past.

Beijing also engaged through arms sales to Iran and Iraq during the Iran–Iraq War (1980–87), again in consideration of geostrategic factors. These included distancing Iran from its Soviet orbit, whilst arm sales to Iraq conformed to the policy preferences of Saudi Arabia, then a close US ally with whom China wanted to maintain pragmatic relations after President Nixon's visit in 1971, and energy considerations. The move may also have helped to encourage Riyadh to recognise Beijing in 1990. Until then, Riyadh had recognised Taiwan as the sole representative of the Chinese people.[8] After the Tiananmen Square protests of 1989 and during the Gulf War and the end of the Cold War, arms sales to the Middle East, including to Iraq, Iran and Sudan, increased, partly to help secure oil concessions and low prices.[9] Broader forms of economic statecraft were well received because of China's rising power status and lack of political baggage. Deng Xiaoping adopted a low-profile approach (*taoguangyanghui*) in 1990–91.[10] Beijing has been especially careful to link its energy needs with infrastructure projects from the time that Chinese President Jiang Zemin determined relations with Saudi Arabia to be based on a 'strategic oil partnership' during a 1999 visit to the kingdom.[11]

The Chinese policy of 'going outside' (*Zou Chuqu*) became explicit from 1999, based on the necessity to bring in commodities from all over the world. It also meant that China would promote socialism with Chinese characteristics (the 'China Model'). However, Chinese officials point out that they accept all development models and one approach does not fit all needs. Chinese companies were encouraged to invest abroad in the Tenth Five Year Plan (2001–5), whilst foreign companies were tempted to invest in China through a gradual liberalisation of its legal framework. Stemming from the need to establish a presence in international markets to boost domestic economic growth, China's initiatives concerning the Middle East have boomed in recent years. China has also sought to avoid entanglement, unlike the US and Europe, which, along with Russia, are seen to be geopolitically driven powers which are active in the region's security affairs through military influence and intervention.[12] The position of Chinese envoy to the Middle East was established in 2002, and the China–Arab States Cooperation Forum (CASCF) was established in 2004, with the new forum being described by Wen Jiabao, China's former head of government, as a 'new partnership' as early as 2006.[13] The final communiqué on establishing the forum included agreement to upgrade ties to the strategic level and for China to be more involved in the region's political and security issues. CASCF views all MENA states the same, but has so far failed to deliver on strategic, political and cultural exchanges. In 2006 and 2009 Hu Jintao visited Saudi Arabia, highlighting China's growing energy interests in the country and coordination on regional issues. The Arab uprisings made it harder for both sides, beyond the Gulf, to reap rewards and realise the potential on offer in the partnership,[14] although Yiwu City in Zhejiang Province attracts around 12,000 Arab residents, the largest Arab community in China, due to its status as the largest commodity distribution centre in the world.[15]

As China's GDP surpassed Japan's in 2010 to become the second-largest economy globally and as China experienced rising tensions with the US, Japan, the Philippines and Vietnam, Chinese foreign policy was under pressure to adapt to new political realities. In 2010, China again used the China–Arab Cooperation Forum to express a willingness to upgrade strategic cooperation in areas such as the economy, technology, education and the media.[16] Also in 2010, China established the China–GCC Economic and Trade Cooperation Forum and the China–GCC Strategic Dialogue. China and Saudi Arabia signed two cooperation agreements on security and law enforcement in the same year and consulted closely. China was also pushing for a Free Trade Agreement with the GCC in 2011. Beijing has, so far, managed to balance the rivalry between Iran and the GCC states, on the one hand, and Israel and the Arab states, on the other, although this has become easier in some cases with the advent of the Abraham Accords.

Chinese policy under Xi Jinping

Xi Jinping became president of the People's Republic of China in 2013. Since this time Chinese foreign policy has shifted, due to a number of initiatives including a Striving for Achievement (*fenfayouwei*) policy.[17] But the initiative with by far the biggest impact and ramifications so far has been the Belt and Road Initiative (BRI), comprising a renaissance of the old Silk Route across Central Asia and a new Maritime Silk Road. Formerly known as One Belt One Road (OBOR), it forms a central plank in China's strategy of rebalancing from its previously Asia-centric focus and has significant implications for China's engagement in the Middle East in the near and longer term. The BRI was launched by President Xi Jinping in September and October 2013 and was added to the Chinese Communist Party's constitution in 2017. Since it is publicly connected to President Xi, it is a convenient justification for his presidency to continue into the future without a specified end date. The announcement of the removal of the two-term limit on the presidency, effectively allowing Xi Jinping to remain in power for life, was made in 2018.

The BRI was followed in 2014 with a 1 (energy) + 2 (construction and infrastructure, trade and investment) + 3 (nuclear energy, aerospace and new energy) framework for China–Arab cooperation.[18] By 2015, five cooperation priorities had been identified, including: policy coordination (working together on political issues), infrastructure connectivity (spanning hydroelectric dams, steel mills, cement factories, ports and airports), unimpeded trade, financial integration and connecting people (cultural, personnel and academic exchanges, media cooperation, youth and women exchanges and volunteer services).[19] Also announced in 2015 was the Digital Silk Road, which aims to improve digital connectivity between participating countries and interoperability of critical infrastructure. There is growing interest in the Middle East in BeiDou, China's global positioning system. Like the BRI, it involves actors at different levels across the Chinese public and private sectors as well as official and unofficial projects, said to total $79 billion by 2018.[20] China is already developing projects in the Middle East, in states such as Egypt, Morocco,[21] UAE (5G roll-out), Lebanon and Pakistan, and so-called 'safe cities' in Saudi Arabia, UAE, Bahrain, Oman, Iraq, Egypt, Algeria, Tunisia and Morocco.[22]

This was followed by a relaunch of the Health Silk Road in the context of COVID-19 in 2020, including a widespread public diplomacy campaign and sending medical aid worldwide. Chinese ambitions for economic engagement in the Middle East also became more pronounced, with confident expectations that it would be expanded from $240 billion in 2013 to reach $600 billion by 2023.[23] Policy coordination, connectivity of infrastructure, unimpeded trade, financial integration and people-to-people bonds were important features of the 2015 Vision and Actions on Jointly Building the Silk Road Economic Belt and the 21st Century Maritime Silk Road.

In 2016, the Arab Policy Paper was launched. It features comprehensive cooperation and development, including political consultation and cooperation through bilateral and multilateral mechanisms (such as the China–Arab States Cooperation Forum, Arab League and GCC), with emphasis on independence, equality, non-interference in internal affairs and the one-China principle.[24] Investment and trade cooperation also features, with a note on generating employment, as do energy cooperation on the basis of reciprocity and mutual benefit, infrastructure, space, civilian nuclear and financial cooperation.[25] Social cooperation references healthcare and climate change-related cooperation as well as people exchanges, media cooperation, military and security cooperation.[26] The paper was published as President Xi Jinping undertook a trip to the Middle East and Asia, travelling to Egypt, Saudi Arabia, Pakistan and Indonesia to celebrate the sixtieth anniversary of the Bandung Conference. The visit was also designed to strengthen relations and expand economic cooperation.

Although the Middle East in general continues to represent a periphery to more immediate Chinese concerns such as relations with the US, territorial issues such as Taiwan, Hong Kong, Tibet and Xinjiang, and developing its sphere of influence in the South China Sea, the Gulf is an important part of the BRI, especially so in terms of energy security (at least, until China is expected to become carbon neutral by 2060[27]), other trade and investment and strategic arms sales. This makes 'complex interdependence'[28] increasingly apt in modelling China–Gulf relations, albeit in the context of a balance of power that favours China.

As Sun notes, China has already established a second 'artificial frontier' through a 'soft' military presence overseas, especially in the wider Middle East, to protect its commercial interests, provide public goods for the international community and minimise damage to its multilateral relations.[29] China has a naval base in Djibouti. Operational since 2017, and reported to have a ten-year lease on the site, its military facilities are reported to include barracks which could house several thousand troops, a paved area and eight hangars for helicopters and UAVs, and naval facilities, including access to the nearby Doraleh container port.[30] A 450 metre-pier allows for the docking of a large naval flotilla, including warships.[31] By building the China–Pakistan Economic Corridor (CPEC) through the unstable and separatist region of Balochistan, China has also fortified what may become another naval base in Gwadar, Pakistan. Its primary function at this location is to maintain a presence close to the Strait of Hormuz choke point, to access easily obtainable Iranian oil and to serve as a port and major overland trade conduit through Pakistan as an alternative to sailing through South Asia.[32]

China and the Gulf States

China is the top energy importer from Saudi Arabia, Iran, Kuwait and Oman. Trade between China and the GCC states rose from less than $10

billion in 2000 to almost $115 billion in 2016.[33] This was comparable to Gulf–India trade, which was $97 billion in 2016, rising to $104 billion in 2017–18,[34] and continuing to hover around $100 billion in 2020. However, GCC–China has gone on to exceed $180 billion in 2019, accounting for 11 per cent of GCC foreign trade.[35] China became the GCC's largest export market in 2020, replacing the EU, which had dominated trade relations since the early 1990s.[36] China–GCC economic relations are premised not only on China securing energy supplies but on the GCC states importing industrial products such as machinery and electronics, as well as attracting Chinese investment. The GCC states rank as China's sixth-largest export destination and fifth-largest import destination.[37] The Chinese aim was to build up political relations to the point of concluding a free trade area, reflecting lower barriers that already exist among WTO members.[38] This was achieved in December 2016 and has supported enhanced trade and investment patterns.

China's commercial projects in the Gulf, such as Khalifa port in Abu Dhabi, Duqm in Oman and the Jizan Industrial Park in Saudi Arabia, are linked to building a supply chain around the Arabian Peninsula to the Mediterranean via the Red Sea and Suez Canal, which also comprises an important part of the BRI, and in areas which offer most value. In response to growing economic relations, Saudi and UAE, like most of the Arab states, are unwilling to push the Uyghur issue with the Communist Party in Beijing and have actively signed up to a 2019 letter supporting China in this instance.[39] The number of Chinese tourists travelling to the GCC is expected to rise from 1.6 million in 2018 to 2.9 million in 2022, up 81 per cent.[40] Saudi Arabia is expected to experience the highest proportionate increase in arrivals from China, whilst the UAE has traditionally been a popular destination.[41] No doubt this figure will be impacted by COVID-19, but tourism could soon bounce back as flights and hotels resume business. In 2020, enterprises from Saudi Arabia, the UAE and other Gulf states participated in the third China International Import Expo in Shanghai and the 2020 Canton Fair. China reciprocated by attending the 2021 World Expo, the Asian Infrastructure Investment Bank sixth Annual Meeting,[42] and Abu Dhabi IDEX in 2021. Chinese development credit between 2008 and 2019 was about the same as World Bank credit during the same period, at $462 billion versus $467 billion. Apart from Iran in the Gulf, the other states that benefited were from it Venezuela, Pakistan, Russia, Angola, Brazil and Ecuador.[43] This is slowly changing as China has committed $20 billion in loans and $106 million in financial aid to the Middle East over the coming years, including new memorandums of understanding (MoUs) with the UAE, Oman, Kuwait and Bahrain.[44] China is attracted to GCC infrastructure projects which could have a commercial value of up to $2 trillion.[45] Although China has been accused of utilising 'sharp power' against states such as Australia, this is not so far evident in the Gulf,[46] and is unlikely to be so for some time, if ever, in the cases of Saudi Arabia and the UAE, given the relatively symmetrical relations and plethora of options that these states still enjoy. The Ethihad rail deal that links Ghuweifat on the border of Saudi Arabia to Fujairah and Khorfakkan on the UAE's east coast is a good example of the sheer diversity of contracts awarded and the diversity of bilateral relations that large-scale projects can foster.[47]

China concluded comprehensive strategic partnerships with Algeria and Egypt in 2014, with Saudi Arabia and Iran in 2016 and with the UAE in 2018. These partnerships include the full pursuit of cooperation and development on regional and international affairs.[48] An extension of non-alignment, and born out of avoiding antagonistic alliances, these bilateral partnerships with pivotal actors are crucial to the BRI.[49] However, there are questions over how sustainable this approach is in the context of relations with a series of states which have clear fissures between them. China's 2016 Arab Policy Paper details its interest in securing trade agreements and its willingness to trade in defence- and nuclear-related technology. This does not amount to a formal alliance or even a 'quasi alliance' (soft balancing), given the continued focus on Chinese state consolidation, the continuation of Saudi Arabia, the UAE and Egypt in the US sphere of influence (including Saudi Arabia and Egypt as Shanghai Cooperation Organization [SCO] dialogue partners from July 2021[50]) and China's wariness of being entangled in regional tensions and escalations.[51]

Where there have been differences in interaction, China has sought to rebalance relations, for example by concluding a new twenty-five-year trade deal with Iran on 24 June 2020. A leaked draft suggested a focus on interests such as energy, and infrastructure such as airports, railways and subways.[52] It has since expanded to include Bitcoin mining.[53] But, as one US official noted in October 2020, to reach the stated goal of $400 billion, it will require a ten-fold increase on investment levels as they were then. He said 'No one is taking that seriously', and that there was 'nothing concrete' in the deal at the time.[54] In March 2020, Iran had received only $115 million in declared oil payments from China,[55] and bilateral trade was at a ten-year low in 2019, so there is some potential.[56] Al-Monitor reports that apart from a 32 per cent discount in crude oil prices and a two-year payment break, and influence over Iranian islands in the south, China could also deploy 5,000 Chinese troops to safeguard its commercial interests in Iran,[57] although to deploy that number under ordinary circumstances is quite unlikely and speaks more to Iranian frustrations over the relative weakness of its ties, including military ties, to China vis-à-vis its Arab neighbours.[58] Iran was also approved as a full SCO member in September 2021, signalling closer ties to China and Russia, which dominate the bloc containing the largest fuel producers and customers of hydrocarbons, but not necessarily altering its geopolitical position.

Joint Iran–Chinese military exercises and industrial defence cooperation may be a greater concern for Abu Dhabi, which conducted fewer joint drills and technical port calls with China than Iran did in the 2010–19 period.[59] Iran will continue to lean on China for broad cooperation at least the US rejoins the JCPOA, which is by no means certain in the context of President Raisi's election and as Ayatollah Khamenei continues to focus on succession. But the convergence also reflects shared views about the role of the US in the Middle East, including sanctions, which has forced Iran to 'Look East' at a time when China's demand for hydrocarbons has rapidly increased. Both Iran and China have adopted strategies to avoid dependence on the Strait of Hormuz choke point in respectively exporting and importing oil: Iran has opened an oil terminal in the Gulf of Oman[60] and China will be able to import via a port it operates at Gwadar, Pakistan.

Saudi–China relations

The kingdom was an opponent of communism during the Cold War, to the point of implementing a trade ban against China to limit attempts at propaganda;[61] recognised Taiwan over China; and was the only Arab country to vote against the People's Republic of China's admission to the UN in 1971. Chinese leaders saw Gulf monarchies as an imperial legacy and supported the anti-monarchical Dhofar rebellion in Oman in the late 1960s, which caused further ructions.[62] Diplomatic relations commenced in 1990 after Prince Bandar visited Beijing in July 1990. Premier Li Peng visited Saudi Arabia the following year.

But covert relations began a decade earlier, in the context of heightened threat perception of Iran after the 1979 revolution and during the Iran–Iraq War, and also of Israel as it projected force and bombed Iraq's Tuwaitha nuclear power plant in 1981 and the headquarters of the Palestine Liberation Organization in Tunis in 1985.[63] Prince Sultan bin Abulaziz Al Saud, then the Saudi defence minister, asked his sons, Prince Bandar bin Sultan Al Saud, the Saudi ambassador to the US, and Prince Khalid bin Sultan Al Saud, who commanded Saudi Arabia's air defence, to request missiles from Beijing.[64] Details were discussed in Pakistan and during secret visits to China. China armed Saudi Arabia with Dong Feng (DF)-3 or CCS-2/'East Wind 3' medium-range and nuclear-capable missiles, but these were sold to the kingdom in the 1980s with conventional warheads.[65]

They were installed in hidden underground installations where Chinese technicians continued to work. The sites were detected by the CIA in 1988, causing a crisis between President Reagan, who wanted them removed, and King Fahd. Information about the situation leaked, and, under intense pressure from the US, Israel did not attack the missile base. It wasn't until a parade on 29 April 2014 to honour the visiting Pakistani army chief of staff that two missiles, out of the original order of around thirty to fifty, were put on public display.[66] With a range of 3,000 kilometres, the missiles are capable of reaching Iran but were said to have been purchased for defensive reasons. There have been rumours about a Pakistan commitment to supply nuclear warheads. The delivery of CCS-5 or DF-21 missiles with a 2,000-kilometre range and which are considered to be more reliable has never been confirmed.

Jiang Zemin visited Riyadh in 1999 after China had become a net importer of oil in 1993. The visit resulted in the 1999 Strategic Oil Cooperation Agreement which allowed Chinese companies to invest in Saudi Arabia's domestic oil market and Saudi companies to participate in China's downstream refining.[67] Oil sales mushroomed from $1.5 billion in 2000 to $25 billion by 2010. By 2002 Saudi Arabia was the leading supplier to China. By discounting prices during COVID-19, and to undercut rivals such as Russia during an OPEC+ war on pricing, Saudi Arabia exported 2.2 million barrels a day to China in May 2020, more than at any other time, representing approximately a third of crude exports.[68] In 2012, Aramco and Chinese state-owned enterprises established Aramco Asia in Beijing to manage its growing trade and investment in the Asian market. Gas cooperation has been less effective. In 2004, Sinopec successfully bid in a ten-year deal to develop a 38,800-kilometre concession in the Gahwar 'Block B' fields located north of Rub Al-Khail (Empty Quarter) under Saudi Gas Initiative 2.[69] However, there appear to be a number issues surrounding the export of the gas to China.

The period from 2006 to 2009 was a golden age for Saudi–Sino relations, with three state or official visits and a raft of new agreements. King Abdullah's first foreign visit was to China in 2005, in the wake of the US-led intervention in Iraq. He signed a series of agreements on energy, minerals, trade and investment there. During Hu Jintao's visit to the kingdom in April 2006, security issues were on the agenda, with a focus on national sovereignty, territorial integrity, mutual support and cooperation on regional and international affairs. It is at this time that the CCS-5 or DF-21 missiles deal may have been concluded, possibly with US support, since they were conventional weapons.[70] The Saudis have also been active in developing a more sophisticated refining capacity through a series of joint ventures with China's national oil companies and at Yanbu Aramco Sinopec Refining Company in Saudi Arabia, which began in 2014.[71]

China's Comprehensive Strategic Partnership with Saudi Arabia was struck in 2016 and aims for cooperation in all spheres from political and military to energy and security. It is guided by a China–Saudi Arabia High-Level Joint Committee, which links to Saudi Vision 2030, with vice premier Zhang Gaoli and Crown Prince Mohammed bin Salman as co-chairs. It met during Mohammed bin Salman's visit to China in 2016 for the G20 meeting, when a series of MoUs were concluded across areas such as housing, energy, culture, science and technology. King Salman included China in his 2017 Asian trip, which also included Malaysia, Indonesia, Brunei and Japan, focusing on trade and energy deals valued at $65 billion.[72] In August the same year another $60 billion worth of deals were announced, plus a $20 billion Joint Investment Fund linked to the BRI and Saudi Vision 2030. China has similar funds with the UAE and Qatar.[73]

Saudi–China relations, now into their third decade, are rooted in energy relations, the complementary nature of the BRI and Saudi Vision 2030. An extra dimension is what the kingdom can learn from the Chinese industrialisation process, particularly industrial cities. There is a pragmatism, in that internal affairs and relations with political dissidents or regional adversaries, such as China's relations with Iran or Saudi Arabia's war in Yemen, do not feature as irritants. But realising the full scope of bilateral relations within the context of a strong US–Saudi security and defence matrix makes it difficult for China to secure competitive advantage. Nevertheless, US security commitments to the Gulf do enable China to 'free ride' by focusing on economic and development goals.[74] Vision 2030 imperatives such as 'Smart cities' such as Neom, and AI, dovetail nicely with the Digital Silk Road Initiative, and both states have an interest in exploring civil nuclear power infrastructure in the kingdom. China has been the kingdom's top trading partner since 2014. Saudi–China trade amounted to $78 billion in 2019, up 23 per cent from the year before.[75]

There may be an element of Saudi hedging against uncertain relations with the US, but relations with Washington still remain at the core of Saudi defense, including arms sales and intelligence, and Middle East diplomacy. The most significant drivers increasing the pace of economic relations are likely to be global energy transitions to renewable energy, zero-carbon commitments and the kingdom's own economic targets to diversification. Given strong US, UK and French ties to the region, China is likely to pursue a long-term policy of deepening economic and political relations. To this end, Mandarin was added to the curricula of Saudi public schools and universities in 2019. In 2019, Mohammed bin Salman undertook an Asian tour, with visits to Pakistan, India and China, where an agreement was signed to build a joint venture – a refining and petrochemical complex in

Liaoning province – as well as other deals. In March 2022, Saudi Aramco announced that its Chinese joint venture would establish a major new refinery and petrochemical complex in Panjin, Liaoning province, in north-east China.

Other forms of cooperation between China and Saudi Arabia include aspects which are more contentious. China is said to be extending its 'Serbia Model' to the Gulf States, including AI technology exports which could be worth \$320 billion by 2030.[76] China is also helping to build 'Safe and Smart Cities', part of Vision 2030, which are said to be more liveable, intelligent and resource-efficient places. They include cities such as the new capital in Cairo and, in the kingdom, parts of the King Abdullah Economic City north of Jeddah, Yanbu Industrial City, Neom, Makkah, Riyadh, Jeddah, Al-Madinah and Al-Ahsa.[77] They can feature a combination of e-governance systems, public transport, the digitisation of public universities and improving recycling.[78] Whilst extensive tracking and 'smart' face-recognition surveillance systems, smart locks and sensors may address counterterrorism and urban safety concerns, they could also be used for broader surveillance, profiling and repression. Huawei is taking a leading role in Yanbu in three phases: construction of digital services; applications such as security, public services and sensors; and city management and a public portal.[79] Further projects involving smart parking, lighting and video-analytics technology are being rolled out in collaboration with Smart City Solutions Company (SC2), a Saudi service provider, in Al Khobar, Damman and Dhahran.[80] Artificial intelligence is a growth sector for the kingdom and offers numerous training opportunities across healthcare, energy and other sectors in cooperation with Chinese companies such Huawei and Alibaba, as well as western companies such as IBM.[81]

Apart from missiles, China has a rather small arms sales footprint in Saudi Arabia, in contrast to the US and UK, which are highly engaged in providing hardware and services to the kingdom's armed forces as outlined in Chapter 2, and Canada which provides infantry vehicles for the Saudi National Guard. Yet, China still has a clear and growing impact on human security in the kingdom and beyond, where the US and European allies hesitate to sell armed drones. Chinese Wing Loong I and II weaponised drones have been used on the battlefields in Yemen, Iraq and Libya. China and Saudi Arabia jointly produce CH-4 drones, announced in 2017, and China has offered to sell the kingdom the Blowfish 3, a machinegun-equipped helicopter UAV that could potentially employ artificial intelligence to identify targets.[82]

China will also have a disproportionate impact on the trajectory of civil nuclear power in the kingdom. Unlike Japan, which is abandoning civil nuclear power after the Fukushima Daiichi nuclear disaster,[83] China is actively promoting the development of the peaceful use of civil nuclear power. Beijing could assume global leadership of nuclear technology development, nuclear safety and non-proliferation by 2030.[84] This is of particular relevance to the kingdom as part of China's regional '1+2+3' initiative, whereby 1 represents energy, 2 represents infrastructure, trade and investment and 3 represents nuclear energy, space satellite and renewable energy.[85] In terms of upholding non-proliferation norms as a member of the UN Security Council, China will have to consider how far it goes in supporting Saudi uranium enrichment activities. China was alleged to be helping Saudi Arabia in the construction of a mill for producing yellowcake, refined uranium ore, in 2020 at Al-Ula.[86] Saudi Arabia acceded to the Non-Proliferation of Nuclear Weapons treaty in 1988 and signed the Comprehensive Safeguards Agreement in 2005, ratifying it in 2009.[87] However, it qualified this with a Small Quantities Protocol (SQP) which exempts it from regular inspections. As the kingdom develops its civil nuclear programme the SQP will no longer apply.[88] Whether or not the kingdom will pursue a Section 123 Agreement with the US, in the way the UAE did to address enrichment concerns, is also an open question.

Overall, China represents a horizontal relationship with Saudi Arabia, comprising a large export market (97 per cent of trade was oil as of 2018, favouring the kingdom to the tune of $20 billion).[89] A further $42 billion has been attributed to Chinese investments and construction in the kingdom from 2005 to 2021,[90] which does not include new opportunities such as 2021 Chinese investment talks for a stake in Aramco.[91] However, China and Saudi are beginning to compete over trade, especially automotive, construction, metal processing, plastic packaging and consumer goods.[92] Japan, on the other hand, is in a vertical relationship, including technology transfer, inward investment and aid.[93] India is somewhere in between. But, to benefit from growing FDI from Japan and South Korea in future, Saudi Arabia will need to compete effectively with Qatar and Iran on petrochemicals. Sectoral analysis will therefore be needed in future as competitive advantage, state-led policies and FDI patterns shift.[94] Fundamentally, Arab Gulf states such as Saudi Arabia and the UAE are using China as an economic 'bridge strategy' to develop a next-generation market in oil and gas products.[95]

UAE–China relations

Diplomatic ties between China and the UAE were established in 1984, and relations have generally been dominated by trade. The UAE is China's second-largest trading partner in the Arab world. The patterns of economic engagement between China and UAE are different to those of Sino–Saudi ties, in that they have matured and diversified beyond recognition in a short space of time. The UAE is an entrepôt, and Abu Dhabi as well as Dubai's Jabal Ali port are key to China–Arabian trade and investment along the BRI. Although the 'maritime silk Road' is expanding on both sides of the Arabian Peninsula and, indeed, the Gulf, the BRI represents a remarkably complementary strategy to the UAE's own economic agenda of establishing or expanding ports in the Middle East and Africa to benefit from expanding trade between East Africa and South Asia.

Whereas Saudi–Sino trade has mainly comprised energy, Sino–UAE trade has been dominated by sectors such as construction. From 2006 to 2020, Chinese investments and construction projects amounted to $36.1 billion,[96] although after the announcement of the joint $10 billion investment fund in 2015 this is shifting to other sectors such as transport, technology and healthcare. There are similarly overlapping interests in free zone development, where Dubai takes the lead regionally, and on technology, logistics and infrastructure. Deals include a first-of-its-kind Chinese State-Owned Financial Services vehicle that invested in the Abu Dhabi Global Market. Along with Dubai International Financial Centre, the two make the UAE the largest hub for fintech in the Middle East. Other non-oil deals include the $300 million construction and machinery deal which saw Abu Dhabi award a thirty-five-year concession to Cosco Shipping Ports in 2018.[97] Non-oil trade increased by 16.3 per cent in 2019 to reach $50 billion, compared to UAE oil exports to China which amounted to $5.9 billion in 2018.[98] Several Chinese companies have pledged investment in Abu Dhabi's KIZAD industrial hub, which is expected to produce 10 million passenger-car tyres and 1 million truck and bus tyres by 2022.[99]

Both countries signed a three-year currency-swap agreement in 2012 to boost the use of the Chinese yuan to settle international trade (oil transactions).[100] The long-term ambition of China is to unseat the US dollar as the dominant unit of international settlement, especially as China became the world's largest exporting nation in 2009, and overtook the US to become the world's largest importer of oil in 2017.[101] Future oil contracts priced in renminbi, launched on the Shanghai Stock Exchange in 2018, were another effort in this direction, but in order to achieve its objective some analysts believe that China will need to further liberalise its financial markets. Several major oil producers in the Gulf have their currencies pegged to the US dollar, including Saudi Arabia, the UAE, Oman and Qatar, and, despite the changing oil demand and economic conditions in these states, the pegs have so far held.

The Sino–Gulf vision of economic statecraft and governance could reorientate Middle Eastern markets for years to come.[102] Whilst China could help these Gulf states and others to overcome the challenge of boom–bust cycles based on hydrocarbon revenues, it depends to a large extent on the Vision plans being implemented successfully. Economic relations are enhanced by large and growing people-to-people connections, such as a Chinese expatriate population of around 200,000 as well as 6,000 Chinese-run businesses.[103] Dubai has significance as the location of China's largest expatriate population in the whole of the Middle East, with extensive business links attached to it. The Chinese government granted the UAE 'approved destination' status in 2009, and in 2012 and 2013 the Chinese Visitor Summit was held in the UAE, which brought in around seventy-five of China's top outbound tourism companies.[104] Since then, tourism has rocketed. In 2019, Chinese visitors to Dubai alone stood at 989,000,[105] representing about 10 per cent of the whole UAE population. The establishment of Confucius Institutes has also played a part in building ties. For example, Dubai police use the institutes to study Mandarin in order to better communicate with Chinese expats and tourists. They also serve to bolster education exchanges between universities such as Zayed University, which hosts such institutes, and Chinese partners such as Beijing Foreign Studies University.[106] In September 2020, the first Chinese full-time public school outside of China opened in Dubai.[107]

Like Saudi Arabia, the UAE reportedly has bought armed UAVs from China, using them for strikes in Libya.[108] The UAE has boosted its imports of Chinese arms, including twelve L-15 light attack planes, with an option on thirty-six more. Like in Saudi Arabia, China is developing 'safe cities' in the UAE, according to UAE government focus on sustainable development, underpinned by the Dubai 2040 Plan, Abu Dhabi's Economic Vision 2030 strategy and China's '1+2+3' strategy. Projects include the Sustainable City in Dubai, which is run on indigenously produced solar power, and Zayed Smart City Project, which is focused on infrastructure management through information and communication technology.[109] The UAE is also focused on e-governance and comprehensive services through smart applications.

Fintech, smart city technology and AI form a distinct strand of strategic cooperation and it is precisely this digital domain which other states in Asia and the West are concerned about, given the pace of change and China's ability to shape technology-driven agendas. The deployment of Chinese technology to the UAE is more complex than in most other Arab Gulf contexts, due to decision making taking place, in some cases, at the emirate level. For example, in 2016 Dubai South – a new urban centre in the emirate – signed an MoU with Huawei to deploy smart-city solutions in the Dubai South Business Park Free Zone.[110] The Chinese company is also working with Dubai Civil Defence and Dubai Police on the deployment of security-related technology.[111] There is great potential to collaborate through the Mohamed bin Zayed University of Artificial Intelligence. Integrating technology as part of Dubai's economy is a clear extension of both China's familiarity with its deployment in its own free zones and its application to the many free zones in Dubai. Increasingly, there is cooperation in establishing virtual hubs for trade and e-commerce, such as Dubai Virtual Commercial City, ideal for maintaining relevance in China's digital BRI.[112] In August 2020, Nasdaq Dubai signed strategic cooperation agreements to attract Chinese listings to the emirate.[113] This would make it ideally suited to attract some Chinese companies unable to list in the US due to ties to China's military or the surveillance industry.[114] In 2021, the UAE announced the opening of its first regional distribution hub for aircraft logistics in Abu Dhabi with Chinese-state backed defence contractor China National Aero-Technology Import and Export Corporation.[115]

There are also convergences in other Chinese and UAE interests. Both states are concerned about Islamist activism. On the whole, the UAE has been supportive of China's policy in Xinjiang. When Mohammed bin Zayed visited Beijing in July 2019, President Xi Jinping thanked him for his country's 'valuable support' when it comes to Xinjiang.[116] Mohammed bin Zayed is reported to have said to President Xi that the UAE would be willing to work with China to 'jointly strike against terrorist extremist forces'.[117] This would repeat not only a pattern of economic-led diplomacy with China, but the UAE's ability to cement deals with international actors to build military experience, interoperability, soft-power stakes and, ultimately, support for the UAE government against internal and external threats. There are also more subtle links between Chinese and UAE security. China has out-sourced security to protect personnel and facilities in Africa and Asia to private security firms. These include Frontier Services Group, founded and chaired by Erik Prince, formerly of Blackwater, which is accused of committing atrocities in Iraq.[118] Frontier Services Group is also alleged to have set up training camps in Xinjiang and is supported by Chinese state-owned CITIC Group, which has offices in Kenya and Dubai.[119]

In a shock move reported by the *Wall Street Journal* in November 2021, US intelligence agencies had found China earlier in the year to be building a suspected military facility at Khalifa Port, about midway between Abu Dhabi and Dubai.[120] After President Biden was in contact with Mohammed bin Zayed, the project was dropped. The move appears to have been an opportunistic one for China, with a senior UAE official noting that the UAE does not see China as a security provider in the Gulf or the UAE.[121] But it confirms US fears, articulated by General Kenneth F. McKenzie, Jr, Commander CENTCOM, in April 2021 that China has a 'long-term goal of expanding its military presence to secure vital routes of energy and trade'.[122] The dual-use nature of the facility was the highlighted by the fact that the UAE did not view it as a military facility, but took into full consideration the view of the Biden administration in halting it.[123] The episode shows how the Gulf could play into the US and China's growing competition over the coming years.

China and the UAE have collaborated closely during COVID-19 and the UAE has been receptive to China's vaccine diplomacy. Clinical trials of Sinopharm took place,[124] UAE company Group 42 and global genomics leader BGI cooperate on population-scale detection and diagnosis of COVID-19 in the UAE,[125] and there has been a deal to manufacture and distribute a UAE-produced version of the Sinopharm vaccine, called Hayat-Vax.[126] The extent of cooperation during the pandemic highlights a firm foundation for future healthcare and scientific collaboration.

Conclusion

The Gulf states under study have experienced imperial influence, particularly affecting their forms of administration and decision making, which has subsequently been overlaid with other modernising socio-economic pro-grammes. Few will be as consequential to these Vision strategies as China's BRI in the twenty-first century. Chinese–Saudi and Emirati relations are subject to an uncommon urgency, due to the carbon-neutral agenda; the linkage between GCC state economic programmes, notably jobs, and political legitimacy; and the growing imperative to broaden trade and FDI.

Saudi Arabia, the UAE and some individual emirates retain a certain identity and agency in their political economies, such as Dubai's nimble transition from free zones to digital economy and AI, which integrate with Chinas's Digitial Silkroad for long-term growth. Apart from implementing Vision programmes, there are other aspects, notably in their foreign policies, which can maximise Chinese cooperation or retard it. Examples include the opportunity cost of activities such as military or economic intervention, competition or conflict.

As Kamrava notes, the state-led 'China model' (combining social, economic and political resources) may be appealing, but structural challenges and incongruities in Middle East political economies underscore great uncertainty as to whether it can be exported or even adapted.[127] A similar optimism was held by Arab onlookers of Maoist China, who romanticised it as being a model for post-colonial modernity.[128] The UAE may be one of the few states to benefit from the model, because it is well positioned to take advantage of near-term gains, including complementary and broadening trade and investment opportunities. These support new UAE start-ups, industries, status and a growing interdependence. 'Safe and smart' cities or projects across a small territory and population are also likely to have a greater impact on efficiency and state security. Dual-use aspects of interactions, AI in 'smart cities' and civil nuclear development in particular, place emphasis on the Saudi and UAE leaderships with special reference to threat perception and intention.

China's rejection of alliances and preference for a series of bilateral relations stands in contrast to the growing number of 'Quads' that in at least one case are at least partially designed to contain its ambitions and normative influence. Beijing's political development and learning, including consistency of leadership alongside the Gulf monarchies, its demand for oil and investment opportunities, and balancing strategy in the Gulf (perhaps slightly frayed after the UAE military facility issue) are indicative of a durable interaction. However, changes in the international trade regime, difficult relations with the US and other large democracies (the so-called D10) and contentions surrounding China's domestic policies and in the Indo-Pacific region, spell an uncertain period ahead.

Notes

1   Jacqueline Armijo, 'China and the Gulf: The Social and Cultural Implications of their Rapidly Developing Economic Ties', in Tim Niblock and Monica Malik (eds) *Asia–Gulf Economic Relations in the 21st Century: The Local to Global Transformation*. Berlin: Gerlach Press, 2013: 225–240.
2   Louise Levathes, *When China Ruled the Seas: The Treasure Fleet of the Dragon Throne, 1405–1433*. New York: Simon and Schuster, 1994.
3   Ministry of Foreign Affairs of the People's Republic of China, 'The Five Principles of Peaceful Coexistence', 30 July 2014, www.fmprc.gov.cn/mfa_eng/wjb_663304/zwjg_665342/zwbd_665378/t1179045.shtml
4   Walter Rodney, *How Europe Underdeveloped Africa*, London: Bogle-L'Ouverture Publications, 1972.
5   Laleh Khalili, 'Growing Pains', *London Review of Books*, 18 March 2021, https://lrb.co.uk/the-paper/v43/n06/laleh-khalili/growing-pains
6   Tim Niblock, 'China and the Middle East: A Global Strategy Where the Middle East has a Significant but Limited Place', *Asian Journal of Middle Eastern and Islamic Studies*, 18 November 2020: 16.
7   Imad Mansour, 'Treading with Caution: China's Multidimensional Interventions in the Gulf Region', *The China Quarterly*, 239, 2019: 7.
8   Ibid.
9   Sergei Troush, 'China's Challenging Oil Strategy and its Foreign Policy Implications', Brookings, 1 September 1999, www.brookings.edu/articles/chinas-changing-oil-strategy-and-its-foreign-policy-implications/
10 Xuetong Yan, 'From Keeping a Low Profile to Striving for Achievement', *The Chinese Journal of International Politics*, 7 (2), Summer 2014: 153–184.

11 Flynt Leverett and Jeffry Bader, 'Managing China–US Energy Competition in the Middle East', *The Washington Quarterly*, 29 (1): 191.

12 Degang Sun and Yahia H. Zoubir, 'China's Economic Diplomacy towards the Arab Countries: Challenges Ahead?' *Journal of Contemporary China*, 25 (95), 2015: 903–921, at 909.

13 Xinhua, 'China–Arab Strategic Ties Serve Fundamental Interests: Premier Wen', 13 May 2006, available at www.china-embassy.org/eng/xw/t694364.htm

14 Sun and Zoubir, 'China's Economic Diplomacy towards the Arab Countries'.

15 Ibid: 916.

16 Xinhua, 'China, Arab States Agree to Establish Strategic Co-op Relations', 14 May 2010, available at http://en.people.cn/90001/90776/90883/6986096.html

17 There is a debate amongst Chinese IR specialists as to the level of continuity or tension between this policy and those which preceded it under Hu Jintao and Keeping a Low Profile policy (*taoguangyanghui*) under Deng Xiaoping. See Niblock, 'China and the Middle East': 20.

18 Xuming Qian and Jonathan Fulton, 'China–Gulf Economic Relationship under the "Belt and Road" Initiative', *Asian Journal of Middle Eastern and Islamic Studies*, 11 (3), 2017: 18.

19 European Bank for Reconstruction and Development, 'Belt and Road Initiative (BRI)', www.ebrd.com/what-we-do/belt-and-road/overview.html

20 Deloitte, 'BRI Update 2019 – Recalibration and New Opportunities': 12, https://www2.deloitte.com/content/dam/Deloitte/cn/Documents/ser-soe-br/deloitte-cn-bri-update-2019-recalibration-and-new-opportunities-en-190422.pdf (accessed 12 March 2021)

21 US–China Economic and Security Review Commission, 'Hearing on China's Strategic Aims in Africa', 8 May 2020, www.uscc.gov/sites/default/files/Feldstein_Testimony.pdf

22 Jonathan E. Hillman and Maesea McCalpin, 'Watching Huawei's "Safe Cities"', Center for Strategic and International Studies, 4 November 2019, www.csis.org/analysis/watching-huaweis-safe-cities

23 Xi Jinping, 'Promote the Silk Road Spirit, Strengthen China–Arab Cooperation', CPC Central Committee Bimonthly, *Qiushi*, 5 June 2014, http://en.qstheory.cn/2021-02/05/c_607637.htm

24 Ministry of Foreign Affairs of the People's Republic of China, 'China's Arab Policy Paper', January 2016, www.fmprc.gov.cn/mfa_eng/zxxx_662805/t1331683.shtml

25 Ibid.

26 Ibid.

27 Helen Regan, 'China will Become Carbon Neutral by 2060, Xi Jinping Says', *CNN*, 23 September 2020, https://edition.cnn.com/2020/09/22/china/xi-jinping-carbon-neutral-2060-intl-hnk/index.html

28 Robert Keohane and Joseph Nye, 'Power and Interdependence Revisited', *International Organization*, 41 (4), 1987: 725–753.

29 Degang Sun, 'China's Soft Military Presence in the Middle East', Middle East Institute, 11 March 2015, www.mei.edu/publications/chinas-soft-military-presence-middle-east

30　Neil Melvin, 'The Foreign Military Presence in the Horn of Africa Region', SIPRI Background Paper, April 2019: 4, www.sipri.org/sites/default/files/2019-05/sipribp1904_2.pdf

31　Ibid.

32　H. I. Sutton, 'China's New High-Security Compound in Pakistan May Indicate Naval Plans', *Forbes*, 2 June 2020, www.forbes.com/sites/hisutton/2020/06/02/chinas-new-high-security-compound-in-pakistan-may-indicate-naval-plans/?sh=38c4d28e1020

33　Ibid.

34　Rahul Roy-Chaudhury, 'India and the Gulf Region: Building Strategic Partnerships', International Institute for Security Studies, 29 August 2018, www.iiss.org/blogs/analysis/2018/08/india-gulf-strategic-partnerships

35　Abdel Aziz Aluwaisheg, 'Expanding the China–GCC Strategic Partnership', *Al Arabiya News*, 4 January 2021, https://english.alarabiya.net/in-translation/2021/01/04/Expanding-the-China-GCC-strategic-partnership

36　Abdel Aziz Aluwaisheg, 'How to Expand the China–GCC Strategic Partnership', *Arab News*, 30 December 2020, www.arabnews.com/node/1785041

37　Qian and Fulton, 'China–Gulf Economic Relationship': 14.

38　Ministry of Foreign Affairs of the People's Republic of China, 'Third Round of China–Gulf Cooperation Council Strategic Dialogue Held in Beijing', 17 January 2014, www.fmprc.gov.cn/mfa_eng/zxxx_662805/t1121625.shtml

39　Haisam Hassanein, 'Arab States Give China a Pass on Uyghur Crackdown', The Washington Institute for Near East Policy, PolicyWatch 3169, 26 August 2019, www.washingtoninstitute.org/policy-analysis/arab-states-give-china-pass-uyghur-crackdown

40　World Travel Market, 'Chinese Visitors to GCC Will Increase 81% by 2022 Says ATM Report', 16 January 2019, https://hub.wtm.com/press/atm-press-releases/chinese-visitors-to-gcc-will-increase-81-by-2022-says-atm-report/

41　Ibid.

42　AIIB was proposed by China in 2013 and set up in 2014. It is seen as a rival to the World Bank and International Monetary Fund (IMF).

43　Khalili, 'Growing Pains'.

44　David Howlett, 'The 21st Century Maritime Silk Road', *MEED Business Review*, 4 (2), February 2019: 18.

45　Ibid: 16.

46　John Fitzgerald, 'Soft Power and Sharp Power: The View from Australia', *The Asan Forum,* https://theasanforum.org/soft-power-and-sharp-power-the-view-from-australia/

47　MEED, 'Chinese Firm Wins Etihad Wagons Deal', 4 August 2020, www.meed.com/chinese-company-wins-etihad-rail-wagons-deal

48　South China Morning Post, 'Quick Guide to China's Diplomatic Levels', 20 January 2016, www.scmp.com/news/china/diplomacy-defence/article/1903455/quick-guide-chinas-diplomatic-levels

49　Degang Sun, 'China's Partnership Diplomacy in the Middle East', *The Asia Dialogue*, 24 March 2020, https://theasiadialogue.com/2020/03/24/chinas-partnership-diplomacy-in-the-middle-east/

50 Global Times, 'Expanding SCO Can Boost Regional Integration and Post-COVID Recovery', 16 July 2021, www.globaltimes.cn/page/202107/1228822.shtml

51 Degang Sun and Dandan Zhang, *Diplomacy of Quasi-Alliances in the Middle East*. Berlin: Gerlach Press, 2020.

52 Dave Lawler, 'China–Iran Deal Envisions Massive Investments from Beijing', *Axios*, 13 July 2020, www.axios.com/china-iran-investment-deal-oil-infrastructure-c919646d-2ece-4ee5-bfd7-c8a16a7f53b0.html

53 Osato Avan-Nomayo, 'Chinese Investors Reboot Iranian Bitcoin Mining Facility', *Cointelegraph*, 15 April 2021, https://cointelegraph.com/news/chinese-investors-reboot-iranian-bitcoin-mining-facility

54 US official who asked not to be named, 13 October 2020.

55 Orkhan Jalilov, 'Trade Exchange Between Iran and China Drops By 30 Percent', *Caspian News*, 1 May 2020, https://caspiannews.com/news-detail/trade-exchange-between-iran-china-drops-by-30-percent-2020-4-30-45/

56 Bill Figueroa, 'A "$400 Billion" China–Iran Deal? The View from History', *Jadaliyya*, 14 October 2020, www.jadaliyya.com/Details/41852

57 Al-Monitor. 'Iran Government Squeezed Over "Secretive" Deal with China'. 10 July 2020, www.al-monitor.com/pulse/originals/2020/07/iran-government-rouhani-secretive-deal-china.html

58 Lucille Greer and Esfandyar Batmanghelidj, 'Last Among Equals: The China–Iran Partnership in a Regional Context', Occassional Paper 38, Wilson Center, September 2020: 2, www.wilsoncenter.org/sites/default/files/media/uploads/documents/MEP_200831_OCC%2038%20v3%20%281%29.pdf

59 Ibid: 15, 17.

60 Reuters Staff, 'Iran Opens Oil Terminal in Gulf of Oman to Bypass Strait of Hormuz', *Reuters*, 22 July 2021, www.reuters.com/article/us-iran-oil-gulf/iran-opens-oil-terminal-in-gulf-of-oman-to-bypass-strait-of-hormuz-idINKBN2ES0V9

61 Jonathan Fulton, 'China's Relations with Saudi Arabia', *China's Relations with the Gulf Monarchies*. Abingdon: Routledge, 2019: 88.

62 Hashim Behbehani, 'Brief History of the Liberation Movement in Oman', *China's Foreign Policy in the Arab World, 1955–1975: Three Case Studies*. Abingdon: Routledge, 2016: 134–188.

63 Bruce Riedel, 'Saudi Arabia's Relations with China: Functional but Not Strategic', Brookings, 20 July 2020, www.brookings.edu/articles/saudi-arabias-relations-with-china-functional-but-not-strategic/

64 Ibid.

65 Kelsey Davenport, 'Saudi Arabia Displays Missiles', June 2014, www.armscontrol.org/act/2014-06/saudi-arabia-displays-missiles

66 Ibid.

67 Jonathan Fulton, 'Strangers to Strategic Partners: Thirty Years of Sino-Saudi Relations', Atlantic Council, August 2020: 6, www.atlanticcouncil.org/wp-content/uploads/2020/08/Sino-Saudi-Relations_WEB.pdf

68 Anthony Di Paola, 'Undercutting Rivals Helps Saudis Grow Share in Key Oil Markets', *World Oil*, 5 June 2020, www.worldoil.com/news/2020/5/6/undercutting-rivals-helps-saudis-grow-share-in-key-oil-markets

69 Mohammed Turki Al-Sudairi, 'Sino-Saudi Relations: An Economic History', Gulf Papers, August 2012, Gulf Research Centre, 10, available at www.files.ethz.ch/ isn/156677/Final_Completed_Sino_Saudi_Economic_History_Report_3778.pdf

70 Jeff Stein, 'Exclusive: CIA Helped Saudis in Secret Chinese Missile Deal', *Newsweek*, 29 January 2014, www.newsweek.com/exclusive-cia-helped-saudis-chinese-missile-deal-227283

71 Xinhua, 'Yanbu's Joint Venture Refinery Shines as Example for Beneficial China–Saudi Energy Cooperation', 9 July 2018, www.xinhuanet.com/ english/2018-07/09/c_137312287.htm

72 Ben Blanchard, 'China, Saudi Arabia Eye $65 Billion in Deals as King Visits', *Reuters*, 16 March 2017, www.reuters.com/article/us-saudi-asia-china/china-saudi-arabia-eye-65-billion-in-deals-as-king-visits-idUSKBN16N0G9

73 Fulton, 'Strangers to Strategic Partners': 9.

74 See Jonathan Fulton, 'Situating Saudi Arabia in China's Belt and Road Initiative', *Asian Politics and Policy*, 12 (3), 2020: 362–383.

75 Chen Yurong, 'Graphics: How Is BRI Bolstering China–Saudi Arabia Ties?', *CGTN*, 20 November 2020, https://news.cgtn.com/news/2020-11-20/Graphics-How-is-BRI-bolstering-China-Saudi-Arabia-ties–VzqqKFdXSo/index.html

76 Wendy Robinson, 'The Rise of Chinese AI in the Gulf: A Renewal of China's "Serbia Model"', Fikra Forum, The Washington Institute of Near East Policy, 13 October 2020, www.washingtoninstitute.org/policy-analysis/ rise-chinese-ai-gulf-renewal-chinas-serbia-model

77 Rahma M. Doheim, Alshimaa A. Farag and Samaa Badawi, 'Smart City Vision and Practices Across the Kingdom of Saudi Arabia – A Review', in Anna Visvizi and Miltiadis Lytras (eds) *Smart Cities: Issues and Challenges: Mapping Political, Social and Economic Risks and Threats*. Amsterdam: Elsevier, 2019: 309–332.

78 Ibid.

79 Huawei, 'Yanbu: A Smart Industrial Oil Kingdom City', https://e.huawei.com/ za/publications/global/ict_insights/201708310903/manufacturing/201712061133

80 Smart Cities World, 'Huawei and SC2 Strike Agreement to Collaborate on Saudi Smart Cities', 29 June 2020, www.smartcitiesworld.net/news/huawei-and-sc2-strike-agreement-to-collaborate-on-saudi-smart-cities-5418

81 Reuters Staff, 'Saudi Arabia Signs MoUs with IBM, Alibaba and Huawei on AI', Reuters, 22 October 2020, www.reuters.com/article/us-saudi-tech-idUKKBN2771LN

82 Ibid.

83 Risa Maeda and Aaron Sheldrick, 'Japan Aims to Abandon Nuclear Power by 2030s', *Reuters*, 14 September 2012, www.reuters.com/article/ us-japan-nuclear-idUSBRE88D05520120914

84 Mark Hibbs, 'The Future of Nuclear Power in China', Carnegie Endowment for International Peace, 14 May 2018: 1, available at https://carnegieendowment. org/2018/05/14/future-of-nuclear-power-in-china-pub-76311

85 Ministry of Foreign Affairs of the People's Republic of China, 'China's Arab Policy Paper', 13 January 2016, www.fmprc.gov.cn/mfa_eng/zxxx_662805/t1331683. shtml

86 Julian Borger, 'Pompeo Pressed on Claims China is Helping Build Saudi Uranium Facility', *The Guardian*, 19 August 2020, www.theguardian.com/world/2020/aug/19/mike-pompeo-alleged-saudi-arabia-uranium-facility-yellowcake-china-democrats

87 Nuclear Threat Initiative, 'Saudi Arabia – Nuclear', July 2016, www.nti.org/learn/countries/saudi-arabia/nuclear/

88 Ibid.

89 Fulton, 'Strangers to Strategic Partners': 12.

90 American Enterprise Institute, 'China Global Investment Tracker', www.aei.org/china-global-investment-tracker/

91 Kane Wu, Alex Lawler and Tom Arnold, 'Exclusive: Major Chinese Investors in Talks to Take Aramco Stake – Sources', *Reuters*, 28 April 2021, www.reuters.com/world/middle-east/exclusive-major-chinese-investors-talks-take-aramco-stake-sources-2021-04-28/

92 Makio Yamada, 'Gulf–Asia Relations as "Post-Rentier" Diversification? The Cases of the Petrochemical Industry in Saudi Arabia', *Journal of Arabian Studies*, 1 (1), 2011: 99–116.

93 Ibid.

94 Ibid.

95 Karen E. Young, 'The Gulf's Eastward Turn: The Logic of Gulf–China Economic Ties', AEI, February 2019, www.aei.org/research-products/report/the-gulfs-eastward-turn-the-logic-of-gulf-china-economic-ties/

96 American Enterprise Institute, 'China Global Investment Tracker', www.aei.org/china-global-investment-tracker/

97 HSBC, 'UAE Economy Offers Increasing Range of Opportunities for Chinese Investors', 14 February 2021, www.business.hsbc.ae/en-gb/insights/growing-my-business/hsbc-china-uae-corridor

98 Ibid.

99 KIZAD, 'Construction Starts on AED 2.2. Billion Tire Manufacturing Plant in Abu Dhabi; First in the UAE', 22 January 2019, www.kizad.ae/2019/01/22/construction-starts-on-aed-2-2-billion-tire-manufacturing-plant-in-abu-dhabi-first-in-the-uae/

100 Reuters Staff, 'China, UAE Sign 35 Billion Yuan Currency Swap: PBOC', *Reuters*, 17 January 2012, https://jp.reuters.com/article/instant-article/idUSTRE80G19020120117

101 David Dollar and Samantha Gross, 'China's Currency Displacing the Dollar in Global Oil Trade? Don't Count on It', Brookings, 19 April 2018, www.brookings.edu/blog/order-from-chaos/2018/04/19/chinas-currency-displacing-the-dollar-in-global-oil-trade-dont-count-on-it/#cancel

102 Young, 'The Gulf's Eastward Turn': 2.

103 Anna Zacharias, 'How a Growing Chinese Community Found a Home Away from Home in the UAE', *The National*, 31 July 2019, www.thenationalnews.com/uae/how-a-growing-chinese-community-found-a-home-away-from-home-in-the-uae-1.889406

104 Muhammad Zulfikar Rakhmat, 'China and the UAE: New Cultural Horizons', Middle East Institute, 19 March 2015, www.mei.edu/publications/china-and-uae-new-cultural-horizons

105 Reuters Staff, 'Dubai Registers 16.7 Million Tourists in 2019, Chinese Visitors Rise', *Reuters*, 21 January 2020, www.reuters.com/article/us-emirates-dubai-tourism-idUSKBN1ZK2L5

106 Rakhmat, 'China and the UAE'.

107 Xinhua, 'First Chinese Public School Outside China Opens in Dubai', 2 September 2020, www.xinhuanet.com/english/2020-09/02/c_139337577.htm

108 Congressional Research Service, 'The United Arab Emirates (UAE): Issues for U.S. Policy', 15 Aril 2021, 18, https://fas.org/sgp/crs/mideast/RS21852.pdf%20 p%2016

109 Elias Aad, 'Why Smart Cities Are Important to the UAE', *Gulf Business*, 15 June 2021, https://gulfbusiness.com/why-smart-cities-are-important-to-the-uae/

110 ITP, 'Dubai South Signs MoU with Huawei for Smart Solutions', 12 July 2016, www.itp.net/infrastructure/608303-dubai-south-signs-mou-with-huawei-for-smart-solutions

111 Government of Dubai, 'DCD and Huawei Collaborate', www.dcd.gov.ae/portal/en/item/198-dcd.jsp; Huawei, 'Huawei and Dubai Police Join Forces to Make Dubai a Safer City through Innovation', 30 May 2016, https://e.huawei.com/ae/news/ae/2015/2016/201605300841

112 UAE Free Zones, 'Dubai Virtual Commercial City', www.uaefreezones.com/dubai_virtual_commercial_city_free_zone.html

113 Emirates News Agency, 'Nasdaq Dubai, Zhongtai Financial International and Beijing Tian Tai Law Firm Sign Agreement to Attract Chinese Listings to Dubai', 26 August 2020, http://wam.ae/en/details/1395302864756%20 %20

114 Jennifer Jacobs and Bloomberg, 'Biden Expands Trump's Investment Blacklist of Chinese Companies to 59 Firms', *Fortune*, 4 June 2021, https://fortune.com/2021/06/04/biden-trump-china-us-investment-blacklist/

115 Chyrine Mezher, 'UAE Conglomerate EDGE Partners with China, US, Unveils New Homegrown Capabilities', *Breaking Defence*, 15 November 2021, https://breakingdefense.com/2021/11/uae-conglomerate-edge-partners-with-china-us-unveils-new-homegrown-capabilities/

116 AFP, 'China Thanks UAE for Backing Beijing's Xinjiang Policies', 22 July 2019, available at https://ph.news.yahoo.com/china-thanks-uae-backing-beijings-xinjiang-policies-112117280.html

117 Ibid.

118 Laleh Khalili, 'Growing Pains', *London Review of Books*, 18 March 2021.

119 Ibid.

120 Gordon Lubold and Warren P. Strobel, 'Secret Chinese Port Project in Persian Gulf Rattles U.S. Relations with U.A.E.', *The Wall Street Journal*, 19 November 2021, www.wsj.com/articles/us-china-uae-military-11637274224

121 UAE official speaking under the Chatham House rule, 9 December 2021.

122 Posture statement of General Kenneth F. McKenzie, Jr, Commander CENTCOM, before the Senate Armed Services Committee. 22 April 2021, www.centcom.mil/ABOUT-US/POSTURE-STATEMENT/

123 UAE official speaking under the Chatham House rule, 9 December 2021.

124 Leng Shumei and Yu Xi, 'Sinopharm to Launch COVID-19 Drug Clinical Trials in UAE', *Global Times*, 9 November 2021, www.globaltimes.cn/page/202111/1238541.shtml

125 BGI, 'G42 and BGI Announce COVID-19 Detection Lab', 31 March 2020, www.bgi.com/global/company/news/g42-and-bgi-announce-covid-19-detection-lab/

126 Gillian Duncan, 'Everything We Need to Know About Hayat-Vax as Distribution of UAE's Covid-19 Vaccine Begins', *The National*, 11 May 2021, www.thenationalnews.com/uae/health/everything-we-know-about-hayat-vax-as-distribution-of-uae-s-covid-19-vaccine-begins-1.1220854

127 Mehran Kamrava, 'The China Model and the Middle East', in James Reardon-Anderson (ed.), *The Red Star and the Crescent*. Oxford: Oxford University Press, 2018: 59–60.

128 Mohammed Turki Alsudairi, 'Arab Encounters with Maoist China: Transnational Journeys, Diasporic Lives and Intellectual Discourses', *Third World Quarterly*, 42 (3), 2021: 503–524.

8

Relations with Europe: conditionality and unity

Introduction

This chapter focuses on UK and French interactions with Saudi Arabia and the UAE. Beginning with a brief summary of British and French colonial-era influences in the Arabian Peninsula, the British withdrawal 'East of Suez', engagement during the Cold War and moving on into the contemporary era, the chapter highlights convergence and divergences in their foreign policies. The chapter is significant because the UK and France spearhead European involvement in the region which has directly or indirectly affected the Gulf States. Areas of activity include participation in the 1990/91 Gulf War, in the Middle East peace process, diplomatic engagement with Iran from the 1990s and participation in the US-led intervention in Afghanistan from 2001. The UK and France also took contrasting approaches to the invasion of Iraq in 2003, and France took a leading position in the NATO intervention of Libya in 2011. After the UK's return to 'East of Suez' in 2014 and a French defence cooperation agreement with the UAE in 2019, there is evidence to suggest a continuation of colonial-era policies.

The rentier states of Qatar, the UAE and to some extent Saudi Arabia have been active in pursuing an entrepreneurial economic statecraft and state branding policy in which expanding soft-power opportunities in sport, and especially but not exclusively in Europe, have been key to extending influence. Qatar has, since 2008, sponsored France's most prestigious horse race, the Prix de l'Arc de Triomphe; Qatar Sports Investments, established in 2005 by Sheikh Al Thani, bought a 70 per cent stake in French football team Paris Saint-Germain FC in 2011 and has invested more than $1 billion in players.[1] Most significantly for geopolitics, Qatar is hosting the 2022 FIFA World Cup. The UAE, Bahrain and Saudi Arabia host the Formula 1 Grand Prix and many GCC states have close ties to British and French horse racing, as is detailed below. Khaldun Al Mubarak, the son of the ambassador to France assassinated in 1984, who is a leading Emirati entrepreneur, power broker and close to Mohammed bin Zayed, helped to oversee the Mansur bin Zayed-led purchase of Manchester City Football Club.[2] Through such purchases and subsequent premier league wins, the UAE is able to extend its soft power or sports statecraft literally into new fields. Al Mubarak is also chairman of the City Football Group, founded in 2013, which owns New York City Football Club, Melbourne City Football Club and Mumbai City Football Club.[3]

The United Kingdom

British imperial policy in the Middle East and Saudi territorial expansion led to the first contact with Ibn Saud in 1902. In the First World War Saudi Arabia remained neutral between Britain and the Turks, and relations with Ibn Saud cooled, due to British support for Sharif Hussein, who proclaimed himself 'King of the Arabs'. To prevent Ibn Saud from lending support to the Turks, Britain extended a monthly stipend of £5,000 and 3,000 rifles – deemed insufficient, especially as Sharif Hussein received more.[4] After the First World War Britain became the major power in the region, in Iraq, Palestine and Trans-Jordan, and was focused on border issues with Ibn Saud. But, after Britain reneged on Arab independence 'in the limits and boundaries proposed by the Sherif of Mecca', Hussein refused to sign the 1919 Treaty of Versailles and subsequent proposals.[5] Britain worried about the impact this would have on opinion across the wider Muslim world. Al-Enazy notes that by withdrawing support from King Hussein and failing to intervene when Ibn Saud's forces conquered Hussein's kingdom in 1924, Britain supported Saudi statehood, but also other objectives of the time such as its own continued occupation of Palestine and the Balfour Declaration.[6]

Control of the Holy Mosques facilitated statehood and removed Ibn Saud from international isolation. He was accepted as king of al-Hijaz in 1926, and the Treaty of Jeddah was signed with the British, recognising his sovereignty over the kingdom of Hejaz and Nejd. Britain used treaties 'as the means to gain the concessions and bases, or any other favourable conditions, believed to be necessary for Empire defence',[7] and this was the first example of a British agreement concluded with an independent Arab state. But it also reflected the growing autonomy of Ibn Saud through the divine power attributed to him through the Saudi–Wahhabi alliance of 1744, and his potential threat to British authority in places such as Kuwait. This made it especially important to protect and consolidate British interests in neighbouring Persia, where the Anglo-Persian Oil Company operated and was effectively nationalised by the British in 1914. Prince Faisal of Saudi Arabia was sent to the UK in 1932, although it was the king's personal adviser, Fuad Bey Hamza, who on 7 May made the offer to Sir Lancelot Oliphant, a senior civil servant at the Foreign Office, of oil drilling rights in exchange for a loan of £500,000 in gold.[8] Oliphant said 'British firms might hesitate to accept a report [on mineral resources] not drawn up by a British expert', and expressed doubt 'as to the readiness of British firms to sink capital in a little-known country at the present time'.[9] Saudi oil was discovered by an American consortium in 1938.

James Barr has found that extra-regional influence in the Arabian Peninsula extends to the US bringing about the end of the British Empire in the Middle East. This stands in contrast to Nasser's Arab nationalism and popular uprisings, which are usually cited as the main causes.[10] Barr points to the US holding opposing opinions to the British on many regional issues such as Saudi oil and the Suez Canal, and which managed to encourage and exploit widespread opposition to the British.[11] The UK had used its influence in the Middle East to secure the route to India and then, after Indian independence in 1947, focused on oil to generate revenue, address a poor balance of payments and enable it to defend itself in any war with the Soviet Union.[12] The 1953 cooperation between the UK and US on overthrowing Mossadegh was in fact an aberration.

The British demise in the Middle East after the Second World War was rooted in economic hardship and delivered by the non-intervention posture of Prime Minister Atlee from 1945 to 1951, the fallout from the Suez Crisis in 1956 and the US pursuit of decolonisation in the 1960s, first articulated by the US and a reluctant Britain in the Atlantic Charter. In 1967 Britain withdrew forces from Aden, pushed out by the National Liberation Front and the Front for the Liberation of Occupied South Yemen. But the Dhofar rebellion in neighbouring Oman from 1963 to 1976 caused Britain, led notably by the Special Air Service, to help push back against rebel forces who were supported at that time by the Soviet Union and China. Britain wasn't the only state to support the Omani sultan: Iran, Pakistan and Jordan also played a role. Britain announced its intention to withdraw 'East of Suez' in 1968, just a few weeks after the devaluation of the pound. Prime Minister Harold Wilson and defence secretary Dennis Healey announced that British troops would be withdrawn by 1971 from military bases in Asia, from Malaysia and Singapore, as well as from the Gulf. There was stern resistance to the British leaving the UAE and Qatar, and Abu Dhabi, Dubai and Qatar all offered to pay for Britain's continuing military presence.[13] The British declined the offer.

Contemporary UK–Saudi/UAE relations

Despite British withdrawal from the Gulf, caused by imperial decline and loss of empire, including India, and with it a scaling-down of British inclusion in great power competition, UK relations with the GCC states remained close. In the smaller Arab Gulf states the UK was highly engaged at security, military and elite levels to secure oil at stable prices, political stability, rational investment of Gulf surplus funds in the West and the steady implementation of social and economic development programmes.[14] These links were accompanied by greater dependence on the US, which served the UK's security and status objectives, and UK membership in the European Economic Community (EEC) from 1973. These developing international connections have reinforced links to the Gulf, notably Iraq, but also led to differences between the positions of the UK, France and Germany on Iran and US containment policies. For the GCC states, the 1973 oil crisis, including a short embargo, fundamentally reshaped the global distribution of economic power in their favour. Saudi Arabia led a softening of the OPEC position on the embargo and took on a leading investment role in the City of London. The GCC states' ongoing search for relative autonomy has created new opportunities for the UK (and a host of other states) to exert influence and gain, maintain or extend a foothold in the region.

The UK has provided military assistance to the SANG for over six decades. The UK defence model is mirrored in the kingdom's reform of the armed forces, although the chain of command is still to the Council of Political and Security Affairs, chaired by Mohammed bin Salman rather than to the National Security Council.[15] The British Military Mission, including military and contracted personnel, is training SANG in counterterrorism, how to deal with improvised explosive devices, hostage rescue, close protection and Hajj security.[16] The Royal Navy has also played an integral role in enhancing UK relations in the Gulf. *HMS Juffair* was a British base established in Bahrain in 1935, but was leased by the US navy after 1971. The May 2011 Business Plan aimed at establishing 'strategic relationships' with the GCC states, followed by the UK government's 'Gulf Initiative' and new defence cooperation agreements.[17] UK initiatives also focused on more high-level visits, trade and culture promotion. The British army would gain experience in a new theatre, provide capacity building to allied states and gain knowledge about how to influence them.[18] It was announced in 2014 that *HMS Juffair* would be re-established as British base and opened in 2018. The base forms the command element of Operation Kipion, the Royal Navy's maritime presence in the Gulf and Indian Ocean, which is designed to help ease concerns about Iranian influence. Four mine counter-measure vessels and one Type 23 frigate are based there, supported by a Royal Fleet Auxiliary Vessel.[19] But after Royal Marines seized an Iranian oil tanker in the Gulf of Gibraltar in 2019, the IRGC responded likewise in the Strait of Hormuz, in an escalation of tensions.[20]

The UK has a fairly light defensive footprint spread across the Arabian Peninsula and Mediterranean. It is also growing steadily in response to changing UK priorities reflecting, amongst other things, UK arms sales and the regional and international security situation. The UK's only Permanent Joint Operating Base is in Cyprus, which supports Operation Shader, the UK's contribution to the global coalition against ISIS. However, army units deployed to Cyprus can be called on to serve in Iraq, Saudi Arabia or other parts of the Gulf.[21] The Royal Air Force has an operational base at Al Udeid in Qatar and access to bases at Al Minhad air base in the UAE and Al Musannah air base in Oman.[22] Oman is becoming increasingly important to the UK since a new Permanent Joint Logistics Support Base was established in Duqm to support new aircraft carriers when they are in the Indian Ocean or Gulf. About 1,350 UK personnel were deployed in the region under Operation Shader, 2,150 personnel are based in Cyprus and just 120 military personnel and 100 Ministry of Defence civilian personnel are in Saudi Arabia. These are working on commercial projects including the Saudi Arabian National Guard Communications Project (SANGCOM) and the Ministry of Defence of Saudi Armed Forces Project.

SANGCOM involves communications and computer equipment, support, consulting and training in a project that has run since 1978 and is estimated to be worth £5 billion up to 2020.[23] Since 2010 it has involved GPT Special Project Management as a partner in phase 3, worth £1.96 billion over ten years. GPT is part of the French company EADS (renamed as Airbus in 2014). The Financial Controller and Programme Director of GPT are said to have uncovered irregular payments of £14.9 million from 2007 to 2010, as well as other unusual costs such as luxury vehicles.[24] In January 2020 the UK Serious Fraud Office (SFO) entered into a €991 million record-breaking Deferred Prosecution Agreement with Airbus as part of a €3.6 billion global resolution deal for failure to prevent bribery across other jurisdictions.[25] In July 2020 this was followed up with SFO charges against three individuals in connection to GPT's activities in Saudi Arabia. GPT subsequently pleaded guilty to one charge of corruption and was ordered to pay a confiscation order of £20.60 million, a fine of £7.52 million and costs of £2.2 million.[26] A trial against the three individuals begins in May 2022. What bearing this will have on SANGOM is unknown and, due to its sensitivity, may yet attract the attention of the UK attorney general or the prime minister. As one former senior UK official noted, corruption is illegal in the UK but is rooted in the Saudi system.[27] These episodes highlight the inherent tension between UK and Saudi Arabia in terms of elite political interests, supporting UK jobs, respect for UK law and public opinion.

The UK deployed troops to Saudi Arabia in May 2018 to assist Saudi ground forces, providing 'information, advice and assistance' during the war in Yemen even during a court-ordered ban on arms sales in February 2020.[28] The UK government believes that President Hadi had legitimacy in the eyes of the UN as leader of Yemen in 2011 and Saudi Arabia has recourse to an assertion of self-defence following widespread Houthi rocket attacks against the kingdom. The troops will have been instrumental in helping Saudi Arabia to shore up its southern border with Yemen after cross-border attacks. UK reliance on a Saudi-led review process to address allegations of violations of international law in Yemen was deemed to be inadequate by a UK parliament review in 2017. A former UK government official acknowledges that mistakes have been made, but the Houthis have also used propaganda and they don't always wear military uniforms, leaving them potentially free to carry out unlawful activities on the battlefield.[29] The UK, under a US military-led effort, was also looking to beef up the security of critical infrastructure such as at Abqaiq and Khurais following the attack in 2019, for which the UK, France, Germany and the US hold Iran accountable.[30] The UK government refuses to confirm whether British troops are operating in Yemen beyond an assistance role. If it proves to be true, another legal case may be brought in addition to the one to stop arms sales to Saudi Arabia. UK arms sales to Saudi Arabia were found to be unlawful in June 2019, but the ban was reversed in July 2020 after a government report found there had been no 'pattern' of Saudi air strikes that breached regulatory law – rather, they were 'isolated incidents'.[31] But non-governmental organisations (NGOs) such as the UK's Overseas Development Institute believe that litigation could still change the situation in Yemen.[32]

On economic and defence cooperation, UK trade with the Middle East amounts to $57.2 billion annually, $50.8 billion of which is with the Gulf region.[33] The UK–Saudi Al-Yamamah (dove) arms deal from 1985 has run to the present day. It is now called As Salaam (peace/greeting), developed in the 2005 'Understanding Document' and subsequent contract for Eurofighter Typhoons with weapon systems. The whole arrangement was said to be worth £40 billion in 2005, and the largest arms deal in UK history.[34] It is said to have been heavily supported by Prime Minister Thatcher's personal cultivation of relations with Prince Sultan, the then Saudi defence minister, and King Fahd.[35] It was helped by Israeli objections to Saudi Arabia securing the Mirage from France or F-15E from the US. The deal has also been subject to a series of accusations concerning overcharges, commissions[36] and kickbacks.[37]

Saudi Arabia has reinvested oil revenue into the UK economy through the stock market, bonds and luxury property, said to amount to £93 billion or equivalent to a fifth of the UK current account deficit during a period of economic instability during Brexit and COVID-19.[38] By the time of the war in Yemen in 2015, the UK was already economically compromised. Dependency increased after the Brexit vote in 2016, After the Brexit vote in 2016 and the UK withdrawal from the EU, the UK faced losing a significant amount of trade with the EU, valued at a total of £292 billion (43 per cent of all UK exports).[39] This immediately put emphasis on other strong trade and investment relationships, particularly those in the Arab Gulf, which might help to plug any potential shortfall. UK trade with the GCC reached £41.4 billion in 2019, with UK exports rising by 48 per cent from 2010 to 2019, to reach £26.1 billion.[40] UK exports to Saudi Arabia alone were estimated to directly or indirectly support 129,000 jobs in the UK in 2016.[41] The then British prime minister made the GCC an integral part of British foreign and economic policy, following visits to India, China, the US and several European countries in an attempt to boost cooperation on trade and investment.[42] The Integrated Security, Defence and Foreign Policy Review might prioritise the Indo-Pacific, but will have little effect on UK policy in the Gulf and Middle East. Alistair Burt, a former minister of state at the Foreign and Commonwealth Office, noted that the region is the third-largest non-EU market for the UK, where the UK can help provide jobs as well as security, and lobby for change.[43]

Saudi investments continue to pour into the UK from Saudi nationals said to have links to Riyadh, including stakes in the *Independent* and *Evening Standard* newspapers which initially attracted a UK government probe into editorial independence.[44] In October 2021, Saudi Arabia's PIF invested £300 million to buy Newcastle United football club.[45] Further public and/or private Saudi investments in UK premier league football clubs could follow, especially due to an opportunity generated by the divestment of Chelsea following UK sanctions in response to Russia's invasion of Ukraine in 2022. Saudi Arabia's pledge to decarbonise its economy is also leading to significant investments in the UK's chemical industry.[46] A number of Saudi tourism and development projects were discussed at the virtual trade summit between the UK and GCC in June 2021.

In March 2022, Prime Minister Boris Johnson, probably in coordination with the Biden administration, visited the UAE and Saudi Arabia to request that they step up oil production to help lower energy prices during the war in Ukraine. He was not successful; furthermore, his visit coincided with the mass execution of eighty-one men on charges of terrorism and holding 'deviant beliefs', three of whom were executed during his visit in an apparent gesture of defiance against western conditionality and alleged values-based foreign policy. However, UK health diplomacy has gained a warmer reception, including the construction of a King's College London hospital, commencing in 2022 and set to open in 2023. The UAE has asserted its red lines against western researchers on particularly sensitive topics related to national security. The 2018 arrest of Matthew Hedges, a Durham University PhD student, being a case in point. After being accused of being a British spy and sentenced to life in prison, he was subsequently released after spending almost six months in solitary confinement. However, decisions about entry into the UAE can include reference to broader considerations. For example, academics who appear to delegitimise UAE allies such as the Bahraini monarchy can also fall foul of the UAE government. This was the case for Dr Kristian Coates Ulrichsen, who was refused entry in 2013 while working for the London School of Economics.[47]

The UAE has shown a keen interest in the UK economy. Abu Dhabi supported Barclays bank during the economic fallout from the global financial crisis in 2008, saving the bank from partial nationalisation. Although the £3.5 billion deal was conducted by Sheikh Mansur bin Zayed, he was in fact working on behalf of the government of Abu Dhabi.[48] Bilateral trade is expected to double by 2020, to £25 billion. The UK is also active in the UAE. More than 5,000 UK businesses operate there such as BP, Shell, Rolls Royce, HSBC, BAE Systems, John Lewis and Standard Chartered. Here the UAE competes with Qatari investments in the UK of upwards of £40 billion in businesses as diverse as Harrods, The Shard, the British Airports Authority (which runs major airports such as Heathrow), and Sainsburys. The UK was represented at the Dubai Expo 2021. Mubadala Investment Company has invested £800 million in UK life sciences through the UK–UAE Sovereign Investment Partnership.[49] There has been follow-up in a proposed £400 million deal with the University of Cambridge, the largest-ever investment to be received by the university, should it go ahead. However, this has once again raised academic freedom and human rights concerns. The university suspended talks in October 2021 following claims about the UAE's use of Pegasus spyware.[50]

The UK has played a leading role since 2012 in selling arms to the UAE that employ cryptography. Dubai's influence in the UK, through the holdings of Sheikh Mohammed bin Rashid Al Maktoum, is similar to Saudi influence, but is more concentrated in London, Scotland and Newmarket property – surpassing the size of Queen Elizabeth II's own estates – as well as a more subtle horse-racing connection with the queen.[51] In March 2020 Sheikh Mohammed was found by the British High Court to have organised the forced repatriation of his two daughters, including Princess Shamsa from Cambridge in England.[52] Possibly more damaging to UK - UAE relations has been the revelation that spyware linked to the UAE was found in on computers in No. 10 Downing Street and in the Foreign, Commonwealth and Development Office in 2020 and 2021.[53] Gulf donors continue to hold a central place in the UK's desire to spread the cost of development spending, especially where interests on forging stability converge, such as in the cases of Afghanistan, Syria and Yemen.

Following Brexit, the UK has made global anti-corruption sanctions a key area of British foreign policy, but in the Saudi case sanctions have been applied against only a few individuals, and this is bound to have been coordinated with the US and European allies, as well as with the Saudi government, in order to minimise any political, economic or diplomatic fallout. Targeted sanctions under the so-called UK 'Magnitsky law' were activated against Ahmed Hassan Mohammed al Asiri, former deputy head of Saudi intelligence services, Saud al-Qahatani, former royal court adviser, and seventeen other Saudis in 2021, all blamed for the death of Jamal Khashoggi.[54] These individuals were fact fired by King Salman back in 2018.[55] Such UK sanctions therefore appear to be designed more to deflect criticism that London is often a preferred destination for the spending of ill-gotten gains, than to punish the kingdom or undermine bilateral relations.

A December 2020 report from the cross-party group of British MPs investigating Mohammed bin Nayef's detention and the denial of access to him found the kingdom's treatment of political detainees a 'threat to the stability of the government of the KSA [Kingdom of Saudi Arabia]' and 'a wider threat to international peace and stability'.[56] A former senior UK government official stated that Saudi Arabia was unlikely to take a cross-party panel decision seriously.[57] Nayef was at the centre of counterterrorism cooperation not only with the US but also with the UK, as Sir Sherard Cowper-Coles noted in 2011: 'I think the strength and depth of UK–Saudi counterterrorism cooperation is truly extraordinary and in large part it is a tribute to Prince Mohammed bin Nayef, the Counter-Terrorist Minister.'[58]

The UK is unlikely to drastically change policy on security issues in the Gulf unless it is forced to scale back due to successful legal action. The Campaign Against Arms Trade did win leave to seek a judicial review of the decision taken by Liz Truss when secretary of state for international trade to restart arms exports to Saudi Arabia in 2020, but a 'clear risk' would have to be demonstrated that a weapon had been used in a serious violation of international humanitarian law. It is unlikely that such a challenge will succeed, given the determination of the UK government to avoid this eventuality due to the costs to itself, its credibility and its relations with the kingdom, and its effect on a UK–GCC or Saudi free trade agreement which was being prepared in 2021. Saudi and UAE trade and investments, either bilaterally or within a GCC free trade framework, are likely to become more widespread in the post-Brexit UK economy, leading to greater interdependency and subordination of other considerations. When considered in the context of rising East Asian influence in the Gulf, notably from China, and conflicting UK political, economic and legal pressures, UK influence may become even more diminished than before.

France

For reasons related to the respective spheres of influence established by the British and French, and assented to by Russia in the 1916 Sykes–Picot Agreement, French interest in the Gulf was nominal. French merchants such as Antonin Besse had developed broad economic interests in the region, in his case, as an agent for Shell Oil in Aden and as a trader in oil, coffee, skins, timber and frankincense across the Indian Ocean and East Africa. French policy was in support of Jewish nationalist movements after 1945 as a way to force the British out. It was further shaped by failed the 1956 Suez Crisis, and by the 1967 Arab–Israeli War. De Gaulle's France distanced itself from Israel by declaring an arms export ban on all the combatants in the conflict, including missile boats (*vedettes*) ready to be exported to Israel. These were 'stolen' by Israel from docks in Cherbourg in 1969, an event that helped to preserve overt French alignment with the Arab states.[59]

Contemporary French–Saudi/UAE relations

Possibly France's biggest role vis-à-vis Saudi Arabia to date was the role it played in ending the 1979 Mecca siege, in which 50,000 pilgrims became trapped when hundreds of heavily armed Bedouin insurgents, led by Saudi preacher Juhayman al Utaybi, fortified the Grand Mosque of Mecca in an attempt to overthrow the Saudi monarchy.[60] Unable to bring the situation under control, dismayed by US inaction against Iran and upset with the US's Carter administration for alerting the world's press of the major incident in Mecca, Saudi King Khalid made a personal request to French President Valerie Giscard d'Estaing.[61] The French president secretly sent five gendarmes from France's elite antiterrorist force.[62] What happened next is subject to serious disagreement between Saudi Arabia and Qatar, the latter's view being based on French testimony in a documentary called *Juhayman: The Other Tale* which aired on the emir of Qatar-owned Al Jazeera television channel in 2020.[63]

The documentary includes a translated interview with the former French military commander Paul Barril, who contradicts previous Saudi statements on a number of points. First, Barril states that the French troops trained Saudi security personnel outside of Mecca, where entry by non-Muslims is prohibited: 'we did not discuss religious aspects [with Saudi authorities], we discussed the military aspects', before being allowed to enter the mosque to take back control.[64] Second, the authorities claimed that twenty-six pilgrims died along with 127 Saudi army personnel and 117 terrorists, while Barril's estimate of civilian deaths is between 3,000 and 5,000 and he says that Saudi soldiers acted with 'extreme cruelty' and 'did not distinguish between the hostages and their captors'.[65] Barril added: 'they [Saudi authorities] wanted 70 tonnes [of tear gas] instead of the seven [I brought with me]', and in return of this 'very secret mission' France received the 'reward' of several deals to supply Saudi Arabia with weapons.[66] This would have helped to support the reconstruction of France's defence industries after the Second World War.

The documentary was aired during the so-called Qatar Crisis, so there may have been an element of *Schadenfreude*, but the evidence hangs on the testimony of Barril and the question of why he would want to lie. French arms sales did grow from 1980, when four F-20005 frigates were ordered. They were delivered in 1985–86. Then, in 1984, Shahine surface-to-air missile systems were ordered. These were delivered in 1986–90.[67] These helped to offset a French arms sales crisis from 1986 to 1995 in many other markets. It is not known whether Barril's testimony will have any effect on Saudi–French arms sales or relations, but when documentary *The Death of a Princess*[68] aired in the UK it caused great controversy and huge damage was done to British economic interests.[69] However, given uncertainties surrounding US policy towards the kingdom, the different configuration of Qatar's economic relations with Saudi Arabia, and Riyadh's intention to maintain stable relations with Doha after the rapprochement at Al Ula, this episode may not receive the same attention or have the same impact.

In 1995, after winning the presidential election, President Jacques Chirac halted payments to intermediaries who had been involved in securing contracts for La Fayette frigates (the Sawari II contract). There was a suspicion that kickbacks from this contract and from the export of Agosta-class submarines might have financed the election campaign of his rival, Edouard Balladur.[70] This had major consequences for French arms sales to the kingdom, which were 'sharply reduced' and restricted to upgrades of existing systems.[71] Arms sales weren't restarted until the Hollande presidency of 2012–17. Former Prime Minister Balladur and François Léotard were both tried for misconduct related to this so-called 'Karachi affair', since the bombing of a bus in Karachi that killed fifteen people, including eleven French naval engineers, may have been related to it. Edouard Balladur was acquitted,[72] whilst François Léotard received a two-year suspended sentence and a fine of €100,000.[73]

From 2000 to 2019 France was the third-largest arms supplier to the kingdom, with an 8.4 per cent share, behind the US (60.6 per cent of all arms sold) and the UK (18.2 per cent).[74] France deployed a radar system as part of the Jaguar Task Force on the eastern coast of Saudi Arabia after missile attacks on the kingdom's oil infrastructure in September 2019, and

President Macron promised the deployment of the *Charles de Gaulle* aircraft carrier and battle group to support Middle East operations from January to April 2020.[75] The French government continues a liberal arms sales policy towards Saudi Arabia and the UAE, in contrast with Germany's approach. Germany's then foreign minister, Sigmar Gabriel, talked about Saudi 'adventurism' in the Middle East, possibly in the context of Prime Minister Hariri's detention in Riyadh and a growing humanitarian crisis in the Yemen conflict.[76] In response to the remarks, Saudi Arabia withdrew its ambassador to Germany and denied accreditation to Germany's ambassador. German exports to the kingdom subsequently dropped by 5 per cent in the first half of 2018.[77] Although a ban on arms exports to the kingdom was put in place since October 2018 and continues up to the time of writing, Berlin did concurrently approve the export of mounted radar systems which track the origin of enemy fire and enable precision counterstrikes.

Macron accused Merkel of 'demagoguery' over German arms export policy.[78] In the context of the war in Yemen, the French National Assembly did authorise a fact-finding mission in 2018, but it had less power than a full parliamentary inquiry.[79] It made a number of recommendations in November 2020, including meaningful legislative oversight which goes beyond 'a statistical approach and the general information it contains' and 'better defining the scope of national defence secrecy, which is sometimes interpreted in an unnecessarily broad manner'.[80] The French approach differs markedly from that of the UK, which appears to rely on a robust legal defence of alleged Saudi war crimes in Yemen rather than a broader assessment of the UK government position.

Abu Dhabi bought sixty-two French Mirage 2000-9 aircraft in 1986 for the UAE Air Force, but it's not clear how many are still in service – perhaps fifty-five, with fourteen used for training.[81] President Sarkozy visited the UAE in May 2009, with economic considerations a foremost interest, including an $11 billion Dassault contract for sixty Rafale fighter jets. There were also rumours when UK Prime Minister David Cameron attended the Dubai Airshow in 2013 that the Eurofighter Typhoon, built by a European consortium, might be sold. Neither of these two deals came to pass. Following a visit by Chuck Hagel, the then US defence secretary, to the UAE in April 2013 to sell more F-16s, the Eurofighter consortium and Dassault were locked in a contest to supply about sixty more jets to replace the ageing Mirage 2000s.[82] But in June 2017 the UAE turned to Russia for Su-27 fighters, and will work with Russia to build a next-generation fighter.

The UAE army has at least 545 tanks, including 380 LeClerc tanks and 370 armoured personnel carriers from France. The LeClerc tanks form part of a $3.5 billion offset programme, one of the UAE's biggest so far. In 2017 the UAE bought two Gowind-class corvettes from France.[83] In the same year the UAE contracted with the Dutch firm Damen, a construction firm in Romania, the French systems company Thales and Abu Dhabi Ship Building (ADSB) to fit out a new powerful offshore patrol vessel.[84] However, ADSB appeared to be going it alone with close to $1 billion order for three Falaj 3-class offshore patrol vessels in 2021.[85] In December the same year, the UAE placed a $19 billion order for eighty Rafale fighter jets and twelve military helicopters..[86] All this fits perfectly with the UAE's attempts to balance its defence contracting, working with allies that are least susceptible to applying political pressure and building a new military-industrial complex which is adaptable to delivering cutting-edge technology for modern warfare.

French policy has been premised on maintaining contacts and guaranteeing a seat at the negotiating table on regional security issues. Although François Mitterrand, president of France from 1981 to 1995, was the first left-wing politician to assume the presidency in the Fifth Republic, he still believed in the Gaullist ideals, including a French role and mission in the world often linked to democracy and human rights, derived from its unique history.[87] In the Middle East, French continuity was also assured on the territorial integrity and unity of Lebanon; the search for peace between Israel and its Arab neighbours; a just settlement of the Palestinian problem; and the promotion of French trading and diplomatic interests.[88] France was also at the forefront in shaping what would become the EU's policy towards the Middle East, through agreements such as the Venice Declaration in 1980 which recognised the PLO as a party to the peace negotiations. France is an important member of NATO and, as the fourth-largest troop contributor, fully reintegrated its troops into NATO's command structure under President Sarkozy in 2009. Paris prefers to work through multilateral institutions to 'legitimise' its actions, from economic sanctions to the use of force. This role conception matters especially in France, where the president is commander-in-chief of the armed forces and has special interests and constitutional provisions in the domains of foreign affairs, security and defence.[89] These have traditionally remained the president's *domaine réservé*.

Arab views of French policy changed with the French participation in Operation Desert Storm, a thirty-nation coalition against the Iraqi invasion of Kuwait. However, France's participation was accompanied by ambiguity on two fronts. First, President Mitterrand tried to negotiate a diplomatic solution with Saddam Hussein right up to almost the last minute, just seventeen days before the launch of Operation Desert Storm. Second, France's credibility was undermined by the resignation of defence minister Jean-Pierre Chevenment as the air campaign began. He was a founding member of the

Franco–Iraqi Friendship Society and was outspoken about the military intervention from the start.[90] France had privileged Iraq in its relations among the Arab Gulf states, given its border with Syria where it had clear interests, and intervention aligned with the US did not fit well with its Arab-policy credentials. Jean-Pierre Chevenment noted the Gulf War as 'America's War' in his resignation, and that the war 'risks driving us further each day from the objectives set by the United Nations'.[91]

After Iraq invaded Kuwait in 1990, France sent a frigate to augment the two French warships already in Gulf waters. Operation Salamandre (Salamander) launched the deployment of the 5th Regiment of Combat Helicopters, and a company of the first Regiment of Infantry on board the French aircraft carrier *Clemenceau*. A cruiser, *Colbert* (named after Jean-Baptiste Colbert), tanker *Var* and the tugboat A696 *Buffle* (Buffalo) were also sent, along with a landing-platform ship *Foudre* (Lightning) to increase French medical capabilities in Kuwait. Operation Daguet (Broket deer) was the codename for French ground operations during the Gulf War, which included the French Foreign Legion and were tasked with guarding the left flank of the allied advance against Iraq in 1991. Although not initially integrated into US command and control, the French nevertheless coordinated closely with the US (including CENTCOM) and the Saudis, and by January 1991 came under the tactical control of the US XVIII Airborne Corps and were reinforced with other divisions of the US army.

As a member of the UN Security Council, France has secured UN resolutions for potential or actual use of force in the Gulf War, Bosnia, Afghanistan, Congo, the Ivory Coast and Haiti and for the NATO mission in Libya. One exception was in 1999 when France, facing a likely Russian veto, failed to get a UN resolution in time, and joined NATO allies in the war against Serbia to prevent ethnic cleansing in Kosovo. Notably, President Chirac opposed the 2003 US intervention in Iraq to oust Saddam Hussein, predicting that it would unleash international terrorism.[92] Aware of the damage done to Franco–US relations and its position in NATO during the Iraq intervention, President Sarkozy fully supported the reintegration France into NATO in 2009, de-emphasised France's traditional role in sub-Saharan Africa and re-emphasised its role in the Middle East. The same year, France set up Camp de la Paix in Abu Dhabi, joining other 'forces of presence' in Djibouti, Ivory Coast, Gabon and Senegal. It was set up after attacks on oil tankers in the Gulf which the US blamed on Iran.[93] The UAE is closer to the sensitive choke point of the Strait of Hormuz than either *HMS Juffair* or the US Fifth Fleet stationed in Bahrain,[94] but will complement their activities. In 2020, the European Maritime Security Mission became operational in the Gulf, based out of Camp de la Paix, with officers from Belgium, Denmark,

Netherlands and France. *Courbet* was the first vessel to take part in the operation, to be joined by the frigate *De Ruyter* from the Netherlands.[95]

President Sarkozy also led the UN arms embargo and economic sanctions against Gadhafi's Libya in 2011. France was the first country to launch airstrikes against the Gadhafi regime and was one the main contributors, along with the UK, to the NATO campaign based on UN Security Council Resolution 1973. Sarkozy was found guilty of trying to bribe a judge in 2014 and received a custodial sentence.[96] He returned to court in March 2021 in relation to the so-called 'Bygmalion affair', a case involving allegations that Muammar Gadhafi sent him a €50 million donation to fund his successful election campaign between November 2006 and January 2007.[97] France, the UAE, Egypt and Russia have a common interest in supporting Libyan strongman, Khalifa Haftar, who lost ground after attempting to advance on Tripoli.

French economic linkages and soft power in the UAE have continued to blossom. President Macron, like his predecessors, is determined for France to assume its rightful place on the international stage. Mubadala established a sovereign investment partnership with France in 2013 and has grown its mid-cap financing in 2020 with Bpifrance, the French national investment bank..[98] Other partnerships between Mubadala and financial services firms such as Barings could bring further investment into France, as well as other European countries.[99] The UAE paid €10 million as a gift to the French government to restore the theatre at château of Fontainebleau, where President Macron met Mohammed bin Zayed in September 2021. On the French side, a branch campus of the Sorbonne university opened in Abu Dhabi in 2006; the Louvre Abu Dhabi opened in November 2017 and is licensed under agreement until 2037; the French company Egis was awarded a project management consultancy contract for the development of the UAE railway network in 2018;[100] and the Guggenheim Abu Dhabi is being constructed. French companies are involved in the UAE's local nuclear supply chain. Various cultural activities also take place and France was represented at the Dubai Expo 2021.

Although France supported the JCPOA with Iran in 2015, in line with establishing stability in the Gulf, this too was done for economic reasons. The French petroleum company Total has maintained a presence in Tehran simply to make sure that it would get paid for previous contracts, and was awarded a new gas contract in 2017.[101] Cooperation in the energy sector could still be an area which contributes to more positive political engagement in the future. Franco-Iranian relations have also been affected by French support for Iraq during the Iran–Iraq War, French participation in the NATO intervention in Afghanistan, support for EU sanctions and a lack of confidence in Iranian decision making.[102] French leverage over Iran, Lebanon and other aspects of regional security has been lacking, beyond President Macron directly intervening in November 2017 to extract then Prime Minister Saad Hariri from Riyadh, where he was being detained by the Saudi government. Having worked together on the Taif Accord, the US, France and Saudi Arabia have held talks on Lebanon's political and economic crises at the foreign minister and head of state levels. Macron directly intervened again during the diplomatic rift between Lebanon and Saudi Arabia caused by Lebanese information minister George Kordahi's comments about Yemen in 2021. The details of the French–Saudi approach remain unknown at the time of writing, but if a deal can be sustained it will enhance post-colonial French influence in Lebanon. This will include safeguarding €100 million which Paris and Washington have each invested as donors following the Beirut port explosion in August 2020, limiting Chinese influence and keeping alive prospects for Saudi re-engagement in Lebanon.

After the Trump administration withdrew from the JCPOA in 2018, France managed to leverage its higher oil purchases from the kingdom into enhanced arms sales. The French expanded cooperation with the UAE through a new defence cooperation agreement in 2019 predicated on securing the Strait of Hormuz and shared concerns about Iran. However, around the same time, Total was the largest shareholder in a Yemen gas plant at Balhaf, which is alleged to have been partly requisitioned and used as a UAE military base and secret prison in 2019, highlighting a potential conflict of interest.[103] Nevertheless, arms sales have increased from €4.7bn between 2010 and 2019.[104] In December 2021 there followed an $18 billion deal between France and the UAE covering eighty upgraded Rafale fighters and Airbus combat helicopters, representing France's largest-ever arms sale.[105] The UK and France were involved in the deployment of Giraffe radars to Riyadh in February 2020, which will help Saudi Arabia to better track and identify objects in its airspace.[106]

In 2021, President Macron continued to attempt to play a mediation role between Iran and the US and attempted to cement gains in Lebanon. He also opted to secure first-mover advantage by being one of the first European heads of state to visit Saudi Arabia after the Khashoggi furore, as part of Gulf tour, and to confirm the Rafale fighters and Airbus combat helicopters deal. This is in the context of the trilateral security pact between Australia, UK and US (AUKUS), which compromised France's multi-billion dollar submarine deal with Australia earlier in the year. However, while the attack on the French consulate in Jeddah in 2020 highlights anger at domestic French policy towards Muslim communities, the suspected Dakar rally terror attack against the French team in Saudi Arabia in January 2022 drew attention to anger against French and Saudi policy with possible intent to embarrass the Saudi security services.

Conclusion

This chapter has drawn attention to British and French imperial rivalry with the overarching imperative of connecting a series of trading posts to maximise global influence. The 1973 oil crisis catalysed greater UK and Saudi Arabia cohesion around oil price moderation, political stability, the recycling of oil revenues in the West and steady social and economic development programmes. Just as the 1973 crisis was considered a great equaliser of economic power, implementation of the Vision strategies could be considered the great enhancer of economic power by raising the number and level of economic stakes, also ensuring continued and consistent support for the political survival of the ruling elites.

Long-standing relations have given the UK preferred status after the US in Saudi Arabia's military-industrial complex, but UK businesses are constantly being caught in the cross-hairs of corruption investigations. Predominantly defence led, and facilitated by Gulf crises, Saudi–European bilateral relations are shrouded in secrecy, but there have been attempts by European media, NGOs, parliamentary committees and lawyers to create a more transparent framework of interaction – attempts which are bound to be resisted at the political level. Retaliation can be costly and has taken the form of suspended arms sales, awards to competitors or eviction from military bases. The negative political consequences can take decades to repair. Whilst such measures are blunt tools, they have been quite effective.

Influence can also be exerted through the tacit knowledge that cooperation, particularly valued intelligence and counterterrorism cooperation, could be at risk if criticism oversteps the mark or if conditionality is introduced. Political consolidation taking place in Saudi Arabia has had little impact when set against the domestic imperatives of European states such as trade and investment, jobs and support for other geostrategic goals in the region and internationally. However, states with more limited interests in the Gulf have been more provocative in their foreign policy debates and responses, including by suspending arms sales and voicing concerns about particular aspects of foreign policy behaviour. But without European solidarity, their position is bound to have a limited effect and will always be susceptible to a change of government.

Saudi Arabia and the UAE could encounter more resistance as their interests in European economies creep into new areas that are more susceptible to public inquiry and pressure. Saudi Arabia and the UAE continue to impact on the UK political economy through significant levels of trade and investment, with the potential for a free trade agreement with the kingdom or GCC giving it/them more weight post-Brexit. The UAE has, so far, invested more broadly, fostered elite connections through soft power and attracted a wider array of British businesses to the Emirates. A growing level of economic interdependence and less weight attributed to oil and arms could eventually normalise relations and integrate these Gulf economies into more familiar global economic patterns.

Notes

1 Adam Reed, 'Paris Saint-Germain's Qatari Owners Have Spent $1.17 Billion on Players, but the Champions League is Still Out of Reach', *CNBC*, 18 September 2018, www.cnbc.com/2018/09/18/paris-saint-germains-qatari-owners-on-players-and-champions-league.html

2 Christopher M. Davidson 'Establishing Control: Political Patronage Networks', *From Sheikhs to Sultanism: Statecraft and Authority in Saudi Arabia and the UAE*. London: C. Hurst & Co., 2021: 113–142, at 123.

3 Ibid.

4 Mohammad Zaid Al-Kahtani, 'The Foreign Policy of King Abdulaziz: A Study in the International Relations of an Emerging State', PhD Thesis, University of Leeds, October 2004: 35.

5 Sahar Huneidi, *A Broken Trust: Sir Herbert Samuel, Zionism and the Palestinians*. London: I. B. Tauris, 2001: 65–70.

6 See Askar H. Al-Enazy, *The Creation of Saudi Arabia*. Abingdon: Routledge, 2013.

7 Clive Leatherdale, 'Historical Background', *Britain and Saudi Arabia 1925–1939: The Imperial Oasis*. Abingdon: Frank Cass, 1983: 26.

8 BBC News, 'The Diplomat Who Said "No" to Saudi Oil', 8 November 2014, www.bbc.com/news/blogs-magazine-monitor-29954567

9 Ibid.

10 James Barr, *Lords of the Desert: The Battle Between the United States and Great Britain For Supremacy in the Modern Middle East*. New York: Basic Books, 2018.

11 Ibid.

12 Ibid: 3.

13 James Onley, 'Britain and the Gulf Sheikhdoms, 1820–1971: The Politics of Protection', CIRS Occasional Papers, Georgetown University Qatar, 2009: 22.

14 Gerd Nonneman, 'Constants and Variations in Gulf-British Relations', in Lawrence Potter and Gary Sick (eds) *The Gulf States and the Iran-Iraq War: Pattern Shifts and Continuities*. New York: Palgrave Macmillan, 2004: 329.

15 Neil Partrick, 'Saudi Arabia's Elusive Defense Reform', Carnegie Endowment for International Peace, 14 November 2019, https://carnegieendowment.org/sada/80354

16 Ibid.

17 Gareth Stansfield and Saul Kelly, 'A return to East of Suez? UK Military Deployment to the Gulf', RUSI briefing paper, April 2013: 8–9.

18 David B. Roberts, 'British National Interest in the Gulf: Rediscovering a Role?', *International Affairs*, 90 (3), May 2014: 670–671.

19 UK Parliament, House of Commons Library, 'UK Forces in the Middle East Region', 15 January 2020, https://commonslibrary.parliament.uk/research-briefings/cbp-8794/

20 AP News, 'The Latest: UK Rejects Iran's "Tit for Tat" View of Tanker', 21 July 2019, https://apnews.com/article/europe-persian-gulf-tensions-jeremy-hunt-tehran-international-news-b9dff688564341dcbdaffe737731598c

21 UK Parliament, House of Commons Library, 'UK Forces in the Middle East Region'.

22 Ibid.

23 World Peace Foundation, 'GPT and the Saudi National Guard', https://sites.tufts.edu/corruptarmsdeals/gpt-and-the-saudi-national-guard/

24 Ibid.

25 Serious Fraud Office, 'SFO Charges GPT and Three Individuals Following Corruption Investigation', 30 July 2020, www.sfo.gov.uk/2020/07/30/sfo-charges-gpt-and-three-individuals-following-corruption-investigation/

26 Serious Fraud Office, 'GPT Pleads Guilty to Corruption', 28 April 2021, www.sfo.gov.uk/2021/04/28/gpt-pleads-guilty-to-corruption/

27 Author's interview with a former senior UK government official who asked not to be named, 18 November 2021.

28 Neil Partrick, 'Saudi Arabia's Elusive Defense Reform', Carnegie Endowment for International Peace, 14 November 2019.

29 Author's interview with a former senior UK government official who asked not to be named, 18 November 2021.

30 Edith M. Lederer and Jill Lawless, 'UK, France, Germany Blame Iran for Saudi Oil Attacks', *AP*, 24 September 2019, https://apnews.com/article/persian-gulf-tensions-france-iran-saudi-arabia-united-nations-ee973164333e44f4b94ea590590f4ed2

31 Stephen Castle, 'Britain Says It Will Resume Arms Sales to Saudi Arabia', *The New York Times*, 7 July 2020, www.nytimes.com/2020/07/07/world/europe/britain-arms-sales-saudi-arabia.html

32 Gemma Davies, 'Can a New Legal Case Stop UK Arms Sales to Yemen?', ODI, 26 March 2021, https://odi.org/en/insights/can-a-new-legal-case-stop-uk-arms-sales-to-yemen/

33 Arab News, 'Virtual Summit to Explore GCC–UK Trade Opportunities', 8 May 2021, www.arabnews.com/node/1855756/corporate-news

34 Arron Merat, '"The Saudis Couldn't Do It without Us": The UK's True Role in Yemen's Deadly War', *The Guardian*, 18 June 2019, www.theguardian.com/world/2019/jun/18/the-saudis-couldnt-do-it-without-us-the-uks-true-role-in-yemens-deadly-war

35 David Pallister, 'The Arms Deal They Called the Dove: How Britain Grasped the Biggest Prize', *The Guardian*, 15 December 2006, www.theguardian.com/world/2006/dec/15/bae.saudiarabia

36 The issue of commissions has also been raised in relation to King Carlos in connection to a contract awarded to Spanish companies to build a high-speed railway connecting Mecca and Medina. King Carlos is alleged to have received $100 million from Saudi Arabia in 2008. On 3 August 2020 King Carlos (who abdicated in 2014) announced he would leave Spain. He left to live in Abu Dhabi, UAE, where he is said to be friendly with Crown Prince Mohamed bin Zayed al Nahyan. Die Welt, 'Spain Probes Ex-King Juan Carlos over Alleged Saudi Bribe', 8 June 2020, www.dw.com/en/spain-probes-ex-king-juan-carlos-over-alleged-saudi-bribe/a-53733202; BBC News, 'Juan Carlos: Spain's Former King Confirmed to Be in UAE', 17 August 2020, www.bbc.com/news/world-europe-53810323.

37 Siri Schubert, 'More on the Al-Yamamah Arms Deal', PBS Frontline, 7 April 2009, www.pbs.org/frontlineworld/stories/bribe/2009/04/al-yamamah.html

38 Merat, 'The Saudis Couldn't Do It Without Us'.

39 UK Parliament, House of Commons Library, 'Statistics on UK–EU Trade', 10 November 2020, https://commonslibrary.parliament.uk/research-briefings/cbp-7851/#:~:text=The%20EU%2C%20taken%20as%20a,2002%20to%2043%25%20in%202019.

40 UK Department for International Trade, 'An Information Note for the Consultation Relating to a Free Trade Agreement Between the United Kingdom and the Gulf Cooperation Council': 10, https://assets.publishing.service.gov.uk/government/uploads/system/uploads/attachment_data/file/1024032/dit-gcc-uk-consult-info-note.pdf

41 Ibid.

42 UK Government, 'Prime Minister Seeks New Chapter in Relations with Gulf on Visit to Bahrain', 4 December 2016, www.gov.uk/government/news/prime-minister-seeks-new-chapter-in-relations-with-the-gulf-on-visit-to-bahrain

43 The Foreign Policy Centre, 'Shifting Sands: The UK's Role in the Middle East and the Changing International Order', 16 June 2021, available at https://hi-in.facebook.com/ForeignPolicyCentre/videos/493745161833269/

44 Patricia Nilsson, 'Government Ends Probe of Evening Standard Stake Sale', *Financial Times*, 16 September 2019, www.ft.com/content/dc0e6050-d891-11e9-8f9b-77216ebe1f17

45 Rick Kelsey, 'Newcastle United Takeover: What is PIF, the Main Owner of the Club?', *BBC News*, 10 October 2021, www.bbc.com/news/newsbeat-58842557

46 BBC News, 'Saudi Chemical Giant to Invest Nearly £1bn in Teeside Plant', 29 October 2021, www.bbc.com/news/business-59070025

47 Kyle Sinclair, 'Why London Academic Was Banned from UAE', *The National*, 25 February 2013, www.thenationalnews.com/uae/government/why-london-academic-was-banned-from-uae-1.302935

48 Eric Ellis, 'Revealed: The Truth about Barclays and the Abu Dhabi Investment' *Euromoney*, 30 May 2013, www.euromoney.com/article/b12kjth9h0p0xf/revealed-the-truth-about-barclays-and-the-abu-dhabi-investment

49 Mubadala, 'UAE and UK Launch Sovereign Investment Partnership with Initial £1 Billion in Life Sciences', 24 March 2021, www.mubadala.com/en/news/uae-and-uk-launch-sovereign-investment-partnership

50 Richard Adams, 'Cambridge University Halts £400m Deal with UAE over Pegasus Spyware Claims', *The Guardian*, 14 October 2021, www.theguardian.com/education/2021/oct/14/cambridge-university-halts-400m-deal-with-uae-over-pegasus-spyware-claims

51 David Conn, Harry Davies and Sam Cutler, 'Revealed: The Huge British Property Empire of Sheikh Mohammed', *The Guardian*, 14 April 2021, www.theguardian.com/world/2021/apr/14/revealed-the-huge-british-property-empire-of-sheikh-mohammed

52 Owen Bowcott and Haroon Siddique, 'Dubai Ruler Organised Kidnapping of His Children, UK Court Rules', *The Guardian*, 5 March 2020, www.theguardian.com/world/2020/mar/05/dubai-ruler-sheikh-mohammed-organised-kidnapping-of-his-children-uk-court-finds

53 Gordon Corera, 'No 10 Network Targeted with Spyware, Says Group', *BBC News*, 18 April 2022, www.bbc.com/news/uk-61142687

54 Office of Financial Sanctions Implementation, HM Treasury, 16 July 2021, https://assets.publishing.service.gov.uk/government/uploads/system/uploads/attachment_data/file/1003139/Global_Human_Rights.pdf

55 Reuters Staff, 'Saudi Arabia Modified Intelligence Service Following Khashoggi Murder', *Reuters*, 20 December 2018, www.reuters.com/article/us-saudi-khashoggi-idUSKCN1OJ2AG

56 Bindmans, 'British Parliamentarians and International Lawyers Publish Report into the Detention of Saudi Arabian Royals', 16 December 2020, www.bindmans.com/insight/updates/fact-finding-panel-of-british-parliamentarians-and-international-lawyers-publish-report-into-the-detention-of-saudi-arabian-royals

57 Author's interview with a former senior UK government official who asked not to be named, 18 November 2021.

58 Author's interview with Sir Sherard Cowper-Coles former British Ambassador to Saudi Arabia 2003–6, London, 4 June 2011.

59 Lucie Béraud-Sudreau, 'Introduction', *French Arms Exports: The Business of Sovereignty,* Abingdon: Routledge, 2020: 11–19.

60 BBC News, 'Mecca 1979: The Mosque Siege that Changed the Course of Saudi History', 27 December 2019, www.bbc.com/news/stories-50852379

61 Joseph Fitchetz and International Herald Tribune, 'Paris Aid to Saudis Cited in Ending Mosque Siege', *The Washington Post*, 28 January 1980, www.washingtonpost.com/archive/politics/1980/01/28/paris-aid-to-saudis-cited-in-ending-mosque-siege/001469e6-c2da-4c07-97e1-772c46fe7966/

62 Ibid.

63 Al Jazeera, 'Juhayman: The Other Tale', aired 2 January 2020, www.aljazeera.net/programs/the-hidden-is-more-immense/2020/2/2/%D9%85%D8%A7-%D8%AE%D9%81%D9%8A-%D8%A3%D8%B9%D8%B8%D9%85-%D8%AC%D9%87%D9%8A%D9%85%D8%A7%D9%86-%D8%A7%D9%84%D8%B1%D9%88%D8%A7%D9%8A%D8%A9-%D8%A7%D9%84%D8%A3%D8%AE%D8%B1%D9%89

64 Ibid.

65 Ibid.

66 Ibid.

67 Lucie Béraud-Sudreau, 'The Ambiguity of French Arms-Export Policy in the Post-Cold War Era', *French Arms Exports: The Business of Sovereignty*, Abingdon: Routledge, 2020: 72.

68 'Death of a Princess' was a British 1980 drama-documentary about the true story of Princess Mishaal, a young Saudi princess and her lover who had been publicly executed for adultery.

69 Interview with Sir Sherard Cowper-Coles, former British Ambassador to Saudi Arabia 2003–6, London, 4 June 2011.

70 Béraud-Sudreau, 'Introduction', *French Arms Exports*: 16.

71 Ibid.

72 HHR Paris, 'HHR Paris Wins Acquittal for Former French PM in Corruption Trial', 5 March 2021, www.hugheshubbard.com/news/la-cour-de-justice-de-la-republique-a-relaxe-monsieur-edouard-balladur-defendu-par-felix-de-belloy-dans-le-volet-financier-de-laffaire-dite-de-karachi

73 ANI, 'Ex-French Defence Minister Leotard Given 2-Year Suspended Sentence in "Karachi Affair" Case', 4 March 2021, www.aninews.in/news/world/asia/ex-french-defence-minister-leotard-given-2-year-suspended-sentence-in-karachi-affair-case20210304183038/

74 Congressional Research Service, 'Arms Sales in the Middle East: Trends and Analytical Perspectives for U.S. Policy', 23 November 2020: 23, https://fas.org/sgp/crs/mideast/R44984.pdf

75 Sharq Al-Awsat, 'Macron Says Jaguar Task Force Deployed to Boost Arabian Peninsula Security', 18 January 2020, https://english.aawsat.com//home/article/2088306/macron-says-jaguar-task-force-deployed-boost-arabian-peninsula-security

76 Die Welt, 'Germany, Saudi Arabia End Diplomatic Row', 25 September 2018, www.dw.com/en/germany-saudi-arabia-end-diplomatic-row/a-45638974

77 Ibid.

78 The Local, '"Pure Demagoguery": Macron Clashes with Merkel Over Saudi Arms Exports After Khashoggi Murder', 26 October 2018, www.thelocal.fr/20181026/pure-demagoguery-macron-clashes-with-merkel-over-saudi-arms-exports-after-khashoggi-murder/

79 Lucie Béraud-Sudreau, 'The Policy Model for French Arms Exports', *French Arms Exports: The Business of Sovereignty*, Abingdon: Routledge, 2020: 47.

80 European Center for Constitutional and Human Rights, 'France's Extraterritorial Obligations Under the International Covenant on Civil and Political Rights', 18 May 2021: 22, www.ecchr.eu/fileadmin/Juristische_Dokumente/ECCHR_WILPF_FRANCE_ICCPR.pdf

81 Defence Aerospace, 'UAE Launch $929M Upgrade of Mirage 2000–9 Fleet', 25 November 2019, www.defense-aerospace.com/articles-view/feature/5/207711/uae-launch-%24929m-upgrade-of-mirage-2000_9-fleet.html

82 GlobalSecurity.org, 'Emirati Air Force – Fight Aircraft', www.globalsecurity.org/military/world/gulf/uae-af-fighters.htm

83 Naval Technology, 'UAE to Buy Two Gowind-Class Corvettes from France', 14 November 2017, www.naval-technology.com/news/uae-buy-two-gowind-class-corvettes-france/

84 Christopher P. Cavas, 'New UAE Patrol Ship Presents a Striking Profile', *Defense News*, 22 February 2017, www.defensenews.com/digital-show-dailies/idex/2017/02/22/new-uae-patrol-ship-presents-a-striking-profile/

85 Agnes Helou, 'Emirati Shipbuilder Receives Record $1B Order for Navy Ships', *Defense News*, 18 May 2021, www.defensenews.com/industry/2021/05/18/emirati-shipbuilder-receives-record-1b-order-for-navy-ships/

86 John Irish, 'Cementing Ties with France, UAE Pledges $19 bln Order for Warplanes, Helicopters', Reuters, 3 December 2021, www.reuters.com/business/aerospace-defense/frances-macron-nears-uae-rafale-fighter-jet-deal-2021-12-03/

87 Jonathan Marcus, 'French Policy and Middle East Conflicts: Change and Continuity', *The World Today*, 42 (2), February 1986: 27–30.

88 Ibid: 27.

89 French Constitution, 4 October 1958, www.conseil-constitutionnel.fr/sites/default/files/as/root/bank_mm/anglais/constitution_anglais.pdf

90 Jim Bitterman, 'France – the Ambiguous Ally', *CNN*, 17 January 2001, http://edition.cnn.com/2001/WORLD/europe/01/16/France.Iraq/

91 Howard LaFranchi, 'France Tries to Reconcile Role in Gulf War with History of Strong Arab Ties', *The Christian Science Monitor*, 1 February 1991, www.csmonitor.com/1991/0201/ofren.html

92 NPR, 'Jacques Chirac, French President Who Opposed U.S. Iraq War, Is Dead at 86', 26 September 2019, www.npr.org/2019/09/26/764561501/jacques-chirac-french-president-who-opposed-u-s-iraq-war-is-dead-at-86

93 Reuters Staff, 'France Says Abu Dhabi to Host HQ for European Naval Mission for the Gulf', 24 November 2019, www.reuters.com/article/us-emirates-france-idUSKBN1XY0AO

94 David Axe, 'Commentary: Here's How the U.S. Navy Will Defeat Iran's Speedboats', *Reuters*, 30 August 2016, www.reuters.com/article/us-navy-iran-commentary-idUSKCN1151SB

95 French Government, 'The European Mission Is Now Operational in the Arabian–Persian Gulf', 5 February 2020, www.gouvernement.fr/en/the-european-mission-is-now-operational-in-the-arabian-persian-gulf

96 BBC News, 'Sarkozy: Former French President Sentenced to Jail for Corruption', 1 March 2021, www.bbc.com/news/world-europe-56237818

97 Kim Willsher, 'Gaddafi "Gave Nicholas Sarkozy €50 Million for 2007 Presidential Campaign"', *The Guardian*, 15 November 2016, www.theguardian.com/world/2016/nov/15/muammar-gaddafi-allegedly-gave-nicolas-sarkozy-50m-euros-2007-presidential-campaign

98 Mubadala, 'Our History', www.mubadala.com/en/who-we-are/our-history

99 Saeed Azhar, 'Mubadala, Barings Partner to Finance European Mid-Market Cos', Reuters, 22 September 2020, available at www.zawya.com/en/wealth/mubadala-barings-partner-to-finance-european-mid-market-cos-n03o8igw

100 Egis, 'Egis Supports the Development of the United Arab Emirates Railway Network', 23 May 20118, www.egis-group.com/action/news/egis-supports-development-united-arab-emirates-railway-network

101 Associated Press, 'Iran Signs $5 Billion Deal with France's Total and Chinese Oil Company to Develop Natural Gas Field', *Los Angeles Times*, 3 July 2017, www.latimes.com/world/la-fg-iran-gas-deal-20170703-story.html

102 Interview with a European Official, Tehran, 24 February 2011.

103 Orient XXI, 'From Yemen to Arms Sales: Unworthy Agreement Between France and the United Arab Emirates', 10 September 2020, https://orientxxi.info/magazine/unworthy-agreement-between-france-and-the-united-arab-emirates,4129

104 Ibid.

105 Barbara Surk and John Gambrell, AP, 'France Signs $18B Weapons Deal with UAE', *Defense News*, 3 December 2021, available at www.defensenews.com/global/mideast-africa/2021/12/03/france-signs-18b-weapons-deal-with-uae/

106 Jon Stone, 'Government Secretly Deployed British Troops to Defend Saudi Arabian Oil Fields', *The Independent*, 27 November 2020, www.independent.co.uk/news/uk/politics/uk-troops-saudi-arabia-arms-oil-fields-mod-parliament-secret-b1762474.html

9

Russia: arms, energy and ideology

Introduction

This chapter sketches out Russia's historically limited channels of influence in the Gulf, from the Russian Empire to the Soviet era. It also charts the disconnect in the Soviet era on issues such as revolutionary policy, energy and religion. It explains Gorbachev's preoccupation with domestic matters during the collapse of the Soviet Union and the emergence of the Russian Federation in the unipolar world, achieving détente with the US and the Arab Gulf states. The chapter covers the evolving balance of Russian domestic and foreign policy priorities, in particular Russia's uneven relations with the West and President Putin's strong response to the violent Islamist threat, which have been highly consequential to its re-engagement in the Middle East and Asia. It then moves on to contemporary energy and economic interactions, especially the attempted energy diplomacy between Russia and Saudi Arabia. This is set against a backdrop of shifting Saudi and UAE foreign policy and regional and international tensions, Russian relations with Iran, the conflicts in Syria and Ukraine and the changing global balance of power. In conclusion, the chapter conceptualises the pivot points for Russia's ongoing relations with Saudi Arabia and the UAE.

Relations during the imperial and Soviet eras

Russia's foreign policy interests have generally been more concerned with its immediate neighbourhood, such as the Turkish and Persian territories. During the imperial and Soviet periods, Russia built a loose cross-border Hajj infrastructure on railroad and steamship routes to support the movement of Muslims between Russian-ruled lands and Arabia. The maritime route was made possible by the opening of the Suez Canal in 1869 and the establishment of Russia's Jeddah consulate in 1891, which was a hub, and was later joined by Tiflis (Tblisi, Georgia), Damascus, Tashkent and Odessa, through Jeddah to Bombay (Mumbai, India),[1] This route was established due to officials' fears about the spread of infectious disease, Islamic revolt and interethnic conflict.[2] Russia also exhibited opportunism in such links with the Arabian Gulf through managing its Muslim population, harnessing the economic opportunity which the Hajj created, advancing state propaganda and creating connections to other parts of the world through which Russia might project its influence.[3] Russia was further motivated by the German empire's planned railway from Berlin to Baghdad, with a terminus in Kuwait. Moscow sought to capitalise on setbacks to Britain's influence in the Gulf such as during the Boer War. For example, in 1900, without aggressive intent or plans for territorial acquisition, Tsar Nicholas II authorised the gunboat *Gilyak* to sail into the Gulf in order to assert that the Russian empire regarded the Gulf as open to vessels of all nations. Russia was seeking to establish a sea route between Odessa and ports in the Gulf, opening consulates in Basra and Bushehr to support this objective.

Imperial Russia was also holding discussions with Persia about a harbour deal in Bandar Abbas. Notwithstanding benign possibilities, the passage of the *Gilyak* still raised hackles among Prime Minister Lord Salisbury's colleagues in London, where there was a fear on two counts: first, that the Russians might hoist their flag, and second, that they would occupy the Bandar Abbas once the gunboat docked there.[4] Neither eventuality occurred. Russia was interested in setting up a coaling station, rather than depend on coal shipments from India.[5] This trip was followed by the cruiser *Varyag*, which was sent to Kuwait in December 1901. The Emir was expecting a Wahhabi attack and wanted to enlist Russia's protection, which Russia declined so as not to antagonise the British.[6] Nevertheless, the government in St Petersburg wanted to establish a coaling station in Kuwait for its navy so as to be able to access the warm waters of the Indian Ocean. This enabled it to compete with the British in and around India, until the Anglo-Russian Convention of 1907 divided their respective spheres of influence in West and Central Asia.[7] Russia was also aware of the importance of the Arabian Peninsula as a centre for Islam, which was relevant for many subjects of the Russian empire.

Following the onset of the Russian Revolution in 1917, the leadership of the newly formed Soviet Union (USSR) assumed that revolution was easy, and so urged the 'toiling masses of the East' to overthrow their imperialist masters.[8] But, given that there were relatively few communists in the region at that time, a new policy sought to secure temporary collaboration between the nationalist bourgeoisie and the revolutionary communists.[9] A more targeted approach also saw individual treaties concluded with Turkey, Persia and Afghanistan in 1921. The USSR was the first state to recognise the kingdom of Hejaz and Nejd in 1923 even though the kingdom had an established relationship with the British, and quickly moved to establish diplomatic relations with Ibn Saud in 1926. The official note carried from the USSR by Karim Khakimov, the first consul general, to Ibn Saud noted: 'the people's right to self-determination and out of respect for the Hijazi people's will as expressed in their choice of you as their king, the government of the USSR recognizes you as King of Hijaz and Sultan to Nejd and her dependencies. On this ground, the Soviet government considers that it is in normal diplomatic relations with Your Majesty's government.'[10] Karim Khakimov befriended Ibn Saud. As a Muslim of Bashkir origin who had worked in Iran and was familiar with Arab culture and language, he quickly became known as 'the Red Pasha'.[11] The USSR also signed a treaty of commerce and friendship with Imam Yahya of Yemen in Moscow in November 1928. Yahya was considered anti-imperialist, partly due to his long-standing border dispute with the British over Aden. The treaty was said to be the first equal treaty between an Arab government and a great power.[12]

By 1930, there was a close trading relationship between the USSR and Yemen, including the deployment of Soviet medical doctors to Yemen and some efforts to build cultural relations. At the same time Ibn Saud showed the US that he was adept at balancing his country's interests for relative autonomy by opening the Saudi market to Soviet goods.[13] However, Ibn Saud grew wary of Soviet activities in the Hejaz, and the Soviet trade mission failed, probably due to the cheap goods flooding the market in Jeddah, which led 'to the cry of protests from the Hejazi merchants, and, no doubt, the British'.[14] In May to June 1932 Ibn Saud sent his son, the future King Faisal bin Abdel Aziz, to Moscow on an official visit to consolidate ties and resolve the issue of Muslim endowments (*awqaf*) which had been nationalised and the facilitation of Hajj for Russian Muslims.[15] The kingdom also demanded that a trade agreement should include a stipulation that the Saudi market not be flooded with Soviet goods and that commercial credits be extended to the kingdom, although these were not agreed to at the time.[16] The Moscow visit followed Faisal's visit to Britain in early May 1932, where the offer of oil concessions in exchange for a loan was turned down (see Chapter 8). Prince Faisal also visited France, Poland and Turkey on the same trip. Apart from the obvious economic incentive to form closer relations, Ibn Saud also appreciated the Bolsheviks' release of secret treaties, such as the Sykes-Picot Agreement printed in *Pravda* and reprinted in Central Power countries as well as in the UK and US.[17] Khakimov's successor, Nazir Tyurykulov, another Muslim Soviet diplomat, agreed a deal with Ibn Saud on the supply of Soviet gas and kerosene in the early 1930s.

However, as the 1930s wore on, the USSR became more concerned about the rise of Nazi Germany. In 1937–38 both Khakimov and Tyuryakulov were recalled to Moscow during the so-called 'Great Terror', were convicted of spying and were shot. Both consuls general were posthumously rehabilitated in the 1950s.[18] After this, Ibn Saud refused to accept a replacement Soviet consul general, and in May 1938 the USSR closed its offices in Saudi Arabia and Yemen. Competition for newly discovered oil in the kingdom was impossible, due to the USSR's literal execution of its direct line to the Saudi king, the centrally planned nature of their economy and the lack of appropriate technology. So, although for different reasons, both Britain and the USSR failed to gain a purchase on the Saudi oil bonanza. Nikita Khrushchev attempted to redress the issue in the 1950s, but to no avail, and, despite the Kremlin's arguments that both powers were critical of Israeli policy and the USSR could help the kingdom to leverage its relations with the US, the approaches fell flat.[19]

After Ibn Saud died in 1952, a rapprochement in Soviet–Saudi relations became possible in August 1956 when King Saud fell out with Egypt's President Nasser. King Saud could have gained sway over Cairo by forming closer relations with Moscow. But, in the context of the Cold War, when the Communist Party had its own International Department to develop relations with revolutionary movements in the Middle East, this was not a natural match. When an arms deal was about to be struck between the kingdom and the USSR around 1962, Arab nationalists supported by Egypt and, in turn, by the USSR, overthrew the North Yemen monarchy and called for revolution throughout the Arabian Peninsula. Soviet–Saudi relations were affected,[20] and so too were Soviet–UAE relations, with Abu Dhabi taking an equally dim view of the revolutionary policies being supported by the USSR in its neighbourhood. Thus, diplomatic relations were established after the UAE's independence in 1971, but embassies were not opened.[21]

The oil crisis of 1973 was a key factor leading Moscow to reconsider its oil policy in relation to new market opportunities in Western Europe. This also coincided with a period of détente with the West which encouraged trade at the expense of Soviet trade with socialist states. Oil exports to Western Europe during the 1970s increased from 44 million tons to 63.6 million tons, the spike occurring against a backdrop of inflated prices. [22] The effect was increased competition with the Gulf States in global energy markets. The USSR became the largest oil exporter by 1980, amplifying tensions with the Gulf States and giving rise to the term 'energy diplomacy'.[23] The USSR also played a key role in the development of energy infrastructure or associated projects in Eastern Europe as well as in Egypt, Angola, Iraq, Syria, Yemen and Libya.[24] The USSR had particularly close political and economic relations with Egypt, which received significant levels of support.

This lasted until 1972, when President Sadat expelled Russian military advisers from Egypt, due to their ambivalence over Egypt's interests against Israel, refusal to provide offensive weapons and quest for stable or improved relations with the US.[25] Relations turned sour again after Egypt signed its peace agreement with Israel in 1978, which brought Egypt under greater US influence than during the Arab nationalism period of Nasser. Syria now became the USSR's most important partner in the region, based on pragmatic concerns: Hafez al-Assad needed an ally to boost his leadership credentials in the Arab world and the USSR needed a new foothold in the Middle East. This was a dynamic which would be repeated in the twenty-first century.

In 1977–78, bilateral Soviet–Saudi relations were once again close to fruition, but were again quickly undermined, this time by the Soviet–Cuba intervention in the Horn of Africa. In 1979, the Soviet intervention in Afghanistan put paid to an entente and became a major area of contention. The invasion reversed Saudi foreign policy calculations and relations with the US, which had been poor following the 1973 Arab–Israeli War. In 1973–74 the Organisation of Arab Petroleum Exporting Countries, led by Saudi Arabia, had imposed an oil embargo on states which supported Israel, including the US. The Saudis now needed US support to tackle the USSR and its alleged attempt to control Middle East oil, with Afghanistan as a first step.[26] In April 1984 the Saudi foreign minister identified four aspects of the invasion which needed addressing in order to improve bilateral ties: Soviet withdrawal from Afghanistan, an end to hostile propaganda in the kingdom, the withdrawal of Soviet forces from Ethiopia and South Yemen and freedom for Muslims to practise their religion in the USSR.[27] Against the odds, Gorbachev managed to address all these issues when he came to power in 1985, also enabling relations with the UAE to improve to the point of reciprocal embassy openings in 1986–87. After the Iraqi invasion of Kuwait, Saudi Arabia established diplomatic relations with the USSR in 1990, and pledged $1 billion in humanitarian aid to the USSR in the final months before its dissolution.[28]

The kingdom may have played a role in the collapse of the USSR through 'oil-market machinations'.[29] More specifically, Yegor Gaidar, former acting prime minister of Russia (15 June to 14 December 1992), cited the combination of aid to the mujahideen and the ramping up of Saudi oil exports to prolong suppressed international oil prices as corresponding to the USSR's decline, and possibly decisive.[30] More likely, it was the combination of reduced economic resources and the planned economy which were to blame. The planned economy was 'spectacularly inefficient' in the face of resource scarcity, especially since oil production declined 30 per cent from 1988 to 1992, when the break-up and capitalist transformation of the USSR were occurring.[31]

Contemporary relations

Katz notes that Russia views Saudi Arabia as a revolutionary regime which operates akin to the Comintern, in that the Saudi state engages other states, whilst the foundations of the state (Wahhabism in this case) undermine those same state relations.[32] To counter religious extremism, Russia has worked with Chechen president Ramzan Kadyrov – controversially, given his alleged human rights abuses[33] – and the UAE's Tabah Foundation.[34] Kadyrov is head of one of Russia's autonomous regions but also plays a role at the federal level in the role of a national diplomat, especially on sensitive issues such as the S-400 missile defence system.[35] By 2015 he had attracted enough investment from the UAE into Chechnya to make Grozny look more like Dubai.[36] This has been part of UAE attempts to leverage soft power to address religious issues and tensions in Russia.

There is said to be a pro-Saudi lobby in Russia, including Aleksandr Novak, the minister of energy, and Kirill Dmitriev, the head of the Russian Direct Investment Fund.[37] Russia banned the MB as a terrorist organisation in 2003, although it signalled briefly that it might ease the ban in light of Morsi's victory in Egypt's presidential election in 2012. Russia has continued to tackle a domestic and regional insurgency of jihadi fighters, some with a background in Saudi Arabia or a strong Wahhabi influence. Many have fought in Afghanistan and gone on to fight in the Tajikistan civil war, Bosnian War, First Chechen War, Dagestan War and Second Chechen War. These include individuals such as Ibn al-Khattab[38] and Shamil Basayev, who was said to be involved in the Budyonnovsk hospital hostage crisis in 1995, the terror attack on the school in Beslan in 2004 and the 2004 Russian aircraft bombings.[39]

The 9/11 attacks could have provided a strategic opening for Russia in the US Global War on Terror. Indeed, President Putin was one of the first foreign leaders to respond by phone to President G. W. Bush to offer his condolences, and by telegram in which he expressed 'anger and indignation' over the 'series of barbaric terrorist acts directed against innocent people'.[40] In a national television address the same day he said the attacks were 'an unprecedented act of aggression on the part of international terrorism' and an event that 'goes beyond national borders'.[41] Putin declared: 'we entirely and fully share and experience your pain. We support you.'[42] This was a strategic choice, as part of Russia's policy pursued in the UN and elsewhere to urge the international community to join the US in its efforts in fighting terrorism. Russia offered the US intelligence and the use of its airspace for through-flights of aircraft carrying humanitarian supplies, and for the first time accepted US bases in Central Asia for the purpose of conducting operations against international terrorism.[43] This was an unparalleled offer of cooperation, not witnessed since the US and Russia had worked together in the contact group on Bosnia and Serbia in the 1990s. By focusing on the US at this time, Putin appeared to be all for cooperation against terrorism, to be fought on the battlefield 'in the strangest of places – in the mountains of Afghanistan, the mosques of Egypt, and the airwaves of Saudi Arabia'.[44] In this endeavour he had strong domestic support.[45] In September 2021, after the US withdrawal from Afghanistan, President Putin floated the idea of Russian bases in Central Asia for the Pentagon to use in order to monitor emerging terrorist threats in Afghanistan. However, it was not an explicit offer, and at the time of writing had not been pushed forward, although General Mark Milley, chairman of the Joint Chiefs of Staff, did discuss it with Russian chief of general staff Valery Gerasimov.[46]

A US–Russian common cause has never truly been realised. Russian foreign policy was reorientated again in the 2000s, in the context of NATO enlargement. Russia's tensions with the West have risen over interventions such as Kosovo in 1999 and in line with a more assertive policy since Putin became president from 2000 to 2008, and again from 2012. There was further antagonism over western responses to the Colour Revolutions in the 2000s, especially the Rose Revolution in Georgia in 2003, and the Orange Revolution in Ukraine in 2004 and the Tulip Revolution in Kyrgyzstan in 2005. Russian relations with the US also deteriorated following the G. W. Bush administration's withdrawal from the 1972 Anti-Ballistic Missile Treaty on 13 December 2001, and there was political opposition during the lead-up to the US-led war in Iraq in 2003, the Ukraine revolution in 2014 and the ensuing civil unrest including the secession of Crimea and Donbas to Russia.

Russian countermeasures against NATO in Kaliningrad in 2016 provided a new strategic context for more positive Russian relations with Saudi Arabia. At first this was not fully reciprocated. But already, following Al Qaeda-launched attacks inside the kingdom in 2003, the Al Saud had turned to support the Russian crackdown in Chechnya; Crown Prince Abdullah had visited Moscow later in 2003, marking better relations; and President Putin had also visited Riyadh in 2007 with a focus on trade and investment.

As well as geostrategic and geopolitical issues, energy considerations have been key in Russian decision making. The 2009 'National Security Strategy of the Russian Federation up to 2020' shows the onus is on Russia's energy resources as tools of Russian foreign policy and that energy, including control over energy resources in the Middle East, is where future conflicts will arise.[47] President Putin, by focusing on rebuilding the Russian economy in the 2000s, put energy at the heart of this effort, the accomplishment of which was reliant on close personal ties within the economy and abroad.[48] The energy issue was further highlighted by tensions over Crimea which spurred the EU to reduce its dependence on Russian oil and gas. Due to sanctions, Russia had to reorientate energy relations to the Middle East and Asia.

Moscow has built stronger economic relations with Turkey, including signing the 2014 Turkish Stream project which is expected to carry 63 billion cubic meters of natural gas per annum and gives Russia access to the Turkish gas market as well as to the EU.[49] However, it pits Russia against Iran, which is also attempting to supply the EU via Turkey.[50] This situation is managed because, like China, Russia engages Saudi Arabia and Iran on both sides of the Gulf. To address this unsatisfactory situation, the Saudis tried to impose conditionality on the relationship, seeking to shift Moscow away from relatively strong relations with Tehran. Similarly, Saudi Arabia, and to some extent the UAE, have tried to reinsure with Russia, China and European states when their relations with the US have been poor. This was notably so at the onset of the Arab uprisings, when President Mubarak was forced to resign, over Syria, the JCPOA, during the attacks on Saudi oil facilities and, at the outset of the Biden administration, over Yemen and human rights. But this has not worked in terms of effecting much of a US policy change.

Given Russia's strong relations with Iran, the Kremlin was nervous that the 2015 JCPOA could lead to a rapprochement between the US and Iran and therefore diminished relations with Russia, taking an economic toll by contributing to lower international oil and gas prices and potentially marginalising Russia as a great power.[51] The timing was also off for Russia, which in 2015 might have been left to defend Assad alone if Iran had withdrawn its forces and militia from the Syrian battlefield.[52] Although pleased with US withdrawal from the JCPOA in 2018, Moscow might have been concerned about Trump's interest in getting a better deal with Iran beyond the nuclear issue, had it not been for the effect that the 'maximum pressure' policy had on Iranian decision making.[53] Russia learnt from the USSR's breaking off of relations with Israel after the 1967 war that being an interlocutor or principal international partner has its advantages.

After recent experiences of perceived US unilateralism, NATO enlargement and interventionism, concerns about returning terrorists from Syria, and in order to divert attention from the annexation of Crimea, Moscow moved quickly to buttress the Assad regime and extend its traditional influence in Syria. From holding a series of consultative conferences in Moscow in 2015 to deploying military assets, and then establishing the 'Astana format' from 2017, President Putin pre-empted western intervention and diplomacy. Instead, he is working more closely with Syria, Turkey and Iran, including on the delivery of the S-300 missile system to Syria in 2018 and to Iran in 2016, and the S-400 to Turkey in 2019.[54] Both Qatar and Saudi Arabia have discussed buying the S-400, which would give them a qualitative edge over Iran's system. Sergei Lavrov was in Riyadh to see Mohammed bin Salman in March 2021, probably to discuss this.[55] But for Saudi Arabia, the choice between acquisition of the F-35 or the S-400 is complex, reflecting high military, intelliegnce and political stakes. According to a White House official, the F-35 'cannot coexist with a Russian intelligence collection platform' such as the S-400.[56] Furthermore, the S-400 lacks interoperability with most of the regional air defence network, which is US made, it would not recognise transponders which enable US and partner aircraft to 'see' each other, and it could not pass on data to the air surveillance network or missile battalions in the country that are US made.[57] It could seriously jeopardise Saudi–US relations and involve Saudi Arabia in the Countering America's Adversaries Through Sanctions Act (CAATSA).

The Syria conflict gave Russia a foothold in the Levant which could be coupled with further attempts to participate in matters of regional security, but also with US relations in mind. Russia's leverage from Syria into Libya is one example of such connectivity. Syria also builds on Putin's security credentials after the Second Chechen War, a domestic issue for Putin, as well as being seen as a reliable regional ally. The Saudis appeared to change tack on Russia in 2017, given that Riyadh's policy in Syria had failed. Riyadh moved to drive a wedge between Moscow and Tehran by expressing the desire to secure more advanced military hardware from Russia, such as indicating interest in the S-400 missile defence system.[58] By 2021, Saudi Arabia was still in discussions to purchase the S-400, which could represent a tipping point in Saudi–US relations, especially in the US Congress. If Russia sells Iran the S-400, this could complicate matters. These are likely to be bargaining chips. Russia held off from sending Iran the S-300 for years after it was paid for. It might also hold off on selling the S-400 if Moscow can make a deal with the US on easing sanctions, although during a war in Ukraine this seems unlikely. Much depends on Saudi calculations.

President Putin has also used the Syrian context to extend Russian interest back into the Gulf, to address insecurity and to try to sell more military hardware in the Gulf. For example, Russia again tabled a vision for collective security in the Gulf in 2019,[59] a proposal which has been promoted since the late 1990s during periods of tension such as Israel–Palestine crises, the US-led intervention in Iraq in 2003 and Iran's stated non-compliance with the IAEA in 2006.[60] The 2019 proposal was supported by China, intent on undermining US influence in the Gulf and maximising opportunities in the region with a minimum commitment. For Iran, the Russian proposal, if a serious one, represents an unacceptable encroachment of another foreign power into the region. For the GCC states, it would impose rules and therefore limit their autonomy. President Putin also tried to seal a missile defence deal with the kingdom after the attacks at Abqaiq and Khurais in September 2019 by saying that 'They [the Saudis] should make clever decisions, as Iran did by buying our S-300, as Erdoğan did by deciding to buy the most advanced S-400 air defence systems. These kinds of systems are capable of defending any kind of infrastructure in Saudi Arabia from any kind of attack.'[61]

Throughout the Syria campaign, Russia has been a de facto member of the resistance axis and is developing relations with Iranian-aligned militia groups, including Hezbollah and Hashd al-Shaabi (Popular Mobilisation Forces) in Iraq, and negotiates with the Houthis on ending the war in Yemen.[62] It is therefore unlikely that Russia will be successful in bringing Saudi Arabia to invest in Syria's reconstruction (via Russian companies) and facilitate Syria's return to the Arab League when the war is not over, even if the UAE would like to move in that direction in order to secure more influence over the country than Iran has. Russia's intervention has given 85 per cent of commanders of large military formations and regiments in the Russian army combat experience.[63] This is a statement of serious intent, given that Putin believes force may again need to be employed in places such as Afghanistan or Central Asia over the coming years.[64]

Since 2020, Russia is also attempting to build up a naval presence in Port Sudan, after unilaterally deploying on an anti-piracy mission to the Horn of Africa from 2008.[65] Whilst probably undertaken with competition with other international actors in mind, this reflects a growing Russian interest in African resources, a connection back to Russia's naval facility at Tartus on Syria's Mediterranean coast and the possibility to project force into the Red Sea and Indian Ocean. Similarly, the UAE has benefited by engaging former Soviet states that have re-entered the international fold, such as Uzbekistan under President Mirziyoyev. This bilateral relationship covers key UAE national security priorities such as projecting influence into Central Asia and addressing food security, as well as building upon traditional economic aspects such as energy, tourism and retail.

In summary, there have been three areas of major concern in Russian–Saudi/UAE relations from 2015. The first is Russia's intervention in Syria in 2015. Improved relations between Russia and Israel as de facto neighbours during the Syria conflict have supported Saudi and UAE interests through, for example, Russia cancelling arms sales to states antagonistic towards Israel, such as Iran.[66] However, should Russia be able to exert influence directly on Syria or Iran, or through Israel, on certain aspects of policy, the repercussions for Saudi Arabia and the UAE could be significant.[67]

The second area is Russia's decision to join the OPEC+ format in 2016 to cut oil output so as to prop up prices. Iran's OPEC representative complained in 2018 that by cooperating on production cuts they were taking the oil market 'hostage'.[68] Saudi Arabia spent more than a decade trying to elicit cooperation from Russia on oil policy, specifically restricting production to enhance oil prices. In light of lower demand from China, a key oil market for both states, the Saudi decision to flood the market and drive the price down below $20 per barrel worked. It forced Moscow to agree to production cuts in 2016, and so was a victory of sorts for Riyadh. But since Russia produced 11.2 million barrels a day by November 2016, versus 10.6 million barrels from Saudi Arabia, production cuts really benefited Russia.[69] It could produce less but probably make the same or even greater profit than it did before. The opening of an oil pipeline between Siberia and China helped Russia to overtake Saudi Arabia to become China's biggest crude oil supplier in 2016.

The third area is Russia's invasion of Ukraine in 2022. Russia's military cooperation agreement with the kingdom, signed in August 2021, intervention in Syria and Gulf diplomacy mean relatively little when stacked up against a Russian military which has been, at least initially, relatively ineffective against organised and western-backed Ukrainian forces. As two states with close economic relations with Russia, concerns about US security provision in the Middle East and without any vested interests in the conflict, Saudi Arabia and the UAE initially appeared unwilling to accept the US position on Russia. The UAE, along with China and India, abstained in the first UN Security Council vote on 25 February 2022 aimed at denouncing the Russian invasion, but backed a similar UN General Assembly resolution on 2 March. NATO–Russia tensions over the 2022 war in Ukraine initially made it less likely that Russia would push Iran to support a new JCPOA with the US, and Russia sought assurances that US sanctions would not affect its trade with Iran. With US acquiescence, the crisis was resolved, but the linkage between different theatres of conflict and diplomacy could yet lead to further difficulties and problems in advancing US–Russian diplomacy in the Middle East.

Economic relations

Modest bilateral economic relations have continued throughout the 1990s and 2000s. The biggest deal for Russia in the GCC was the December 2016 $5 billion investment deal between Rosneft and Qatar. Companies such as Rosneft, Gazprom and Lukoil will continue to seek deals in the Gulf for reasons related to both domestic economy and Kremlin-led foreign policy. The Russian Direct Investment Fund (RDIF) is setting up a number of partnerships with GCC SWFs. For example, Mubadala Petroleum and Rosneft signed a strategic cooperation deal in 2014 to develop Rosneft assets in

Eastern Siberia and give Rosneft participation in international projects carried out by Mubadala Petroleum.[70] On 24 May 2018, the RDIF, Mubadala Petroleum and Gazprom Neft announced a joint venture to develop Siberian oil fields.[71] So there is space to develop Russian–GCC energy policy at the bilateral and multilateral levels. Russia is also building on old Soviet links, with new energy-related projects in Egypt, Iraq, Libya and Iran. Rosatom, the Russian state nuclear energy company, is also looking to build links across the region, and in 2016 set up its first regional office in Dubai, overseeing projects in Egypt, Iran, Jordan, Turkey and the UAE.[72] It will be a pivotal time to engage Saudi Arabia, which is seeking to build multiple civil nuclear reactors.

Saudi trade with Russia in 2019 was just $1.6 billion,[73] whilst UAE trade with Russia during the same period was $1.7 billion, making it the biggest trade partner in the Middle East.[74] In 2019, Saudi investment in Russia was $2.5 billion, but there exists a 2015 agreement for the PIF to invest $10 billion in Russia.[75] Investment discussions are ongoing about this, aided by the RDIF having set up an office in Saudi Arabia in October 2019, just before President Putin's visit.[76] In 2019, the UAE and Russia were set to invest $1.3 billion through ten deals signed by President Putin on a visit in 2019.[77] The UAE appear to have made particular efforts to stand out during Putin's short visit. There are other links with the UAE, such as tourism – 1 million Russians spent $1.3 billion in the UAE in 2018;[78] there are opportunities in the space sector; and deals in the energy sector continue, such as the $200 million paid in 2021 by Mubadala to Russian billionaire Oleg Deripaska's ex-wife for 2.86 per cent of En+, a hydropower and aluminium company.[79]

On 1 June 2018, Crown Prince Mohammed bin Zayed of the UAE and President Putin signed a 'Declaration of Strategic Partnership' to cooperate across politics, security, economy and culture, including regular consultations at the foreign minister level. That effort appears to be matched by increasing economic investment. For example, Mubadala Investment Company has invested $3 billion in a portfolio of Russian investments since 2010, and in 2021 announced its largest investment in Russia, a 1.9 per cent stake in Sibur, the largest integrated petrochemicals company in Russia.[80] The UAE was mulling the purchase of a squadron of Su-35s in 2017; but, as a useful workaround to possibly opening itself up to penalties under CAATSA and to boost its domestic military-industrial capacity, it has entered into the joint development of a fifth-generation 'Checkmate' fighter with Rostec of Russia. For Russia, joint development spreads the cost with another partner. It highlights that the future interest for Saudi Arabia and the UAE will not necessarily be in buying arms per se, but in foreign state willingness to assist in the development, expansion and advancement of Gulf-based defence industries, which in turn will support jobs, military development and exports from 2026.[81] Already Saudi Arabia has signed a contract with Rosoboronexport for the domestic production of TOS-1A heavy flamethrower systems based on the Soviet T-72 battle tank. Saudi Arabian Military Industries has also licensed the 9M133 Kornet, an anti-tank guided missile, and is looking to licence modern AK rifle variants such as the AK-103.[82] Along with discussions on the Su-35 and the S-400, the kingdom is likely to remain heavily engaged with Russia on arms sales.

At the G20 in Argentina in November/December 2018, the personal rapport between Mohammed bin Salman and President Putin appeared to be good. Putin clearly took the opportunity to contrast his friendliness and the West's lukewarm reception after the Khashoggi incident. Russia sent a large contingent to the Saudi investment conference in October 2018 and President Putin visited the kingdom in 2019. Both states pledged bilateral deals worth $2 billion, and more than twenty agreements were announced[83] – yet many of these remain to be confirmed.

Notwithstanding economic deals, Syria still represents a return to the Middle East for Putin, and another reason for Saudi Arabia, the UAE and Qatar to engage with Russia on mutual interests such as Libya, Sudan, Israel–Palestine and Iran. A Russian base in Sudan may extend that rationale for engagement to the Horn of Africa. Saudi Arabia and the UAE will be looking to diversify their IR at a time when US and European pressure on human rights and suspended arms sales could have forced them into a more acquiescent posture. As Albadr Alshateri, a former professor at Abu Dhabi's National Defence College, put it: 'the UAE sees Russia as a very reliable partner as opposed to western countries who have to defer to parliaments and civil society pressure'.[84] Russian participation at IDEX 2021 was huge, as was China's, even though Russia appears on the US CAATSA list. Their high-profile presence stood in contrast to that of the lower-key US delegation, visually representing some of the key trends in Gulf affairs.

Conclusion

Russian political interactions have historically been predisposed to other great power engagement, for reasons related to maintaining or expanding established spheres of influence. Whilst Russian interests are evolving in line with trade and other opportunities, they also evolved in the Soviet era along ideological lines. In opposition to Saudi Arabia's Wahhabi-led policies during the Soviet era, along with Saudi and Emirati concerns about Soviet-supported revolutionary groups in the Arabian Peninsula, relations appeared destined to fail. Whilst the Soviet–Afghan War cemented US–Saudi relations, it soured Soviet–Saudi relations, and along with Saudi Arabia's possible role in the dissolution of the USSR this is bound to reverberate in Putin's psyche and in his search for lost Russian status and influence. Similarly, the Saudis and Emiratis have not forgotten domestic imperatives and US policies, which have accelerated their drive to secure international allies. Whilst the 1973 oil crisis drove and expanded Soviet energy diplomacy towards Europe, more recently Russian energy diplomacy is targeting the Middle East and Asia. This is bound to be reinforced by western sanctions after the Russian invasion of Ukraine.

Economic deals to consolidate Russia's position in global (non-western) energy markets, including boosting its flagship businesses in line with Russian foreign policy, are the key to future relations with Saudi Arabia, along with cooperation on a number of primarily regional interests, especially Iran, Syria and Libya. The frequency of Sergei Lavrov's and Ramzan Kadyrov's visits to the Gulf stands testament to this. For the kingdom and the UAE, their positions with Russia rest on arms sales and building indigenous arms capacity (but which could be costly in the context of Ukraine and CAATSA), shifting priorities in the international oil market and Russian relations with Israel, Iran and Syria. Whilst they are not yet self-sufficient, the small steps which Saudi Arabia and the UAE have accomplished towards building their respective military-industrial complexes raise fundamental questions about shifting alliance patterns and core–periphery relations. They also raise further questions about political consolidation, hyper-nationalism, artificial intelligence and human rights concerns. At face value, the UAE is further along in its military-industrial transition through the joint venture with Russia on the fifth-generation fighter jet. But the S-400 negotiations between Russia and Iran, and perhaps Saudi Arabia, draw our attention back to the fact that Russia can gain leverage through its ability to delay, constrain, hamper or interrupt strategic relations between regional and international powers.

Following its 2022 action against Ukraine, although Russia has lost a great deal of soft power and access to western markets, making it more reliant on China, Saudi Arabia and the UAE maintain an authoritarian, economic and military kinship with Russia, not least in OPEC+, where Russia's participation helps Saudi Arabia to continue to dominate the international oil market, versus the US which has become a vital producer on the back of the shale boom. Russia is also importantvis-à-vis Iran. Nevertheless, their search for international allies is likely to favour those states which can more capably demonstrate their ability to project force, whilst avoiding western sanctions. Saudi Arabia and the UAE require increasing connectivity with the global economy, and being caught up in secondary sanctions could compromise their economic growth prospects. China may become a key beneficiary in the Gulf and Red Sea, especially if it is able to prove itself to be a more credible military ally over time. This would presuppose that Beijing itself is not caught up in a robust western response, should China invade Taiwan, and that the US and other western allies consent to closer military and security ties.

The evolution of UAE–Russian joint arms deals signifies converging interests around economised and militarised secularism. This underscores the kingdom's limited strategic investments in comparison, but belies the more profound potential that Riyadh and Moscow have in shaping the energy and security landscape of the Middle East over the longer term on deals such as the S-400, civil nuclear power and missile defence. Saudi Arabia also maintains centrality in the oil market and in the past has proven its ability to exert influence through changes to its oil policy. Whether that will be possible in the future is another core question and one which will dominate debate about riyal politik, economic statecraft, Saudi political economy, Saudi–Russian relations and core–periphery relations.

Notes

1 Eileen Kane, 'Imperialism through Islamic Networks', *Russian Hajj: Empire and the Pilgrimage to Mecca*. Ithaca, NY: Cornell University Press, 2015: 46.
2 Ibid.
3 Ibid.
4 Briton Cooper Busch, 'The Russian Danger', *Britain and the Persian Gulf: 1894–1914*. Berkeley: University of California Press, 1967: 128–131.
5 Ibid.
6 Andrej Kreutz, 'Russia and the Arabian Peninsula', *Journal of Military and Strategic Studies*, 7 (2), Winter 2004: 3
7 Britain promised to stay out of northern Persia and extended loans and some political support. Russia recognised southern Persia as part of the British sphere of influence, British influence in Afghanistan, and that neither country would interfere in the internal affairs of Tibet. The British assumption was that it would keep an *entente* with Russia rather than being definite or binding. D. W. Sweet and R. T. B. Langhorne, 'Great Britain and Russia, 1907–1914', in F. H. Hinsley (ed.), *British Foreign Policy Under Sir Edward Grey*, Cambridge: Cambridge University Press, 1977: 247
8 John Baldry, 'Soviet Relations with Saudi Arabia and the Yemen 1917–1938', *Middle Eastern Studies*, 20 (1), 1984: 53.
9 Ibid.
10 Alexei Vassiliev, *The History of Saudi Arabia*. London: Saqi, 2000: 265.

11 Oleg Yegorov, 'How Stalin Lost His Chance to Make a Fortune on Saudi Oil', *Russia Beyond*, 23 September 2019, www.rbth.com/history/331017-stalin-saudi-arabia-ussr

12 Vassiliev, *The History of Saudi Arabia*: 17.

13 Kreutz, 'Russia and the Arabian Peninsula': 7.

14 David Holden and Richard Johns, 'The Coming of Mammon', *The House of Saud*. London: Sidgwick and Jackson, 1981: 97.

15 Badr Alkhorayef, 'Faisal Laid Foundations of Strong Saudi–Russian Ties', *Arab News*, 7 May 2008, www.arabnews.com/node/311670

16 Ibid.

17 Manley O. Hudson, 'The Registration and Publication of Treaties', *American Journal of International Law*, 19 (2), 1925: 273–292.

18 Yegorov, 'How Stalin Lost His Chance'.

19 Mark N. Katz, 'Better than Before: Comparing Moscow's Cold War and Putin Era Policies Towards Arabia and the Gulf', Durham Middle East Paper No. 96, Sir William Luce Publication Series, Durham University, 2018: 12.

20 Jesse Ferris, 'Soviet Support for Egypt's Intervention in Yemen, 1962–1963', *Journal of Cold War Studies*, 10 (4), 2008: 5–36.

21 United Arab Emirates Ministry of Foreign Affairs and International Cooperation, 'The Russian Federation–UAE Relationships: Bilateral Relationship', www.mofaic.gov.ae/en/Missions/Moscow/UAE-Relationships/Bilateral-Relationship

22 Yury Barmin, 'Russian Energy Policy in the Middle East', *Insight Turkey*, 19 (4), 1 October 2017, www.insightturkey.com/articles/russian-energy-policy-in-the-middle-east

23 Ibid.

24 Ibid.

25 Edward R. F. Sheehan, 'Why Sadat Packed Off the Russians', *The New York Times*, 6 August 1972, www.nytimes.com/1972/08/06/archives/why-sadat-packed-off-the-russians-egypt.html

26 Yegor Gaidar, 'The Soviet Collapse: Grain and Oil', American Enterprise Institute, April 2007, www.aei.org/wp-content/uploads/2011/10/20070419_Gaidar.pdf

27 Mark N. Katz, 'Prince Sa'ud Al Faysal: A Remembrance', Mark Katz Travels and Observations blog, 9 July 2015, https://katzeyeview.wordpress.com/2015/07/09/prince-saud-al-faysal-a-remembrance

28 Patrick E. Tyler, 'Saudi Arabia Pledges $1 Billion to Soviet Union', *The New York Times*, 9 October 1991.

29 Bernard Haykel, 'Saudi Arabia's Radical New Oil Strategy', Project Syndicate, 23 March 2020, www.project-syndicate.org/commentary/saudi-arabia-oil-production-mbs-new-strategy-by-bernard-haykel-2020-03

30 Gaidar, 'The Soviet Collapse'.

31 Douglas B. Reynolds, 'Soviet Economic Decline: Did an Oil Crisis Cause the Transition in the Soviet Union?' *The Journal of Energy and Development*, 24 (1), Autumn 1998: 65.

32 Mark N. Katz, 'Saudi Arabian Foreign Policy: Conflict and Cooperation', Arab Gulf States Institute in Washington, 23 March 2016, https://agsiw.org/saudi-arabian-foreign-policy-conflict-and-cooperation-2/

33 Carol Morello and Paul Sonne, 'U.S. Blacklists Strongman of Chechnya for Human Rights Abuses', *The Washington Post*, 20 July 2020, www.washingtonpost.com/national-security/us-blacklists-strongman-of-chechnya-for-human-rights-abuses/2020/07/20/1a1b2d4a-caa6-11ea-89ce-ac7d5e4a5a38_story.html

34 The Tabah Foundation offers a 'renewed Islamic discourse that engages the critical methodologies of the shariah disciplines with issues of concern to the global community'. Tabah Foundation, www.tabahfoundation.org/en/

35 Nikolay Kozhanov, 'Diversifying Relationships: Russian Policy in the Middle East and its Impact on the GCC', Bussola Institute, 24 November 2020, www.bussolainstitute.org/research/diversifying-relationships-russian-policy-in-the-middle-east-and-its-impact-on-the-gcc

36 Theodore Karasik, 'Russia's Financial Tactics in the Middle East', The Jamestown Foundation, 20 December 2017, https://jamestown.org/program/russias-financial-tactics-middle-east/#_ednref51

37 Ibid.

38 Muhammad al-'Ubadydi, 'Khattab', Jihadi Bios Project, Combating Terrorism Center at Westpoint, https://ctc.usma.edu/khattab-jihadi-bios-project/

39 Robert Parsons, 'Basayev's Death Confirmed', Radio Free Europe, 10 July 2006, www.rferl.org/a/1069732.html

40 US Department of State, 'Archive – The International Response: Global Condolences', 15 August 2002, https://2001-2009.state.gov/coalition/cr/fs/12710.htm

41 President of Russia, 'Statement on Terrorism Attacks in the USA', 11 September 2001, http://en.kremlin.ru/events/president/transcripts/21328

42 Ibid.

43 John O'Loughlin, Gearóid Ó Tuathail and Vladimir Kolossov, 'A "Risky Westward Turn"? Putin's 9–11 Script and Ordinary Russians', *Europe-Asia Studies*, 56 (1), January 2004: 3.

44 Michael McFaul, 'U.S.–Russia Relations After September 11, 2001', Carnegie Endowment for International Peace, 24 October 2001, https://carnegieendowment.org/2001/10/24/u.s.-russia-relations-after-september-11-2001-pub-840

45 Michael McFaul, 'U.S.–Russia Relations After September 11, 2001', Carnegie Endowment for International Peace, 24 October 2001, https://carnegieendowment.org/2001/10/24/u.s.-russia-relations-after-september-11-2001-pub-840

46 Michael McFaul, 'U.S.–Russia Relations After September 11, 2001', Carnegie Endowment for International Peace, 24 October 2001, https://carnegieendowment.org/2001/10/24/u.s.-russia-relations-after-september-11-2001-pub-840

47 Roman Kupchinsky, 'Energy and Russia's National Security Strategy', Atlantic Council, 19 May 2009, www.atlanticcouncil.org/blogs/new-atlanticist/energy-and-russias-national-security-strategy/

48 Yuri Barmin, 'Russian Energy Policy in the Middle East', *Insight Turkey*, 19 (4), Fall 2017, www.insightturkey.com/articles/russian-energy-policy-in-the-middle-east

49 Ibid.

50 Ibid.

51 Mark N. Katz, 'Russia Secretly Feared the Iran Nuclear Deal. Here's Why', *IranSource*, Atlantic Council, 28 April 2021, www.atlanticcouncil.org/blogs/ iransource/russia-secretly-feared-the-iran-nuclear-deal-heres-why/

52 Ibid.

53 Ibid.

54 The Moscow Times, 'Turkey to Send Home Russian S-400 Missile System Experts in Signal to U.S. – Reports', 3 June 2021, www.themoscowtimes.com/2021/06/02/ turkey-to-send-home-russian-s-400-missile-system-experts-in-signal-to-us-reports-a74078

55 Schmidt, 'The Saudi Air Defense Problem'.

56 Bradley Bowman and Andrew Gabel, 'Russia's S-400: An Offer US Partners Should Refuse', *Defense News*, 22 July 2019, www.defensenews.com/opinion/ commentary/2019/07/22/russias-s-400-an-offer-us-partners-should-refuse/

57 Patrick Schmidt, 'The Saudi Air Defense Problem is a U.S. Opportunity', The Washington Institute for Near East Policy, PolicyWatch 3450, 17 March 2021.

58 Robert Mason, 'Saudi Visit to Moscow: Is Saudi Arabia Driving a Wedge Between Russia and Iran?', *The Globe Post*, 10 October 2017, https://theglobepost. com/2017/10/10/saudi-salman-russia-iran/

59 The Ministry of Foreign Affairs of the Russian Federation, 'Presentation on Russia's Collective Security Concept for the Persian Gulf Region', 23 July 2019, www.mid.ru/en/liga-arabskih-gosudarstv-lag-/-/asset_publisher/0vP3hQoCPRg5/ content/id/3733593

60 Nikolay Kozhanov, 'Russia and the Issue of a New Security Architecture for the Persian Gulf', LSE Middle East Centre, 4 August 2021, https://blogs.lse. ac.uk/mec/2021/08/04/russia-and-the-issue-of-a-new-security-architecture-for-the-persian-gulf/?fbclid=IwAR3sfkMr5b4YLeMr4hFXqhYFp5RaZ-vxB6WV5sIJ7Qy2ZIeQK8wXyteKp6k

61 Mark N. Katz, 'He's Serious: Putin Offers to Sell Air Defense Missiles to Saudi Arabia', Atlantic Council, 17 September 2019, www.atlanticcouncil.org/blogs/ new-atlanticist/hes-serious-putin-offers-to-sell-air-defense-missiles-to-saudi-arabia/

62 Samuel Ramani, 'Russia's Growing Ties with Iran-Aligned Militia Groups', Middle East Institute, 26 March 2021, www.mei.edu/publications/russias-growing-ties-iran-aligned-militia-groups

63 TASS, 'Over 85% of Russian Army Commanders Gained Combat Experience in Syria, Says Putin', 25 May 2021, https://tass.com/defense/1293675

64 Dmitri Trenin, 'Russia in the Middle East: Moscow's Objectives, Priorities, and Policy Drivers', Carnegie Endowment for International Peace, 25 March 2016, https://carnegieendowment.org/files/03-25-16_Trenin_Middle_East_Moscow_ clean.pdf

65 Neil Melvin, 'The Foreign Military Presence in the Horn of Africa Region', SIPRI Background Paper, April 2019: 13.

66 Times of Israel, 'Russian Nixed Arms Sales to Israel's Enemies at its Request, PM's Advisor Says', 2 November 2019, www.timesofisrael.com/ russia-nixed-arms-sales-to-israels-enemies-at-its-request-pms-adviser-says/

67 There is a possibility this topic came up in conversations between Erik Prince, Trump donor and Blackwater founder who has ties to the UAE, and Kirill Dmitriev, the head of Russian Direct Investment Fund who has ties to Vladimir Putin, at a secret meeting in the Seychelles in 2017. Andrew Prokop, 'The Secret Seychelles Meeting Robert Mueller is Zeroing in on, Explained', *Vox*, 10 April 2018, www.vox.com/2018/3/7/17088908/erik-prince-trump-russia-seychelles-mueller

68 Reuters Staff, 'Iran Says Saudi Arabia and Russia Have Taken Oil Market "Hostage": SHANA', 15 September 2018, www.reuters.com/article/us-iran-oil-opec/iran-says-saudi-arabia-and-russia-have-taken-oil-market-hostage-shana-idUSKCN1LV05B

69 Yuri Barmin, 'Russian Energy Policy in the Middle East', *Insight Turkey*, 19 (4), Fall 2017.

70 Rosneft, 'Rosneft Signs a Strategic Cooperation Agreement with Mubadala Petroleum', 24 May 2014, www.rosneft.com/press/releases/item/153291/

71 Mubadala, 'RDIF, Mubadala Petroleum and Gazprom Neft Announce Joint Venture to Develop Siberian Oil Fields', 24 May 2018, www.mubadala.com/en/news/rdif-mubadala-petroleum-and-gazprom-neft-announce-joint-venture-develop-siberian-oil-fields

72 Zawya, 'ROSATOM Opens a Regional Office in Dubai', 10 April 2016, www.zawya.com/mena/en/press-releases/story/ROSATOM_opens_a_regional_office_in_Dubai-ZAWYA20160410110115/

73 Marianna Belenkaya, 'Russia–Saudi Roller Coaster: From a High Five to a Price War', 8 July 2020, https://carnegieendowment.org/2020/07/08/russia-saudi-roller-coaster-from-high-five-to-price-war-pub-81896

74 President of Russia, 'Russian–UAE Talks', 15 October 2019, http://en.kremlin.ru/events/president/transcripts/61806

75 Arab News, 'Davos 2019: Saudi Investment in Russia 'Hits $2.5bn''', 23 January 2019, www.arabnews.com/node/1440521/business-economy

76 Reuters Staff, 'Russian Sovereign Fund Opens Office in Saudi', *Reuters*, 9 October 2019, www.reuters.com/article/us-russia-saudi-rdif/russian-sovereign-fund-opens-office-in-saudi-idUSKBN1WO0JO

77 Nik Pratt, 'Russia to Invest More than $1.3 Billion in UAE', Funds Global MENA, 18 October 2019, www.fundsglobalmena.com/news/russia-to-invest-more-than-13bn-in-uae

78 Yury Barmin, 'Putin's Visit Draws UAE, Russia Closer', *Al-Monitor*, 17 October 2019, www.al-monitor.com/originals/2019/10/russia-uae-putin-visit.html

79 Arab News, 'Abu Dhabi's Mubadala Buys En+ Stake from Billionaire Oleg Deripaska's Ex-Wife', 24 June 2021, www.arabnews.com/node/1882411/business-economy

80 Arabian Business, 'Abu Dhabi's Mubadala Announces Largest Investment in Russia', 9 December 2021, www.arabianbusiness.com/industries/energy/abu-dhabis-mubadala-announces-largest-investment-in-russia

81 Military Watch Magazine, 'The New Checkmate Stealth Jet is the Result of a Russia–UAE Joint Fighter Program – Report', 22 July 2021, https://militarywatchmagazine.com/article/sukhoi-light-stealth-jet-russia-uae-joint-program-report

82 Mark Episkopos, 'Five Weapons Saudi Arabia Would Love to Buy from Russia', *The National Interest*, 28 January 2021, https://nationalinterest.org/blog/buzz/five-weapons-saudi-arabia-would-love-buy-russia-177251

83 Frank Gardner, 'Saudi Arabia Warms to Russia's Embrace', BBC News, 16 October 2019, www.bbc.com/news/world-middle-east-50054546

84 Samuel Ramani, 'Putin, Mohamed bin Zayed Seek to Reclaim Common Ground on Libya', *Al-Monitor*, 15 July 2020, www.al-monitor.com/originals/2020/07/russia-uae-libya-policy-hifter-egypt.html

10

The Horn of Africa: security on the western flank

Introduction

The Arabian Peninsula and the Horn of Africa, comprising the states of Djibouti, Eritrea, Ethiopia, Sudan and Somalia, have common connections that span millennia. Contact was facilitated by the *Hijrat* or Muslim migration from western Arabia to places such as Abyssinia (Ethiopian empire) with the Axumites, whose empire spanned Eritrea, northern Ethiopia, most of Sudan and southern/eastern Yemen at its peak between 80 AD and 825 AD. Both before and since, there has been a constant rejuvenation of communication through sailors, conquerors, traders and slaves crossing the Red Sea. In another major development, mostly Arabs from Oman and the Arabian Peninsula travelled across the Arabian Sea and Indian Ocean to what is modern-day Mozambique, Kenya and Tanzania. In many cases there are clear links between Muscat, Basra, Qalhat and Bandars in Persia to Shanga, Qanbalu and Mombasa.[1] Traders and merchants of African and Arab origin established the 'Swahili Coast' from around the ninth to fourteenth centuries, including trading centres such as Mogadishu, Lamu, Malindi, Mombasa, Zanzibar, Kilwa, the island of Mozambique and Sofala. Gold and ivory from the interior of Africa were transported through ports such as Kilwa, in present-day Tanzania, ruled by Persians from Shiraz in the ninth century.[2] African slaves were used as sailors in Persia, pearl divers in the Gulf, soldiers in the Omani army and workers on the salt pans of Mesopotamia (Iraq).[3] Many were used as domestic slaves in rich households.

Whilst Sultan Seyyid Said had begun to rule over the island of Zanzibar from 1856 by moving his entire court there from Muscat, it came under British authority through the Heligoland-Zanzibar Treaty of 1890. The East Africa campaign, from June 1940 to November 1941 during the Second World War, defeated the Comando Forze Armate dell'Africa Orientale Italiana (Italian East African Armed Forces Command) in Italian Somalia, Italian Eritrea and the occupied Ethiopian empire after the Second Italo-Ethiopian

War (1935–37). British control of the Suez Canal was crucial in cutting off Italian forces from resupply.

Decolonisation in the 1960s and 1970s further altered the dynamics of the region. King Faisal (1964–75) is credited with establishing diplomatic relations with African states after the Six Day War in 1967 in an attempt to isolate Israel, then as part of its Cold War strategy aligned with the US and later as a mediator in conflicts.[4] Livestock exports from British Somaliland/ Somalia, which have traditionally and mainly gone to Saudi Arabia, developed according to political conditions, local population growth and price. For example, exports peaked during Mogadishu's urbanisation in the 1970s and 1980s.[5] Supplies of livestock are particularly important for sacrifice during the Hajj, but have been interrupted on occasion due to quarantines imposed by the kingdom in 1983 and 1999, and by COVID-19 restrictions in 2020.

Growing energy linkages between Africa, the Middle East and Asia are refocusing international attention on the Indian Ocean as a strategic space. Renewed and enhanced maritime trade and market access (including that linked to China's BRI), politics and state building,[6] anti-piracy (usually with a focus on Somalia)[7] and counterterrorism operations[8] reflect the opportunity, challenges and threats in the littoral states of the Horn of Africa and beyond. The Arab uprisings as well as the Gulf crises between Saudi Arabia, Bahrain, the UAE and Egypt, on the one hand, and Qatar, Turkey and Iran, on the other, have incentivised GCC state competition in the Horn of Africa, especially in states undergoing transition, such as Sudan and Somalia. Recent conflicts such as the Eritrean–Ethiopian War from to 2000 with a final peace agreed only in 2018, and operational considerations surrounding the Saudi-led coalition intervention in Yemen from 2015, including base considerations, have been of paramount concern.

From 2005 to 2013 Iranian President Ahmadinejad pushed for closer relations with African states to bolster his position and standing in the world. This was also designed to escape international isolation and build an anti-sanctions consensus among non-permanent UN Security Council members at the time, in light of developments in the Iranian nuclear programme. Iranian concerns about attracting FDI and technological expertise mirror, to a degree, Horn interests. Iranian traction in the Horn has been rather weak, reflecting very small Shia populations of less than 10 per cent. But Iran has been active in places such as Sudan and, more opportunistically, in Somalia, given the US military presence there in the early 1990s.

For Qatar, its interests in the Horn tend to rest on issues such as food security and alliance with Turkey, which has come under intense scrutiny since 2017 and could be viewed as driving UAE regional ambitions across the Red Sea, especially in Somalia. Turkey has expanded its relations in the

Horn since 2002, especially in Sudan, Somalia and Djibouti. Diplomatic ties, direct air connections and loosened visa restrictions are encouraging contacts at the elite, business and tourism levels. The removal of US sanctions on Sudan in 2017 has helped, and Turkish investments and presence in Sudan and Somalia are particularly noticeable. Given that 'Turkey's policy in Africa in general and in Somalia in particular will help [give it] a sustainable presence',[9] the focus is bound to remain on this country as a strategic point of influence. The precise dynamics in each Horn state are detailed in the following sections.

Djibouti

The UAE's first foray into Africa was the development of the Doraleh Container Terminal concession in 2006. However, maritime logistics company DP World was forced out by presidential decree in 2018, following which the UAE won a tribunal ruling against Djibouti's port company, Port de Djibouti S.A., in July 2021.[10] The UAE considered getting Djibouti on side a geostrategic necessity, given the Houthi gains around Bab al-Mandab. Saudi Arabia signed a security cooperation agreement with Djibouti in 2016, including allowing the Gulf state to build a military base on its territory.[11] As one Saudi diplomat noted in 2018, the Houthi presence 'made us very serious about controlling the Red Sea Coast. We should not leave this for any militia. We have to protect it from Iran, the Houthis and any militia'.[12] However, around the same time President Abdrabuh Mansour Hadi Mansour also saw that the UAE was playing off Aden against Djibouti, thereby representing a 'high tide of UAE ambition in the Red Sea'.[13]

Eritrea

Eritrea had offered its port at Assab to the Iranian navy, in return for Iranian support. In 2015, Saudi Arabia established a GCC base at Assab, ending Iran's naval access. The UAE built a port and expanded an airstrip in Assab and used it to train and equip 4,000 Yemeni fighters, including Hadrami Elite Forces and Security Belt Forces – some of who may have been involved in disappearances and/or abuse of detainees during their ground operations – and also as a point of transit for soldiers arriving from Sudan and Senegal.[14] The base was also used to enforce the naval blockade on Yemen prior to being dismantled by the UAE following its withdrawal from the Yemen conflict in 2020.[15] Saudi Arabia and the UAE secured Eritrea's participation in the Saudi-led coalition in Yemen with money and fuel. In 2016, 400

Eritrean troops were said to have been embedded with the UAE contingent in Yemen.[16] Riyadh started a dialogue between Eritrea and Djibouti over their border conflict in 2018.

Ethiopia

In 2018, Saudi Arabia and the UAE took leading roles in negotiating between Ethiopia and Eritrea and providing aid to end the war which had rolled on for 20 years. The UAE pledged $3 billion, of which $1 billion was earmarked for a central bank deposit.[17] There has also been a $28.7 million project by Sanad Aerotech, owned by Mubadala, for aircraft engine maintenance in partnership with Ethiopian airlines, and a $646 million real estate deal in November 2018, conducted by Dubai-based Eagle Hills, for a mixed land-use project.[18] Saudi Arabia pledged $140 million for infrastructure and energy projects in 2019.[19] It has also been returning around 400,000 irregular Ethiopian migrants from Ethiopia – a plan of action that was suspended briefly in 2020 due to COVID-19.[20]

Ethiopian Prime Minister Abiy Ahmed faces international condemnation over his handling of the Tigray War in November 2020, and it appears that the UAE, Turkey and Iran have been caught up in that through their supply of armed drones. The UAE appears to have the upper hand by deploying Chinese made Wing Loong drones, which have a longer range than their Turkish equivalents. Ethiopia says that it foiled an attack on the UAE embassy in February 2021, and there may have been a similar planned attack on the UAE embassy in Khartoum.[21] Mohammed bin Zayed had a telephone conversation with Prime Minister Ahmed shortly after the capital, Mekelle, fell to the Tigray Defence Forces in June 2021, and earlier welcomed a ceasefire in Tigray region.[22] Saudi Arabia and the UAE may be more cautious going forward, also in light of Turkey's inroads into Ethiopia through soft power such as the popularity of Turkish television shows, trade and development aid. As Yaprak Alp, the Turkish ambassador to Ethiopia noted in 2021, Turkish policy in Africa is predicated on the idea that Africa 'had not been paid enough attention, that there was huge potential here for humanitarian and development efforts, first of all, and then also for economic ties, of course'.[23]

Ethiopia has the second-largest population in Africa, and is home to the African Union, making it a regional power. Ottoman naval missions have been sent to the Horn as far back as the sixteenth century, and Turkey in 2021 was the third-biggest investor of capital in Africa after China and Saudi Arabia.[24] The Ethiopian economy grew by 10 per cent annually from 2005 to around 2018, and Prime Minister Ahmed's privatisation plans are luring further investment. The number of Turkish companies has increased from three in 2005 to 200 in 2021.[25] Turkey has also been bolstered by the tension between Addis Ababa and Cairo over the GERD, which had been helped by UAE mediation and coordination with Egypt in 2018 but appears to have had a limited effect so far. Further Saudi and UAE diplomacy and aid could still stabilise the deterioration of Egypt–Ethiopian relations and seek a way out of the GERD impasse in a similar manner to the brief attempt at UAE mediation in the Sudan–Ethiopia border dispute in 2021, but a lack of leverage remains a key concern.

Sudan

Iran benefited from the autocratic Islamist Al-Ingaz regime under Hassan Al-Turabi, from 1989 until 1999–2000, who was a polarising and extremist force in the region, allying himself with Al Qaeda, Hezbollah and Carlos the Jackal whilst pursuing the overthrow of the Chad, Ethiopian and Egyptian governments. By refusing to participate in the 1990–91 Gulf War to expel Iraqi forces from Kuwait, offering Osama bin Laden sanctuary after he was stripped of Saudi citizenship and refusing to recognise Saudi Arabia's ulema, Sudan quickly became a pariah state. Without ties of significant amounts of aid, Tehran was able to engage Sudan. Tehran was also motivated to engage Sudan due to the US presence in Somalia in the early 1990s, where it wished to prosecute a proxy campaign, including by taking a leading role in establishing the Somalia Revolutionary Guard, who were trained using Iranian and Hezbollah experts in Sudan.[26] Iran also sent anti-aircraft missiles to Sudan for possible use in Somalia.[27]

Turabi's policies were unsustainable, given the heavy economic toll, and thus Omar al-Bashir implemented a coup and repaired relations with the GCC states. However, intra-GCC competition developed and, following the 2005 Comprehensive Peace Agreement and the 2011 secession of South Sudan, tensions developed with Saudi Arabia, the EU and the US over debt and sanctions relief. Sudan then became embroiled in arms trafficking to Hamas, and a military factory in Khartoum linked to such activities was the subject of an Israeli air strike in 2012.[28] Amid the first Qatar Crisis in 2014, Sudan moved to close Iranian cultural centres, possibly looking for increased Saudi funding. But still, Iran formed a Gulf of Aden anti-piracy task force in 2014 based out of Port Sudan. Tehran continues to send naval forces to the Gulf of Aden and the entrance to the Red Sea.

The storming of the Saudi embassy in Iran in response to the Saudi execution of Nimr al-Nimr, an activist Shia cleric in the kingdom, in 2016 provided a firmer basis on which Saudi Arabia was able to mobilise regional support to achieve its objectives in Yemen and against Iran. Beyond calling for the Arab world to cut diplomatic relations with Iran, Saudi Arabia secured Sudanese troop and air force participation in the Yemen conflict in exchange for $2 billion to $4 billion worth of aid and a possible promise to push the US to lift sanctions against Sudan.[29] Sudanese troops and mercenaries, estimated to be more than 70,000 at their peak, were vital to the Saudi war effort and played into the changing balance of power in Sudan in favour of General Mohamed Hamdan Degalo (Hemedti).[30] The normalisation of diplomatic relations, where then President Omar al-Bashir was once Khartoum's military attaché in Abu Dhabi[31] but was also close to Ankara, was expected to enhance Saudi investments in the country and ease the process of sending remittances from Sudanese labourers working in the kingdom.

Saudi Arabia and the UAE attempted to play a role in shaping the political transition in Sudan after the revolution in April 2019, through $500 million sent in cash and $2.5 billion in commodities. But they are said to have cut support to the government in December 2019 after having paid only half this amount.[32] Their association with Hemedti, deputy head of the Transitional Military Council, after visits to Riyadh, Cairo and Abu Dhabi, has raised questions in light of the June 2019 massacres carried out in Sudan.[33] This was articulated by the US and the UK, who engaged Saudi Arabia and the UAE, noting that it represented further possible reputation damage after the Yemen conflict and the US arms suspension. Furthermore, in light of the persistence of the Sudanese protestors, in contrast to Bahrain where repression worked quickly, and in Egypt where the army was able to take control, a power-sharing agreement between Sudan's military and civil leaders was able to be formulated in July 2019.[34]

The stakes were also high for Saudi Arabia and the UAE, as the incumbent regime was Islamist and any delayed transition could favour extremists. As de Waal notes, Egypt has different interests in Sudan compared to Saudi Arabia and the UAE, focusing on handing over Islamists in exile, suspending a deal for a Turkish naval base and ceding its territorial claim over the Halaib Triangle.[35] Qatar has been heavily engaged on Darfur, and its role vis-à-vis Islamists in the country could be harnessed in a joined-up strategy. It is perhaps unsurprising, then, that Khartoum reinstated its diplomatic relations with Qatar in April 2021, withstanding pressure not to do so from Saudi Arabia, Egypt and the UAE. Following the military coup in October/November 2021 led by General Abdel Fattah al-Burhan, Saudi Arabia and the UAE officially stood against the coup, perhaps due to European influence. But the interests of Riyadh and Abu Dhabi are not necessarily in supporting the civilian leadership, but in finding the best method of guaranteeing stability. The UAE, to which al-Burhan made his first publicly announced official trip in March 2022, will remain vital in terms of its economic support for the military elite. This has already borne fruit, including new projects such as a new Red Sea port in Sudan, part of a $6 billion investment package announced by the UAE and Sudanese businessman Osama Daoud Abdel-latif in June 2022,[36] at a time when international donors have suspended financial assistance and investments in Sudan to compel the coup leaders to restore civilian rule and support the democratic transition process in the country.

Somalia

Beyond Saudi riyal politik in Somalia and important livestock imports for the Hajj (which were adversely affected by COVID-19, highlighting the necessity of diversification in this industry), UAE and Turkish engagement in Somalia has been more evident. Overall, there remains potential in Saudi Arabia encouraging closer relations by building greater trade and investment ties.

Anwar Gargash, the former minister of state for foreign affairs, has noted that UAE policy in Somalia can be viewed as an extension of its policy towards Afghanistan because terror groups know no boundaries, and that there are connections between Al Qaeda and al Shabab.[37] The UAE was training the Somali government forces in its darkest years and, furthermore, maritime piracy developed because of the lack of economic opportunity in Somalia.[38] The UAE also helped to create more awareness of piracy and to galvanise international support for anti-piracy activities.[39] Erik Prince's private army have helped to clarify the limits of UAE engagement, mainly by drawing unwanted press attention to the UAE's anti-piracy force in Puntland.[40]

In 2018 Abu Dhabi invested $336 million to expand the port of Bosaso in the semi-autonomous region of Puntland in Somalia.[41] During the Qatar Crisis, in which the central government maintained links to Qatar and Turkey, the UAE explored links at the federal state level, exacerbating tensions with Mogadishu. The UAE moved to develop economic and military links to semi-autonomous regions such as Somaliland, Jubaland and Puntland. The Emirates also had plans to build a military base at Berbera in Somaliland, before agreeing to turn it into a civilian airport in 2019, according to the region's president.[42] As of March 2021, DP World was expanding and developing the Port of Berbera.[43] The UAE is also building up influence in Somaliland through the appointment of Abdullah Muhammad Al Naqbi as director of a new UAE Trade Office.[44] This could boost cooperation on anti-piracy and counterterrorism initiatives. The UAE has also been involved in training the region's military forces. For example, from 2014 until 2018 it trained hundreds of Somali troops, until Somali security forces seized millions of dollars and temporarily held a UAE plane.[45]

Turkey has poured more than $1 billion into Somalia since 2011, including $2.4 million that Somalia owed to the IMF, and has built hospitals and schools and provided scholarships.[46] It has had a base, Camp Turksom, its largest overseas military facility so far, plus a defence university in Mogadishu, since 2017. The camp was attacked by Al Shabab in 2021.[47] In 2020 Turkey took control of the country's second-largest port, at Hobyo in Galmudug state, on a fourteen-year contract.[48] The UK also has a small British Security Training Centre in Somalia, based in Baidoa and Mogadishu.[49] Both sites have been operational since 2017 and operate within the UN-mandated African Union Mission in Somalia,[50] although the military component is comprised of only African states: Ugandan, Burundian, Djiboutan, Kenyan and Ethiopian troops are deployed across south and central Somalia.[51]

Conclusion

The long-standing relations between the Arab Gulf monarchies and the Horn of Africa states reflect deep social, economic, political and religious ties. These have at times been temporarily compromised, usually by ideologically based actions at the elite level in the Horn which have favoured Saudi and UAE adversaries such as Iran. Economic concerns, including broader international interests in sanctions relief and improved relations with the US and EU, have occasionally favoured Saudi Arabia and the UAE as important interlocutors. Both Saudi Arabia and the UAE have been able to extend their brand of economic intervention to maximise influence in the political marketplaces of the Horn states, including through aid, investment and other financial arrangements. This has been done to great effect in the cases of Eritrea and Ethiopia, and perhaps less so during the political transition in Sudan, in conjunction with Egypt.

When the kingdom engaged Horn states over relations with Iran, Turkey or during the Qatar Crisis, and encouraged balancing with upfront economic and energy payments, Saudi policy was effective. However, in the absence of follow-through by the kingdom, the situation could change. As the ruling elite focuses on Vision 2030 and seeks closure to the war in Yemen, Saudi interests look set to be focused increasingly on economic channels (e.g. mega projects such as Neom) and potential new regional connections such as a causeway across the Tiran Strait to Egypt (more likely to occur than the 'Bridge of the Horn of Africa' between Djibouti and Yemen). These will be supplemented by diplomatic channels such as the Red Sea Council, which it established in January 2020 and which is focused on addressing shared security threats, with its membership including Sudan, Djibouti, Somalia, Eritrea, Egypt, Yemen and Jordan. Although this is another step towards providing a coordinated regional approach, it is missing some key states which could enhance its efficacy.

UAE influence in the Horn appears to have followed a policy of gradualism in Somaliland, exploiting island opportunities such as Socotra and Mayun in its pivot around the Arabian Peninsula, and extending a maritime security model which reflects its core interests as a trading nation. Its influence addresses national security threats from internal/hinterland insecurity, including from Islamist groups such as Al Shabab, and is in concordance with international actors with limited resources to effect radical change and development in the region. Whilst the Yemen conflict served to facilitate tactical base agreements, security training programmes and deployments from the region, the Emirati withdrawal from the conflict has also served to right-size the UAE footprint in the Horn by, for example, dismantling the airstrip at Assab or turning the military base in Berbera, Somaliland into a civilian airport. UAE arms relations with the US may also have a bearing on its engagement in places such as Ethiopia.

Saudi and UAE relations with Hemedti and General Fattah al-Burhan (after the Sudan military coup in 2021), like the UAE's courting of Haftar in Libya, illustrate their joint interest in generating near-term stability. This extends to securing vital trade and tourism projects on the Red Sea, at the expense of support for foreign concepts such as democratisation, the outcome of which, in security terms, is neither predictable, linear nor guaranteed.

Gulf intervention and broader competition encompassing key Egyptian national security issues and the presence of Turkey in Somalia and Ethiopia have also created aspects of instability. This could have a particularly grave effect in places such as Somalia which are already suffering from the effects of drought and disintegration. The duality of instability – that from competing GCC and other interests being superimposed on the Horn as well as domestic and regional challenges – could further compromise local cooperation through intergovernmental organisations such as the Intergovernmental Authority on Development (IGAD). IGAD already lacks capacity and operates amid divergent state agendas (notably Ethiopia and Djibouti during the Somali peace process), state collapse and political contestation in Somalia, civil war in Darfur (Sudan), civil war in Tigray (Ethiopia) and fragile Eritrea–Ethiopia relations.

Notes

1 Allen Fromherz, 'Oman, the Gulf, and East Africa', 6 May 2016, www.oxfordbibliographies.com/view/document/obo-9780199846733/obo-9780199846733-0159.xml

2 Michael N. Pearson, 'Introduction: Locating Coastal East Africa', *Port Cities and Intruders: The Swahili Coast, India, and Portugal in the Early Modern Era*. Baltimore, MD: Johns Hopkins University Press, 1998: 21.

3 BBC World Service, 'The Story of Africa: Slavery', www.bbc.co.uk/worldservice/africa/features/storyofafrica/9chapter3.shtml

4 Jens Helbach, 'Sub-Saharan Africa: A Theater for Middle East Power Struggles', *Middle East Policy*, 27 (2), Summer 2020: 71.

5 Cedric Barnes, 'The Ethiopian–British Somaliland Boundary', in Dereje Feyissa and Markus Virgil Hoehne (eds) *Borders and Borderlands as Resources in the Horn of Africa*. Woodbridge, Suffolk: James Currey, 2010: 144.

6 See Christopher Clapham, *The Horn of Africa: State Formation and Decay*. Oxford: Oxford University Press, 2017; Alex de Waal, *The Real Politics of the Horn of Africa: Money, War and the Business of Power*. Cambridge: Polity Press, 2015; Peter Woodward, *Crisis in the Horn of Africa: Politics, Piracy and the Threat of Terror*. London: I. B. Tauris, 2012.

7 See Christopher L. Daniels, *Somali Piracy and Terrorism in the Horn of Africa*. London: Scarecrow Press, 2012; Martin N. Murphy, *Somalia: The New Barbery? Piracy and Islam in the Horn of Africa*. New York: Columbia University Press, 2011; Awet Tewelde Weldemichael, *Piracy in Somalia: Violence and Development in the Horn of Africa*. Cambridge: Cambridge University Press, 2019.

8 The US increased counterterrorism operations in the Horn of Africa after 9/11 with the establishment of Operation Enduring Freedom-Horn of Africa (OEF-HOA) in October 2002 and Combined Joint Task Force-Horn of Africa (CJTF-HOA) which covers Djibouti, Eritrea, Ethiopia, Kenya, the Seychelles, Somalia and Sudan. Camp Lemonnier, serves as a base of operations for US allies to engage, especially those without their own bases in the Horn, such as the UK. Neil Melvin, 'The Foreign Military Presence in the Horn of Africa Region', SIPRI Background Paper, April 2019: 19–20.

9 Interview with a Turkish diplomat who asked not to be named, 14 October 2020.

10 Reuters, 'DP World Says Wins Ruling Against Djibouti's Port Company', 12 July 2021, www.reuters.com/world/middle-east/dp-world-says-wins-ruling-against-djiboutis-port-company-2021-07-12/

11 John Aglionby and Simeon Kerr, 'Djibouti Finalising Deal for Saudi Arabian Military Base', *Financial Times*, 17 January 2017.

12 International Crisis Group, 'The United Arab Emirates in the Horn of Africa', Briefing 65, 6 November 2018, www.crisisgroup.org/middle-east-north-africa/gulf-and-arabian-peninsula/united-arab-emirates/b65-united-arab-emirates-horn-africa

13 Interview with Gerald M. Feierstein, 23 April 2021.

14 Rahma Hussein, 'The UAE's Military and Naval Reliance on Eritrea Makes the War in Yemen Even Riskier for the U.S.', Just Security, 31 March 2017, www.justsecurity.org/41450/uaes-military-naval-reliance-eritrea-war-yemen-riskier-u-s/

15 Jon Gambrell, 'UAE Dismantles Eritrea Base as it Pulls Back after Yemen War', *AP News*, 18 February 2021, https://apnews.com/article/eritrea-dubai-only-on-ap-united-arab-emirates-east-africa-088f41c7d54d6a397398b2a825f5 e45a

16 Salem Solomon, 'Observers See Several Motives for Eritrean Involvement in Yemen', *VOA News*, 9 January 2016, www.voanews.com/middle-east/ observers-see-several-motives-eritrean-involvement-yemen

17 Reuters, 'UAE to Give Ethiopia $3 Billion in Aid and Investments', 16 June 2018, available at www.arabnews.com/node/1322591/business-economy

18 Karen E. Young, 'Iraq Wants Aid, but Saudi Arabia and the UAE See Investment Opportunity', *Foreign Policy*, 30 April 2021, https://foreignpolicy.com/2021/04/30/ saudi-arabia-uae-iraq-investment-energy/

19 Reuters Staff, 'Ethiopia to get $140mln in Loans from Saudi Arabia', 19 December 2019, www.reuters.com/article/ethiopia-economy-idUSL8N28T2EG

20 IOM, 'Post Arrival Emergency Life Saving Assistance to Kingdom of Saudi Arabia Returnees – Flash Update', 16 July 2021, https://reliefweb.int/report/ ethiopia/post-arrival-emergency-life-saving-assistance-kingdom-saudi-arabia-returnees-flash-0

21 Reuters, 'Ethiopia Says it Foiled Attack on UAE Embassy in Addis Ababa', 3 February 2021, https://news.trust.org/item/20210203174729-af8eo/

22 AFP, 'US, Ireland, UK Request UN Security Council Meeting on Tigray, Diplomats Say', *Gulf News*, 29 June 2021, https://gulfnews.com/world/africa/us-ireland-uk-request-un-security-council-meeting-on-tigray-diplomats-say-1.80294254

23 Andres Schipani and Laura Pitel, 'Erdogan's Great Game: Turkey Pushes into Africa with Aid, Trade and Soaps', *Financial Times*, 18 January 2021, www.ft.com/ content/0e3cec2a-bd80-499c-a6ab-e5d1a1e768cf

24 Ibid.

25 Ibid.

26 Shaul Shay, 'Iranian Involvement in Somalia', *The Red Sea Terror Triangle: Sudan, Somalia, Yemen, and Islamic Terror.* Abingdon: Routledge, 2005: 76.

27 Ibid.

28 BBC News, 'Sudan Blames Israel for Khartoum Arms Factory Blast', 24 October 2012, www.bbc.com/news/world-africa-20050781

29 International Institute of Security Studies, *The Military Balance 2017.* IISS, 2017: 491

30 Alex de Waal, 'Cash and Contradictions: On the Limits of Middle Eastern Influence in Sudan', *African Arguments*, 1 August 2019, https://africanarguments.org/2019/08/ cash-and-contradictions-on-the-limits-of-middle-eastern-influence-in-sudan/

31 International Crisis Group, 'The United Arab Emirates in the Horn of Africa', Briefing 65, 6 November 2018.

32 Jean Baptiste-Gallopin, 'Bad Company: How Dark Money Threatens Sudan's Transition', European Council on Foreign Relations, 9 June 2020, https://ecfr.eu/publication/ bad_company_how_dark_money_threatens_sudans_transition/#_ftnref25

33 Camille Lons, 'Gulf Countries Reconsider their Involvement in the Horn of Africa', IISS, 1 June 2021, www.iiss.org/blogs/analysis/2021/06/gulf–horn-of-africa

34 Declan Walsh, 'In Sudan, a Power-Sharing Deal Propelled by a Secret Meeting and Public Rage', *The New York Times*, 5 July 2019, www.nytimes.com/2019/07/05/world/africa/sudan-power-sharing-deal.html

35 de Waal, 'Cash and Contradictions'.

36 Nafisa Eltahir, 'Exclusive: UAE to Build Red Sea Port in Sudan in $6 Billion Investment Package', Reuters, 21 June 2022, www.reuters.com/world/middle-east/exclusive-uae-build-red-sea-port-sudan-6-billion-investment-package-2022-06-20/

37 Council on Foreign Relations, 'A Conversation with Anwar Gargash', 29 September 2020, www.cfr.org/event/conversation-anwar-gargash

38 Ibid.

39 Ibid.

40 Mark Mazzetti and Eric Schmitt, 'Private Army Formed to Fight Somali Pirates Leaves Troubled Legacy', 4 October 2021, *The New York Times*, www.nytimes.com/2012/10/05/world/africa/private-army-leaves-troubled-legacy-in-somalia.html

41 Maggie Fick, 'Harbouring Ambitions: Gulf States Scramble for Somalia', *Reuters*, 1 May 2018, www.reuters.com/article/us-somalia-gulf-analysis-idUSKBN1I23B4

42 Reuters Staff, 'Somaliland UAE Military Base to be Turned into Civilian Airport', 15 September 2019, www.reuters.com/article/us-somalia-emirates-idUSKBN1W00FI

43 Jochebed Menon, 'DP World, Somaliland Launch New Terminal at Berbera Port', *Construction Business News*, 27 June 2021, www.cbnme.com/logistics-news/dp-world-somaliland-launch-new-terminal-at-berbera-port/

44 Emirates News Agency, 'Somaliland President Receives Credentials of Director of UAE Trade Office in Somaliland', 17 March 2021, https://wam.ae/en/details/1395302918982

45 Reuters Staff, 'UAE Denounces Seizure of Cash and Plane in Somalia', *Reuters*, 10 April 2018, www.reuters.com/article/us-somalia-politics-emirates-idUSKBN1HH21V

46 Schipani and Pitel, 'Erdogan's Great Game'.

47 Hussein Mohamed and Megan Specia, 'Suicide Blast at Military Training Camp in Somalia Targets New Recruits', *The New York Times*, 15 June 2021, www.nytimes.com/2021/06/15/world/africa/somalia-shabab-attack-turkey.html

48 Africa Intelligence, 'Ankara's Ports Offensive', 11 November 2020, www.africaintelligence.com/eastern-and-southern-africa_business/2020/11/11/ankara-s-ports-offensive,109620346-art

49 Neil Melvin, 'The Foreign Military Presence in the Horn of Africa Region', SIPRI Background Paper, April 2019: 19.

50 Ibid.

51 AMISOM, 'AMISOM Military Component', https://amisom-au.org/mission-profile/military-component/

11

India and Pakistan: shifting tides of interaction and dependency

Introduction

India and Pakistan's dependence on the kingdom for energy imports, Hajj access, migrant labour opportunities and associated remittances has been an enduring feature of their engagement with Saudi Arabia and the UAE. These ties have been supplemented since the Mumbai attacks in 2008 by a converging Saudi and Indian interest in security and defence cooperation, rooted in counterterrorism. India's rising naval power in the Indian Ocean and a co-dependency in avoiding criticism or interference in domestic and some regional affairs has further strengthened political relations. Following the fallout from the Khashoggi affair, Asia has been a welcoming region for Mohammed bin Salman, versus the more cautious approach pursued by the Biden administration and some European states. For example, in Pakistan he received a 21-gun salute and a fly-past by the country's air force on arrival in 2019, followed by the gift of a gold-plated submachine gun from Pakistani senators.[1]

In New Delhi, Prime Minster Modi broke protocol and met Mohammed bin Salman at the airport on arrival and gave him a bear hug, something he tends to reserve for close allies and those states with which he intends to build strategic relations, especially after the Pulwama attack in Kashmir in February 2019.[2] It is notable that as bilateral relations between Riyadh and New Delhi have blossomed, so has the Indian Hajj quota, rising from 170,000 in 2018 to 200,000 in 2019 and 2020, whilst Pakistan received only an additional 5,000 places each year in the three years up to 2020, reaching 189,210 that year.[3] New Delhi's relations with Israel (which are at their most efficient when transport connections are facilitated by access through the kingdom's territory) have added another reason to advance a common agenda. Saudi and UAE relations with India and Pakistan, and Asia more widely, are becoming increasingly complex and dynamic as Saudi Arabia shifts its focus from Islamic to economic credentials and as these GCC states continue to implement their Visions strategies. Whilst relations with India and Pakistan are durable, a number of potential hurdles remain at the regional level, especially their policies and respective threat perceptions over Kashmir.

The following sections survey Saudi and UAE relations with India and Pakistan. The chapter concludes with remarks concerning the conceptualisation of shifts and transitions taking place bilaterally and interregionally between South and West Asia.

Saudi–Indian relations

India's historical connections to the Gulf span millennia, dating from trading between the Indus Valley and Dilmun, an ancient civilisation in Eastern Arabia on the trade route from Mesopotamia.[4] The Bombay Presidency determined and pursued British imperial interests in the Gulf.[5] After partition in 1947, King Saud made the first official Saudi visit to India in 1955, primarily to guarantee the safety of Muslims who remained within Indian territory.[6] India's close connections with the USSR during the Cold War and Saudi support for Pakistan effectively froze relations until Indira Ghandi's visit to the kingdom in 1982. It wasn't until 2006 that a Saudi king again travelled to India.

Every GCC head of state or government travelled to India between 2005 and 2007, recognising their role as principal suppliers of India's energy needs, primary trade and investment partners, and major destinations for Indian human resources, and also the longer-term economic opportunities in the East. The 'Delhi Declaration' signed in 2006 during former Saudi King Abdullah bin Abdulaziz's visit to India, where he was chief guest at India's Republic Day celebrations, announced a 'strategic energy partnership' between the two states. It covers diversification of trade and investment, oil, political cooperation, counterterrorism, money laundering and organised crime.[7] Following the 2008 Mumbai attacks, which highlighted regional exposure to violent extremism, the 'Riyadh Declaration' signed in 2010 by King Abdullah and Prime Minister Dr Manmohan Singh envisaged close cooperation in security, defence, economic and cultural areas. A Saudi–Indian extradition treaty signed in 2010 enabled the transfer of an Indian nationalist, Zabiuddin Ansari, to face prosecution in New Delhi in 2012. He was suspected of being the 'handler' of ten terrorists involved in the 2008 Mumbai terror attacks.[8]

The Arab uprisings and growing Saudi–US differences over political and security issues involving Egypt, Syria and Iran coincided with India becoming the world's fastest-growing major economy from around 2014 to 2018.[9] India's consistent passive opposition to the overthrow of President Assad in Syria, where it was forced to abandon oil investments, ties in well with the UAE's interest in 2021 to rehabilitate Assad in the League of Arab States. India's passive stance during the wars in Yemen and Libya was also largely for economic reasons, in that they have constrained opportunities for the Indian diasporas there to work and send remittances.[10] The advantage of this approach has been that India has avoided confrontation the Saudi Arabia and the UAE on issues deemed critical to their respective national security calculations. New Delhi adopted a similarly neutral stance to the 2017–21 Qatar Crisis without reprisals, which was all the more important, given the stakes for Indian expatriate labour in the Gulf.

Prime Minister Narendra Modi began his first term with visits to the GCC state capitals of Saudi Arabia, the UAE, Qatar and Iran in 2015 and 2016, followed by visits to Oman in 2018 and Bahrain in 2019, showing his intention to maintain close contact with the strategic region. Besides affirming ties in the traditional areas of energy, trade, investments and human resources, the joint statements signed during these visits have high-lighted interest in exploring new frontier areas for bilateral cooperation: food security, renewable and nuclear energy, education, defence industry, biotechnology, space, electronics, cyber security, innovation and support for business start-ups.[11] Saudi–Indian ties have been less high profile than Saudi–Sino ties but are still critical to extending Saudi energy exports, especially in light of the fact that in 2020 the US Energy Information Administration predicted that India would overtake China as the world's largest importer of oil.[12] China and India will be primarily responsible for global oil sales growth at least up to 2030. In 2021, the kingdom slipped as India's leading oil supplier, behind Iraq and then the US, as it implemented an OPEC production cut.[13] However, as recently as 2018, the kingdom made up 20 per cent of India's total oil imports,[14] and, far from declining oil sales, it is likely Saudi Arabia will make up lost ground following changes in OPEC policy over the coming years. Prime Minister Modi has pledged that India will cut emissions to net zero by 2070, longer than the mid-century cut-off date aimed for at the 2021 UN Climate Change Conference (COP26). It is also a decade later than Saudi Arabia's pledge to reach net zero emissions. The UAE is an important oil exporter to India, and Qatar is a key state for liquefied natural gas.

Saudi Arabia is India's fourth-largest trading partner after China, the US and the UAE. The GCC is the most important trading bloc in the world for India, beating Indian–EU trade of $102 billion in 2017–18 by $2 billion, even though there is no free trade treaty.[15] Between 1999 and 2018, Saudi–Indian trade increased from $3.2 billion to $31.7 billion, most of it based on Saudi oil exports.[16] Saudi–Indian trade was up slightly in 2020, to reach $33.09 billion,[17] but a contracting economy is bound to take a toll in the economic sphere in 2021–22. The oil-led relationship has facilitated Aramco support for the second-largest oil refinery in Asia after China, Jamnagar Refinery. Saudi Arabia has committed to investing $100 billion in India's energy, infrastructure and other sectors over the coming years.[18]

Indian businesses have also invested in Riyadh's metro, and India is part of Saudi food security through the export of basmati rice to the kingdom, although this appears to have been negatively impacted from 2018 to 2019 by the introduction of more stringent food quality rules by the kingdom (including controls on the use of pesticides).[19] Iran, another major Indian basmati rice destination, also appears to be reducing its imports in line with balancing trade with its crude oil exports to India.[20] India–Saudi investments in non-oil sectors remain low. Indian investments in the kingdom amounted to just $1.5 billion in 2020, whilst Saudi investments in India were $1.8 billion.[21] But there are signs of growth. In June 2020, PIF announced a $1.5 billion investment in Jio Platforms, India's leading telecommunication and digital services company, and $1.3 billion in Reliance Retail Ventures Limited, alongside $600 million from Alfanar into two wind projects in India.[22] In a meeting between Prime Minister Modi and Saudi foreign minister Prince Faisal bin Farhan Al Saud in New Delhi in September 2021, alongside discussions on Afghanistan, Modi expressed his interest in attracting further Saudi investment into Indian energy, IT and defence manufacturing.[23] It is conceivable that further cooperation in the fields of space, AI, cyber technologies and renewable energy will also take place.

Following oil price declines and economic slowdown since 2014, wage increases in India and Saudi policies favouring domestic labour in sectors traditionally dominated by migrants (including increases in work permit fees and taxes), the kingdom has reduced migrant labour opportunities. For example, in 2015 there were 306,000 registered workers from India in the kingdom, but by 2019 this number had tumbled to just 143,000.[24] Remittances still grew by 14 per cent year on year in 2018, to reach $78.6 billion, reflecting the depreciation of the rupee, transfers from unregistered migrants, better-paid jobs and/or repatriation of funds before leaving the country. This trend, similar across other GCC states, will no doubt lead to new and more diverse economic substance in bilateral relations and wider regional relations between the GCC states and sources of foreign labour in South Asia. This could to some extent adversely impact on the employment prospects of many of the 8.5 million non-resident Indians working in the Gulf.[25] Further cooperation such as in higher education exchange could help to mitigate this trend, as could more cooperation on renewable energy, water, food security, information technology (IT) and possibly shifting supply chains if they come to favour more local production.[26] Other economic opportunities may present themselves as more strategic cooperation develops.

At the Shangri-La Dialogue in Singapore on 1 June 2018, Prime Minister Modi put the Indo-Pacific region (spanning from the coast of Africa to the Americas and inclusive of the Gulf) at the centre of India's foreign policy.[27] Backed by fellow democratic states – the US, Japan and Australia (India being part of the so-called Quad) – but highlighting strategic autonomy in terms of maintaining relations with Russia and stable relations with China, India will be key to managing emerging threats in this new strategic theatre. Its approach has, so far, been to work with the Quad states, France and other island nations in building capacity and addressing constraints. In light of growing Indian competition with China over ties to islands such as the Maldives, Mauritius, Seychelles and Sri Lanka, the Gulf states could assume a growing role in serving Indian interests in the Indian Ocean, especially as some GCC states grow their military capabilities and autonomy.

There is already significant Indian–GCC defence and naval cooperation, including joint exercises, regular ship visits and GCC armed forces who train in Indian defence and military academies. There are Indian anti-piracy patrols off the Somali coast and in 2008 India set up the Indian Ocean Naval Symposium (IONS) as a dialogue forum for navy chiefs from across the Indian Ocean littoral. However, India does not want to be drawn into Gulf security in the way the US has been, and does not take sides in intra-regional disputes. It also has relations with Iran, Qatar and Israel, but had to respond to US demands during the Trump administration to reduce oil imports from Iran and earlier had voted against Iran at the IAEA in 2005 and 2009 when it was negotiating its nuclear deal with the US. Iran is nevertheless an important partner, especially after India invested $500 million in the development of Chabahar port in Iran and related connectivity projects to Afghanistan, the Central Asian republics and to Russia from this port, avoiding Pakistan. Operations were supposed to begin at the end of May 2021.

The US and Israel strengthened relations with India during the Kargil crisis of 1999. Israel became an important supplier of arms, with sales amounting to $2.2 billion from 2000 to 2015,[28] becoming India's second-largest arms supplier in 2019.[29] Israel was also India's tenth-largest trade partner in 2014. Israel provides cyber-security solutions for Indian critical infrastructure, trains Indian special forces on counterterrorism and police officers in Indian administered Kashmir. Between 2014 and 2021, India has abstained from various votes against Israel in the UN Human Rights Council.[30] Apart from importing high-technology products and arms, generating investment and possibly gaining some leverage over the Israel–Palestine conflict, the impact of the growing Indian–Israel nexus extends to the kingdom in terms of building a greater sense of regional connectivity. For example, an Air India flight on 23 March 2018 was the first commercial flight to transit Saudi Arabia airspace to Israel, saving two hours of flight time.[31]

Saudi–Indian ties could have been threatened at times due to a history of intercommunal and Hindu-supremacist vigilante-led violence targeting Muslims in India, with little by way of official Indian condemnation in recent years.[32] Further action, such as the India Citizenship Amendment Act in December 2019, which critics labelled unconstitutional,[33] could also have become a source of tension. But this has not transpired. COVID-19 created opportunities for Indian doctors and the supply of personal protective equipment in the kingdom and the wider Gulf, whilst India welcomed medical aid, including oxygen from the kingdom, the UAE and Qatar in May 2021.[34] Although the pandemic has caused the kingdom to repatriate Indian and Pakistani migrants for a mixture of health and economic reasons, none has been due to diplomatic clashes or escalations.

Yet there have been mounting exchanges which have created friction, mainly at the social level, between India and some GCC states. Muslim missionaries in New Delhi were blamed for a cluster of cases of COVID-19 in mid-March 2020 and were subjected to physical and verbal abuse. Some Indians, including members of the Bharatiya Janata Party, called some events run by Tablighi Jamaat 'corona jihad'.[35] Member of the Sharjah royal family and businesswoman Sheikha Hend Faisal Al Qassimi called out Saurabh Upadhyay, an Indian national working in the UAE in April 2020, for being 'openly racist and discriminatory'.[36] She went on to publish a front-page opinion piece in the *Gulf News* titled 'I pray for an India without hate and Islamophobia'.[37] In response to the growing Islamophobia linked to COVID-19, the Jeddah-based OIC did urge the Indian government to 'take urgent steps to stop the growing tide of Islamophobia in India and protect the rights of persecuted Muslim minority as per its obligations under int'l HR [human rights] law'.[38] To which Prime Minister Modi responded by noting that COVID-19 'does not see race, religion, colour, caste, creed, language or borders before striking'.[39] This was followed by the Indian external affairs minister, S. Jaishankar, responding to Saudi Arabia, the UAE and other GCC members to reassure and thank them for taking care of their Indian communities.[40] The Indian ambassador to the UAE, Pavan Kapoor, also followed this up with a reminder to Indians in the UAE against hate speech.[41]

UAE–Indian relations

The UAE has drawn exceptional interest from Prime Minister Modi. As a regional entrepôt, it was India's third-largest trading partner in 2019–20 after China and the US. It was also the first Gulf country the Indian prime minister visited in August 2015. The UAE had pledged to boost Emirati investments in the Indian economy (mainly in infrastructure and petrochemical projects) to $75 billion over five years from 2015[42] and then to $115 billion in five years from 2021.[43] In the context of difficulties experienced by Etisalat after the Indian Supreme Court cancelled 2G licences in 2012 and other difficulties experienced by Emaar, the real estate developer, the Indian commerce and industry minister, Piyush Goyal, said both sides are letting 'bygones be bygones'.[44] The UAE is also active in pursuing soft-power opportunities in India. For example, as part of its 'year of giving', the UAE National Archives, a subsidiary of the Ministry of Presidential Affairs, launched a charity initiative with the Emirates Red Crescent to construct fives mosques in 2017.[45] One was to be constructed in each of Mauritania, Somalia, Burkina Faso, Mali and India, each capable of accommodating 800 worshippers, along with a well in Mali and India.[46] As part of its 'year of tolerance' in 2019, Abu Dhabi announced that it would open its first official Hindu temple in 2020.[47]

Similar to Saudi Arabia, Mubadala invested $1.2 billion in Jio Platforms in June 2020, and Reliance plans to invest $2 billion in Abu Dhabi TA'ZIZ Industrial Chemicals Zone, a joint venture between Abu Dhabi National Oil Co. and SWF ADQ.[48] This push for post-COVID-19 economic recovery has been on the agenda for some months. As Navdeep Suri, former Indian ambassador to the UAE, put it in March 2020: 'COVID-19 is having a devastating impact on economic activity around the globe and I don't think any country is going to escape it. We see the lockdown in India and we have seen the reports about the likely postponement of the Dubai Expo 2020 by a year. I believe that we have to see this difficult period through and rework our plans once we have overcome the impact of COVID-19.'[49]

The UAE–India High Level Joint Task Force on Investments shows how serious both parties are about increasing economic ties, which are expected to include roads, railways and logistics and also potentially an increase in the number of flights, as well as Indian monetisation and divestment programmes.[50] UAE–Indian economic cooperation appeared to take on a greater possible strategic dimension following the establishment of a new joint economic forum between India, Israel, the US and the UAE, announced in October 2021.[51] A new Quad could tie India more closely into the Saudi–UAE nexus in the Gulf versus Iran or Qatar/Turkey, for example, which may expose India to economic fallout down the line. It's not clear if or how this would interact with the main Quad in the Indian Ocean: the US, Japan, Australia and India. Being an informal grouping focused on issues such as maritime security, counterterrorism, climate change and sustainable development, it is likely that cooperation will be on an ad hoc basis. At a minimum,

India would also like to extend economic cooperation to other parts of the world where China has had more impact, such as Africa. For example, Navdeep Suri noted in 2020: 'Both India and UAE have significant development assistance programmes in Africa and there was a feeling that we could perhaps create some synergy. The IT Centre for Excellence in Ethiopia was conceived as a trilateral project where the Ethiopian side provides the land, the UAE side constructs the building and we bring in all the hardware, software and trainers. We are ready to take up other similar projects in Africa.'[52] There is also considerable potential at the sub-national level within the framework of a possible Comprehensive Economic Partnership Agreement. For example, there was also a panel on 'The Sub National Opportunities in the Indian Story, Realising the Trillion-Dollar Economy Vision' organised as part of the Dubai 2020 Expo with a focus on Maharashtra.[53] This is bound to be aided by close personal connections between the UAE and India in the ruling elite, including, for example, Sheikh al-Qasimi, ruler of Sharjah, who is said to be an Indophile and understands Malayalam as he was looked after by a Malayali nanny from Kerala during childhood.[54]

Similar to Saudi Arabia, India and the UAE also cooperate on defence. For example, in 2016, a bilateral air force exercise was conducted between the states at Al-Dhafra air base in the UAE (Exercise Desert Eagle II).[55] Exercise Desert Eagle I took place in the same location in 2008. Controversially, in 2020, Indian commandoes were said to have been involved in the forced repatriation of Princess Latifa, daughter of the vice-president and prime minister of the UAE and ruler of Dubai, Sheikh Mohammed bin Rashid al-Maktoum, as she fled across the Indian Ocean in 2018.[56] Following the establishment of UAE bases in the Horn of Africa, it is not beyond the realm of possibility to envisage military cooperation with India being extended to include cooperation in the wider region, including UAE investments in new Indian bases such as on Agalega island in Mauritius.[57]

The ongoing conflict between India and Pakistan has impacted on closer India–Gulf ties, mainly in religious forums such as the OIC, where Pakistan has prevented India from joining even though it hosts the second-largest Muslim population in the world.[58] However, India was invited as 'Guest of Honour' to the OIC's plenary session in Abu Dhabi in March 2019.[59] The UAE ambassador to the US, Yousef Al Otaiba, confirmed in April 2021 that his country is mediating between India and Pakistan on the issue of Kashmir. The UAE objective is to thaw relations that were frozen after the suicide bombing of an Indian military convoy in Kashmir in 2019[60] and after Prime Minister Modi withdrew Indian-ruled Kashmir autonomy later in the same year. This led to the downgrading of diplomatic relations and the suspension of bilateral trade with Pakistan.[61] A senior UAE official has noted that the UAE will use its 'reservoir of goodwill' but lacks the historical, legal or emotional experience to decrease tensions, and therefore its activities do not amount to mediation.[62] In August 2019 Prime Minister Modi was awarded the Order of Zayed for promoting friendship and cooperation with the UAE, and helped to launch a special commemorative stamp in the UAE marking the 150th anniversary of Mahatma Gandhi's birth.[63] The UAE has thus done its utmost to build strategic relations with India at this critical juncture.

Saudi and UAE relations with Pakistan

Pakistan's political economy and recent history has received consistent attention in volumes such as *Pakistan on the Brink: The Future of Pakistan, Afghanistan and the West*[64] and in policy-orientated papers from notable analysts such as Bruce Riedel.[65] T. V. Paul, professor of political science at McGill University, notes that Pakistan has teetered on the brink of becoming a failed state. The country relies heavily on international aid, the Taliban were said to occupy 30 per cent of the country in 2015 and there is an ever-present danger of nuclear weapons falling into terrorist hands.[66] Weak economic growth and lack of jobs are key areas of concern.[67] More recent works such as *Pakistan under Siege* deal with Islam and paranoia about India and their effect on narratives, laws and curricula, which have shaped attitudes.[68] There are also ongoing issues surround extremism, with Pakistan being added to the intergovernmental FATF terror-financing watch list in June 2018, against attempts by Turkey, China and Saudi Arabia to block the move.[69]

Pakistan, home to the world's third-largest Muslim population,[70] has long appreciated links to the Muslim world, and especially Saudi Arabia, which have provided respite from feared Indian hegemony and international calls for reform.[71] Saudi–Pakistan relations have been defined by cordial and complementary relations spanning society, politics and economics, and also military, security and intelligence cooperation, which are especially desirable because they don't pose a threat to Saudi Arabia's position in the regional order. Saudi–Pakistan ties go back to the early days of the Cold War, when Pakistan air force pilots flew RSAF Lightnings in 1969 to repel South Yemeni incursions over Saudi's southern border. The Iranian Revolution in 1979 and Soviet invasion of Afghanistan in the same year increased Saudi influence in Pakistan. Mainly private Saudi funding and influence over teaching a puritanical version of Islam in Ahl-e-Hadith and Deobandi madrassas predated these events, but was operationalised to encourage the Afghan jihad. These continue to contribute to anti-Iranian sentiment and sectarian tension in the country, which spills over into regular attacks against Ithna Ashari Shias, including ethnic Hazaras.[72]

During the 1970s and 1980s Pakistan also stationed up to 15,000 troops in the kingdom, mainly from the majority Sunni region of Balochistan, in a brigade combat force near the Israeli–Jordanian–Saudi border.[73] Most were recalled after the Iran–Iraq War, but military ties continue. During the 2014 Saudi military display, when CSS-2 ballistic missiles from China were paraded with other Saudi military hardware, the guest of honour was the chief of army staff of Pakistan.[74] Although bilateral ties were tested in 2015 when Pakistan's parliament unanimously rejected a Saudi request for Pakistani troops to support its intervention in Yemen, a Pakistani brigade was operating on the kingdom's southern border with Yemen from 2017 and Saudi troops participated in the Pakistan Day Parade in the same year. A retired Pakistani general, Rahil Sharif, was selected in 2017 to become the head of the Saudi-sponsored 'Islamic Military Counterterrorism Coalition' based in Riyadh. Enhanced military ties in the face of Pakistani parliamentary concern suggest the extent of Pakistani military fears about the growing Indian footprint in the Middle East.

Unlike the decades-old rift which existed with India, Saudi Arabia and Pakistan have enjoyed a consistent number of high-level visits since Pakistani independence in 1947. King Abdullah's high-profile Asian tour in 2005, which took in China, India, Malaysia and Pakistan, was an important marker for relations with India and China but also a natural continuation of interactions with Pakistan. The religious interests of Pakistan, a Muslim-(Sunni) majority state, dovetailed naturally with Saudi Islamic leadership. This was especially the case when Pakistan lost what was then East Pakistan after the Bangladesh Liberation War and therefore sought to re-establish national identity and security by emphasising Islam under President Zulfighar Ali Bhutto[75] and during a period of military rule under General Muhammad Ziaul Haq.

For many years this bond has also been supplemented by close economic ties, particularly involving Saudi aid and energy contributions, expatriate labour opportunities in the kingdom and associated remittances, which amounted to a little over $2 billion in 2021–22.[76] Bilateral trade increased markedly, from $2.1 billion in 2003–4 to $3.8 billion in 2014–15, with the majority being Saudi oil exports.[77] Saudi Arabia has funded a $10 billion oil refinery in Gwadar, near Pakistan's border with Iran, fitting into the CPEC project to develop Pakistan's energy and transport infrastructure.[78] The kingdom was well placed to contribute to the China-led initiative at a point when Saudi Arabia itself was seeking to attract Chinese participation in a number of domestic economic projects.

Since 2015, as the kingdom began to move away from an Islamic-orientated foreign policy in favour of a more nationalist and secular focus on economics and geostrategic advantage, and as Pakistan refused to participate in the Saudi intervention in Yemen, relations have become increasingly strained. The Pakistani parliament voted unanimously against sending troops to Yemen, for fear of upsetting the country's domestic sectarian balance. The assumption that the Saudi and UAE air forces would combine with Egyptian and Pakistani troop deployments against the Houthis was unfounded and has no doubt affected the war's progress, whilst drawing attention to Saudi manpower issues. Nevertheless, Pakistan did attempt to mediate between Saudi Arabia and Iran amid worsening tensions in 2016. Prime Minister Imran Khan participated in the 2018 Future Investment Initiative summit in Riyadh, despite a global boycott following the Khashoggi murder, and the Pakistan military did agree in 2018 to send 1,000 troops to the kingdom on a 'training and advice mission'.[79]

Pakistan's hesitancy on Yemen could have fundamentally undermined the bilateral relationship, including the level of aid and Saudi confidence in Pakistan providing nuclear warheads if deemed necessary during a period of duress.[80] In the short term at least, following Mohammed bin Salman's visit to Pakistan in 2019, when $20 billion of Saudi investments were announced, economic relations appeared to be unaffected by such political issues.[81] But questions over Pakistani reliability may have shifted calculations in Riyadh concerning its civil nuclear power programme, as well as associated calculations regarding domestic uranium enrichment and other potential nuclear capabilities. The death of Abdul Qadeer Khan in October 2021 and his legacy of assistance to Iran, among other states, underscores the role that Pakistan has played in supporting Iranian proliferation that has helped to undermine Gulf security to this day.

Saudi–Pakistani tensions continued to rise in 2019, when Aramco announced plans to invest in a refinery in Gujarat, India, a week after New Delhi revoked Indian-administered Kashmir's special legal status.[82] Temporary special status was granted to the state of Jammu and Kashmir – the only Muslim-majority region to join India at partition – under Article 370 of the Indian Constitution, which acknowledges the state's special status in terms of autonomy and its ability to formulate laws for its residents.

While on a visit to Saudi Arabia in December 2019, Prime Minister Imran Khan, who was supposed to co-convene the 2019 Kuala Lumpur summit, announced that Pakistan was pulling out, just one day before he was supposed to arrive in Malaysia to assuage Saudi concerns over the summit. Then, in 2020, the Pakistani foreign minister, Shah Mahmood Qureshi, criticised the kingdom for not convening a special session of the OIC to discuss India's legal initiatives to change the status of the state of Jammu and Kashmir, and even threatened to work with like-minded states, such as Turkey, on the issue.[83] (Turkey's President Erdoğan had visited Pakistan in February 2020 and spoken in favour of Pakistan's stance on Kashmir). Saudi Arabia was displeased by the outburst, especially the threat to work with one of the kingdom's rivals in the region. It suspended a \$3.2 billion oil credit facility in May of that year and cancelled a \$3 billion loan, asking for the loan to be repaid in full.[84] The package totalling \$6.2 billion had been announced in November 2018 as Pakistan was waiting for an IMF bailout, which was approved in July 2019. Without Saudi backing, Pakistan was forced to approach China for a \$1 billion bridging loan.

Within months, Islamabad realised its miscalculation and sent army chief of staff General Qamar Javed Bajwa (who has overseen closer military ties[85]) to Riyadh in August 2020 to begin work on repairing relations.[86] By February 2021, around the same time that Pakistan's foreign minister visited Egypt, Saudi Arabia agreed to roll over the \$1 billion due to service its loan to Pakistan.[87] In June 2021, Pakistani Prime Minister Imran Khan visited Saudi Arabia to establish the Saudi–Pakistan Supreme Coordination Council and reset relations. The kingdom also agreed to restart \$1.5 billion in annual oil aid to Pakistan.[88] But this is nowhere near the pledges of 2019. Furthermore, Pakistani expatriate labour has been affected. From October 2020 to June 2021 there were reports of at least four Pakistani Shia residents being forcefully deported from the UAE.[89] In November 2020, the UAE suspended work visas for visiting Pakistani labourers, among other countries. Although the Kafala system which placed contractual restrictions on foreign labour was being eased in the kingdom at the same time, still 400,000 Pakistani labourers remain affected by the COVID-19 restrictions in place.[90] This is a large proportion of the approximately 1 million Pakistanis usually employed in the kingdom and represents an existential threat to the \$32 billion in remittances flowing from Saudi Arabia and the UAE in 2021–22.[91] Also in 2020, as Samuel Ramani noted in a tweet, the Saudi Arabian Monetary Authority was showing Jammu and Kashmir as independent from India and Pakistan on the twenty-riyal note.[92]

The pace of future Saudi–Pakistani relations will likely reflect the promise of improved personal relations with Prime Minister Shehbaz Sharif, brother of Nawaz Sharif who fled to the kingdom after being deposed by General Musharraf. Shehbaz Sharif succeeds Imran Khan, who was forced out of power after a no confidence vote in March 2022. Riyadh will further seek to contain Iran in the Gulf and in Central and South Asia,[93] to support any future role for the kingdom in Afghanistan, especially in averting a humanitarian disaster, and possibly to build goodwill with the Biden administration. Should the US conclude a new JCPOA with Iran, burgeoning Iranian–Pakistani trade ties could once again threaten Saudi interests. Riyadh will continue to seek influence over Pakistan's security policy and also drive a wedge into its relations with other states such as Turkey and Malaysia which vie for influence over the Islamic world and in relation to Pakistan through their support on the Kashmir issue. However, with the pivot away from Wahhabism, Saudi soft-power leverage may become weakened, leaving military–military relations at the core of their interactions. As of 2021 these included the Royal Saudi Air Force taking part in Pakistan's 'Aces Meet-2021' multinational air exercise at Pakistan air force base Mushaf.[94] A first-time consortium of Pakistani companies which invested $305 million in offshore oil exploration in the UAE in August 2021 could set the tone for broader economic relations, should they be sustainable,[95] but since Shehbaz Sharif became prime minister, the UAE will have to adapt, since it has generally enjoyed better relations with the Bhutto family.

Conclusion

India–Saudi relations and Saudi–Pakistan relations reached a possible inversion point in the 2015–20 period after Pakistan proved unreliable in sending troops to support Saudi objectives in Yemen and indirectly criticised Saudi Arabia over Kashmir. The new Al Saud leadership has become more attuned to criticism and less attached to traditional forms of interaction. As political issues have intervened in Saudi–Pakistan relations, so economic pledges appear to have fallen by the wayside. In contrast, Riyadh has signalled engagement with India in the widest possible terms, extending to security cooperation after its AQAP insurgency and bolstered by papering over cracks that might have been caused by Hindu nationalist rhetoric and actions, as well as Kashmir. India–Saudi relations have been building, particularly since 2006, using the 2008 Mumbai attacks to extend political and security cooperation. Both sides have managed to avoid entanglements during the Arab uprisings and on human rights.

The rise of India represents an opportunity for Saudi and UAE to extend economic relations, and also to benefit from longer-term geostrategic relations with a growing international power. Like Pakistan, India remains exposed to the GCC states on jobs, remittances and inward investment, and therefore a degree of economic dependency exists. India, being vital to extending Saudi oil supplies over the coming decades, will assume a special significance for the kingdom, creating a firm bond, and will possibly cause a fundamental and long-term rebalancing in Saudi relations between Pakistan and India. The UAE has re-engaged in the Indian economy and established joint ventures and military-military connections that have benefited Dubai's internal (elite) security interests, although the federal composition of the UAE has also created space for some diversity of political opinion about Indian politics.

Contemporary relations with India have become less ideologically driven and more 'normalised' as part of the global economy. This appears to be increasingly so during COVID-19 and as India has become a major actor in terms of energy imports, as a defence partner and in terms of realising synergies in Africa. A free trade agreement between India and the GCC states could provide further opportunities to expand non-oil trade and investment in the coming years. Harmonising procedural measures, for example a similar level of protections in food standards, could significantly boost trade, especially when considering that non-tariff measures can impact more than tariffs. Future commercial relations depend on how quickly these GCC states can reorientate their economies to maximise value from every element of the bilateral relationship and how quickly India can extract value from the Arab–Mediterranean corridor to compete more effectively with other powers such as China. More strategic naval relations could come to the fore as India plays an important role through defence and military academies and continues to develop its blue-water naval capacity and cooperation in the Indian Ocean.

In the short term, Saudi and UAE relations with Pakistan hinge on a deal for Pakistani labour to return to pre-COVID-19 levels. One of the few options for Pakistan, beyond China (which is unlikely to invest in the amount Pakistan needs to maintain a balanced political economy), Turkey and Malaysia (an alliance which the kingdom was determined to prevent, as illustrated by Pakistan's withdrawal from the 2019 summit in Malaysia), would be to develop economic relations with Iran. This could happen only if and when a revitalised JCPOA could be concluded with the US, and represents a highly uncertain option. Pakistan's economic dependence on the oil-rich kingdom therefore looks set to continue and, without a fundamental reformulation of its political economy, its agency is bound to remain latent.

South Asia–Gulf connectivity is subject to many variables: changes in Iranian and Pakistani relations with the US, Pakistan–China relations, Pakistan–Turkey/Malaysia relations, the evolving issue of Kashmir and leadership in South and West Asia. India's good historic relations with the GCC states, coupled with good relations with Iran and Israel, will no doubt enhance relations further. On the other hand, this could easily be offset by India's capacity as a developing state, any failure to expand economic relations during GCC state diversification and spillover from growing competition or conflict in the Gulf, between India and China or between India and Pakistan. It will be especially interesting to see if the UAE's de-escalation experience between India and Pakistan can be applied back home in the Gulf.

Notes

1 Jack Guy, 'Saudi Crown Prince Gifted Golden Submachine Gun in Pakistan', *CNN*, 20 February 2019, https://edition.cnn.com/2019/02/20/asia/saudi-pakistan-golden-gun-scli-intl/index.html

2 Jyoti Malhotra, 'Wooing Saudis After Pulwama was Important and Modi did the Right Thing by Hugging MBS', *ThePrint*, 22 February 2019, https://theprint.in/opinion/modi-monitor/wooing-saudis-after-pulwama-was-important-modi-did-the-right-thing-by-hugging-mbs/196376/

3 James Piscatori, 'Allocating "God's Guests": The Politics of Hajj Quotas', HH Sheikh Nasser al-Mohammad al-Sabah Publication Series 32, May 2021: 10. www.durham.ac.uk/media/durham-university/departments-/school-of-government-amp-int-affairs/Allocating_Gods_Guests_JP_updated_27_April_2021.pdf

4 Rahul Roy-Chaudhury, 'India and the Gulf Region: Building Strategic Partnerships', International Institute of Strategic Studies, 29 August 2018, www.iiss.org/blogs/analysis/2018/08/india-gulf-strategic-partnerships

5 Ibid.

6 A. K. Pasha, 'India and West Asia: Challenges and Opportunities', in Anjali Ghosh et al., *India's Foreign Policy*. Delhi: Longman, 2009: 317.

7 Government of India Ministry of External Affairs, 'Delhi Declaration, Signed by King Abdullah bin Abdulaziz Al Saud of the Kingdom of Saudi Arabia and Prime Minister Dr. Manmohan Singh of India', 27 January 2006, https://mea.gov.in/bilateral-documents.htm?dtl/5969/Delhi+Declaration+Signed+by+King+Abdullah+bin+Abdulaziz+Al+Saud+of+the+Kingdom+of+Saudi+Arabia+and+Prime+Minister+Dr+Manmohan+Singh+of+India

8 BBC News, 'Mumbai Attacks: "Planner Abu Jundal was in Control Room"', 27 June 2012, www.bbc.com/news/world-asia-india-18605817

9 BBC News, 'India Loses Place as World's Fastest-Growing Economy', 31 May 2019, www.bbc.com/news/business-48478028

10 Kadira Pethiyagoda, 'India–GCC Relations: Delhi's Strategic Opportunity', Brookings Doha Center Analysis Paper No. 18, February 2017: 11, www.brookings.edu/wp-content/uploads/2017/02/india_gcc_relations.pdf

11 Talmiz Ahmed, 'India-Gulf Ties Over the Next Decade: Navigating Frontier Areas for Cooperation', Observer Research Foundation, 26 April 2021, www.orfonline.org/expert-speak/india-gulf-ties-next-decade-navigating-frontier-areas-cooperation/#_ednref3

12 Nidhi Verma and Promit Mukherjee, 'India's Oil Demand Growth Set to Overtake China by mid-2020s: IEA', *Reuters*, 10 January 2020, www.reuters.com/article/us-india-energy-iea/indias-oil-demand-growth-set-to-overtake-china-by-mid-2020s-iea-idUSKBN1Z90CD

13 The Economic Times, 'U.S. Becomes India's Second Biggest Oil Supplier, Saudi Plunges to No. 4', 15 March 2021, https://economictimes.indiatimes.com/industry/energy/oil-gas/u-s-becomes-indias-second-biggest-oil-supplier-saudi-plunges-to-no-4/articleshow/81506917.cms?from=mdr

14 Roy-Chaudhury, 'India and the Gulf Region'.

15 Ibid.
16 IMF, 'Direction of Trade Staatistics', https://data.imf.org/?sk=9D6028D4-F14A-464C-A2F2-59B2CD424B85
17 Embassy of India, Riyadh, Saudi Arabia. 'Indo-Saudi Arabia Economic and Commercial Relations', www.eoiriyadh.gov.in/page/india-saudi-business-relations/
18 Irina Slav, 'Saudi Arabia to Invest $100 Billion in India's Energy Sector', Oilprice. com, 21 February 2019, https://oilprice.com/Energy/Energy-General/Saudi-Arabia-To-Invest-100-Billion-In-Indias-Energy-Sector.html
19 Dilip Kumar Jha, 'India's Rice Exports Hit as Saudi Arabia Makes Quality Rules More Stringent', *Business Standard*, 24 September 2019, www.business-standard.com/article/economy-policy/india-s-rice-exports-hit-as-saudi-arabia-makes-quality-rules-stringent-119092401288_1.html
20 Indronil Roychowdhury, 'Basmati Exports to Take a Hit this Fiscal due to Low Buying from Iran and Saudi Arabia', *Financial Express*, 30 January 2020, www.financialexpress.com/market/commodities/basmati-exports-to-take-a-hit-this-fiscal-due-to-low-buying-from-iran-and-saudi-arabia/1839414/
21 Embassy of India, Riyadh, Saudi Arabia, 'Indo-Saudi Arabia Economic and Commercial Relations', n.d., www.eoiriyadh.gov.in/page/india-saudi-business-relations/
22 Ibid.
23 The Hindu Business Line, 'Modi Meets Saudi Prince Al Saud, Seeks Greater Investments in Energy, IT, Defence', 21 September 2021, www.thehindubusinessline.com/news/modi-meets-saudi-prince-al-saud-seeks-greater-investments-in-energy-it-defence/article36581677.ece
24 John Calabrese, 'India–Gulf Migration: A Testing Time', Middle East Institute, 14 April 2020, www.mei.edu/publications/india-gulf-migration-testing-time
25 Ibid.
26 Ahmed, 'India–Gulf Ties Over the Next Decade'.
27 India Global Business, 'Modi Spells Out Free, Open, Inclusive Indo-Pacific Policy', 17 July 2018, www.indiaglobalbusiness.com/igb-archive/modi-spells-out-free-open-inclusive-indo-pacific-policy
28 Guy Burton, 'India's "Look West" Policy in the Middle East Under Modi', Middle East Institute, 6 August 2019, www.mei.edu/publications/indias-look-west-policy-middle-east-under-modi#_ednref12
29 Pieter D. Wezeman et al., 'Trends in International Arms Transfers, 2019', SIPRI Factsheet, March 20200: 6, www.sipri.org/sites/default/files/2020-03/fs_2003_at_2019.pdf
30 Suhasini Haidar, 'India Abstains from UNHRC Vote against Israel', *The Hindu*, 3 July 2015, www.thehindu.com/news/india-abstains-from-unhrc-vote-against-israel/article7383796.ece; Scroll, 'India Abstains from Voting as UN Human Rights Council Adopts Resolution to Investigate Gaza Violence', 28 May 2021, https://scroll.in/latest/996068/india-abstains-from-voting-as-un-human-rights-council-adopts-resolution-to-investigate-gaza-violence
31 Stephen Weizman, 'In World First, Air India Crosses Saudi Airspace to Israel', *The Times of Israel*, 22 March 2018, www.timesofisrael.com/in-world-first-air-india-crosses-saudi-airspace-to-israel/

32 Geeta Pandey, 'Beaten and Humiliated by Hindu Mobs for Being a Muslim in India', *BBC News*, 2 September 2021, www.bbc.com/news/world-asia-india-58406194

33 BBC News, 'Citizenship Amendment Bill: India's New "Anti-Muslim" Law Explained', 11 December 2019, www.bbc.com/news/world-asia-india-50670393

34 Nidhi Verma, 'Oil for Oxygen: Covid-hit India Welcomes Saudi Medical Aid, Boosts Oil Imports', *Reuters*, 7 May 2021, www.reuters.com/world/asia-pacific/india-oil-minister-thanks-saudi-other-countries-oxygen-supplies-2021-05-07/

35 ThePrint, 'BJP's Karanataka MP Calls Delhi's Tablighi Jamaat Event "Corona jihad"', 5 April 2020, https://theprint.in/politics/bjps-karnataka-mp-calls-delhis-tablighi-jamaat-event-corona-jihad/395511/

36 Hend F. Q. on Twitter, 15 April 2020, https://twitter.com/LadyVelvet_HFQ/status/1250502022228566016

37 Hind Al Qassemi, 'I Pray for an India Without Hate and Islamophobia', *Gulf News*, 26 April 2020, https://gulfnews.com/opinion/op-eds/i-pray-for-an-india-without-hate-and-islamophobia-1.71169436

38 OIC-IPHRC on Twitter, 19 April 2020, https://twitter.com/OIC_IPHRC/status/1251826491094073344?ref_src=twsrc%5Etfw%7Ctwcamp%5Etweetembed%7Ctwterm%5E1251826491094073344&ref_url=https%3A%2F%2Fthewire.in%2Fcommunalism%2Findias-coronavirus-related-islamophobia-has-the-arab-world-up-in-arm

39 PMO India on Twitter, 19 April 2020, https://twitter.com/PMOIndia/status/1251839308085915649

40 Jyoti Malhotra, 'As Gulf Calls for an "India without Islamophobia," Jaishankar Works the Phones', *ThePrint*, 28 April 2020, https://theprint.in/opinion/global-print/gulf-calls-india-without-islamophobia-jaishankar-works-phones/410159/

41 Amb Pavan Kapoor on Twitter, 20 April 2020, https://twitter.com/AmbKapoor/status/1252189495199518720?ref_src=twsrc%5Etfw%7Ctwcamp%5Etweetembed%7Ctwterm%5E1252189495199518720%7Ctwgr%5E%7Ctwcon%5Es1_&ref_url=https%3A%2F%2Fgulfnews.com%2Fuae%2Findia-and-uae-share-value-of-non-discrimination-says-ambassador-1.71075552

42 Rajeev Sharma, 'PM Modi Extracts $75 Bn Investment Pledge from UAE but Celebrations are Premature', *Firstpost*, 18 August 2015, www.firstpost.com/business/pm-modi-extracts-75-bn-investment-pledge-from-uae-but-celebrations-are-premature-2396208.html

43 Hindustan Times, '"Aggressive" Plan for $115 Billion India, UAE Trade in 5 Years: Goyal', 23 September 2021, www.hindustantimes.com/india-news/aggressive-plan-for-115-billion-india-uae-trade-in-5-years-goyal-101632335739709.html

44 The Times of India, 'India, UAE Chalk Out Road Map for Investment', 3 October 2021, https://timesofindia.indiatimes.com/business/india-business/india-uae-chalk-out-road-map-for-investment/articleshow/86718315.cms

45 WAM, 'UAE to Build Mosques in India, Four Other Countries', *Khaleej Times*, 5 August 2017, www.khaleejtimes.com/uae/uae-to-build-mosques-in-india-four-other-countries

46 Ibid.

47 Ramola Talwar Badam, 'UAE's First Hindu Temple to Partially Open to the Public Next Year', *The National*, 23 April 2019, www.thenationalnews.com/uae/heritage/uae-s-first-hindu-temple-to-partially-open-to-the-public-next-year-1.852651

48 Dania Saadi, 'India's Reliance to Invest $2 Billion in ADNOC Chemical JV, its First Deal in Gulf Region', *S&P Global Platts*, 29 June 2021, www.spglobal.com/platts/en/market-insights/latest-news/petrochemicals/062921-indias-reliance-to-invest-2-bil-in-adnoc-chemical-jv-its-first-deal-in-gulf-region

49 Author's interview with Navdeep Suri, former Indian Ambassador to the United Arab Emirates, 31 March 2020.

50 The Times of India, 'India, UAE Chalk Out Road Map'.

51 Dipanjan Roy Chaudhury, 'A New Quad? India, Israel, US and UAE Agree to Establish Joint Economic Forum', *The Economic Times*, 20 October 2021, https://economictimes.indiatimes.com/news/economy/foreign-trade/india-israel-us-and-uae-agree-to-establish-joint-economic-forum/articleshow/87139659.cms?from=mdr

52 Author's interview with Navdeep Suri, former Indian Ambassador to the United Arab Emirates, 31 March 2020.

53 'CEPA Will Be a Game Changer in Regional Cooperation Between India and the UAE', *Mint*, 9 December 2021, www.livemint.com/economy/cepa-will-be-game-changer-in-regional-cooperation-between-india-and-uae-11638988274403.html

54 The Times of India, 'When the Sheikh Spoke in Malayalam', 28 September 2017, https://timesofindia.indiatimes.com/city/kochi/when-the-sheikh-spoke-in-malayalam/articleshow/60857017.cms

55 Global Security, 'Emirati Air Force', www.globalsecurity.org/military/world/gulf/uae-af-fighters.htm

56 Owen Bowcott and Haroon Siddique, 'Dubai Ruler Organised Kidnapping of His Children, UK Court Rules', *The Guardian*, 5 March 2020, www.theguardian.com/world/2020/mar/05/dubai-ruler-sheikh-mohammed-organised-kidnapping-of-his-children-uk-court-finds

57 The Economic Times, 'India Believed to be Building Naval Facility on Mauritian island of Agalega: Report', 3 August 2021, https://economictimes.indiatimes.com/news/defence/india-believed-to-be-building-naval-facility-on-mauritian-island-of-agalega-report/articleshow/85017163.cms?from=mdr

58 Expected to be the first-largest Muslim population by 2060. Jeff Diamant, 'The Countries with the 10 Largest Christian Populations and the 10 Largest Muslim Populations', Pew Research Center, 1 April 2019, www.pewresearch.org/fact-tank/2019/04/01/the-countries-with-the-10-largest-christian-populations-and-the-10-largest-muslim-populations/

59 Nayanima Basu, 'India Warns OIC against Use by "Vested Interests" after Muslim Nation Group's Kashmir Remarks', *ThePrint*, 8 July 2021, https://theprint.in/diplomacy/india-warns-oic-against-use-by-vested-interests-after-muslim-nation-groups-kashmir-remarks/692519/

60 Reuters, 'UAE is Mediating Between India and Pakistan, Says Senior Diplomat', 15 April 2021, www.reuters.com/world/india/uae-is-mediating-between-india-pakistan-says-senior-diplomat-2021-04-15/

61 Ibid.

62 UAE official speaking under the Chatham House rule, 9 December 2021.

63 Gulf News, 'Narendra Modi Conferred with Order of Zayed', *Gulf News*, 24 August 2019, https://gulfnews.com/uae/narendra-modi-conferred-with-order-of-zayed-1.65990341

64 Ahmed Rashid, *Pakistan on the Brink: The Future of Pakistan, Afghanistan and the West*. Ontario: Penguin, 2013.

65 For example: Bruce Riedel, 'Enduring Allies: Pakistan's Partnership with Saudi Arabia Runs Deeper', Brookings, 9 December 2011, www.brookings.edu/articles/enduring-allies-pakistans-partnership-with-saudi-arabia-runs-deeper/

66 T. V. Paul, *The Warrior State: Pakistan in the Contemporary World*. Oxford: Oxford University Press, 2015.

67 United States Institute of Peace, 'Pakistan Faces a Long Road to Sustainable Growth', 7 October 2020, www.usip.org/publications/2020/10/pakistan-faces-long-road-sustainable-growth

68 Madiha Afzal, *Pakistan under Siege: Extremism, Society, and the State*. Washington, DC: Brookings Institution Press, 2018.

69 Saeed Shah and Ian Talley, 'Saudi Arabia Stymies U.S. Over Pakistan Terror List', *The Wall Street Journal*, 21 February 2018, www.wsj.com/articles/pakistan-avoids-inclusion-on-international-terror-financing-watch-list-1519257040

70 Diamant, 'The Countries with the 10 Largest Christian Populations and the 10 Largest Muslim Populations'.

71 Marvin G. Weinbaum and Abdullah B. Khurram, 'Pakistan and Saudi Arabia: Deference, Dependence and Deterrence', *Middle East Journal*, 68 (2), Spring 2014: 211–228.

72 Simon Wolfgang Fuchs, 'Faded Networks: The Overestimated Saudi Legacy of Anti-Shi'i Sectarianism in Pakistan', Special Issue: Transnational Religious Networks and the Geopolitics of the Muslim World, *Global Discourse*, 9 (4), 2019: 703–715.

73 Bruce Riedel, 'Saudi Arabia: Nervously Watching Pakistan', *Brookings*, 28 January 2008, www.brookings.edu/opinions/saudi-arabia-nervously-watching-pakistan/

74 Bruce Riedel, 'Obama and Trump, Abdullah and Salman, 2009 to 2017', *Kings and Presidents: Saudi Arabia and the United States Since FDR*. Washington, DC: Brookings Institution Press, 2018: 173.

75 Shireen T. Hunter, 'Iran's Relations with Saudi Arabia: Rivals for Regional Supremacy', *Arab-Iranian Relations: Dynamics of Conflict and Cooperation*. New York: Rowman and Littlefield, 2019: 207–244, at 213.

76 Shahid Iqbal, 'Pakistan Gets Record $8bn Remittances in July–Sept', *Dawn*, 9 October 2021, www.dawn.com/news/1650949

77 Embassy of Pakistan, Kingdom of Saudi Arabia, 'Pakistan-Saudi Arabia Relations', www.pakembassyksa.com/PakSRel.aspx (accessed 15 March 2021).

78 Gul Yousafzai, 'Saudi Arabia to Set Up $10 Billion Oil Refinery in Pakistan', *Reuters*, 12 January 2019, www.reuters.com/article/us-saudi-pakistan-economy/saudi-arabia-to-set-up-10-billion-oil-refinery-in-pakistan-idUSKCN1P60OU

79 Baqir Sajjad Syed, 'Army Says Troops Being Sent to Saudi Arabia', *Dawn*, 16 February 2018, www.dawn.com/news/1389722

80 BBC News, 'Saudi Nuclear Weapons "On Order" From Pakistan', 6 November 2013, www.bbc.com/news/world-middle-east-24823846

81 Hillary Leung, 'Saudi Crown Prince Pledges $20 Billion in Deals with Pakistan on the First Stop of His Asia Tour', *Time*, 18 February 2019, https://time.com/5531657/saudi-crown-prince-mbs-pakistan-20-billion/

82 Vindu Goel, 'As Saudis and Indians Grow Closer, a $15 Billion Deal Blooms', *The New York Times*, 12 August 2019, www.nytimes.com/2019/08/12/business/reliance-india-saudi-aramco-oil.html

83 Syed Fazl-E-Haider, 'As Pakistan and Saudi Arabia Drift Apart, China Moves In', *The Interpreter*, 19 August 2020, www.lowyinstitute.org/the-interpreter/pakistan-saudi-arabia-drift-apart-china-moves

84 Nikkei Asia, 'Saudi Arabia Pulls Support for Pakistan as Kashmir Tiff Widens', 10 August 2020, https://asia.nikkei.com/Politics/International-relations/Saudi-Arabia-pulls-support-for-Pakistan-as-Kashmir-tiff-widens

85 Umer Karim, 'Pakistan's Military Steps in to Manage Tense Ties with Saudi Arabia', Arab Gulf States Institute in Washington, 1 September 2020, https://agsiw.org/pakistans-military-steps-in-to-manage-tense-ties-with-saudi-arabia/

86 Marwa Rashad and Asif Shahzad, 'Pakistani Army Chief Visits Saudi Arabia to Revive Ties Strained Over Kashmir', *Reuters*, 17 August 2020, www.reuters.com/article/us-pakistan-saudi-arabia/pakistani-army-chief-visits-saudi-arabia-to-revive-ties-strained-over-kashmir-idUSKCN25D10H

87 Adnan Aamir, 'Saudi Arabia Wins Back Pakistan', *The Interpreter*, 3 June 2021, www.lowyinstitute.org/the-interpreter/saudi-arabia-wins-back-pakistan

88 Daily Times, 'Saudi Arabia Agrees to Restart $1.5bn Annual Oil Aid to Pakistan in July: FT', 22 June 2021, https://dailytimes.com.pk/777067/saudi-arabia-agrees-to-restart-1-5bn-annual-oil-aid-to-pakistan-in-july-ft/

89 Human Rights Watch, 'UAE: Arbitrarily Targeting of Pakistani Shia Residents', 22 June 2021, www.hrw.org/news/2021/06/22/uae-arbitrary-targeting-pakistani-shia-residents

90 Dawn, 'Pakistan, Saudi Arabia to Work on Easing Travel Restrictions', 27 July 2021, www.dawn.com/news/1637227/pakistan-saudi-arabia-to-work-on-easing-travel-restrictions

91 Muzaffar Rizvi, 'Pakistan to Exceed $31 Billion Remittances Target', *Khaleej Times*, 9 October 2021, www.khaleejtimes.com/business/pakistan-to-exceed-31-billion-remittances-target

92 Samuel Ramani on Twitter, 31 October 2020, https://twitter.com/SamRamani2/status/1322651458358136835?s=20

93 Having allegedly offered Pakistan $1 billion to forgo the Iran–Pakistan–India pipeline and supported Baluchi dissidents, which has raised tensions between Tehran and Islamabad at times. Shireen T. Hunter, 'Iran's Relations with Saudi Arabia: Rivals for Regional Supremacy', *Arab–Iranian Relations: Dynamics of Conflict and* Cooperation: 214.

94 Airforce Technology, 'PAF, RSAF and USAF Conclude Multinational Air Exercise Aces Meet 2021–1', 12 April 2021, www.airforce-technology.com/news/paf-rsaf-and-usaf-conclude-aces-meet-2021-1/#:~:text=Share%20Article-,The%20

Pakistan%20Air%20Force%20(PAF)%20has%20successfully%20completed%20
the%20multinational,1%20at%20PAF%20base%20Mushaf.&text=The
%20exercise%20included%20the%20employment,control%20aircraft%20
and%20military%20satellites.

95 Anthony di Paola, 'Pakistan Invests in Middle East Oil with $305 Million UAE
    Deal', *Bloomberg*, 31 August 2021, www.bloomberg.com/news/articles/2021-08-31/
    pakistan-invests-in-middle-east-oil-with-305-million-uae-deal?sref=zEzFg8RN

12

Japan and the Republic of Korea: institutionalising ties amid strategic uncertainty

Introduction

Japan and the Republic of Korea (ROK) are both noted for their large imports of Middle East energy supplies. Alongside China, their economic relations with Saudi Arabia and the UAE grew rapidly in the 1980s. However, strategic realities in Asia continue to dominate intra-Asian relations, whether the demise of the USSR, security relations with the US, the rise of China, growing regionalism, energy considerations and new trade and investment opportunities due to the Arab Gulf Vision strategies. Always present is the threat posed by nuclear weapons in frozen conflicts involving ROK (with US support) and North Korea, India and Pakistan, with further potential proliferation risks and conflict between Iran and Saudi Arabia. The Asian geo-economic and security landscape is complex, interwoven and constantly shifting, making bilateral relations a more favourable channel than pursuing such interests wholly through multilateral fora.

This chapter details the broadening bilateral relations between Saudi Arabia, the UAE, Japan and ROK, assesses the interplay of energy, East Asian contributions to, and benefits from, Saudi and UAE Vision strategies and attempts to conceptualise their contemporary relations and effects on the wider region.

Saudi and UAE relations with Japan

Saudi–Japan ties expanded considerably throughout the twentieth century, with the main initial contacts being the Muslim Kotaro Yamaoka, who, along with a Mongolian group of Muslim pilgrims, visited Mecca in 1909. This was followed by the visit to Japan of Saudi envoy to the UK, Hafiz Wahba, to attend the opening of the Tokyo mosque in 1938.[1] In 1939, Yokoyama, then the Japanese envoy to Egypt, visited Saudi Arabia and had an audience with King Abdulaziz (Ibn Saud).[2]

From the late nineteenth century to the 1940s, the Japanese economy sourced most of its commodities within Asia, due to cost and taste. Even oil was imported from the Dutch East Indies until the Second World War, although the majority, about 80 per cent, was imported from the US.[3] Following the US oil embargo against Japan in the summer of 1941, due to Japan's war against China, Japan attacked Pearl Harbour on 7 December 1941 as a precursor to invasions that included Hong Kong, Singapore, Thailand and the Philippines. Japan invaded Java (Indonesia) in early 1942 for its oil resources.[4] The US campaign in the Asia-Pacific theatre of war underscored the vulnerability of Japan's oil supply chain. After the war, Japan aimed for economic modernisation based on expanding its internal market. In the 1950s the steel industry was responsible for most of the energy demand, followed by power stations, with strong demand also from the transport and the petrochemical industries from the 1960s. In 1953 oil accounted for 23 per cent of Japanese energy consumption, 60 per cent in 1963 and 80 per cent by 1973.[5] In this latter period there was an abundance of cheap oil. But Japan's classification as an unfriendly state during the first oil crisis in October 1973, and the rise in the oil price during a recession in Japan, underscored its vulnerability to price hikes.[6] Following the second oil crisis in 1979, after the Iranian Revolution, Japan had more options with regard to oil stockpiles lasting more than 100 days, energy-saving measures and gas and nuclear power.[7] But still Japan's dependence on oil remained high and Gulf states continued to supply approximately 90 per cent of Japan's oil well into the twenty-first century.[8] Japan's role in the Middle East has been predicated on an oil for manufactured goods, capital and technology exchange, with aid available for the non-oil exporters in the region. It is due to Japanese exports of automobiles, consumer electronics, heavy machinery and computers to the Middle East and the West that it has been able to sustain high oil imports at a vast cost. The pattern of trade appears to have been that Saudi and UAE oil income from states such as Japan were generally invested in the West, in the US and Europe.[9] Lessons from Japanese economic growth, especially rapid economic growth experienced between 1955 and 1973, including urbanisation and, eventually, a 1 per cent unemployment rate,[10] could be a shining example to the GCC states as they seek to traverse late rentierism[11] into the post-oil era.

Since the establishment of Saudi–Japanese diplomatic relations in 1955, oil has been a major component in the relationship, although oil imports from the kingdom were dominated by American Aramco and thus formed a major plank in US–Japan rather than Japan–Saudi relations.[12] Japan's Arabian Oil Company (AOC) in the Neutral Zone – in the onshore and offshore territory shared by Saudi Arabia and Kuwait at their border – was an exception, but Japanese economists have maintained that it was unnecessary, as Aramco could supply oil to Japan if needed.[13] Japan recognised the UAE as an independent state in 1971. By 1997, in the context of extending Japan's AOC concession, which ultimately failed, Prime Minister Ryutaro Hashimoto was calling for a Saudi–Japanese 'Comprehensive Partnership toward the 21st Century'.[14] With regular high-level visits between Japan and the Saudis and Emiratis, Tokyo aimed at expanding cooperation. The launch of the Visions strategies has united these states in their pursuit of human capital development, trade and investment opportunities. This is what Heng calls a 'sustainability turn' in the UAE case, given the mutual interests of both parties.[15]

Although Japanese oil consumption and oil used for electricity production have both been declining since 2005, Saudi Arabia still has a leading role in energy relations with Japan. Iranian oil exports have been affected by a series of political and security issues over the past decades, including the 1979 revolution, the Iran–Iraq War and the US-led sanctions regime against Iran. In 2003 Iran supplied about 16 per cent of Japan's crude oil,[16] but by 2019 this had dropped to about 3 per cent.[17] Decades of Iraqi instability have undermined Japan–Iraqi relations, but Iraqi oil exports have been salvaged by long-term contracts between the Iraqi National Oil Company and Japan for the stable supply of crude oil.[18] Since 2003, oil exports have rapidly increased as western firms managed to secure favourable concession terms during the G. W. Bush administration.[19]

Japanese dependence on GCC-state oil has also grown following the Fukushima Daiichi nuclear disaster in 2011, even though some nuclear reactors were restarted in 2015. Nuclear power was supposed to generate around 20 per cent of Japan's electricity by 2030, but the disaster has instead forced it to switch back to relying more on coal-fired power stations.[20] Hence Japan's lobbying, along with Saudi Arabia, Australia and others prior to COP26 in 2021 to play down the need to move away from fossil fuels.[21] Japan has offered civil nuclear energy cooperation to the kingdom, mainly with a view to confirming Saudi Arabia as a key oil supplier.[22] The move could also have been motivated to encourage flexibility in Saudi export volumes, should it be required. In 2015 Saudi Arabia represented more than 35 per cent of Japanese oil imports, with the UAE in second place at around 25 per cent, although the UAE also exports some gas.[23] But Australia, Malaysia, Russia, Indonesia and Qatar (which doubled exports after the disaster[24]) all export more gas to Japan than does the UAE.

Saudi Arabia has invested in Japanese oil companies since the 1990s, with stakes in Showa Oil and Idemitsu Kosan. Japan is Saudi Arabia's third-most important trading partner and, according to Dr Abed Al Saadoun, Saudi deputy minister for petroleum and gas, bilateral trade amounted to $38 billion in 2018.[25] But Japan has traditionally had a very low number of investments in the Gulf, compared to western small and medium-sized enterprises (SMEs) active in the GCC market. In terms of capital deployed, Japan fares better. For example, Sumitomo Chemical and Saudi Aramco formed a $10 billion joint venture, Petro Rabigh, in 2005.[26] King Salman's four-day visit to Japan in 2017, part of a wider tour to Malaysia, Indonesia, Brunei, China and the Maldives, was the first by a Saudi monarch in forty-six years, and necessary to boost trade and investment. Both he, and King Faisal before him, arrived in Japan in the context of changing economic conditions in the kingdom.[27] The PIF has since concluded a $45 billion investment in Japan's Softbank Vision Fund, in 2018, raising its investment in Softbank, which has a focus on the technology and start-ups, to $90 billion.[28] However, most Japanese companies have been located in the UAE, due to the 100 per cent foreign ownership permitted in Dubai's free zones. Japan did not invest in the Aramco initial public offering (IPO) in 2020 but instead prefers to invest in new opportunities which track Saudi diversification policies.

Japan's pursuit of opportunities in the UAE, where cooperation has generally taken place in the oil industry, including research and development and human resource development, has also shifted. In 2020 there was greater emphasis on climate change, food security, peace, social engineering through IT and joint responses to COVID-19.[29] As a clear indicator of the direction of increasingly technical and nuanced cooperation, the UAE probe to Mars was carried on a Japan-made Mitsubishi H2A rocket, launched from Tanegashima Space Center in Kagoshima Prefecture.[30] Teaching Japanese as a second language is beginning to take place in some UAE schools, possibly to rival Chinese language training, which has had a successful roll-out. Manga and judo are becoming popular among Emiratis,[31] and Dubai has become an important Japanese tourist destination in the Middle East.

Japan is also well placed to contribute to clean energy policies in Saudi Arabia and the UAE. Saudi Arabia shipped blue ammonia to Japan for power generation in September 2020 and ENEOS, Japan's largest refiner, signed an agreement with Saudi Aramco to develop a carbon-free hydrogen and ammonia supply chain for use in the transport sector.[32] Japan and the UAE signed an MoU on hydrogen on 5 July 2021.[33] This was still a pilot project at the survey stage, as of 2021, and very much dependent on security of demand in Japan, as well as on supply of hydrogen and ammonia (the Abu Dhabi National Oil Company [ADNOC] began to ship ammonia to Japan in June 2022).[34] As Akihiko Nakajima, the Japanese ambassador to the UAE, stated, it is hard to compare a gas station and a hydrogen station, especially as there is no clear vision about the future of this area.[35] Masdar and Mitsubishi were working closely on the development of an electric vehicle pilot in 2011.[36] As of 2018, ten Mitsubishi electric vehicles were functional in Masdar City, although by 2019 Masdar and ekar had announced a tie-up to bring a Tesla car-share operation to the region..[37]

Saudi Vision 2030 is built on a series of pillars (diversity, innovation and soft values) and themes (competitive industry, energy, entertainment and media, healthcare and medicals, quality infrastructure, agriculture and food security, SMEs and capacity building, culture, sports and education, and investment and finance).[38] These are joined by enablers (regulation, incentives, organisational support and human capital).[39] The joint vision also includes the 'Saudi–Japanese Vision 2030 Group', which has sub-groups studying opportunities across trade and investment, finance, energy and industry, SME policy and culture and education.

In Saudi–Japan Vision 2030, Yamada notes that new concepts have been introduced: 'enabler', 'Kaizan' and 'Cool Japan, Warm Saudi'. 'Enabler' explains an environment conducive to further cooperation, including regulations, incentives, organisational support and human capital. 'Kaizan' refers to 'improvement' – the Japanese method of continuous improvement – which Yamada notes could be adopted in the kingdom, notably during the *Nitāqāt* labour nationalisation programme. Some firms, such as Abdul Latif Jameel, have taken it on board. 'Cool Japan, Warm Saudi' refers to Japanese soft power such as media, technology and know-how, developing Saudi content through manga, anime and computer games or joint-venture animated films such as *The Journey* (2021). Other opportunities include entertainment expos, at the same time that the kingdom is emphasising its hospitality credentials.[40]

The 'Saudi–Japan Vision 2030 Business Forum', with its first online meeting in December 2020, could drive further economic cooperation, with particular interest from the Saudi side in attracting regional headquarters, business cooperation, investment in tourism and innovation.[41] Japanese companies are considering the intentions of the Saudi government in making stipulations such as setting up a regional headquarters in the kingdom, and hope that the guidelines are not overly burdensome. There is also considerable potential and/or interest in information and communications technology, robotics, automation, big data and cloud computing, artificial intelligence, genomics and bioengineering, renewable energy, electrical storage and other future-orientated sectors.[42]

In October 2019, Saudi–Japan Vision 2030 2.0 was announced, projects increased from thirty-one to sixty-nine and participating ministries or institutions participating increased from forty-one to sixty-five.[43] Enabling projects include Vision Office Riyadh, established in early 2020, SAGIA Office Tokyo in the Saudi Arabian embassy, which opened at the end of 2019, and a Cooperation Programme between the National Industrial Development and Logistics Programme and the Saudi–Japan Vision Office in Riyadh from October 2019.[44] Saudi–Japan Vision 2030 2.0 also includes a joint venture, Toho Titanium Sponge Titanium Factory, Japanese business missions to the Special Economic Zone in the kingdom, the 'Future Shapers' student exchange programme, an International Agreement for Cost-Sharing Technical Cooperation, and Cooperation on Intellectual Property.[45] Higher education exchange is beginning to be realised, as hundreds of Saudi students are studying at Japanese universities.[46] The Joint Crude Oil Storage Project in Okinawa, supplying Japan with crude oil for an emergency, was also renewed in October 2019. SAGIA has already signed agreements in the sectors of finance, industry and education.[47] Following the UAE–Japan Investment Forum in 2018[48] and the UAE–Japan Comprehensive Strategic Partnership signed in 2018, one could expect a UAE–Japanese Vision Group similar to that of the Saudi–Japan group.

As an extension to Japanese dependence on Gulf oil and the growing portfolio of other commercial relations, Japan is keenly interested in stability in the region. Japan's peace constitution has caused it to take a passive role in international affairs, evident in the Gulf War. But there have been Japanese anti-piracy operations around the Horn of Africa since 2008[49] and Tokyo established a military base in Djibouti in 2011. This was its first overseas base since the Second World War, to protect its shipping and energy flows. Although Tokyo supports UN-backed peace initiatives and has deployed the Japanese Self-Defence Forces (SDF) to, *inter alia*, the Gulf (1991), Golan Heights (1996–2013), Iraq (2004–8), Sudan (2008–11) and South Sudan (2011–17), it is unlikely that Japan will involve itself in Gulf security issues. Prime Minister Yoshihiko Noda did speak about the need to deploy Japanese SDF on minesweeping and escort operations in 2012,[50] and in 2015 a law was passed allowing the SDF to engage in military operations targeting foreign combatants.[51] This is bound to be with ISIS and Al Qaeda in mind, which have killed several Japanese nationals. Japan's approach to regional security has varied between prime ministers. Prime Minister Shinzo Abe, for example, was more proactive in establishing the Quadrilateral Security Dialogue in 2007, launching unprecedented joint naval exercises (Exercise Malabar) and engaging the Gulf States and the US up to the end of his second term in 2020. He visited Tehran in 2019 to help mediate rising tensions between the US and Iran during the Trump administration.[52] However, this faced resistance from the IRGC, who, during his visit, may have placed limpet mines on the Japanese-owned tanker *Kokuka Courageous* on 13 June 2019.[53]

Tokyo has traditionally relied on the US to take the lead on Gulf security issues, mainly because it lacks leverage. Amid rising Gulf tensions, Japan decided in December 2019 not to deploy with a US-led task force in the Strait of Hormuz because the task force had been criticised by Iran. Instead,

Japan aimed to safeguard the potential of positive bounce in economic relations with Tehran after a new JCPOA is agreed, and deployed a destroyer and two patrol planes unilaterally to protect its shipping off the coast of Iran.[54] As a member of the Quad, re-established in 2017, Japan, along with the US, India and Australia, is showing solidarity for a free and open Indo-Pacific. It is also looking ahead to infrastructure changes in the Gulf, including on data, and waiting to see how well placed China will be to set the technological norms and influence rules within states such as Saudi Arabia and the UAE. The result, depending on the outcome, could either enhance or undermine Japanese businesses in this field.

The development of human capital and a knowledge-based economy in the kingdom will have a huge bearing on Japan's relations with Saudi Arabia and UAE, especially if these economies manage to integrate further. Given Japan's continuing dependence on the kingdom for energy, the stakes are high for Tokyo and Riyadh to make Vision 2030 a success. As Japan draws down oil consumption, growing oil consumption in India and China fill the void, although both India and China will be wary about increasing their energy dependence on the Gulf states. Still, this transition is taking place as part of a 'natural trend' in relations and there may be potential in sales to third-party Asian states via storage facilities in Japan.[55] Bilateral Japan–UAE relations have gone from oil- and energy-dependent relations prior to 1998, to more engineering projects post-2000, and, since the Joint Declaration in 2018, have included a greater focus on manufacturing, infrastructure and space cooperation.[56] However, these were in support of Japanese oil concessions in Abu Dhabi which have been in effect since the 1970s. Since about 60 per cent of concessions expired in March 2018, questions arise as so how strong non-oil cooperation might continue without the strong oil-based relationship to sustain it, if concessions are not renewed.[57] Since the UAE economy is also shifting, oil sales remain important – especially as the price remains high – up to 2030. But oil accounts for just 30 per cent of UAE GDP and, with its small population, core expertise will remain outside of the UAE's borders. It will therefore need to maintain an 'inviting' policy.[58]

Saudi and UAE relations with South Korea

Diplomatic relations between Saudi Arabia and the ROK were established in 1962. Chaebols (large, family-owned businesses) such as Hyundai and Daewoo, supported by the ROK government, had early success in establishing entrepreneurial contacts and market penetration in the kingdom. They were especially effective at winning bids on large construction projects, making ROK firms some of the most successful in Saudi Arabia in the 1970s and early 1980s.[59] This has created a positive historic lens for both states through which to view current interactions, and perhaps especially for the ROK, which was recovering from the Korean War (1950–53). However, since these contracts were subject to the oil price, when that price declined in the 1980s and 1990s, the contracts followed suit. By the 2000s, fortunes returned and Seoul engaged on political issues as well, including regular presidential visits to the kingdom and discussions at the G20. Seoul's approach reflected a mercantilist approach, reinforced by former South Korean President Lee Myung-bak (2008–13) who had worked in the kingdom as a Hyundai executive.

However, despite then Prime Minister Hwang Kyo-ahn recognising Vision 2030 to be 'a perfect matching-project to Korea' in May 2016,[60] the momentum of economic cooperation was lost later that year, following the onset of a political scandal involving former ROK President Park Geun-hye which was not resolved until her impeachment in March 2017. The impeachment proceedings against President Park had such a destabilising effect that ROK was unable to accommodate King Salman during his Asian tour in 2017.[61] This was an unusual situation, given that the country was at the time one of the largest consumers of Saudi, oil and potentially a major investor in Vision 2030.[62] However, it is unlikely to remain a major issue, given the goodwill that Korean President Moon Jae-In created with the kingdom when he hosted Mohammed bin Salman in Seoul in June 2019, just after the UN released a report linking the Saudi government to the Khashoggi incident.

ROK will continue to build strong links in the new economic milieu, which may be boosted further since free trade negotiations resumed with the GCC in October 2021 after a decade-long hiatus.[63] Seoul and Saudi Arabia already have strong credentials: close and complementary economic relations, and little by way of political baggage over the past decades. Indeed, the growth of ROK's trading relationship with the kingdom – its top trading partner in the Middle East – is even more impressive than that of the kingdom and Japan, rapidly accelerating to reach $30.4 billion in 2018, including an increase of 21 per cent from the previous year.[64] Even though trade is still dominated by oil (around 90 per cent), the recent increase reflects a growth in non-oil trade.[65] However, Yamada makes a good point that, due to some electronics assembly shifting from Japan to ROK, what is 'Made in Korea' may also have a positive trade impact on Japan, but this may be hidden in trade statistics.[66]

In terms of investments, Samsung C&T Corporation won a $1.97 billion contract to build part of the Riyadh metro in 2013. Saudi Arabia was the number one FDI destination for ROK, at around $3 billion from 2014 to 2016, mostly in the oil industry.[67] In April 2019, Saudi Aramco bought a

17 per cent stake in ROK refiner Hyundai Oilbank for $1.24 billion.[68] In June 2019, during Mohammed bin Salman's first visit to Seoul, an $8.3 billion economic cooperation pact was signed, but again mainly reinforcing the $6 billion deal between Saudi Aramco and S-Oil to build a refinery and downstream facilities in South Korea.[69] Relations between these two companies stretch back decades.

The 'Korea–Saudi Vision 2030 Committee' was established in 2017 and has institutionalised cooperation. It proposes to leverage Saudi Arabia's energy, capital, location, consumer and infrastructure market, which serves ROK's demand for energy, FDI opportunities and major markets for manufacturing and infrastructure companies, in particular. ROK offers a skilled labour pool and experience of trade and development relevant to the Saudi case.[70] Common ground in strengthening the Saudi–Korean Vision 2030 plan for 2017–22 appears to lie in a number of key areas, extending to energy and manufacturing (including shipyard construction, auto production, solar assembly, renewable energy development, power-plant upgrades and new nuclear power plants).[71] ROK will also assist the kingdom in local arms production, including armoured vehicles, precision-guided munitions and air-defence technology transfer.[72]

Both states will aim to cooperate on smart infrastructure and digitisation (including smart city applications, Dahiyat Al-Fursan New City Project and information modelling), capacity building, healthcare and life sciences, SMEs and investment.[73] Similar to Japan, there is recognition of 'enablers' being important. A Vision realisation office will formulate proposals and manage the pipeline and interaction with relevant ministries, with scope to escalate key requirements such as regulations. Another element of cooperation is the creation of a Saudi–Korean Vision 2030 Investment Fund. As an informal or soft-power tool, K-pop band BTS became the first foreign artist to play a solo stadium show in Saudi Arabia, highlighting the cultural bonds that can facilitate further cooperation aimed at youth, such as education exchange.[74]

Khalid al-Falih, then Saudi Arabian minister of energy, industry, and mineral resources, met with President Moon Jae-In on 4 May 2018, followed by a visit to Paik Un-gyu, then Korean minister of trade, industry and energy. Paik and a former presidential secretary were subsequently investigated for alleged abuse of power and interference with business by pushing for the early closure of Wolsong-1, ROK's second-oldest nuclear reactor.[75] Korean President Moon Jae-in, elected in 2017, had favoured removing nuclear power from the country's energy mix after Japan's Fukushima disaster, to be replaced with renewables.[76] This led to ROK nuclear fuel companies searching for opportunities abroad. President Moon's pledge for ROK to be carbon neutral by 2050 has fuelled debates on how to remove nuclear and coal simultaneously. ROK energy policy still aims for growth over environmentalism, as the two new nuclear power stations being constructed on the country's south-eastern coast attest. By maintaining a small civil nuclear industry, ROK is well placed to feed into a nascent Saudi civil nuclear programme. Saudi Arabia is interested only in the latest nuclear power technology, such as fourth-generation reactors to be constructed after 2025.[77] The South Korean firm Korea Electric Power Corporation is already constructing nuclear reactors for the Emirates Nuclear Energy Corporation, at a cost of $24.4 billion.[78] The first of the four plants at Barakah went online in August 2020, and the second in August 2021.[79] Apart from generating a quarter of the UAE's electricity requirement, offsetting 21 million tonnes of greenhouse gas emissions each year,[80] the status gained from such engineering prowess and the experience of maintaining a nuclear programme will continue to be abundant for the UAE. ROK's state-run nuclear research institute and the country's shipbuilder joined forces in 2021 to develop a marine molten salt reactor as part of efforts towards the development of small modular reactors which help to achieve carbon neutrality in shipping and power generation.[81] This may be of interest to the kingdom in the same way that companies such as Rolls Royce, which is developing small nuclear reactors to generate cleaner energy, may also be of interest.[82]

ROK's business credentials in contributing to economic development and diversification in the kingdom reflect its successful activity elsewhere in the Gulf. In 2009 the South Korea–UAE Strategic Partnership was established to move the states, which had established diplomatic ties only in 1980, away from focusing on energy and construction. By 2018, relations were upgraded further to 'special strategic partners', whereby dialogue would henceforth take place at the diplomatic and defence vice-ministerial level, talks between foreign ministers and a joint panel to discuss economic issues.[83] New areas being explored include cooperation on science and IT, renewable and new sources of energy, cooperative channels for industries, investment, tourism and the knowledge economy. Trade is likely to be further enhanced once a new free trade deal between ROK and the GCC is concluded. Samsung C&T helped to build Burj Khalifa in Dubai with Belgian company BESIX and Arabtec from the UAE. ROK bilateral trade with the UAE was $9.4 billion in 2020, with non-oil trade at $2.1 billion in the first six months of 2021.[84] There have been a range of energy-related investments, partly spurred on by the Abu Dhabi Investment Forum in Seoul in 2017.[85] In March 2018, Samsung Engineering signed two contracts worth $3.5 billion with ADNOC on a major upgrading of the UAE's Ruwais refinery, part of the transformation of Ruwais from a small town outside Abu Dhabi into a refining, petrochemical and conversion hub.[86] In 2019, ADNOC awarded South Korea's SK Engineering & Construction a Dh 4.4 billion (around $1.2 billion) contract to build the world's largest single-site underground crude storage facility.[87] Mubadala was among a consortium of investors which purchased 47 per cent of ROK Botox maker Hugel for $2.5 billion in 2021.[88]

In parallel to building ties to the kingdom and the UAE, Prime Minister Chung Sye-kyun travelled to Iran in April 2021 to deal with Hankuk Chemi – impounded by the IRGC in response to Seoul, under US pressure, having frozen $7 billion in oil payments to Iran – and to try to revive the JCPOA.[89] By February, Iran appeared to be de-escalating the situation by releasing the ROK crew, whilst the ROK government agreed to expedite a review of the monies owed.[90] Seoul continues to balance its economic interests in Iran (which could be reinvigorated if a new JCPOA is signed with the US) and its close security relations with the US in relation to North Korea, including compliance on US-led sanctions against Iran. In an attempt to force Iran out of the East Asian oil market during the Trump presidency, both the US and Saudi Arabia increased their oil sales to South Korea. ROK naval forces have been operating in the Gulf of Aden since 2009, its first operational deployment away from the Korean Peninsula. It has been building up its presence in the Middle East and associated itself with the EU's anti-piracy mission in the Horn of Africa, called Operation Atalanta.[91] As part of deepening security relations with the UAE, around 1,600 special forces have been on a training mission there, which may have been part of open-secret military pact linked to KEPCO's successful bid in the UAE civil nuclear programme.[92] However, that military pact is most likely to be limited to civil nuclear installation security, leveraging ROK's experience and expertise in protecting its own critical infrastructure from potential North Korean attack.[93] Elsewhere in the Gulf, ROK forces are bound to come under the US security umbrella.

Conclusion

Japanese and ROK relations with Saudi Arabia and the UAE have undergone an emphasis shift, primarily since 2018, and broadening in the composition of their relations. Whilst oil dependence remains a defining characteristic in their interaction, leading to unquestioning support for the kingdom, especially as Iranian and Iraqi oil exports remain compromised by sanctions and insecurity, zero-carbon policies and Vision strategies are driving new economic interests, innovations and institutionalisations. Growing oil-refining operations with Saudi participation[94] might be a feature over the coming decades, but this is complicated by the growth of renewables and clean-energy policy which favours the UAE.

Asian diversification into strategic industries such as nuclear, complementary to the UAE demand for such expertise, has brought with it the opportunity to enhance some military relations, as the circumstances surrounding the KEPCO agreement suggest. The decree to which this model exists or is transferable remains unclear, but, given the security-centric priorities and balancing strategies of many of the GCC states, including Saudi Arabia and the UAE, this approach is certainly consistent with their foreign policy imperatives and behaviour.

Japanese and ROK engagement on Vision strategies is important to these respective economies but could be revolutionary in terms of pushing the kingdom and the UAE past post-rentierism and into fully fledged diversified states. The Korean chaebol model of business operations that are often politically connected and family owned would sit well with the GCC monarchies, where they could be integrated into a patronage network. But there are some major differences between these states. The long-standing institutional foundations of government–chaebol relations from the Japanese colonial era, during which powerful rent-seekers had been purged, do not exist in the Gulf. Furthermore, intra-chaebol competition was intense and their competitiveness relied on the efficiency of the state regulator. The signs so far are of UAE attracting international competition and of an end to state monopolies as it tries to attract more investment. If the joint Vision 2030 committees succeed in achieving substantial diversification, they will have considerable impact on the participating states, but this is not an assured outcome.

In the short term, Saudi Arabia and the UAE are blurring core–periphery relations and aspects of dependency, and will do so further, should they be successful in delivering the range and depth of projects to build capacity outlined by the joint vision groups. They are bound to have a growing influence over the political economy of the Middle East through normative influence, associated exports and possible technology transfer to third parties, and new joint ventures or investments in other regions, notably Africa. There is evidence of more East Asian soft-power penetration as East and West Asia mesh in a globalised society. In terms of alliance patterns, Saudi Arabia, the UAE, ROK and Japan have been, and continue to be, dominated by US strategic calculations. Japan and ROK favour Saudi Arabia and the UAE for pragmatic reasons, with an ongoing view to balancing relations with China and in their support for free trade policies.

Notes

1　Ministry of Foreign Affairs of Japan, 'Japan-Saudi Arabia Relations (Basic Data)', www.mofa.go.jp/region/middle_e/saudi/data.html

2 Ibid.

3 Daniel Yergin, 'Blood and Oil: Why Japan Attacked Pearl', *The Washington Post*, 1 December 1991, www.washingtonpost.com/archive/opinions/1991/12/01/blood-and-oil-why-japan-attacked-pearl/1238a2e3-6055-4d73-817d-baf67d3a9db8/

4 Ibid.

5 Kaoru Sugihara, 'Japan, the Middle East and the World Economy: A Note on the Oil Triangle', in J. A. Allan and Kaoru Sugihara (eds) *Japan and the Contemporary Middle East*. London: Routledge: 1993: 4.

6 Loftur Thorarinsson, 'A Review of the Evolution of the Japanese Oil Industry, Oil Policy and its Relationship with the Middle East', The Oxford Institute for Energy Studies, February 2018: 9, www.oxfordenergy.org/wpcms/wp-content/uploads/2018/02/A-Review-of-the-Evolution-of-the-Japanese-Oil-Industry-Oil-Policy-and-its-Relationship-with-the-Middle-East-WPM-76.pdf

7 Ibid: 10.

8 Yoshio Minagi, 'Japan and the Gulf: Balancing the Business Relationship', in Tim Niblock and Monica Malik (eds), *Asia–Gulf Economic Relations in the 21st Century: The Local to Global Transformation*. Berlin: Gerlach Press, 2013: 343.

9 Sugihara, 'Japan, the Middle East and the World Economy': 2.

10 Makio Yamada, 'How Did Japan Achieve a 1% Unemployment Rate? Facilitating the Education-to-Employment Transition', *Dirasat*, 30, King Faisal Center for Research and Islamic Studies, December 2017, www.kfcris.com/pdf/251e9fe51db9047dae97f66750401c355b0679375f7de.pdf

11 Late rentierism is an extension of rentier state theory which seeks to explain the impacts of external rents on state-society relations and governance. See Matthew Gray, 'A Theory of "Late Rentierism" in the Arab States of the Gulf', Center for International and Regional Studies, Georgetown University Qatar, 2011, https://repository.library.georgetown.edu/bitstream/handle/10822/558291/CIRSOccasionalPaper7MatthewGray2011.pdf

12 Makio Yamada, 'Japan's Relations with Saudi Arabia: The Evolution of Energy Diplomacy in Response to the Developmental Shift in the Rentier State', in Satoru Nakamura and Steven Wright (eds) *Japan and the Middle East: Foreign Policies and Interdependence*. Singapore: Palgrave Macmillan, 2022.

13 Ibid.

14 Ministry of Foreign Affairs of Japan, 'Japan–Saudi Arabia Relations (Basic Data)'.

15 Yee-Kuwang Heng, 'The Sustainability Turn in UAE–Japan Relations', *Contemporary Arab Affairs*, 13 (4), December 2020: 88–107.

16 Garrett Nada and Alex Yacoubian, 'Iran and Japan Struggle Over Ties and Trade', United States Institute of Peace, The Iran Primer, 20 December 2019, https://iranprimer.usip.org/blog/2019/dec/17/iran-and-japan-struggle-over-ties-and-trade

17 Reuters Staff, 'Japan Expects Little Impact from U.S. Scrapping Iran Oil Waivers', *Reuters*, 23 April 2019, www.reuters.com/article/us-usa-iran-oil-japan-idUSKCN1RZ024

18 Akiko Yoshioka, 'Japan's Expanding Relations with Iraq in 1970s–80s', JIME-IEE Japan, 18 July 2019: 5, www.iraq.emb-japan.go.jp/files/000500191.pdf

19 Antonia Juhasz, 'Why the War in Iraq was Fought for Big Oil', *CNN*, 15 April 2013, https://edition.cnn.com/2013/03/19/opinion/iraq-war-oil-juhasz/index.html

20 Florentine Koppenborg and Ulv Hanssen, 'Japan's Growing Dependence on Coal', East Asia Forum, 22 March 2020, www.eastasiaforum.org/2020/03/22/japans-growing-dependence-on-coal/

21 Justin Rowlatt and Tom Gerken, 'COP26: Document Leak Reveals Nations Lobbying to Change Key Climate Report', *BBC News*, 21 October 2021.

22 Reuters Staff, 'Japan Offers Nuclear Help to Saudi to Free up Oil', *Reuters*, 10 February 2013, www.reuters.com/article/us-japan-saudi-idUSBRE91907520130210

23 Loftur Thorarinsson, 'A Review of the Evolution of the Japanese Oil Industry, Oil Policy and its Relationship with the Middle East', The Oxford Institute for Energy Studies, February 2018: 11.

24 Akiko Yoshioka, 'Relations between Japan and the Middle East', International Institute for Asian Studies, Newsletter 80, Summer 2018, www.iias.asia/the-newsletter/article/relations-between-japan-middle-east

25 Abed Al Saadoun, 'Strengthening Ties Between Saudi Arabia and Japan in the Era of Vision 2030', Speech to JCCP Symposium, 30 January 2020, www.jccp.or.jp/international/conference/docs/K1Saudi.pdf

26 RAWEC, 'Petro Raabigh', www.rawec.com/our-client/

27 Makio Yamada, 'King Salman's Visit to Tokyo: In Search of New Concepts for Saudi-Japanese Bilateral Relations', King Faisal Center for Research and Islamic Studies, Commentaries: 1, www.kfcris.com/pdf/52cc88cac443932dffe9a0e44fc969b2591303118791d.pdf

28 Isobel Asher Hamilton, 'Saudi Arabia is Investing Another $45 Billion with Softbank', *Business Insider*, 8 October 2018, www.businessinsider.com/saudi-arabia-45-billion-with-softbank-2018-10

29 Embassy of Japan in the UAE, 'Message from H.E. Akihiko Nakajima, Ambassador of Japan on Mars Mission 2020', July 2020, www.uae.emb-japan.go.jp/Mars%20Mission%202020/Message%20from%20Ambassador%20of%20Japan%20on%20Mars%20Mission_20200720.pdf

30 Arab News, 'Mars Hope Probe Success Strengthens UAE–Japan Partnership', 12 February 2021, www.arabnews.com/node/1808041/business-economy

31 Arabian Business, 'New Japanese Envoy Seeks Deeper Ties with the UAE', 1 August 2019, www.arabianbusiness.com/education/425170-new-japanese-envoy-seeks-deeper-ties-with-the-uae

32 Narayanappa Janardhan, 'Japan's Oil Diplomacy in the Gulf: Old Idea, New Approaches', 15 April 2021, https://agsiw.org/japans-oil-diplomacy-in-the-gulf-old-idea-new-approaches/

33 International Energy Agency, 'Memorandum of Cooperation (MoC) on Hydrogen between Japan and the UAE', 5 July 2021, www.iea.org/policies/13316-memorandum-of-cooperation-moc-on-hydrogen-between-japan-and-uae

34 Some hydrogen is produced as a by-product from refining oil. Ammonia is produced by combining hydrogen with nitrogen.

35 Author's interview with Ambassador Akihiko Nakajima, Japanese Ambassador to the UAE, 9 November 2021.

36 Mitsubishi, 'Masdar Launches Electric-Vehicle Pilot', 17 January 2011, www.mhi.com/news/110127.html

37 Khalifa University, 'Zero-Emission Electric Motorcycle Visits Masdar City on Tour of UAE', 21 September 2018, www.ku.ac.ae/zero-emission-electric-motorcycle-visits-masdar-city-on-tour-of-uae; Masdar News, 'Masdar and Ekar Announce Strategic Partnership to Bring First Tesla Car-Share Operation to the Middle East', 20 October 2019, https://news.masdar.ae/en/news/2019/10/20/10/47/masdar-city-and-ekar-announce-strategic-partnership#:~:text=UAE%2Dfounded%20ekar%20has%20announced,Masdar%20City%20in%20Abu%20Dhabi

38 Saudi Japan Vision 2030, 'Compass of a New Partnership', March 2017, www.mofa.go.jp/files/000237093.pdf

39 Ibid.

40 Yamada, 'King Salman's Visit to Tokyo'.

41 Japan External Trade Organization, 'First Online "Saudi-Japan Vision 2030" Business Forum', December 2020, www.jetro.go.jp/en/jetro/topics/2020/2012_topics1.html

42 Abed Al Saadoun, 'Strengthening Ties between Saudi Arabia and Japan in the Era of Vision 2030', Speech to JCCP Symposium, 30 January 2020, www.jccp.or.jp/international/conference/docs/K1Saudi.pdf

43 Saudi Vision 2030 2.0 Updated, 'Compass of a New Partnership', October 2019, www.meti.go.jp/press/2019/10/20191024005/20191024005-2.pdf

44 Ibid: 5–7.

45 Ibid.

46 Arab News, 'Saudi–Japanese Relations Continue to Evolve and Grow, Says Former Ambassador', 1 July 2019, www.arabnews.com/node/1518596/saudi-arabia

47 Al Saadoun, 'Strengthening Ties between Saudi Arabia and Japan.

48 WAM, 'UAE Looks to Woo More Foreign Direct Investment from Japan', 15 December 2018, available at https://emirates-business.ae/uae-looks-to-woo-more-foreign-direct-investment-from-japan/

49 Fouad Farhaoui, 'Japan's Interests between the Gulf of Aden, Africa and Yemen – Analysis', *Eurasia Review*, 29 February 2016.

50 Takeo Kumagai, 'Japan Mulls Sending SDF Escort Vessels to Strait of Hormuz: Report', S&P Global, 16 February 2012, www.spglobal.com/platts/en/market-insights/latest-news/oil/021612-japan-mulls-sending-sdf-escort-vessels-to-strait-of-hormuz-report

51 Farhaoui, 'Japan's Interests between the Gulf of Aden, Africa and Yemen'.

52 Daniel Hurst, 'What Did Japanese Prime Minister Shinzo Abe Accomplish in Iran?', *The Diplomat*, 14 June 2019, https://thediplomat.com/2019/06/what-did-japanese-prime-minister-shinzo-abe-accomplish-in-iran/

53 Jon Gambrell, 'US Says Video Shows Iran Removing Mine from Stricken Tanker', *Yahoo! News*, 14 June 2019, https://ph.news.yahoo.com/us-says-iran-removed-unexploded-020504854.html

54 Deutsche Welle, 'Japan to Deploy Warship and Planes to Middle East', 27 December 2019, www.dw.com/en/japan-to-deploy-warship-and-planes-to-middle-east/a-51804992

55 Author's interview with Ambassador Akihiko Nakajima, Japanese Ambassador to the UAE, 9 November 2021.

56 Ibid.

57 Japan Bank for International Cooperation, 'JBIC Signs Facility Agreement with ADNOC', 16 January 2018, www.jbic.go.jp/en/information/press/press-2017/0116-010442.html

58 Author's interview with Ambassador Akihiko Nakajima, Japanese Ambassador to the UAE, 9 November 2021.

59 Chung In Moon, 'Korean Contractors in Saudi Arabia: Their Rise and Fall', *Middle East Journal*, 40 (4), Autumn 1986: 614–633.

60 Theodore Karasik, 'Saudi Arabia's Substantial, Expanding Ties with South Korea', *Arab News*, 26 June 2019, www.arabnews.com/node/1516391/%7B%7B

61 Inwook Kim, 'Saudi Vision 2030 and Saudi–South Korean Relations', King Faisal Center for Research and Islamic Studies, July 2018: 6, https://kfcris.com/pdf/6b34ff6e8faf3c3752cf2245ddf7395f5b4209e5d5ee8.pdf

62 Ibid.

63 Kuwait News Agency, 'S. Korea Eyes Resumption of New FTA with GCC', 6 September 2021, www.kuna.net.kw/ArticleDetails.aspx?id=2996291&language=en

64 The Arab Weekly, 'Saudi Arabia, South Korea Expanding Trade Ties', 3 August 2019, https://thearabweekly.com/saudi-arabia-south-korea-expanding-trade-ties

65 Xinhua, 'Saudi-South Korean Trade Volume up 21 pct in 2018: Report', 27 June 2019, www.xinhuanet.com/english/2019-06/27/c_138176502.htm

66 Interview with Makio Yamada, Senior Adviser, King Faisal Center for Research and Islamic Studies, 24 November 2021.

67 Kim, 'Saudi Vision 2030 and Saudi–South Korean Relations': 10.

68 Reuters Staff, 'Hyundai Heavy Says Aramco Buys 17 Percent Stake in South Korean Refiner Unit for $1.2 Billion', *Reuters*, 15 April 2019, www.reuters.com/article/us-saudiaramco-hyundai-oilbank-idUSKCN1RR0EI

69 AFP, 'South Korea, Saudi Sign $8 bln Economic Cooperation Pact', 26 June 2019, www.france24.com/en/20190626-south-korea-saudi-sign-8-bln-economic-co-operation-pact

70 Kim, 'Saudi Vision 2030 and Saudi–South Korean Relations': 7.

71 Saudi Korean Vision 2030: 7, www.mep.gov.sa/Documents/Content/KSA_Korean.pdf

72 Ibid.

73 Ibid: 8–12.

74 Asia Society, 'Interview with H.E. Sami M. Alsadhan, Saudi Arabian Ambassador to the Republic of Korea', 24 September 2021, https://asiasociety.org/korea/interview-he-sami-m-alsadhan-saudi-arabian-ambassador-republic-korea

75 Yonhap, 'Ex-Minister Indicted Over Alleged Abuse of Power in Reactor Shutdown Decision', *The Korea Herald*, 30 June 2021, www.koreaherald.com/view.php?ud=20210630001113

76 Ibid.
77 Makio Yamada, 'GCC–East Asia Relations in the Fields of Nuclear and Renewable Energy: Opportunities and Barriers', The Oxford Institute for Energy Studies, September 2016: 16, www.oxfordenergy.org/wpcms/wp-content/uploads/2016/09/GCC-East-Asia-Relations-in-the-Fields-of-Nuclear-and-Renewable-Energy-MEP-14.pdf
78 Robert Mason and Gawdat Bahgat, 'Civil Nuclear Energy in the Middle East: Demand, Parity and Risk', Arab Gulf States Institute in Washington, 11 April 2019: 8, https://agsiw.org/wp-content/uploads/2019/04/Mason_Bahgat_Civil-Nuclear_ONLINE-1.pdf
79 Reuters, 'UAE's Only Nuclear Power Plant Begins Operations at 2nd Unit', 27 August 2021, www.reuters.com/world/middle-east/uaes-only-nuclear-power-plant-begins-operations-2nd-unit-2021-08-27/
80 Power Technology, 'Barakah Nuclear Power Plant', www.power-technology.com/projects/barakah-nuclear-power-plant-abu-dhabi/
81 Charles Lee, 'South Korea Companies Develop Molten Salt Reactor for Shipping, Power Generation', S&P Global, 22 June 2021, www.spglobal.com/platts/en/market-insights/latest-news/metals/062221-south-korea-companies-develop-molten-salt-reactor-for-shipping-power-generation
82 BBC News, 'Rolls-Royce Gets Funding to Develop Mini Nuclear Reactors', 9 November 2021, www.bbc.com/news/business-59212983
83 President of the Republic of Korea, 'Korea, UAE Agree to Become Special Strategic Partners', 26 March 2018, https://english1.president.go.kr/Media/News/293
84 Khaleej Times, 'UAE, South Korea Begin Talks to Boost Trade Ties', 14 October 2021, www.khaleejtimes.com/economy/uae-south-korea-to-launch-free-trade-talks
85 KIZAD, 'Abu Dhabi Ports Presents FDI Opportunities at Seoul Investment Forum', 10 May 2017, www.kizad.ae/2017/05/10/abu-dhabi-ports-presents-fdi-opportunities-seoul-investment-forum/
86 Reuters Staff, 'UAE's ADNOC Awards $3.5 Billion Contracts to Samsung Enginerring', *Reuters*, 26 March 2018, www.reuters.com/article/us-emirates-adnoc-samsung/uaes-adnoc-awards-3-5-billion-contracts-to-samsung-engineering-idUSKBN1H217C
87 Fareed Rahman, 'UAE and South Korea in Talks to Deepen Trade Ties', *The National*, 12 September 2021, www.thenationalnews.com/business/economy/2021/09/12/uae-and-south-korea-to-resume-trade-talks/
88 Ibid.
89 Hyonhee Shin, 'South Korean PM Arrives in Iran to Help Try to Revive Nuclear Deal', *Reuters*, 12 April 2021, www.reuters.com/world/asia-pacific/south-korean-pm-arrives-iran-help-try-revive-nuclear-deal-2021-04-12/
90 Choe Sang-Hun and Fernaz Fassihi, 'Iran Agrees to Free South Korean Ship's Crew', *The New York Times*, 2 February 2021, www.nytimes.com/2021/02/02/world/asia/iran-south-korea-crew.html#:~:text=SEOUL%2C%20South%20Korea%20%E2%80%94%20Iran%20has,the%20vessel%20a%20month%20ago

91 Neil Melvin, 'The Foreign Military Presence in the Horn of Africa Region', SIPRI, April 2019: 12, www.sipri.org/sites/default/files/2019-05/sipribp1904_1.pdf

92 June Park and Ali Ahmad, 'Risky Business: South Korea's Secret Military Deal with UAE', *The Diplomat*, 1 March 2018, https://thediplomat.com/2018/03/risky-business-south-koreas-secret-military-deal-with-uae/

93 Interview with a former senior UK official who asked not to be named, 18 November 2021.

94 The top five oil-refining countries in Asia are: China, India, South Korea, Japan and Singapore. NS Energy, 'Top Five Countries in Asia-Pacific Region for Oil Refining Capacities', 1 January 2020, www.nsenergybusiness.com/features/countries-oil-refining-asia-pacific/#:~:text=With%20a%20capacity%20of%20592%2C000,refining%20facility%20in%20the%20country.

13

Indonesia and Malaysia: transnationalism and Islamic leadership

Introduction

The commercial and religious links between the Middle East and Indian Ocean routes to Southeast Asia stretch back centuries. Arab merchants set sail with rosewater, madder (a herb), indigo, raisins, silver and seed-pearls.[1] They came mainly from Hadramaut (comprising most of present-day Yemen), introduced Islam to the wider region including Nusantara (modern-day Indonesia) and Malaya (modern-day Malaysia). In both cases there has been some mixing between Islam and local customs to form distinct aspects of religious expression, whilst some groups have resisted this. Although the process of direct engagement was interrupted by Portuguese occupation, followed by the Dutch and British in the seventeenth century, it was normalised again in the nineteenth century after the British removed customs duties, which attracted Arab (and Chinese) traders once again.[2]

As Al Rasheed notes in *Transnational Connections and the Arab Gulf*, most literature on globalisation and transnationalism with reference to the Gulf has focused on foreign labour, the Gulf state's legal and social restrictions, and local resistance to integrating expatriate communities.[3] Although there is a great distance between the Gulf and Southeast Asia, transnationalism has been evident in a myriad of ways, mainly between peoples and institutions. Much of it has been based on religious influence emanating from Umm Al Qura (Makkah), the Islamic University of Madinah, Muhammad bin Saud Islamic University (Riyadh) and the newly named Ibn Khaldun International Institute of Advanced Research in Malaysia. Educational institutions in Indonesia include the Pondok Pesantren Modern Darussalam Gontor in East Java, Pondok Pesantren Sarang in Central Java and Pesantren Darun Najah in Jakarta.

Having sat on the periphery of Gulf politics and Islam for decades, the region is becoming a hotbed of local and interregional activity once more, partly spurred on by Iran's having filled the vacuum. The growth of Al Qaeda and ISIS in the Middle East, and the Taliban becoming the dominant power once again in Afghanistan, have reignited debates surrounding violent Islamism and Islamic fundamentalism, respectively, to which these states are responding. Indonesia, like Saudi Arabia and the UAE, is a member of the GCTF and has led on the Detention and Reintegration Working Group.[4] These states are also members of the IONS, an initiative to increase naval cooperation.

As Indonesia develops as an emerging power, a range of questions abound. They include the nature of the shift in Indonesian dependency, participation in Asian and US-led alliances and the government's ability to continue to promote a distinctive Islam Nusantara[5] and Pancasila,[6] which will be vital to consolidating and enhancing soft-power capabilities over the coming years. This chapter provides an overview of Saudi and UAE engagement with Indonesia and Malaysia, referencing changes in the domestic politics of these Southeast Asian nations and the evolving bases of their long-standing interregional interaction.

Saudi–Indonesian relations

For centuries, Muslims on the Malay–Indonesian archipelago have travelled to the Hijaz for pilgrimage or Islamic learning, along with more recent intellectual-, tourism- and labour-related exchanges. Indonesia is the largest Muslim-majority nation, but also a constitutionally secular state which incorporates six major religions. Saudi Arabia was one of the first countries to recognise Indonesia as an independent state, in 1947, and the countries established diplomatic relations in 1950. Whilst the Saudi embassy opened in Jakarta in 1955, Indonesia first opened its embassy in Jeddah in 1964, relocating it to Riyadh in 1985.

Islamic leaders have been included in the political process since the Dutch created a colonial People's Council and the Japanese established the Council of Indonesian Muslim Associations (the Masyumi, incorporating leaders from leading Islamic non-governmental organisations Nahdlatul Ulama [NU] and Muhammadiyah).[7] The Masyumi Party was a major Islamic political party during the Liberal Democracy Era in Indonesia (1950–58), but was banned by President Sukarno in 1960 for supporting the Revolutionary Government of the Republic of Indonesia rebellion – a revolutionary government set up in Sumatra in 1958 to oppose the central government. In its place, the Saudis established Lembaga Ilmu Pengetahuan Islam dan Bahasa Arab (LIPIA) in 1980, the Jakarta-based branch of Riyadh's Imam Muhammad ibn Saud Islamic University, which served as a well-funded bridge back to the kingdom for the top students.[8] LIPIA is said to serve as a 'Saudi microcosm' which also provides a gateway to all of Southeast Asia.[9]

NU is one of the largest religious institutions serving the masses[10] and has produced moderate intellectuals who now play major roles in the democratisation process, including through a range of political parties such as National Awakening Party, United Development Party, Indonesian Democratic Party of Struggle, Partai Golkar, Partai Demokrat, Nasional Demokrat, and Prosperous Justice Party. NU is represented through high-profile figures such as the Ma'ruf Amin, vice-president, and Yaqut Cholil Qoumas, religious affairs minister, and Mahfud MD, the coordinating minister for political, legal, and security affairs, in the government of President Joko Widodo (also known as Jokowi).

It is germane to this chapter to dwell on the political development of Indonesia, which has enabled Saudi Arabia to project religious influence among the vast majority of the 87 per cent or so of the 273 million inhabitants (as of 2020) who identify as Sunni Muslim. Islamic conservatism is widely associated with influences from the Middle East, especially Salafism, the MB,[11] India's Jamaah Tabligh and Hizbut Tahrir. Political and religious activities on university campuses became increasingly restricted under Suharto after the Iranian Revolution in 1979, banning books related to Shia or Islamic books containing politics. Restrictions were also put in place following the Tanjung Priok riots in 1984, after which alternative religious-political currents started to develop whereby Islamic *dakwah* groups, similar to Christian missions, discussed religious and political issues and applied their new-found knowledge in the local community.[12] They hoped to be in a position of political strength at the end of the Suharto era through the Justice Party (now Justice and Welfare Party), but, whilst its tenets are popular among many students, their transition to political power remains elusive.

A growing following of conservative Islam was also evident in the massive demonstrations that erupted after Basuki Tjahaja Purnama (also known as 'Ahok'), Jakarta governor and a Christian from the minority Chinese community, was accused of insulting Islam in 2016. He was subsequently sentenced to two years in jail.[13] Two of the primary organisers of the protests against Ahok within the Gerakan Nasional Pengawal Fatwa Majelis Indonesia (National Movement to Uphold the Fatwa of Indonesian Council of Ulama) were Bachtiar Nasir and Muhammad Zaitun Rasmin, both educated in Saudi Arabia.[14] Representatives from hard-line Islamist groups have also been implicated in the mass demonstrations, such as Rizieq Shihab from the Islamic Defenders Front,[15] who also graduated from a Saudi university.

A number of Indonesian politicians have come through the Islamic Educational Institute, Gontor, in East Java, where figures such as Nasir teach, but which also maintains a mainstream approach. The key issue appears to be between Indonesian Islamism versus western liberalism, with evidence of increasingly mainstream hostility towards the Shia.[16] Hizbut Tahrir, which aims to revive the Muslim world, liberate Muslims from the thought and systems of unbelievers and restore the Islamic Caliphate, has also benefited from Indonesia's democratisation process and strong adherence to Islam. It was pushed out of the Middle East after coup attempts in Jordan, Syria and Egypt, and, after the Cold War, members moved from the West to Central Asia, the Caucasus and Southeast Asia.[17] In Indonesia, it was free to mobilise until the government revoked its permit to operate in 2017. With representation on the Indonesian Ulama Council, which declared that secularism, liberalism and pluralism violate Islamic teachings, Hizbut Tahrir is firmly aligned with Islamist-nationalists.[18] It is its ability to mobilise supporters on a range of domestic and international issues which maintains its relevance, but the actions of a limited number of members such as Bahrum Naim who have joined ISIS represent a threat to Indonesian national security.[19] The future stability of Indonesia and engagement with states in the Middle East such as Saudi Arabia and the UAE, and with the West, depend on offshoot groups such as Forum Umat Islam and whether they can successfully roll back or reinterpret Pancasila[20] by mobilising a broad swathe of society and the military against it.

Mainstream groups continue to emphasise Pancasila and the constitution as a key unifying elements.[21] Bachtiar Nasir helps to link the Islamic University of Madinah in Saudi Arabia with Indonesian Islamic organisations such as the Persatuan Islam, Nahdlatul Ulama and Muhammadiyah, of which he is a member. As an Islamic scholar, he also holds sway through running an Islamic school in Jakarta, as chairman of the Aliansi Cinta Keluarga, which promotes family values, and as a commentator in newspapers and on television.[22] Muhammad Zaitun Rasmin, leader of Wahdah Islamiyah, a Salafi organisation with over 120 branches worldwide, is another graduate of the Islamic University of Madinah, aiming to walk a 'middle' path in Indonesia between communism/liberalism on the left and Islamic militancy on the right, whilst differentiating between Muslims and non-Muslims.[23]

Indonesia has, so far, done well to contain the violent Islamist threat through a combination of broad-based social institutions and democratisation. But, as Caruso notes, Indonesian democracy is only two decades old, and policies of 'appeasement' could yet tip the balance back in the favour of extremists.[24] To underscore the level of uncertainty over national security in the coming years, ISIS foreign fighters are found to be relocating out of Syria and Iraq to join other jihadist front lines around the world, and Indonesia and Malaysia are becoming 'priority relocation destinations'.[25] A new university, Universitas Islam Internasional Indonesia, opened its doors to graduate students in 2021 to promote what former Indonesian Vice-President

Jusuf Kalla called a 'more modern interpretation of religion'.[26] For this approach to work, a whole network of universities which share the same commitment is needed.

Saudi Arabia's soft-power influence in Indonesia has been built on religious universities, scholarships for Indonesians to study in the kingdom and the supply of teachers and textbooks to hundreds of *pesantren* (boarding schools).[27] However, after the 2014 oil price decline, this appears to be waning. Various schemes have been introduced whereby the financial burden is now shared between the kingdom and Indonesia, or is even fully funded by Indonesian Islamic organisations or the government. Whilst proselytisation is still at the heart of their bilateral relations, Esam Abid Al-Thagafi, the Saudi ambassador to Indonesia, has also said that 'Everything we [the Saudis] do here, from Qur'an competitions to Ramadan iftars, is at the request of Indonesian Muslim groups.'[28]

After Suharto, the democracy was decentralised to the district level, which has in some cases incorporated Sharia law into bylaws related to dress (including headscarves in government services), homosexuality and Ramadan closing times.[29] But Al Qurtuby noted in 2021 that Saudi-trained Indonesian Islamic scholars vary quite considerably in terms of religious orientation, political affiliations, social networks and academic backgrounds, raising questions about the plurality and shifting bases of Saudi Arabia's religious impact in Indonesia.[30] The alternative is that Saudi influence may just be more diffuse in Indonesia amid district-level decision making and a national-level political transition involving a large population.

On the back of high oil prices, Saudi Arabia and Indonesia signed a defence cooperation agreement covering training, education, counterterrorism and defence industry cooperation in January 2014. But Saudi–Indonesian trade has since been hit by falling oil prices from later that year. Bilateral trade dropped from $8.7 billion in 2014 to $4 billion in 2016,[31] recovering slightly in 2018 to reach $6.13 billion and reducing again in 2019 to $5.07 billion.[32] Although a $6 billion joint venture was announced between Saudi Aramco and Pertamina in December 2016, non-oil investments have been poor, plummeting from $30 million in 2015 to just $900,000 in 2016.[33] Saudi Arabia has barriers to trade, including tariffs, which, if lessened or removed, could encourage Indonesia to export more of its halal products, fisheries produce, medicines, textiles and garments to the kingdom. The MoU on counterterrorism and extremism could segue into a broader dialogue on the positive role that Indonesia can play in managing relations between Muslim-majority states and the West.

Economic relations were rejuvenated by King Salman's visit in 2017, the first such visit since King Faisal bin Abdulaziz Al Saud met with President Suharto in Jakarta in 1970.[34] The visit was therefore eagerly anticipated.

King Salman concluded eleven memorandums of understanding in the areas of trade, education, health, culture, pilgrimage, tourism, information sharing (including on SME programmes), science and technology, civil aviation, fisheries, security, defence and counterterrorism. He also held a series of interfaith meetings, met representatives of the Chinese community, including businesspeople and political figures, posed for selfies and shook hands with female leaders, thus bringing a human dimension to the Saudi state and continuing to build on a policy of tolerance established by his predecessor, King Abdullah.

No major breakthroughs on domestic workers or compensation for families of victims of Hajj tragedies were announced at the time, no deals on tourism (beyond the extended stay of the entourage in Bali) and no major investment deals were concluded, although King Salman did pledge $6.71 billion in investment[35] and $1 billion in development finance.[36] Four investment deals were proposed totalling $2.4 billion.[37] Wijaya Karya signed an MoU with Saudi Adil Abdul Munif Makki Group to create 8,000 housing complexes costing $2 billion, whilst Alfanar Energy planned to invest $100 million in a biomass plant in Indonesia.[38] In 2018, Saudi Arabia had forty-three projects in Indonesia worth $5.36 million. An SME initiative was set up in 2021 to realise potential for generating up to $60 million in trade.[39] Saudi ambassador Esam Althagafi said in 2020 that Indonesia 'is a member of Vision 2030'.[40] Should the successful implementation of Vision 2030 accompany Indonesia's economic transition to a global top-ten economy by 2030,[41] there could be significant opportunities to expand trade and investment. The Saudi embassy has put resources into Arabic-language programmes, said to put it on a par with the British Council or Alliance Française.[42] In Jeddah, Indonesians have also implemented language training in the form of the Bahasa Indonesia Untuk Penutur Asing programme.

Indonesia is able to boast good relations with the kingdom, and also good formal and informal people-to-people connections, in terms of historic links and the number of Indonesians living in the kingdom, which was around 400,000 in 2019, as well as those settled as Saudi nationals.[43] However, the treatment of Indonesian domestic workers has been a near constant irritant in the relationship, highlighting the conditions and patterns of discrimination, power asymmetry and ongoing socio-economic drivers. Following the execution of two female Indonesian domestic workers found guilty of murder in 2015, the government in Jakarta imposed a moratorium on sending new domestic workers to the Middle East.[44] The main issue as the then Indonesian minister of manpower, Muhammad Hanif Dhakiri, said at the time is that 'there are no standardized labor regulations that bind the said [Middle East] countries, to the detriment of migrant workers'.[45] A new deal was reached in October 2018, including the introduction of a new electronic system to better recruit and track workers and protect their contractual rights,[46] reflecting possible changes to the construct of domestic labour and geography of state power.[47] During the intervening period, agents/traffickers had continued to supply the kingdom, using Indonesians sent there under false pretences who either defied the ban or were unaware of it.[48]

Indonesia is also dependent on Saudi Arabia to increase the Hajj quota, which rose by only 10,000 in 2019 to 231,000, even though the Hajj waiting list in Indonesia can stretch to twenty-five years or more. Officials have at times used the promise of bypassing long queues for political patronage and corruption.[49] Approximately 100,000 Indonesians go on Umrah each month.[50] These trips were temporarily affected by the kingdom closing its borders in 2020, due to COVID-19.

Being a front-line state in the US's efforts to challenge China in the South China Sea, Indonesia has taken on a new relevance and, in October 2019, the US removed some of its tariffs as part of ongoing trade negotiations.[51] Jakarta remains wary of US policy in the region, including the AUKUS trilateral security pact between Australia, the UK and US. The combination of changes to its regional foreign policy, including taking a harder line on China's repression of the Uighurs, and internal efforts at reforming Islam (including addressing anti-Shia sectarianism) could suggest a mutually reinforcing dynamic which aims to boost Indonesian state power and status[52] but also cuts against some Saudi and UAE interests.

As a Muslim state sensitive to Saudi national security interests, Indonesia has highlighted its concerns to Iran over its nuclear programme, has emphasised respect for the NPT and supported the JCPOA. On at least two occasions Indonesia has offered to mediate between Saudi Arabia and Iran, mainly to boost its Islamic credentials among Muslim-majority states and provide new opportunities to expand trade with Iran.[53] The Indonesian government distanced itself from a 1996 fatwa against Shias which sanctioned official persecution, and in 2007 allowed Iran to set up an 'Iranian corner' at a branch of the National Islamic University outside Jakarta.[54]

Indonesia has had a markedly different policy on Qatar than on Saudi Arabia and the UAE, preferring to end to the crisis early, and welcomed Kuwait's mediation efforts. In Yemen, Indonesia's neutral response was initially conditioned by the number of expatriates, mainly students, living there. Jakarta declined to participate in the war in Yemen, focusing its efforts on the repatriation of its nationals. It then modified its stance, from abstention to voting in October 2021 against a measure in the UN Human Rights Council to extend the independent war crimes investigation in Yemen. Riyadh is alleged to have warned Indonesia that if it did not do so, it would create obstacles (such as not recognising COVID-19 vaccination certificates) for Indonesians travelling to Mecca.[55] If Hajj *politik*, or leveraging access to the Hajj as a source of political influence, has occurred, it will have been targeted towards Indonesia, due to its action on an issue vital to the kingdom where there are few other sources of direct leverage. It may also have been with knowledge that there is a need on a political level to cut long waiting times to participate in the Hajj. However, for a state whose Basic Law references the Qur'an and Sunna (Traditions of the Prophet) as its constitution, using the Hajj quota as a source of leverage could be interpreted as dubious.[56]

UAE–Indonesian relations

The UAE has emerged as a new pole with which Indonesia can balance to effect change to the status quo in relation to Saudi Arabia. Non-oil trade grew 100 per cent from 2010 to 2019, and by 23 per cent in 2019,[57] reaching $2 billion in 2020.[58] The UAE has an opportunity to exert influence through a broad sweep of economic statecraft, including $23 billion in deals signed during Crown Prince Mohammed bin Zayed's visit to Indonesia in 2019.[59] This will help to extend ADNOC's energy supplies in the region, but also included education, health, agriculture and counterterrorism.[60] President Widodo, re-elected in 2019, is concerned with economic growth for the country, and especially with providing jobs through foreign investment. The UAE stated in March 2021 that it is also investing $10 billion in Indonesia's SWF, the Indonesia Investment Authority.[61] ADIA is also investing $400 million in Indonesia's GoTo Group (formed by a merger between Tokopedia and Gojek in May 2021) as part of pre-IPO fundraising for the technology unicorn. It is ADIA's first principal investment in Southeast Asia and its biggest investment in Indonesia.[62] The UAE agreed to invest $32.7 billion in Indonesia following President Widodo's 4 November 2021 visit to the UAE. Projects are expected to include DP World investment in port infrastructure with the Indonesian Investment Authority, a deal with Pertamina on floating solar panels with Masdar and G42 (an AI and cloud computing company founded in Abu Dhabi in 2018) investment in smart-city projects, telecoms and genomics laboratories.[63]

Perhaps the most significant form of cooperation is Sheikh Mohammed bin Zayed's agreement to chair a committee that will oversee the construction of a new Indonesian capital in East Kalimantan at an estimated cost of $34 billion. With just 19 per cent funding of from the Indonesian state budget, expectations will be high that the committee, including former British Prime Minister Tony Blair and Masayoshi Son, billionaire founder and chief executive of SoftBank, will be able to attract significant foreign investment.[64]

In September 2021 the UAE and Indonesia launched talks on a Comprehensive Economic Partnership and established the United Arab Emirates

Comprehensive Economic Partnership Agreement to expand economic ties and build cooperation.[65] President Widodo stated in October 2021 that 'I see that religious moderation and diversity in the UAE are widely respected. And that is the area of cooperation we would like to explore more because we both share the closeness in the vision and characters of moderate Islam that propagates tolerance.'[66] He also noted that 'our relationship with the UAE is not just like friends, we are like brothers'.[67] Their economic association is reinforced through other modes of cooperation such as their respective membership of the Indian Ocean Rim Association, in which the UAE was chair from 2020 to 2021.

The UAE is also making headway in challenging established Saudi support for religious institutions in Indonesia. A $20 million replica of the UAE's largest mosque, Sheikh Zayed mosque, was gifted to Indonesia and construction began in March 2021 in Central Java province. It is expected to be completed in 2022 and shows that the near-monopoly on mega mosque construction (this one has capacity for 10,000 worshippers) is no longer occupied by the kingdom. There is also likely to be further cooperation in this area, such as digital education programmes for madrassas.[68] In April 2021 the UAE was also suggesting that it might invest in Indonesian COVID-19 vaccine production.[69] The convergence between Indonesia and the UAE has been a long time coming. In the economic sphere, the investment opportunities in a large market fit well with the UAE's search for diversification and influence, especially in an Asian Muslim-majority nation. The political relationship appears to be warm, as underscored by President Widodo's comments about Indonesia and the UAE being brothers. Should bilateral trade continue to flourish and triple, as planned, over the four years from 2021, the UAE could become one of the top five trading partners with Indonesia, currently dominated by China, the US, Japan, Singapore and India.

Saudi–Malaysian relations

Malaysia, a multicultural and multi-confessional country with a 2020 population of around 32 million, has made its official religion Islam, enabling a more favourable entry for the kingdom into what was a non-aligned and remains a neutral state. Saudi Arabia's relations with Malaysia have been closely paired under successive Malaysian premiers, including Tunku Abdul Rahman al-Hajj (in office 1957–70), who was a close friend of King Faisal's. Tunku was appointed as the first secretary general of the OIC during the king's visit to Malaysia in 1970.[70] Financial assistance, usually in the form of low-interest loans, was provided by the kingdom during the following two Malaysian premierships through the Saudi Fund for Development (aimed at supporting religious institutions such as Pertubuhan Kebajikan Islam Malaysia (the Muslim Welfare Organization Malaysia) and the International Islamic University of Malaysia). Bilateral funds have been aimed at educational and economic development, with an emphasis on land development, the construction of palm oil mills and district hospitals. Other elements of soft power have included distribution of the Qu'ran and 'Nidah Ul-Islam' (the voice of Islam) in Malay.[71]

Whilst Malaysia's regional collaboration was a logical consequence of military conflict with Indonesia between 1963 and 1966, the country has been expanding ties with the Middle East and focused on expanding relations with Japan during the Mahathir bin Mohamad premiership of 1981–2003. During this time Malaysia underwent a period of rapid economic development and has been active in cultivating its IR. For example, its number of diplomatic missions have grown to number eighty-five by 2021, compared with Saudi Arabia, which has a GDP twice as large as Malaysia's but with about half (forty-six) the number of diplomatic missions abroad.[72]

Malaysia also sought to lessen its trade deficit and subsequent dependence on the kingdom for oil imports. Saudi oil still represented 30 per cent of Malaysian oil imports in 2016, costing $774 million.[73] Kuala Lumpur made a series of reforms to equalise economic activity, including allowing the National Shipping Company of Saudi Arabia access to Malaysian ports from 1985.[74] The 1997 Asian financial crisis confirmed the need for Malaysia to enter new markets in the Middle East to balance its exposure to Association of Southeast Asian Nations economies. This trend had already begun during the Mahathir premiership from 1981 to 2003. Bilateral trade subsequently rose from $260 million in 1990 to $3.6 billion in 2012.[75] Saudi Arabia's Al-Rajhi bank established a regional office in Malaysia in 2009, with sixteen branches, highlighting its interest in, and growth the potential of, the Islamic financial market.[76] Islamic banking companies from other states also operating in Malaysia include Kuwait Finance House and Qatar General Insurance and Reinsurance Group. Under the premiership of Abdullah Ahmad Badawi (prime minister from 2003 to 2009), Malaysia turned to the Gulf for investment and concluded the 2011 Framework Agreement on Economic, Commercial, Investment and Technical Cooperation with the GCC. After this, investments rose further. Aramco and Malaysia's state-owned oil company, Petronas, set up a $7 billion joint refining operation in Malaysia in 2017.[77]

The nature of the bilateral relations shifted, based on the kingdom's 'Look East' policy under King Abdullah, reflecting changes in international energy markets and global power shifts more broadly. King Abdullah visited China, India, Malaysia and Pakistan in 2006. By 2009 Prime Minister Najib

Razak was in office (until 2018), and he developed a close relationship with King Salman. In 2010 Prime Minister Razak received Saudi Arabia's highest award, the King Abdulaziz Sash Order of Merit of the First Class, granted to crown princes and prime ministers of 'brotherly and friendly countries'.[78] Their personal connection helped to facilitate King Salman's visit to Malaysia in 2017 before he travelled to Brunei, Japan, China and the Maldives. Memorandums of understanding worth $3 billion were signed in Malaysia, mainly in the fields of science, education, the halal industry, aerospace, construction, labour and news exchange. Saudi tourism had also flourished up to this time, with the number of Saudi visits rising 60 per cent between 2007 and 2016 to reach 123,878.[79]

King Salman would invite Prime Minister Razak for a royal audience every time he visited the kingdom.[80] But from 2010, bilateral relations were compromised by corruption through the 1Malaysia Development Berhad (1MDB), a sovereign investment vehicle set up by Prime Minister Razak to finance infrastructure, with an estimated $4.5 billion embezzled between 2009 and 2014.[81] The fallout from this scandal included Malaysia's then attorney general Abdul Gani Patail linking $681 million in Najib Razak's bank account to firms associated with or bodies with links to 1MDB; but Adel al-Jubeir, the Saudi foreign minister, confirmed that this was a personal donation from the Saudi royal family.[82] According to Datuk Syed Omar Alsagoff, the former Malaysian ambassador to Saudi Arabia, Najib Razak had said that the Saudi donation was to pay for the 2018 election campaign, although he was not privy to communication between King Abdullah and the Malaysian prime minister at the time.[83] Prime Minister Razak subsequently lost the 2018 election and was sentenced to twelve years in jail and fined $50 million in 2020 for his part in the 1MDB scandal.[84]

After the 2018 election, the Malaysian cabinet withdrew Malaysia's armed forces from Saudi Arabia, which had been there on standby to evacuate Malaysians from Yemen.[85] Nonetheless, some argued that Malaysia's involvement served as a clear sign of support to the kingdom and went against Malaysia's non-alignment policy.[86] In addition, the King Salman Centre for International Peace, established just over a year earlier, ceased operations immediately and its functions were subsumed into the Malaysian Institute of Defence and Security. Mahathir bin Mohamad, who won the 2018 election, moved to 'do something' to improve the lives of Muslims and overcome Islamophobia.[87] As an emergent middle power in the Islamic world, Malaysia has championed various causes including the Iran–Iraq War, the Gulf War, Rohingya humanitarianism and Palestine. However, by snubbing the Kuala Lumpur summit, ostensibly because it was 'outside the aegis of the OIC', and by putting pressure on Pakistan not to attend, Saudi Arabia quickly reinforced the perception that Malaysia was forming an Islamic axis with those who did attend, such as Iran, Qatar and Turkey.[88] This alliance was reinforced in 2019 when Turkey, Iran, Qatar and Malaysia were to create an economic alliance that sought to use gold and bartering as a way to trade outside of sanctions targeting 'Muslim' countries (i.e. Iran).[89]

Saudi relations with Malaysia have continued to improve following the election in March 2021 of Ismail Sabri Yaakob, who comes from the same political party as Razak, the United Malaysia National Organisation. Trade ties are being expanded from their low level. YB Dato' Seri Mohamed Azmin Ali led a trade mission to Saudi Arabia and the UAE in May 2021 after the former Malaysian prime minister, Muhyiddin Yassin, paid an official to visit to both countries in March 2021. As a result, Saudi Arabia aims to increase its imports of palm oil from 318,000 tonnes in 2020 to 500,000 tonnes in 2021, adding more than $100 million to Malaysian export income.[90] Also in 2021, Saudi Arabia took another step to enhance tourism relations with Malaysia by opening the Saudi Tourism Authority's first commercial office in Southeast Asia in Malaysia.[91] This may represent a new commercial era in Saudi–Malaysian relations aimed at recovering and extending Saudi influence. There is also potential in third parties contributing to Malaysian trade and investment relations. For example, Katsuhiko Takahashi, ambassador of Japan to Malaysia, stated that 'I want to explore the possibility of Japan and Malaysia to identify joint ventures in the Middle East. Malaysia offers lots of good advice to Japan in doing business with [the] Muslim world such as halal and Islamic banking. And countries in the Gulf can learn a lot from development experience from Malaysia, in the area of energy, creating manufacturing industries, and sustainable society.'[92]

UAE–Malaysian relations

The relationship between the UAE and Malaysia has expanded rapidly from the 1980s, after a Cultural and Scientific Cooperation Agreement and Economic and Technical Cooperation Agreement were signed in 1975. Bilateral cooperation was further strengthened through the Economic and Technical Cooperation Agreement of 1981. Malaysia opened an embassy in the UAE in 1983. Relations are dominated by 'commercial religious elements' such as religious education, halal food, Islamic finance, investment and tourism.[93] UAE religious influence looks set to increase after the UAE gifted the construction a mosque complex inspired by the Sheikh Zayed Grand Mosque in Abu Dhabi. But this plan was not realised. This is most likely due to the project's being tied to the Razak premiership; and since he was defeated in the 2018 election, this may have caused a delay in the construction. The UAE continues to acts as a gateway for Malaysian products in the Middle East, supported by its non-aligned posture, whilst Malaysia is a gateway for these GCC states in Southeast Asia, with the added advantage of countering Iranian influence in the region.

UAE relations with Malaysia have been centred on Mubadala Petroleum, which has invested heavily in the Southeast Asian state's oil industry, including exploration and oil storage at Johor. Bilateral trade was about $2 billion in 2006[94] but has risen in recent years to reach $5.7 billion in 2018.[95] An 'Invest in Malaysia' event in Abu Dhabi in 2017 yielded a joint committee for the economy, trade, investment and technological cooperation. In the UAE, in 2021 meetings with retail conglomerates Landmark Group and Lulu Group, commitments were reached from both companies to increase their sourcing and to broaden the range of products from Malaysia.

Other personal connections also exist between the UAE and Malaysia. For example, in June 2019 the king of Malaysia, Sultan Abdullah Sultan Ahmad Shah, arrived for his first visit to the UAE.[96] In July 2019 Mohammed bin Zayed attended the official coronation of his long-time friend and Sandhurst classmate Sultan Abdullah Ahmad Shah, sixth sultan of Pahang, who is traditionally head of Islam and the source of all titles and honours in the state.

Of greater concern to the UAE going forward will be any repeat of the visits to Malaysia by Ismael Haniyeh, head of the Hamas 'Political Bureau', which occurred during the Mahathir Mohamad administration in 2019. Following the change of government from Razak to Mahathir, one of the new coalition partners, Anwar Ibrahim, had close connections to Yusuf Qaradawi, a MB exile in Doha. Whilst these connections have since diminished, the potential for Malaysia to leverage its activist Islamic credentials again cannot be discounted. The results could equally affect the kingdom by posing a threat to its Islamic leadership, and the UAE if it empowers pro-Islamist adversaries.

Conclusion

Islam continues to shape Saudi soft-power deployment in Southeast Asia, but as a legitimising factor, as a possible source of leverage and as an attractive incentive for tourism. Indonesia is a good example of where the legacy of Saudi soft-power deployment continues to achieve resonance. Superimposed on these traditional but diminished links are the commercial deals that the UAE has signed, coupled with Sheikh Mohammed bin Zayed's agreement to chair a committee that will oversee the construction of a new Indonesian capital city. The replica of the Sheikh Zayed mosque is a symbol of the UAE's growing soft power and triumphant growth in the Indonesian market. In just over two decades the economic component in UAE–Indonesian relations has been transformed by state-led, SWF-led, emirate-led and now private sector-led trade and investment. The UAE position is rooted in having national champions such as DP World poised to commit to deals, with state backing, to enhance its economic statecraft approach, which is especially geared towards rapidly developing economies. In building more dynamic economic relations and taking a leading role in the new Indonesian capital, UAE influence, lack of conditionality and safe-city technology may reinforce the authoritarian tendencies of President Widodo.

Malaysia has a low-level trading relationship with Saudi Arabia and the UAE, focused on palm oil exports. However, religious tourism could yet create a new robust linkage and industry which continues to tie Malaysia to the kingdom. Saudi influence in Malaysia, a smaller nation than Indonesia, has been more highly personalised through leaders such as President Razak, similar to elite interactions in the GCC. The loss of Razak as a strategic ally, and his subsequent conviction in connection with the 1MDB case, has tarnished the kingdom in Malaysia. The push by Mahathir to launch a summit effectively put Malaysia in the same challenger bracket as regional actors such as Qatar and Turkey. It underscores an emerging geostrategic and ideological fault line developing between those states which turn a blind eye to Islamophobia and those which seek to challenge it, those which tolerate political Islam and those that do not, and those that seek to marginalise the Shia and those states with constitutional protections in place. The divergent approach reflects the amount of control each state has over the Ummah, patterns in the global economy and regional and international relations.

As middle powers operating in a different geography, Indonesia and Malaysia are several steps removed from the intense politicking of the Middle East, and lack leverage. Yet their identity and close associations with Mecca, and with the Arabian Peninsula more broadly, has created a series of robust linkages as a key source of dependency. But as democratic states these Southeast Asian states are susceptible to the will of their populations with diverse interests. They are not necessarily the all-weather friends that can be relied upon in a crisis, which could be problematic into the future. Since Indonesia and Malaysia are both addressing a series of public policy issues and aim to achieve rapid economic development, Saudi Arabia and UAE can help them to achieve their ambition in achieving middle-powerhood and status, but it possibly with new forms of dependency over the coming years. Only Indonesia has a diversified economy, ready to digest major economic opportunities, and yet, as a democratic state with a liberal foreign policy agenda it could find itself embroiled in Middle East and Asian regional security issues not of its own making.

Notes

1 Armando Cortesao, *The Suma Oriental of Tome Pires: An Account of the East, From the Red Sea to Japan, written in Malacca and India in 1512–1515.* Vol. II, Series II. London: The Hakluyt Society, 1944.

2 Asmady Idris, 'Malaysia–Saudi Arabia Relations: Roots, Dimensions, and Prospects', Middle East Institute, 18 June 2013, www.mei.edu/publications/malaysia-saudi-arabia-relations-roots-dimensions-and-prospects#_ftnref5

3 Madawi Al-Rasheed, 'Introduction: Localizing the Transnational and Transnationalizing the Local', in Madawi Al-Rasheed (ed.), *Transnational Connections and the Arab Gulf*. Abingdon: Routledge, 2005: 2.

4 Ministry of Foreign Affairs of the Republic of Indonesia, 'Indonesia and Counter-Terrorism Efforts', 7 April 7 2019, https://kemlu.go.id/portal/en/read/95/halaman_list_lainnya/indonesia-and-the-counter-terrorism-efforts

5 Indonesian Islamic model: A distinctive brand of Islam developed in the Indonesian archipelago since at least the sixteenth century that resulted from interaction, indigenisation, interpretation and the venacularisation of Islam.

6 The official foundational philosophy of Indonesia, consisting of: belief in God, a just and civilised humanity, the unity of Indonesia, democracy through unanimity from deliberations, and social justice.

7 M. C. Ricklefs, 'Islamisation in Java to c. 1930', *Islamisation and its Opponents in Java: A Political, Social, Cultural and Religious History, c. 1930 to Present.* Singapore: NUS Press, 2012: 3–20, at 62.

8 Ibid.

9 Amanda Kovacs, 'Saudi Arabia Exporting Salafi Education and Radicalizing Indonesia's Muslims', GIGA Focus 7, 2014, available at www.files.ethz.ch/isn/184727/gf_international_1407.pdf

10 Nahdlatul Ulama, a charitable body which funds schools, hospitals and poverty-reduction programmes, claimed to have a membership of 60 million in Indonesia and 30 million more worldwide in 2017, making it the largest independent Islamic organisation in the world. Faried F. Saenong, 'Nahdlatul Ulama (NU): A Grassroots Movement Advocating Moderate Islam', in *Handbook of Islamic Sects and Movements*. Leiden: BRILL, 2021: 129–150.

11 Chris Chaplin, 'Political Protests, Global Islam and National Activism: Deciphering the Motivations Behind Indonesia's "Conservative Turn"', Middle East Institute, 23 January 2018, www.mei.edu/publications/political-protests-global-islam-and-national-activism-deciphering-motivations-behind

12 Mathias Diederich, 'A Closer Look at *Dakwah* and Politics in Indonesia: The *Partai Keadilan*', Archipel, 2002: 103.

13   Kate Lamb, 'Ahok, Jakarta's Former Governor, Released after Jail Term for Blasphemy', *The Guardian*, 24 January 2019, www.theguardian.com/world/2019/jan/24/ahok-jakartas-former-governor-released-after-jail-term-for-blasphemy

14   Chaplin, 'Political Protests, Global Islam and National Activism'.

15   When the then Saudi Ambassador to Indonesia tweeted a picture of a rally of Shihab's supporters with a caption that suggested NU was a heretical organisation, he created a flashpoint in Saudi–Indonesian relations for alleged interference in Indonesia's internal affairs and underscored Saudi influence over public figures such as Shihab Krithika Varagur, 'How Saudi Arabia's Religious Project Transformed Indonesia', *The Guardian*, 16 April 2020, www.theguardian.com/news/2020/apr/16/how-saudi-arabia-religious-project-transformed-indonesia-islam; Jarryd de Haan, 'Saudi Strategies for Religious Influence and Soft Power in Indonesia', Future Directions International, 2 July 2020, www.futuredirections.org.au/publication/saudi-strategies-for-religious-influence-and-soft-power-in-indonesia

16   Paul Marshall, 'The Ambiguities of Religious Freedom in Indonesia', *The Review of Faith and International Affairs*, 16 (1), 2018: 85–96.

17   Ali Abdullah Wibisono, 'Hizbut Tahrir in Indonesia: Riding the Wave of the Islamization Agenda', Middle East Institue, 27 February 2018, www.mei.edu/publications/hizbut-tahrir-indonesia-riding-wave-islamization-agenda

18   Ibid.

19   Mohamed Nawab Mohamed Osman, 'Insight: Is Hizbut Tahrir a Threat to Indonesia?', *The Jakarta Post*, 20 June 2019, www.thejakartapost.com/academia/2019/06/20/is-hizbut-tahrir-a-threat-to-indonesia.html

20   Fahlesa Munabari, 'Reconciling *Sharia* with "Negara Kesatuan Republik Indonesia": The Ideology and Framing Strategies of the Indonesian Forum of Islamic Society (FUI)', *International Area Studies Review*, 20 (3) 2017: 242–263.

21   Dewi Fortuna Anwar, 'Indonesia's Democratization Underpinned by Major Islamic Groups and Consensus on National Ideology', Middle East Institute, 26 February 2019, www.mei.edu/publications/indonesias-democratization-underpinned

22   Ibid.

23   Chris Chaplin, 'Salafi Islamic Piety as Civic Activism: Wahdah Islamiyah and Differentiated Citizenship in Indonesia', *Citizenship Studies*, 22 (2), 2018: 208–223.

24   Phil Caruso, 'Indonesia and Terrorism: Success, Failures, and an Uncertain Future', Middle East Institute, 6 February 2018, www.mei.edu/publications/indonesia-and-terrorism-success-failure-and-uncertain-future

25   Francesco Milan, 'The Return of ISIS? Jihadis Fleeing into Asia and Detainees in Syria and Iraq Pose a Greater Danger than Terrorists Returning Home', King's College London, 16 July 2020, www.kcl.ac.uk/news/the-return-of-isis-jihadis-fleeing-into-asia-and-detainees-in-syria-and-iraq-pose-a-greater-danger-than-terrorists-returning-home

26   Dio Suhenda, 'New State-of-the-Art Islamic University to Begin Maiden Academic Year', *The Jakarta Post*, 21 September 2021, www.thejakartapost.com/news/2021/09/21/new-state-of-the-art-islamic-university-to-begin-maiden-academic-year.html

27 Carolyn Nash, 'Saudi Arabia's Soft Power Strategy in Indonesia', Middle East Institute, 3 April 2018.

28 Varagur, 'How Saudi Arabia's Religious Project Transformed Indonesia'.

29 Nash, 'Saudi Arabia's Soft Power Strategy in Indonesia'.

30 Sumanto Al Qurtuby, 'Saudi Arabia and Indonesian Networks: On Islamic and Muslim Scholars', *Islam Nusantara Journal for the Study of Islamic History and Culture*, 2 (2), 2021: 17–44.

31 Siwage Dharma Negara, 'The Impact of Saudi King's Visit to Indonesia', ISEAS-Yusof Ishak Institute *Perspective*, No. 16, 10 March 2017: 2, www.iseas.edu.sg/images/pdf/ISEAS_Perspective_2017_16.pdf

32 Indonesian Palm Oil Association, 'Palm Oil Safe From Saudi Arabia's Trade Policy', https://gapki.id/en/news/18750/palm-oil-safe-from-saudi-arabias-trade-policy

33 Negara, 'The Impact of Saudi King's Visit to Indonesia': 2, 6.

34 Sumanto Al Qurtuby, 'King Salman's Historic Visit to Indonesia: Mirror of a Changing Saudi Arabia', Middle East Institute, 16 January 2018, www.mei.edu/publications/king-salmans-historic-visit-indonesia-mirror-changing-saudi-arabia#_ftnref1

35 Asian Correspondent, '"Disappointed": Jokowi Upset that Saudi Invests in China More than Indonesia', 15 April 2017, https://asiancorrespondent.com/2017/04/disappointed-jokowi-upset-saudi-invests-china-indonesia// (accessed 18 February 2019)

36 VOA News, 'Saudi Arabia Announces Indonesia Investments as King Visits', 1 March 2017, www.voanews.com/a/saudi-arabia-announces-indonesia-investment-as-king-vists/3745381.html

37 Rahajeng Kh and Imam Suhartadi, 'Saudi Businesses Invest $2.4b in Indonesia During King Salman's Visit', *Jakarta Globe*, 3 March 2017, https://jakartaglobe.id/context/saudi-businesses-invest-2-4b-in-indonesia-on-the-heels-of-king-salmans-visit/

38 Ibid.

39 Ismira Luftia Tisnadibrata, 'Indonesia Campaign Helps SMEs Enter Saudi Market', *Arab News*, 19 January 2021, www.arabnews.com/tags/saudi-indonesian-trade

40 Varagur, 'How Saudi Arabia's Religious Project Transformed Indonesia'.

41 Hannover Messe, 'Indonesia Economy and Investment', 1 July 2019, www.hannovermesse.de/en/news/news-articles/indonesia-economy-and-investment

42 Varagur, 'How Saudi Arabia's Religious Project Transformed Indonesia'.

43 Mohamed Hery Saripudin, 'Paving the Way for a Meaningful Strategic Indonesia–Saudi Partnership', *Arab News*, 17 August 2019, www.arabnews.com/node/1541096/saudi-arabia

44 Hilary Whiteman, 'Indonesia Maid Ban Won't Work in Mideast, Migrant Groups Say', *CNN*, 6 May 2015, https://edition.cnn.com/2015/05/06/asia/indonesia-migrant-worker-ban/index.html

45 Ibid.

46 Arab News, 'Saudi Arabia, Indonesia Reach Agreement Over Domestic Workers', 13 October 2018, www.arabnews.com/node/1386861/saudi-arabia

47 Rachel Silvey, 'Transnational Domestication: State Power and Indonesian Migrant Women in Saudi Arabia', *Political Geography*, 23 (3), 2004: 245–264.

48 Arabian Business, 'Survey Shows Indonesian Women Defy Ban to Work as Maids in Middle East', 21 June 2016, www.arabianbusiness.com/survey-shows-indonesian-women-defy-ban-work-as-maids-in-middle-east-635697.html; Beh Lih Yi, 'Trafficked and Abused: Indonesia's Middle East Maid Ban Backfires', *Reuters*, 6 March 2017, www.reuters.com/article/us-indonesia-labour-trafficking-idUSKBN16D1F6

49 James Piscatori, 'Allocating "God's Guests": The Politics of Hajj Quotas', HH Sheikh Nasser al-Mohammad al-Sabah Publication Series 32, May 2021: 9

50 Saripudin, 'Paving the Way for a Meaningful Strategic Indonesia–Saudi Partnership'.

51 Reuters, 'U.S. Removes Tariffs for Five Indonesian Products', 30 October 2019, www.reuters.com/article/us-indonesia-usa-trade-idUKKBN1X90OW

52 James M. Dorsey, 'Indonesia Potentially Set to Take on China and Claim Leadership of "Moderate" Islam', *Mideast Soccer blog*, 1 January 2021, https://mideastsoccer.blogspot.com/2021/01/indonesia-potentially-set-to-take-on.html

53 Donald Greenlees, 'To Gain among Muslims, Indonesia Offers to Mediate Middle East Disputes', *The New York Times*, 8 June 2007, www.nytimes.com/2007/06/08/world/asia/08indo.html; Time, 'Could Indonesia Mediate in the Saudi-Iranian Conflict?', 20 January 2016, https://time.com/4186427/indonesia-saudi-arabia-iran-diplomacy-sunni-shia/

54 Peter Mandaville and Shadi Hamid, 'Islam as Statecraft: How Governments Use Religion in Foreign Policy', *Brookings*, November 2018: 17, www.brookings.edu/wp-content/uploads/2018/11/FP_20181116_islam_as_statecraft.pdf

55 Stephanie Kirchgaessner, 'Saudis Used "Incentives and Threats" to Shut Down UN Investigation in Yemen', *The Guardian*, 1 December 2021, www.theguardian.com/world/2021/dec/01/saudi-arabia-yemen-un-human-rights-investigation-incentives-and-therats

56 Hajj quotas and access have been an issue before, notably during the Qatar Crisis in 2018, when Qatar and Saudi Arabia blamed each other for disruption to a dedicated website for Qatari pilgrims and not allowing unimpeded travel. There were also concerns raised by United Malays National Organisation of Malaysia that the Islamic Summit which the Malaysian government hosted in December 2019 had undermined efforts to increase the Malaysian Hajj quota. Picatori, 'Allocating "God's Guests"': 11, 13.

57 'UAE and Indonesia 45 Years of Cooperation, Strategic Relationships, and Growing Partnerships', UAE International Investors Council, 24 April 2021, https://uaeiic.ae/en/news/details/493

58 Georgia Tolley, 'UAE Leaders Meet Indonesian President', *The National*, 4 November 2021, www.thenationalnews.com/uae/government/2021/11/04/sheikh-mohammed-bin-rashid-meets-indonesian-president-joko-widodo-at-expo-2020-dubai/

59 Reuters, 'Indonesia, UAE Sign Business Deals Worth About $23 Billion: Widodo', 13 January 2020, www.reuters.com/article/us-indonesia-emirates-deals/indonesia-uae-sign-business-deals-worth-about-23-billion-widodo-idUSKBN1ZC08R

60 Ibid.

61 Binsal Abulkader, 'Exclusive: Indonesia, UAE "Like Brothers", Can Work Together to Promote Moderate Islam, Says Joko Widodo', *Emirates News Agency*, 4 November 2021, http://wam.ae/en/details/1395302988994

62 Chad Bray, 'Abu Dhabi Investment Authority to Invest US$400 Million in Indonesia's GoTo Group', *South China Morning Post*, 20 October 2021, www.scmp.com/business/banking-finance/article/3153047/abu-dhabi-investment-authority-invest-us400-million

63 The Strait Times, 'UAE to Invest $32.7b in Indonesia', 7 November 2021, www.straitstimes.com/asia/se-asia/uae-to-invest-327b-in-indonesia

64 Associated Press, 'Indonesia: UAE Crown Prince to Lead New Capital Construction', 14 January 2020, available at www.voanews.com/a/east-asia-pacific_indonesia-uae-crown-prince-lead-new-capital-construction/6182565.html

65 Emirates News Agency, 'UAE, Indonesia Launch Talks on Comprehensive Economic Partnership Agreement', 6 September 2021, www.wam.ae/en/details/1395302967399

66 Bray, 'Abu Dhabi Investment Authority to Invest US$400 Million'.

67 Ibid.

68 Nugraha Romadhan, 'Bidik Madrasah, Indonesia dan UEA Jajaki Kerjasama Digital Education', *TQN News*, 20 December 2019, www.tqnnews.com/bidik-madrasah-indonesia-dan-uea-jajaki-kerjasama-digital-education/

69 Reuters, 'UAE May Invest in Indonesian COVID Vaccine Production Facility – Minister', 12 April 2021, www.reuters.com/world/middle-east/uae-may-invest-indonesian-covid-vaccine-production-facility-minister-2021-04-12/

70 Idris, 'Malaysia–Saudi Arabia Relations'.

71 Ibid.

72 Sharifah Munirah Alatas, 'A Malaysian Perspective on Foreign Policy and Geopolitics: Rethinking West-Centric International Relations Theory', *Global Studies Quarterly*, 1, 2021: 4.

73 United Nations Comtarde Database, 'Malaysia's Import from Saudi Arabia 2016', https://comtrade.un.org/data/

74 Ibid.

75 Rodolfo C. Estimo Jr, 'Malaysian Envoy Ends Tour of Duty', *Arab News*, 11 September 2013, www.arabnews.com/news/464242

76 The Asian Banker, 'Saudi Arabia Tops Islamic Bank Ranking, Malaysia Dominates Share of Assets', 29 October 2019, www.theasianbanker.com/updates-and-articles/saudi-arabia-tops-islamic-bank-ranking,-malaysia-dominates-share-of-assets; Al Rajhi Bank, 'Our Position Today', www.alrajhibank.com.my/page/about-us/corporate-info-92/overview

77 P. Prem Kumar, 'Saudi Aramco Stands by Malaysia Mega-Refinery, Petronas Says', *Nikkei Asia*, 20 September 2019, https://asia.nikkei.com/Business/Energy/Saudi-Aramco-stands-by-Malaysia-mega-refinery-Petronas-says#:~:text=Saudi%20Aramco%20acquired%20a%2050,commercial%20production%20later%20this%20year

78 The Prime Minister's Office, Malaysia, 'Malaysian Prime Minister Receives Saudi Arabia's Highest Award by Saudi King Abdullah', 19 January 2010, available at

www.newswire.ca/news-releases/malaysian-prime-minister-receives-saudi-arabias-highest-award-by-saudi-kingabdullah-539214101.html

79 Castlereagh Associates, 'GCC-Malaysia Relations: Part III: Political and Economic Relations Between Malaysis and GCC Countries', *Economic Risk Series* No. 2, May 2019: 13, https://castlereagh.net/wp-content/uploads/Malaysia-Report-III.pdf

80 Ahmad Naqib Idris, 'Witness: Najib was the one who told me Saudi Donation was for Election', *The Edge Markets*, 10 February 2020, www.theedgemarkets.com/article/witness-najib-was-one-who-told-me-saudi-donation-was-election

81 Callum Burroughs and Yusuf Khan, 'The Bizarre Story of 1MDB, the Goldman Sachs-Backed Malaysian Fund that Turned into One of the Biggest Scandals in Financial Hisstory', *Business Insider*, 9 August 2019, www.businessinsider.com/1mdb-timeline-the-goldman-sachs-backed-malaysian-wealth-fund-2018-12

82 BBC News, 'Malaysia 1MDB: Saudi Minister Says Najib Funds Were a Donation', 15 April 2016, www.bbc.com/news/world-asia-36051474

83 Idris, 'Witness: Najib Was the One Who Told Me Saudi Donation was for Election'.

84 Yen Nee Lee, 'Former Malaysian PM Najib Razak Sentenced to 12 Years in Jail, Fined $50 Million Over 1MDB Scandal', *CNBC*, 28 July 2020, www.cnbc.com/2020/07/28/former-malaysian-prime-minister-najib-razak-found-guilty-in-1mdb-trial.html

85 Yiswaree Palasamy, 'Malaysian Troops to Withdraw from Saudi, Defence Minister Confirms', *Malay Mail*, 28 June 2018, www.malaymail.com/news/malaysia/2018/06/28/malaysian-troops-to-withdraw-from-saudi-defence-minister-confirms/1646478

86 Asmady Idris and Asri Salleh, 'The Role of Systemic Leadership Factors in Influencing Malaysia's Joint Military Involvement in the Saudi-Led Coalition in Yemen, 2015–2018', *Contemporary Review of the Middle East*, 8 (3), 2021: 13.

87 Joseph Sipalan and Stephen Kalin, 'Saudi Arabia, Pakistan Snub Malaysia's Muslim Summit', *Reuters*, 18 December 2019, www.reuters.com/article/us-malaysia-muslimalliance-idUSKBN1YM0G3

88 Ibid.

89 Seth J. Frantzman, 'Turkey–Iran–Qatar–Malaysia Alliance to Seek Own Gold Trade Standard', *The Jerusalem Post*, 21 December 2019, www.jpost.com/international/turkey-iran-qatar-malaysia-alliance-to-seek-own-gold-trade-standard-611665

90 Bloomberg Law, 'Malaysia Gets Saudi Pledge to Boost Palm Oil Imports, Plans Hub', 14 March 2021, https://news.bloomberglaw.com/international-trade/malaysia-gets-saudi-pledge-to-boost-palm-oil-imports-plans-hub?utm_source=rss&utm_medium=ITNW&utm_campaign=00000178-33f4-d55c-af79-3bf4e1240003

91 TTG Asia, 'Saudi Tourism Opens First SE Asia Office in Malaysia', 20 August 2021, www.ttgasia.com/2021/08/20/saudi-tourism-opens-first-se-asia-office-in-malaysia/

92 Author's interview with Katsuhiko Takahashi, Ambassador of Japan to Malaysia, 12 December 2021.

93 Mohd Fauzi Abu-Hussin, Asmady Idris, Mohd Rizal Mohd Yaakop and Mohd Afandi Salleh, 'Essential Factors Influencing Malaysia's Relations with the United Arab Emirates', *Contemporary Review of the Middle East*, 8 (4), 2021: 1–19.

94 Lucia Dore, 'UAE Expands Exports to Malaysia', *Khaleej Times*, 8 November 2006, www.khaleejtimes.com/business/uae-expands-exports-to-malaysia

95 Malay Mail, 'Malaysia Eyes Stronger Bilateral Ties with UAE', 22 October 2019, www.malaymail.com/news/malaysia/2019/10/22/malaysia-eyes-stronger-bilateral-ties-with-uae/1802687

96 The National, 'Sheikh Mohamed bin Zayed and Malaysian King Perform Friday Prayers Together', 15 June 2019, www.thenationalnews.com/uae/government/sheikh-mohamed-bin-zayed-and-malaysian-king-perform-friday-prayers-together-1.874399

Conclusion

This book has covered a wide number of thematic issues and bilateral relations with the objective of shedding further light on the foreign policies and IR of Saudi Arabia and the UAE. It has noted the impacts at the state level and the feedback effect into contemporary Saudi leadership style from an oscillating existential threat to monarchical survival and stability, faced over centuries and across three kingdoms. The Al Saud have addressed these threats often by forming close ties to groups such as the Wahhabi, Ikhwan and MB. Thus, the rationale of mobilising and disbanding forces that enhance Saudi leadership and consolidate power is a clear one, but is riddled with potential difficulties in rolling back entrenched and emboldened interests.

The book has highlighted elements of youth, background, perceived past policy failings or caution and lack of affinity with western allies as relatively understudied aspects of political assertiveness and consolidation which have had a significant bearing on the construct and conduct of domestic, regional and international politics. The findings support the notion of a rapid economic transition taking place that favours closer interaction with rising powers. Mohammed bin Salman has harnessed liberalisation, political consolidation, hyper-nationalism and secularisation in this effort, reflecting some of the same risks of rapidly implemented reforms implemented by the shah of Iran. These policy traits are to varying degrees also found in the UAE, motivated by a similar need to maintain the political status quo and forge a common sense of unity against the perceived Islamist threat, whilst attracting highly qualified expatriate labour and investment and appealing to the US as its preferred security partner. Its smaller population, managed federal structure and more diversified economy help to reduce the risks from its rapid pace of reforms.

In both cases, policy is being dominated by youthful decision makers who often hold economic as well as pan-regional political briefs, blurring the parameters of foreign and domestic policy, ministries and personalities. These states' search for regional leadership, international acceptance and economic development is becoming more pronounced now that many of the GCC border issues have been resolved and US hegemonic power is perceived to be unreliable or in decline. Whilst the effect of youth cannot be quantified, a certain self-assuredness and assertiveness has been evident in these regimes as it has been in those of their (former) adversaries such as Qatar. Whilst policy overreach and right-sizing has already occurred in some instances, uncertain economic futures and a fluctuating power differential could lead to the growth of dynastic competition.

The main sources of Saudi Arabia's and UAE's autonomy and external influence reflect their attempts at balancing between the US and China (and to some extent Russia) in the international system. Their interest in maintaining cordial relations with Russia and resisting western attempts to increase oil production levels during the war in Ukraine suggests an inversion point in their historic relations with the West. At the regional level, US–Saudi–Iranian relations have become fused since 1979, with alliance deconstruction and strategic depth having been key drivers of Saudi and UAE foreign policies. Absent effective regional security structures, and with growing questions about US security assistance after the 2019 Abqaiq and Khurais attacks, these states have prioritised the roll-out of their respective military industrial complexes, sub-regional informal security alliances and hedging with a range of international partners as possible solutions. There is evidence, particularly in Saudi foreign policy, of a lack of planning and follow-through, compensated for by its status as a sub-regional hegemon and patron–client relations, or sources of dependency vis-à-vis select allies.

Whilst oil is found to be the dominant source of Saudi external influence, the reasons for this are becoming more diffuse than ever. It reflects the kingdom's continued status as a swing producer, its centrality in the global economy, the energy security considerations of many Asian states and maintaining political stability in weak states through the direction of oil revenues or energy transfers. Riyal politik and economic statecraft have been vital to Saudi Arabia and the UAE in pursuing (counter-)revolutionary objectives during and after the Arab uprisings. But, since the oil price decline in 2014, there is a question as to whether an exclusively economic approach can be replicated, making these states potentially more open to partnerships on major foreign policy issues, especially towards states where they lack leverage.

Economic factors in their foreign policies can be categorised and arranged in a hierarchy, primarily through their strategic deployment, impact or effectiveness on political decision making or alliance formation/deconstruction.

Saudi riyal politik and UAE economic statecraft

Some of these components, incorporating highly targeted financial transfers or in-kind support, have traditionally been employed to uphold the economic integrity of close allies such as Egypt, Lebanon and Pakistan. The personal connections that underpinned these and other relations, whether to Hosni Mubarak, Rafic Hariri or Najib Razak, have been undermined, respectively, by uprising, assassination or election. More recently, in the decade 2011–21, riyal politik has been vital in providing a bridging mechanism to further economic support from the IMF. However, following a reassessment of riyal politik in Lebanon and Iraq, withdrawal of support followed by the pursuit of limited (joint) investments has become the new normal, often driven by other extra-regional states with a greater national interest at stake. UAE economic statecraft has been used as part of a hybrid approach to support border security, an anti-Islamist and pro-authoritarian agenda, notably in North Africa, in Egypt, Libya and Tunisia, but also in other regional theatres such as Sudan. The alleged role of UAE dark money in the attempted coup in Turkey in 2016 and the Saudi detention of Saad Hariri, former Lebanese prime minister, in 2017 highlight the assertiveness of these states. This is especially the case where there has been an extended period of political deadlock. Recourse to such strong-arm tactics is usually reserved for dealing with internal political challenges or dissent. The UAE case shows connectivity between theatres of conflict, mainly through underwriting the mobilisation of mercenaries.

Oil sales, arms sales, soft-power relations and strategic 'dual use' investments

There is ample evidence that these broader economic aspects have been used in multiple attempts to moderate western policy both as a stick, for example oil as an actual or potential weapon (related to supply and production/price), and with other forms of leverage such as damage to, or suspension of, diplomatic relations and broader trade relations. They may also be used as a carrot (e.g. arms sales). For more dependent states the impact of suspended aid has been stark. Strategic economic relations are playing an important role in supporting vision strategies, and attracting increasingly Asian investment into dual-use or overtly security or defence-orientated industries. As the kingdom expands its indigenous military capabilities in terms of industrialisation and training, it may create new forms of Saudi agency in the regional system in a similar vein to 'Little Sparta' (see Chapter 6), although there appears to be some way to go in terms of its structural adaptation. Dual-use aspects of international interactions, such as AI in 'smart cities' or port facilities, continue to place emphasis on the Saudi and UAE leaderships with reference to threat perception and intention. Along with arms sales, the volume has drawn attention to how foreign policy decision making can cascade down to affect close allies, reinforcing relations and creating catchment areas of dependency, soft and hard power. These will tend to national security priorities with the Middle East at the core. But, failing a revitalised JCPOA, we may see increasingly broad investments and/or trading relations with Russia and other former Soviet states in order to project more influence into Central Asia, with containment of Iran and Islamism as primary motivating factors.

The provision of expatriate labour opportunities, associated remittances and the Hajj

These aspects have played important roles in supporting regional relations with non-rentier states and other states predominantly in the Muslim world. Due to internal economic reforms and COVID-19, these relations are under unprecedented downward pressure. The size of such transnational flows shows the extent to which Saudi Arabia and the UAE can affect state and regional political economies, disproportionately in some cases, and the dependency that it generates and sustains. The domestic effects of offering residency to certain expatriates could also create more social tensions between those with and without such benefits. It changes the balance of power between highly qualified (and mobile) expatriates, which these programme favour, and the state. The Hajj retains its status as a key source of connectivity and dependence, increasingly relevant as a source of leverage on specific issues, especially where other sources of leverage are lacking.

New or revitalised trade, aid and investment patterns

These are burgeoning under the direction of the Visions strategies and could be considered a great enhancer of economic power. Economic relations may be enhanced with those states which seek a free trade agreement with Saudi Arabia and/or the GCC as a trading bloc, such as the UK, India or ROK. However, these relations are subject to an uncommon urgency, due to the linkage between GCC state economic programmes and political legitimacy, the growing imperative to broaden trade and FDI and the carbon-neutral agenda, although growing clean energy sales could even out dependency, as these Arab Gulf states are eager to advance their expertise and technologies and develop new markets. States such as China, a leading supplier of rare earth imports, some of which are vital in the development of clean energy technology, may retain relevance here. Here, Saudi investment and diversification strategy appears to be under intense pressure from JASTA in the US, from reputation damage and from a cadre of western journalists, NGOs, parliamentary committees and lawyers seeking to establish a more transparent and accountable framework of engagement. They have been joined by some western states with limited interests in the Gulf which have been more robust in their foreign policy debates and responses. In this context, whilst energy and commercial opportunities in Asia may encourage 'Look East' policies, sometimes the social–legal–political environment in western states might encourage GCC states to 'Push East'. This is moderated only by elite recourse to valued intelligence and counterterrorism cooperation, or interventions based on national security concerns in extreme cases. A closer partnership centred on renewable energy could enhance Saudi and UAE relations with western states in future. Beyond having limited its reputation damage in Yemen, the UAE is also structurally better positioned to take advantage of near-term economic gains, including state-led, SWF-led, emirate-led and private sector-led trade and investment opportunities.

The UAE's relatively early use of oil revenue to underwrite economic projects has afforded it multiple opportunities to diversify its economy and to consolidate its federation and the individual's place within it. UAE external influence is rooted in a crisis vis-à-vis Islamism, which has been a driving force for its hard-power projection. After a decade of assertive responses seen since the Arab uprisings, UAE foreign policy is apparently reverting to favouring economic statecraft as a more efficient method of securing its regional interests.

Saudi Arabia and the UAE have been most effective when they have acted within a permissive international context, for example during high oil prices in the early 2000s and when they acted in concert vis-à-vis the Trump administration during the Qatar Crisis. This could have been dismissed as the exceptional before high oil prices and President Biden's visit to the kingdom and the UAE in 2022 could again serve to enhance their relative autonomy and status. Saudi hegemony in the GCC has been a two-edged sword, capable of delivering a diplomatic fracture with Iran in 2016, an OPEC disagreement in 2020 and a visceral response to Lebanese criticism in 2021. But it has also been the root to GCC collective security advances. Iran, terrorism, air defence and manpower issues continue to unite the GCC states to varying degrees. Concurrently, small-state hedging has been common, particularly in the UAE, where fix-it personalities, mediation and COVID-19 have been used opportunistically to advance state objectives.

Whilst the US–Saudi relationship has experienced numerous periods of cordial and tense relations, the US remains a key security and defence broker. President Trump was highly consequential to the IR of these states. His administration, quite extraordinarily, appeared to reverse the dynamic and privileges of the patron–client relationship through an overemphasis on transactional policies, personal connections and receptivity to lobbying. Renewed efforts by the Biden administration to provide assurances to these Gulf monarchies may have stabilised relations, but they have not yet brought them back from a nadir. Amid the combination of zero-sum perspectives in the Gulf, the past US pursuit of maximalist interests in the region and having become susceptible to global economic structural shifts and competing policy priorities, Saudi–US relations appear to be bogged down in a state of crisis.

Other conceptual insights relate to shifting alliance patterns and 'forced' alliance patterns, for example after the execution of Nimr al Nimr and the storming of the Saudi embassy in Tehran in 2016, or the detention of Saad Hariri in 2017. Thus, offensive realism, mainly with reference to power maximisation and fear of other states, remains highly relevant. In addition, the volume has found an emerging ideological fault line developing. Whereas actual or potential challenger states such as Qatar, Turkey and Iran are confined to the MENA region, where the kingdom and UAE have greater sources of leverage, they have not effectively been isolated, due to a lack of regional and international consensus. However, relations have developed as both sides realise the value, post COVID-19, of economic cooperation over ideational resonance. Malaysia, which entered the realm of challenger state, highlights transnationalism (and its limits) as an important optic through which to view the Islamic world. The continued Saudi search for political legitimacy and Islamic leadership in a crowded and contested field could translate into a revised domestic social contract. It could be expected, especially if hyper-nationalism or other effots prove insufficient in maintaining or managing national unity amid any future economic malaise.

Index